MADAGASCAR

INVESTMENT AND BUSINESS GUIDE

VOLUME 1

STRATEGIC AND PRACTICAL INFORMATION

International Business Publications, USA
Washington DC, USA - Madagascar

MADAGASCAR

INVESTMENT AND BUSINESS GUIDE

VOLUME 1 STRATEGIC AND PRACTICAL INFORMATION

UPDATED ANNUALLY

Cover Design: **International Business Publications, USA**

We express our sincere appreciation to all government agencies and international organizations which provided information and other materials for this handbook

2014 Updated Reprint International Business Publications, USA
ISBN 1-57751-872-1

This handbook provides basic information for starting or/and conducting business in the country. The extraordinary volume of materials covering the topic, prevents us from placing all these materials in this handbook. For more detailed information on issues related to any specific investment and business activity in the country, please contact Global Investment Center, USA
Please acquire the list of our business intelligence and marketing reports and other business publications. We constantly update and expand our business intelligence and marketing materials. Please contact the center for the updated list of reports on over 200 countries.

in the USA: **Global Investment Center, USA.**
P.O.Box 15343, Washington, DC 20003
Phone: (202) 546-2103, Fax: (202) 546-3275, E-mail: rusric@erols.com

For additional analytical, marketing and other information please contact
Global Investment Center, USA

Printed in the USA

MADAGASCAR

INVESTMENT AND BUSINESS GUIDE

VOLUME 1

STRATEGIC AND PRACTICAL INFORMATION

TABLE OF CONTENTS

STRATEGIC & DEVELOPMENT PROFILES

STRATEGIC PROFILE

Capital and largest city	Antananarivo 18°55′S 47°31′E18.917°S 47.517°E
Official languages	Malagasy French
Ethnic groups (2004)	26% Merina 15% Betsimisaraka 12% Betsileo 7% Tsimihety 6% Sakalava 5% Antaisaka 5% Antandroy 24% Others
Demonym	Malagasy
Government	Unitary semi-presidential republic
- President	Hery Rajaonarimampianina
- Prime Minister	Roger Kolo
Legislature	Parliament
- Upper house	Senate
- Lower house	National Assembly
	Independence
- from France	26 June 1960
	Area
- Total	587,041 km^2 (47th) 226,597 sq mi
- Water (%)	0.009%
	Population
- estimate	22,005,222 (53rd)
- 1993 census	12,238,914
- Density	35.2/km^2 (174th) 91.1/sq mi
GDP (PPP)	2011 estimate
- Total	$20.400 billion
- Per capita	$933
GDP (nominal)	2011 estimate
- Total	$10.025 billion
- Per capita	$458
Gini (2010)	44.1 medium
HDI (2013)	0.498 low · 155th
Currency	Malagasy ariary (MGA)
Time zone	EAT (UTC+3)
- Summer (DST)	not observed (UTC+3)
Drives on the	right

Calling code	+261
ISO 3166 code	MG
Internet TLD	.mg

Madagascar, officially the **Republic of Madagascar** and previously known as the Malagasy Republic, is an island country in the Indian Ocean, off the coast of Southeast Africa. The nation comprises the island of Madagascar (the fourth-largest island in the world), as well as numerous smaller peripheral islands. Following the prehistoric breakup of the supercontinent Gondwana, Madagascar split from India around 88 million years ago, allowing native plants and animals to evolve in relative isolation. Consequently, Madagascar is a biodiversity hotspot; over 90 percent of its wildlife is found nowhere else on Earth. The island's diverse ecosystems and unique wildlife are threatened by the encroachment of the rapidly growing human population and other environmental threats.

Initial human settlement of Madagascar occurred between 350 BC and AD 550 by Austronesian peoples arriving on outrigger canoes from Borneo. These were joined around AD 1000 by Bantu migrants crossing the Mozambique Channel from East Africa. Other groups continued to settle on Madagascar over time, each one making lasting contributions to Malagasy cultural life. The Malagasy ethnic group is often divided into eighteen or more sub-groups of which the largest are the Merina of the central highlands.

Until the late 18th century, the island of Madagascar was ruled by a fragmented assortment of shifting socio-political alliances. Beginning in the early 19th century, most of the island was united and ruled as the Kingdom of Madagascar by a series of Merina nobles. The monarchy collapsed in 1897 when the island was absorbed into the French colonial empire, from which the island gained independence in 1960. The autonomous state of Madagascar has since undergone four major constitutional periods, termed Republics. Since 1992 the nation has officially been governed as a constitutional democracy from its capital at Antananarivo. However, in a popular uprising in 2009 president Marc Ravalomanana was made to resign and presidential power was transferred in March 2009 to Andry Rajoelina in a move widely viewed by the international community as a *coup d'état*. Constitutional governance was restored in January 2014 when Hery Rajaonarimampianina was named president following a 2013 election deemed fair and transparent by the international community.

In 2012, the population of Madagascar was estimated at just over 22 million, 90 percent of whom live on less than two dollars per day. Malagasy and French are both official languages of the state. The majority of the population adheres to traditional beliefs, Christianity, or an amalgamation of both. Ecotourism and agriculture, paired with greater investments in education, health and private enterprise, are key elements of Madagascar's development strategy. Under Ravalomanana these investments produced substantial economic growth but the benefits were not evenly spread throughout the population, producing tensions over the increasing cost of living and declining living standards among the poor and some segments of the middle class. As of 2014, the economy has been weakened by the recently concluded political crisis and quality of life remains low for the majority of the Malagasy population.

Formerly an independent kingdom, Madagascar became a French colony in 1896 but regained independence in 1960. During 1992-93, free presidential and National Assembly elections were held ending 17 years of single-party rule. In 1997, in the second presidential race, Didier RATSIRAKA, the leader during the 1970s and 1980s, was returned to the presidency. The 2001 presidential election was contested between the followers of Didier RATSIRAKA and Marc RAVALOMANANA, nearly causing secession of half of the country. In April 2002, the High Constitutional Court announced

RAVALOMANANA the winner. RAVALOMANANA achieved a second term following a landslide victory in the generally free and fair presidential elections of 2006. In early 2009, protests over increasing restrictions on opposition press and activities resulted in RAVALOMANANA handing over power to the military, which then conferred the presidency on the mayor of Antananarivo, Andry RAJOELINA, in what amounted to a coup d'etat. Following a lengthy mediation process led by the Southern African Development Community (SADC), Madagascar held UN-supported presidential and parliamentary elections in 2013. Former de facto finance minister Hery RAJAONARIMAMPIANINA defeated RAVALOMANANA's favored candidate Jean-Louis ROBINSON in a presidential runoff and was inaugurated in January 2014. Most international observers, while noting some irregularities, declared polls to be a credible reflection of the Malagasy public's will.

GEOGRAPHY

Location:
Southern Africa, island in the Indian Ocean, east of Mozambique

Geographic coordinates:
20 00 S, 47 00 E

Map references:
Africa

Area:
total: 587,041 sq km
country comparison to the world: 47
land: 581,540 sq km
water: 5,501 sq km

Area - comparative:
slightly less than twice the size of Arizona

Land boundaries:
0 km

Coastline:
4,828 km

Maritime claims:
territorial sea: 12 nm
contiguous zone: 24 nm
exclusive economic zone: 200 nm
continental shelf: 200 nm or 100 nm from the 2,500-m isobath

Climate:
tropical along coast, temperate inland, arid in south

Terrain:
narrow coastal plain, high plateau and mountains in center

Elevation extremes:
lowest point: Indian Ocean 0 m
highest point: Maromokotro 2,876 m

Natural resources:
graphite, chromite, coal, bauxite, rare earth elements, salt, quartz, tar sands, semiprecious stones, mica, fish, hydropower

Land use:
arable land: 5.96%
permanent crops: 1.02%
other: 93.02% (2011)

Irrigated land:
10,860 sq km (2003)

Total renewable water resources:
337 cu km (2011)

Freshwater withdrawal (domestic/industrial/agricultural):
total: 16.5 cu km/yr (2%/1%/97%)
per capita: 1,010 cu m/yr (2005)

Natural hazards:
periodic cyclones; drought; and locust infestation
volcanism: Madagascar's volcanoes have not erupted in historical times

Environment - current issues:
soil erosion results from deforestation and overgrazing; desertification; surface water contaminated with raw sewage and other organic wastes; several endangered species of flora and fauna unique to the island

Environment - international agreements:
party to: Biodiversity, Climate Change, Climate Change-Kyoto Protocol, Desertification, Endangered Species, Hazardous Wastes, Law of the Sea, Marine Life Conservation, Ozone Layer Protection, Ship Pollution, Wetlands
signed, but not ratified: none of the selected agreements

Geography - note:
world's fourth-largest island; strategic location along Mozambique Channel

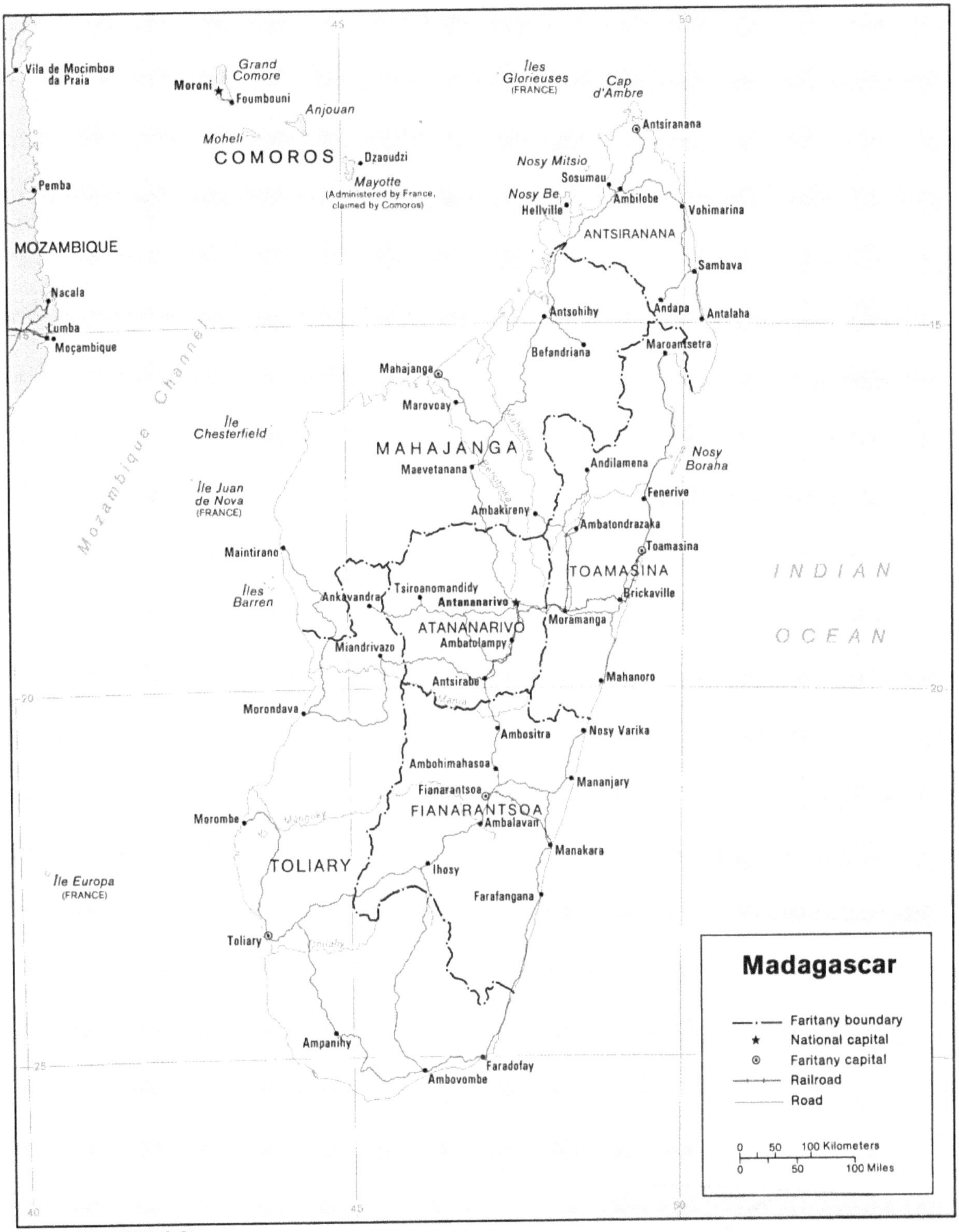

Base 504693 (545856) 3-81

PEOPLE

Nationality:
noun: Malagasy (singular and plural)
adjective: Malagasy

Ethnic groups:
Malayo-Indonesian (Merina and related Betsileo), Cotiers (mixed African, Malayo-Indonesian, and Arab ancestry - Betsimisaraka, Tsimihety, Antaisaka, Sakalava), French, Indian, Creole, Comoran

Languages:
French (official), Malagasy (official), English

Religions:
indigenous beliefs 52%, Christian 41%, Muslim 7%

Population:
23,201,926 (July 2014 est.)
country comparison to the world: 53

Age structure:
0-14 years: 40.7% (male 4,765,523/female 4,685,298)
15-24 years: 20.6% (male 2,394,146/female 2,384,564)
25-54 years: 31.3% (male 3,635,506/female 3,629,204)
55-64 years: 4.2% (male 466,263/female 503,375)
65 years and over: 3.1% (male 334,533/female 403,514) (2014 est.)

population pyramid:

Dependency ratios:
total dependency ratio: 81.4 %
youth dependency ratio: 76.3 %
elderly dependency ratio: 5.1 %
potential support ratio: 19.6 (2014 est.)

Median age:
total: 19.2 years
male: 19 years
female: 19.4 years (2014 est.)

Population growth rate:
2.62% (2014 est.)
country comparison to the world: 25

Birth rate:
33.12 births/1,000 population (2014 est.)
country comparison to the world: 33

Death rate:

6.95 deaths/1,000 population (2014 est.)
country comparison to the world: 135

Net migration rate:
0 migrant(s)/1,000 population (2014 est.)
country comparison to the world: 87

Urbanization:
urban population: 32.6% of total population (2011)
rate of urbanization: 4.73% annual rate of change (2010-15 est.)

Major urban areas - population:
ANTANANARIVO (capital) 1.987 million (2011)

Sex ratio:
at birth: 1.03 male(s)/female
0-14 years: 1.02 male(s)/female
15-24 years: 1 male(s)/female
25-54 years: 1 male(s)/female
55-64 years: 1 male(s)/female
65 years and over: 0.83 male(s)/female
total population: 1 male(s)/female (2014 est.)

Mother's mean age at first birth:
19.5
note:median age at first birth among women 25-29 (2008-09 est.)

Maternal mortality rate:
240 deaths/100,000 live births (2010)
country comparison to the world: 48

Infant mortality rate:
total: 44.88 deaths/1,000 live births
country comparison to the world: 48
male: 48.86 deaths/1,000 live births
female: 40.78 deaths/1,000 live births (2014 est.)

Life expectancy at birth:
total population: 65.2 years
country comparison to the world: 174
male: 63.77 years
female: 66.67 years (2014 est.)

Total fertility rate:
4.28 children born/woman (2014 est.)
country comparison to the world: 33

Contraceptive prevalence rate:
39.9% (2008/09)

Health expenditures:
4.1% of GDP (2011)
country comparison to the world: 161

Physicians density:
0.16 physicians/1,000 population (2007)

Hospital bed density:
0.2 beds/1,000 population (2010)

Drinking water source:
improved:
urban: 78.2% of population
rural: 35.4% of population
total: 49.6% of population
unimproved:
urban: 21.8% of population
rural: 64.6% of population
total: 50.4% of population (2012 est.)

Sanitation facility access:
improved:
urban: 19.2% of population
rural: 11.3% of population
total: 13.9% of population
unimproved:
urban: 80.8% of population
rural: 88.7% of population
total: 86.1% of population (2012 est.)

HIV/AIDS - adult prevalence rate:
0.5% (2012 est.)
country comparison to the world: 73

HIV/AIDS - people living with HIV/AIDS:
58,800 (2012 est.)
country comparison to the world: 57

HIV/AIDS - deaths:
6,200 (2012 est.)
country comparison to the world: 32

Major infectious diseases:
degree of risk: very high
food or waterborne diseases: bacterial diarrhea, hepatitis A, and typhoid fever
vectorborne diseases: malaria and dengue fever
water contact disease: schistosomiasis
animal contact disease: rabies (2013)

Obesity - adult prevalence rate:

1.6% (2008)
country comparison to the world: 187

Children under the age of 5 years underweight:
36.8% (2004)
country comparison to the world: 6

Education expenditures:
2.7% of GDP (2012)
country comparison to the world: 150

Literacy:
definition: age 15 and over can read and write
total population: 64.5%
male: 67.4%
female: 61.6% (2009 est.)

School life expectancy (primary to tertiary education):
total: 10 years
male: 11 years
female: 10 years (2012)

Child labor - children ages 5-14:
total number: 1,827,423
percentage: 28 %
note:data represents children ages 5-17 (2007 est.)

Unemployment, youth ages 15-24:
total: 2.3%
country comparison to the world: 145
male: 1.7%
female: 2.8% (2005)

MAP OF 22 REGIONS AND PROVINCES OF THE FORMER

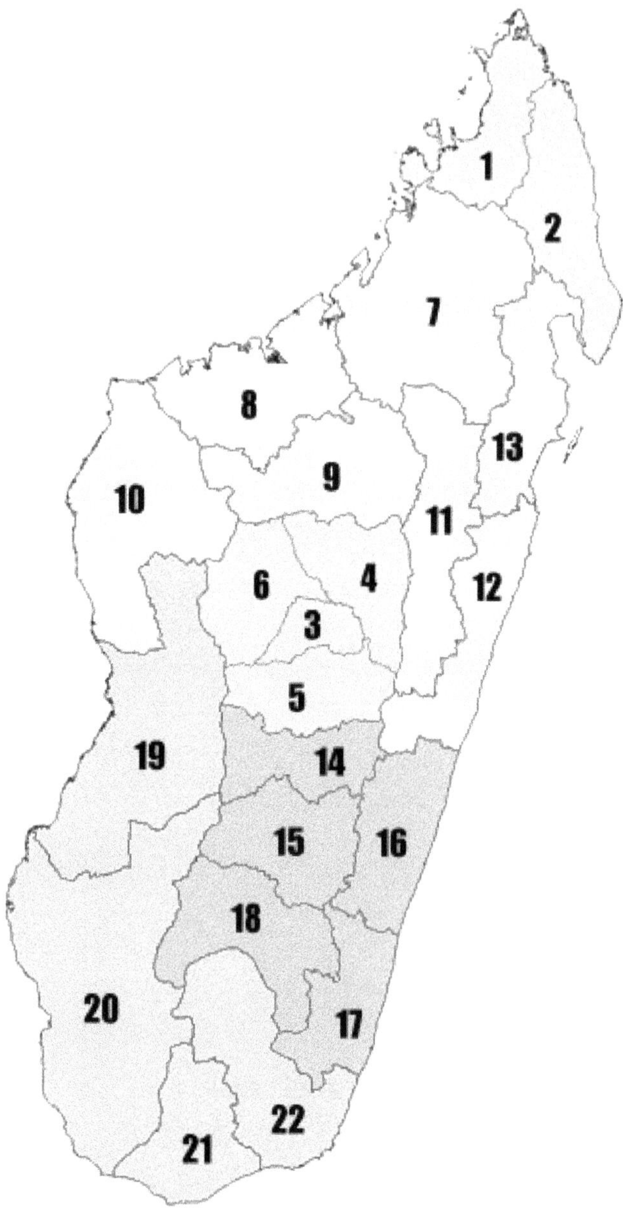

Antsiranana
1. Sava
2. Diana

Antananarivo
3. Itasy
4. Analamanga
5. Vakinakaratra
6. Bongolava

Mahajanga
7. Sofia
8. Boeny
9. Betsiboka
10. Melaky

Toamasina
11. Alaotra-Mangoro
12. Atsinanana
13. Analanjirofo

Fianarantsoa
14. Amoron'i Mania
15. High Matsiatra
16. Vatovavy-Fitovinany
17. Atsimo-Atsinanana
18. Ihorombe

Toliara
19. Menabe
20. Atsimo-Andrefana
21. Androy
22. Anosy

GOVERNMENT

Country name:
conventional long form: Republic of Madagascar
conventional short form: Madagascar
local long form: Republique de Madagascar/Repoblikan'i Madagasikara
local short form: Madagascar/Madagasikara
former: Malagasy Republic

Government type:
republic

Capital:
name: Antananarivo
geographic coordinates: 18 55 S, 47 31 E
time difference: UTC+3 (8 hours ahead of Washington, DC, during Standard Time)

Administrative divisions:
Hi Trent,6 provinces (faritany); Antananarivo, Antsiranana, Fianarantsoa, Mahajanga, Toamasina, Toliara

Independence:
26 June 1960 (from France)

National holiday:
Independence Day, 26 June (1960)

Constitution:
previous 1992; latest passed by referendum 17 November 2010, promulgated 11 December 2010 (2012)

Legal system:
civil law system based on the old French civil code and customary law in matters of marriage, family, and obligation

International law organization participation:
accepts compulsory ICJ jurisdiction with reservations; accepts ICCt jurisdiction

Suffrage:
18 years of age; universal

Executive branch:
chief of state: President Hery Martial RAJAONARIMAMPIANINA Rakotoarimana (since 25 January 2014)
head of government: Prime Minister Roger Laurent Christophe KOLO, M.D. (since 11 April 2014)
cabinet: Council of Ministers appointed by the prime minister
(For more information visit the World Leaders website **)**

elections: president elected by popular vote for a five-year term (eligible for a second term); election last held on 20 December 2013 (next to be held in 2018); prime minister nominated by the National Assembly and appointed by the president
election results: Hery RAJAONARIMAMPIANINA elected president in second round; percent of vote - Hery RAJAONARIMAMPIANINA 53.5%, Jean Louis ROBINSON 46.5%
note:on 17 March 2009, democratically elected President Marc RAVALOMANANA stepped down handing the government over to the military, which in turn conferred the presidency on opposition leader and Antananarivo mayor Andry RAJOELINA; a power-sharing agreement established a 15-month transition period to conclude with a general election in 2010, which failed to occur; a subsequent agreement aimed for an early 2013 election - the first round was held on 25 October 2013 and the second on 20 December 2013

Legislative branch:
bicameral legislature consists of a Senate or Senat (33 seats; 22 elected from each of the 22 regions; the remaining 11 appointed by the president; members to serve six-year terms) and a National Assembly or Assemblee Nationale (151 seats in the December 2013 election; reduced from 160 seats to 127 seats by an April 2007 national referendum - never used; members elected by popular vote to serve four-year terms)
elections: National Assembly - last held on 20 December 2013 (next to be held in 2017); note - a power-sharing agreement in the summer of 2009 established a 15-month transition, concluding in general elections scheduled for late 2013 after repeated delays
election results: National Assembly - percent of vote by party - Party of Andry Rajoelina 17.3%, Ravalomannana Movement 10.8%, Vondrona Politika 8.2%, independents and others 63.7%; seats by party - Party of Andry Rajoelina 49, the Ravalomannana Movement 20, Malagasy Miara Mianinga 13, independents 25, seats with delayed elections 4, other 40

Judicial branch:
highest court(s): Supreme Court or Cour Supreme (consists of 11 members; addresses judicial administration issues only); High Constitutional Court or Haute Cour Constitutionnelle (consists of 9 members)
note - the judiciary includes a High Court of Justice responsible for adjudicating crimes and misdemeanors by government officials including the president
judge selection and term of office: Supreme Court heads elected by the president and judiciary officials to serve single-renewable, 3-year terms; High Constitutional Court members appointed - 3 each by the president, by both legislative bodies, and by the Council of Magistrates; members serve single, 6-year terms
subordinate courts: Courts of Appeal; provincial and city tribunals

Political parties and leaders:
AVANA Party [Jean-Louis ROBINSON]
Economic Liberalism and Democratic Action for National Recovery or LEADER/Fanilo [Manasse ESOAVELOMANDROSO]
Green Party or Parti Vert [Sarah Georget RABEHARISOA]
I Love Madagascar or TIM [Marc RAVALOMANANA]
Judged by Your Work or AVI [Norbert RATSIRAHONANA]
Malagasy Miara-Miainga or MMM [Hajo ANDRIANAINARIVELO]
Malagasy Tonga Saina or MTS [Roland RATSIRAKA]
Movement for Democracy in Madagascar or MDM [Pierrot RAJAONARIVELO]
New Force for Madagascar of FIDIO [Hery RAJAONARIMAMPIANINA]
Renewal of the Social Democratic Party or RPSD [Evariste MARSON]
Socialist and Democratic Party for the Unity of Madagascar or PSDUM [Jean LAHINIRIKO]
Union Party or Tambatra [Pety RAKOTONIAINA]

Young Malagasies Determined or TGV [Andry RAJOELINA]

Political pressure groups and leaders:
Committee for the Defense of Truth and Justice or KMMR
Committee for National Reconciliation or CRN [Albert Zafy]
National Council of Christian Churches or FFKM

International organization participation:
ACP, AfDB, AU, CD, COMESA, EITI (candidate country), FAO, G-77, IAEA, IBRD, ICAO, ICC (national committees), ICRM, IDA, IFAD, IFC, IFRCS, ILO, IMF, IMO, InOC, Interpol, IOC, IOM, ISO (correspondent), ITSO, ITU, ITUC (NGOs), MIGA, NAM, OIF, OPCW, PCA, SADC, UN, UNCTAD, UNESCO, UNHCR, UNIDO, UNWTO, UPU, WCO, WFTU (NGOs), WHO, WIPO, WMO, WTO

Diplomatic representation in the US:
chief of mission: Ambassador (vacant); Charge d'Affaires Velotiana Rakotoanosy RAOBELINA (since 20 June 1011)
chancery: 2374 Massachusetts Avenue NW, Washington, DC 20008
telephone: (202) 265-5525 through 5526
FAX: (202) 265-3034
consulate(s) general: New York

Diplomatic representation from the US:
chief of mission: Ambassador (vacant); Charge d'Affaires Eric WONG note - also accredited to Comoros
embassy: Lot 207A, Point Liberty, Andranoro, Antehiroka, 105 Antananarivo
mailing address: B. P. 620, Antsahavola, Antananarivo
telephone: [261] (23) 480 00/01
FAX: [261] (23) 480 35

Flag description:
two equal horizontal bands of red (top) and green with a vertical white band of the same width on hoist side; by tradition, red stands for sovereignty, green for hope, white for purity

National anthem:
name: "Ry Tanindraza nay malala o" (Oh, Our Beloved Fatherland)

ECONOMY

After discarding socialist economic policies in the mid-1990s, Madagascar followed a World Bank- and IMF-led policy of privatization and liberalization that has been undermined since the start of the political crisis. This strategy placed the country on a slow and steady growth path from an extremely low level. Agriculture, including fishing and forestry, is a mainstay of the economy, accounting for more than one-fourth of GDP and employing 80% of the population. Exports of apparel boomed in recent years primarily due to duty-free access to the US; however, Madagascar's failure to comply with the requirements of the African Growth and Opportunity Act (AGOA) led to the termination of the country's duty-free access in January 2010 and a sharp fall in textile production. Deforestation and erosion, aggravated by the use of firewood as the primary source of fuel, are serious concerns. The current political crisis, which began in early

2009, has dealt additional blows to the economy. Tourism dropped more than 50% in 2009 compared with the previous year, and many investors are wary of entering the uncertain investment environment. Growth was slow during 2010 to 2013 although expansion in mining and agricultural sectors is expected to contribute to more growth in 2014. International organizations and foreign donors are expected to resume development aid to Madagascar once RAJAONARIMAMPIANINA appoints a new government.

GDP (purchasing power parity):
$22.03 billion (2013 est.)
country comparison to the world: 129
$21.47 billion (2012 est.)
$21.06 billion (2011 est.)
note:data are in 2013 US dollars

GDP (official exchange rate):
$10.53 billion (2013 est.)

GDP - real growth rate:
2.6% (2013 est.)
country comparison to the world: 126
1.9% (2012 est.)
1.8% (2011 est.)

GDP - per capita (PPP):
$1,000 (2013 est.)
country comparison to the world: 220
$1,000 (2012 est.)
$1,000 (2011 est.)
note:data are in 2013 US dollars

Gross national saving:
-3.7% of GDP (2013 est.)
country comparison to the world: 153
-5.8% of GDP (2012 est.)
-7.2% of GDP (2011 est.)

GDP - composition, by end use:
household consumption: 84%
government consumption: 12.7%
investment in fixed capital: 14%
investment in inventories: 0%
exports of goods and services: 24.7%
imports of goods and services: -35.3%
(2013 est.)

GDP - composition, by sector of origin:
agriculture: 27.3%
industry: 16.4%
services: 56.3% (2013 est.)

Agriculture - products:
coffee, vanilla, sugarcane, cloves, cocoa, rice, cassava (manioc, tapioca), beans, bananas, peanuts; livestock products

Industries:
meat processing, seafood, soap, beer, leather, sugar, textiles, glassware, cement, automobile assembly plant, paper, petroleum, tourism

Industrial production growth rate:
4% (2013 est.)
country comparison to the world: 73

Labor force:
9.504 million (2007)
country comparison to the world: 50

Population below poverty line:
50% (2004 est.)

Household income or consumption by percentage share:
lowest 10%: 2.2%
highest 10%: 34.7% (2010 est.)

Distribution of family income - Gini index:
47.5 (2001)
country comparison to the world: 26
38.1 (1999)

Budget:
revenues: $2.113 billion
expenditures: $2.356 billion (2013 est.)

Taxes and other revenues:
20.1% of GDP (2013 est.)
country comparison to the world: 165

Budget surplus (+) or deficit (-):
-2.3% of GDP (2013 est.)
country comparison to the world: 95

Fiscal year:
calendar year

Inflation rate (consumer prices):
8.8% (2013 est.)
country comparison to the world: 202
6.4% (2012 est.)

Central bank discount rate:

5% (31 December 2010 est.)
NA% (31 December 2009 est.)

Commercial bank prime lending rate:
44% (31 December 2013 est.)
country comparison to the world: 1
56.25% (31 December 2012 est.)

Stock of narrow money:
$1.839 billion (31 December 2013 est.)
country comparison to the world: 128
$1.492 billion (31 December 2012 est.)

Stock of broad money:
$3.163 billion (31 December 2013 est.)
country comparison to the world: 143
$2.357 billion (31 December 2012 est.)

Stock of domestic credit:
$1.663 billion (31 December 2013 est.)
country comparison to the world: 137
$1.245 billion (31 December 2012 est.)

Market value of publicly traded shares:
$NA

Current account balance:
-$1.945 billion (2013 est.)
country comparison to the world: 141
-$1.989 billion (2012 est.)

Exports:
$644.4 million (2013 est.)
country comparison to the world: 169
$592.1 million (2012 est.)

Exports - commodities:
coffee, vanilla, shellfish, sugar, cotton cloth, clothing, chromite, petroleum products

Exports - partners:
France 23.4%, China 6.6%, US 6.6%, Singapore 5.9%, Canada 5.5%, Germany 5.4%, Indonesia 5.3%, India 5.2%, South Africa 4.5% (2012)

Imports:
$2.794 billion (2013 est.)
country comparison to the world: 151
$2.755 billion (2012 est.)

Imports - commodities:
capital goods, petroleum, consumer goods, food

Imports - partners:
China 17.7%, France 12.4%, South Africa 5.3%, India 5.1%, Mauritius 5%, Bahrain 4.7%, Kuwait 4.6% (2012)

Reserves of foreign exchange and gold:
$1.249 billion (31 December 2013 est.)
country comparison to the world: 131
$1.191 billion (31 December 2012 est.)

Debt - external:
$3.361 billion (31 December 2013 est.)
country comparison to the world: 131
$3.116 billion (31 December 2012 est.)

Stock of direct foreign investment - at home:
$NA

Stock of direct foreign investment - abroad:
$NA

Exchange rates:
Malagasy ariary (MGA) per US dollar -
2,227.8 (2013 est.)
2,195 (2012 est.)
2,090 (2010 est.)
1,956.2 (2009)
1,654.78 (2008)

COMMUNICATIONS

Telephones - main lines in use:
143,700 (2012)
country comparison to the world: 138

Telephones - mobile cellular:
8.564 million (2012)
country comparison to the world: 89

Telephone system:
general assessment: system is above average for the region; Antananarivo's main telephone exchange modernized in the late 1990s, but the rest of the analogue-based telephone system is poorly developed
domestic: combined fixed-line and mobile-cellular teledensity about 40 per 100 persons
international: country code - 261; landing point for the EASSy, SEACOM, and LION fiber-optic submarine cable systems; satellite earth stations - 2 (1 Intelsat - Indian Ocean, 1 Intersputnik - Atlantic Ocean region) (2010)

Broadcast media:
state-owned Radio Nationale Malagasy (RNM) and Television Malagasy (TVM) have an

extensive national network reach; privately owned radio and TV broadcasters in cities and major towns; state-run radio dominates in rural areas; relays of 2 international broadcasters are available in Antananarivo (2007)

Internet country code:
.mg

Internet hosts:
38,392 (2012)
country comparison to the world: 102

Internet users:
319,900 (2009)
country comparison to the world: 127

ENERGY

Electricity - production:
1.211 billion kWh (2010 est.)
country comparison to the world: 143

Electricity - consumption:
1.126 billion kWh (2010 est.)
country comparison to the world: 149

Electricity - exports:
0 kWh (2012 est.)
country comparison to the world: 161

Electricity - imports:
0 kWh (2012 est.)
country comparison to the world: 167

Electricity - installed generating capacity:
430,000 kW (2010 est.)
country comparison to the world: 144

Electricity - from fossil fuels:
65.6% of total installed capacity (2010 est.)
country comparison to the world: 119

Electricity - from nuclear fuels:
0% of total installed capacity (2010 est.)
country comparison to the world: 130

Electricity - from hydroelectric plants:
34.4% of total installed capacity (2010 est.)
country comparison to the world: 65

Electricity - from other renewable sources:
0% of total installed capacity (2010 est.)
country comparison to the world: 196

Crude oil - production:
0 bbl/day (2012 est.)
country comparison to the world: 191

Crude oil - exports:
0 bbl/day (2010 est.)
country comparison to the world: 146

Crude oil - imports:
0 bbl/day (2010 est.)
country comparison to the world: 85

Crude oil - proved reserves:
0 bbl (1 January 2013 est.)
country comparison to the world: 158

Refined petroleum products - production:
0 bbl/day (2010 est.)
country comparison to the world: 167

Refined petroleum products - consumption:
17,480 bbl/day (2011 est.)
country comparison to the world: 136

Refined petroleum products - exports:
365 bbl/day (2010 est.)
country comparison to the world: 115

Refined petroleum products - imports:
12,120 bbl/day (2010 est.)
country comparison to the world: 127

Natural gas - production:
0 cu m (2011 est.)
country comparison to the world: 158

Natural gas - consumption:
0 cu m (2010 est.)
country comparison to the world: 166

Natural gas - exports:

0 cu m (2011 est.)
country comparison to the world: 139

Natural gas - imports:
0 cu m (2011 est.)
country comparison to the world: 90

Natural gas - proved reserves:
2.01 billion cu m (1 January 2012 est.)
country comparison to the world: 99

Carbon dioxide emissions from consumption of energy:
1.843 million Mt (2011 est.)

TRANSPORTATION

Airports:
83 (2013)
country comparison to the world: 66

Airports - with paved runways:
total: 26
over 3,047 m: 1
2,438 to 3,047 m: 2
1,524 to 2,437 m: 6
914 to 1,523 m: 16
under 914 m: 1 (2013)

Airports - with unpaved runways:
total: 57
1,524 to 2,437 m: 1
914 to 1,523 m: 38
under 914 m:
18 (2013)

Railways:
total: 854 km
country comparison to the world: 97
narrow gauge: 854 km 1.000-m gauge (2008)

Roadways:
total: 34,476 km
country comparison to the world: 92
paved: 5,613 km
unpaved: 2,886 km (2010)

Waterways:
600 km (432 km navigable) (2011)
country comparison to the world: 80

Merchant marine:
total: 1
country comparison to the world: 156
by type: cargo 1
registered in other countries: 1 (unknown 1) (2010)

Ports and terminals:
major seaport(s): Antsiranana (Diego Suarez), Mahajanga, Toamasina, Toliara (Tulear)

MILITARY

Military branches:
People's Armed Forces: Intervention Force, Development Force, and Aeronaval Force (navy and air); National Gendarmerie

Military service age and obligation:
18-25 years of age for male-only voluntary military service; no conscription; service obligation is 18 months for military or equivalent civil service; 20-30 years of age for National Gendarmerie recruits and 35 years of age for those with military experience (2012)

Manpower available for military service:
males age 16-49: 4,900,729
females age 16-49: 4,909,061 (2010 est.)

Manpower fit for military service:
males age 16-49: 3,390,071
females age 16-49: 3,682,180 (2010 est.)

Manpower reaching militarily significant age annually:
male: 248,184
female: 246,769 (2010 est.)

Military expenditures:
0.69% of GDP (2012)
country comparison to the world: 119
0.73% of GDP (2011)
0.69% of GDP (2010)

TRANSNATIONAL ISSUES

Disputes - international:
claims Bassas da India, Europa Island, Glorioso Islands, and Juan de Nova Island (all administered by France); the vegetated drying cays of Banc du Geyser, which were claimed by Madagascar in 1976, also fall within the EEZ claims of the Comoros and France (Glorioso Islands, part of the French Southern and Antarctic Lands)

Trafficking in persons:
current situation: Madagascar is a source country for men, women, and children

subjected to forced labor and women and children subjected to sex trafficking; poor Malagasy women hired as domestic workers in Lebanon and Kuwait are vulnerable to abuse by recruitment agencies and employers; an increasing number of Malagasy men were victimized by labor trafficking abroad in 2012; Malagasy children are subjected to domestic servitude, prostitution, forced begging, and forced labor within the country, often with the complicity of family members; coastal cities have child sex tourism trades, with Malagasy men being the main clients
tier rating: Tier 2 Watch List - Madagascar does not fully comply with the minimum standards for the elimination of trafficking; however, it is making significant efforts to do so; law enforcement authorities have made a significant increase in efforts in 2012, resulting in 30 trafficking-related prosecutions and two convictions; public officials complicity in human trafficking, however, remains a significant problem; the government has failed to identify and refer victims to protective services and has not supported NGO-run care facilities; the government also has not engaged any Middle Eastern governments regarding the protection of and legal remedies for Malagasy workers exploited abroad (2013)

Illicit drugs:
illicit producer of cannabis (cultivated and wild varieties) used mostly for domestic consumption; transshipment point for heroin

IMPORTANT INFORMATION FOR UNDERSTANDING THE COUNTRY

OFFICIAL NAME: **Republic of Madagascar**

PROFILE

Geography
Area: 592,800 sq. km. (228,880 sq. mi.).
Cities: *Capital*--Antananarivo (pop. about 1,300,000). *Other cities*--Antsirabe (about 500,000), Mahajanga (about 400,000), Toamasina (about 450,000).
Terrain: Mountainous central plateau, coastal plain.
Climate: Moderate interior, tropical coasts.

People
Nationality: *Noun and adjective*--Malagasy.
Population (2009 estimate): 20,653,556.
Annual population growth rate (2009 estimate): 3%.
Ethnic groups: 18 Malagasy tribes; small groups of Comorans, French, Indians, and Chinese.
Religions: Traditional beliefs 52%, Christian 41%, Muslim 7%.
Languages: Malagasy (official), French (official), English (official).
Education: *Years compulsory*--5. *Attendance*--65%. *Literacy*--68.9%.
Health: *Infant mortality rate*--54.2/1,000. *Life expectancy*--62.89 yrs.
Work force (2000): 7.3 million. *Agriculture*--80%; *industry*--7%.

Government
Type: Republic.
Independence: June 26, 1960.
Constitution: Entered into force in March 1998.
Branches: *Executive*--president, prime minister, cabinet. *Judicial*--Supreme Court, High Court of Justice, Constitutional High Court. *Legislative*--National Assembly and Senate.

NOTE: On March 17, 2009, democratically elected President Marc Ravalomanana stepped down and purported to transfer his authority to a senior military figure, who in turn purported to confer the presidency on opposition leader Andry Rajoelina, who is currently heading the High Transitional Authority (HAT). The United States characterized the transfer of power as tantamount to a military coup d'état and does not recognize the HAT. References to de facto government officials in this text are factual only and do not reflect U.S. recognition of the HAT regime.

Suffrage: Universal at 18.
National holiday: June 26.

Economy
GDP (U.S.$, 2008 est., official exchange rate): $9.729 billion.
GDP per capita (2008 est., purchasing power parity): $1,000.
Unemployment: no reliable data available.
Natural resources: Graphite, chrome, coal, bauxite, ilmenite, nickel, gold, oil, tar sands, precious and semiprecious stones, and hardwoods.
Agriculture (26% of GDP, 2008 est.): *Products*--rice, livestock, seafood, coffee, vanilla, sugar, cloves, cotton, sisal, peanuts, and tobacco.
Industry (15.9% of GDP, 2008 est.): *Types*--processed food, clothing, textiles, mining, paper,

refined petroleum products, glassware, construction, soap, cement, tanning.
Trade: *Exports* (2007, f.o.b.) $989 million: apparel, shrimp, vanilla, coffee, cloves, graphite, essential oils, industrial minerals and gemstones. *Major export markets*--France, U.S., Germany, Italy, U.K. *Imports* (2007, f.o.b.) $1.933 billion: foodstuffs, fuel and energy, capital goods, vehicles, consumer goods and electronics. *Major suppliers*--France, China, Iran, Mauritius, Hong Kong.

PEOPLE AND HISTORY

Madagascar's population is predominantly of mixed Asian and African origin. Research suggests that the island was uninhabited until Indonesian seafarers arrived in roughly the first century A.D., probably by way of southern India and East Africa, where they acquired African wives and slaves. Subsequent migrations from both the Pacific and Africa further consolidated this original mixture, and 18 separate tribal groups emerged. Asian features are most predominant in the central highlands people, the Merina (3 million) and the Betsileo (2 million); the coastal people are of more clearly African origin. The largest coastal groups are the Betsimisaraka (1.5 million) and the Tsimihety and Sakalava (700,000 each).

The Malagasy language is of Malayo-Polynesian origin and is generally spoken throughout the island, with significant regional variations. French is spoken among the educated population of this former French colony. English is becoming more widely spoken, and in 2003 the government began a pilot project of introducing the teaching of English into the primary grades of 44 schools, with hopes of taking the project nationwide.

Most people practice traditional religions, which tend to emphasize links between the living and the dead. They believe that the dead join their ancestors in the ranks of divinity and that ancestors are intensely concerned with the fate of their living descendants. The Merina and Betsileo reburial practice of famadihana, or "turning over the dead" celebrate this spiritual communion. In this ritual, relatives' remains are removed from the family tomb, rewrapped in new silk shrouds, and returned to the tomb following festive ceremonies in their honor.

About 41% of the Malagasy are Christian, divided almost evenly between Roman Catholic and Protestant. Many incorporate the cult of the dead with their religious beliefs and bless their dead at church before proceeding with the traditional burial rites. They also may invite a pastor to attend a famadihana. While many Christians continue these practices, others consider them to be superstitions that should be abandoned. Many of the Christian churches are influential in politics. In the coastal regions of the provinces of Mahajanga and Antsiranana (Diego Suarez), Muslims constitute a significant minority. Muslims are divided between those of Malagasy ethnicity, Indo-Pakistanis, and Comorans.

The written history of Madagascar began in the seventh century A.D., when Arabs established trading posts along the northwest coast. European contact began in the 1500s, when Portuguese sea captain Diego Dias sighted the island after his ship became separated from a fleet bound for India. In the late 17th century, the French established trading posts along the east coast. From about 1774 to 1824, it was a favorite haunt for pirates, including Americans, one of whom brought Malagasy rice to South Carolina.

Beginning in the 1790s, Merina rulers succeeded in establishing hegemony over the major part of the island, including the coast. In 1817, the Merina ruler and the British governor of Mauritius concluded a treaty abolishing the slave trade, which had been important in Madagascar's economy. In return, the island received British military and financial assistance. British influence remained strong for several decades, during which the Merina court was converted to Presbyterianism, Congregationalism, and Anglicanism.

The British accepted the imposition of a French protectorate over Madagascar in 1885 in return for eventual control over Zanzibar (now part of Tanzania) and as part of an overall definition of spheres of influence in the area. Absolute French control over Madagascar was established by military force in 1895-96, and the Merina monarchy was abolished.

Malagasy troops fought in France, Morocco, and Syria during World War I. After France fell to the Germans, the Vichy government administered Madagascar. British troops occupied the strategic island in 1942 to preclude its seizure by the Japanese. The Free French received the island from the United Kingdom in 1943.

In 1947, with French prestige at low ebb, a nationalist uprising was suppressed after several months of bitter fighting. The French subsequently established reformed institutions in 1956 under the Loi Cadre (Overseas Reform Act), and Madagascar moved peacefully toward independence. The Malagasy Republic was proclaimed on October 14, 1958, as an autonomous state within the French Community. A period of provisional government ended with the adoption of a constitution in 1959 and full independence on June 26, 1960.

GOVERNMENT

In March 1998, Malagasy voters approved a revised constitution. The principal institutions of the Republic of Madagascar are a presidency, a parliament, a prime ministry and cabinet, and an independent judiciary. The president is elected by direct universal suffrage for a 5-year term, renewable twice. The last presidential election was held on December 3, 2006.

In Madagascar, the parliament has two chambers; the National Assembly and the Senate. The last National Assembly election was held on September 23, 2007, and marked a significant reform to the parliament. The National Assembly previously had 160 members, elected for a four-year term in single-member and two-member constituencies. However, in July 2007, just before the National Assembly elections, a council of ministers agreed to reduce the number of parliamentarians from 160 to 127. Consequently, few of the 116 districts elected more than one member. Antananarivo's six districts, however, each elected two deputies. The Senate has 33 members, with 22 members elected for a six-year term, 1 for each province by provincial electors, and 11 members appointed by the president.

The prime minister and members of parliament initiate legislation, and the government executes it. The president can dissolve the National Assembly. For its part, the National Assembly can pass a motion of censure and require the prime minister and council of ministers to step down. The Constitutional Court approves the constitutionality of new laws.

In an effort to decentralize administration, the country's six provinces were dissolved in the constitutional referendum of 2007, in favor of 22 regions designated previously in 2004. Decentralization is a key element of Madagascar's development plans, and the transition is an ongoing process.

Principal Government Officials

Office	Name	Party	Since
President	Hery Rajaonarimampianina	Hery Vaovao ho an'i Madagasikara	25 January 2014
Prime Minister	Roger Kolo	Independent	16 April 2014

Ambassador to the U.S.--Jocelyn B. Radifera
Ambassador to the UN--Zina Andrianarivelo-Razafy

Madagascar maintains an embassy in the United States at 2374 Massachusetts Avenue NW, Washington, DC 20008 (tel. 202-265-5525).

POLITICAL CONDITIONS

Madagascar's first President, Philibert Tsiranana, was elected when his Social Democratic Party gained power at independence in 1960 and was reelected without opposition in March 1972. However, he resigned only 2 months later in response to massive antigovernment demonstrations. The unrest continued, and Tsiranana's successor, Gen. Gabriel Ramanantsoa, resigned on February 5, 1975, handing over executive power to Lt. Col. Richard Ratsimandrava, who was assassinated 6 days later. A provisional military directorate then ruled until a new government was formed in June 1975, under Didier Ratsiraka.

During the 16 subsequent years of President Ratsiraka's rule, Madagascar continued under a government committed to revolutionary socialism based on the 1975 constitution establishing a highly centralized state. National elections in 1982 and 1989 returned Ratsiraka for a second and third 7-year presidential term. For much of this period, only limited and restrained political opposition was tolerated, with no direct criticism of the president permitted in the press.

With an easing of restrictions on political expression, beginning in the late 1980s, the Ratsiraka regime came under increasing pressure to make fundamental changes. In response to a deteriorating economy, Ratsiraka relaxed socialist economic policies and instituted some liberal, private-sector reforms. These, along with political reforms like the elimination of press censorship in 1989 and the formation of more political parties in 1990, were insufficient to placate a growing opposition movement known as Hery Velona or "Active Forces." A number of already existing political parties and their leaders, among them Albert Zafy and Rakotoniaina Manandafy, anchored this movement which was especially strong in Antananarivo and the surrounding high plateau.

In response to largely peaceful mass demonstrations and crippling general strikes, Ratsiraka replaced his prime minister in August 1991 but suffered an irreparable setback soon thereafter when his troops fired on peaceful demonstrators marching on his suburban palace, killing more than 30.

In an increasingly weakened position, Ratsiraka acceded to negotiations on the formation of a transitional government. The resulting "Panorama Convention" of October 31, 1991, stripped Ratsiraka of nearly all of his powers, created interim institutions, and set an 18-month timetable for completing a transition to a new form of constitutional government. The High Constitutional Court was retained as the ultimate judicial arbiter of the process.

In March 1992, a widely representative National Forum organized by the Malagasy Christian Council of Churches (FFKM) drafted a new constitution. Troops guarding the proceedings clashed with pro-Ratsiraka "federalists" who tried to disrupt the forum in protest of draft constitutional provisions preventing the incumbent president from running again. The text of the new constitution was put to a nationwide referendum in August 1992 and approved by a wide margin, despite efforts by federalists to disrupt balloting in several coastal areas.

Presidential elections were held on November 25, 1992, after the High Constitutional Court had ruled, over active forces objections, that Ratsiraka could become a candidate. Runoff elections were held in February 1993, and the leader of the Hery Velona movement, Albert Zafy, defeated Ratsiraka. Zafy was sworn in as President on March 27, 1993. After President Zafy's impeachment by the National Assembly in 1996 and the short quasi-presidency of Norbert Ratsirahonana, the 1997 elections once again pitted Zafy and Ratsiraka, with Ratsiraka this time emerging victorious. A National Assembly dominated by members of President Ratsiraka'a political party AREMA subsequently passed the 1998 constitution, which considerably strengthened the presidency.

In December 2001, a presidential election was held in which both major candidates claimed victory. The Ministry of the Interior declared incumbent Ratsiraka of the AREMA party victorious. Marc Ravalomanana contested the results and claimed victory. A political crisis followed in which Ratsiraka supporters cut major transport routes from the primary port city to the capital city, a stronghold of Ravalomanana support. Sporadic violence and considerable economic disruption continued until July 2002 when Ratsiraka and several of his prominent supporters fled to exile in France. In addition to political differences, ethnic differences played a role in the crisis and continue to play a role in politics. Ratsiraka is from the coastal Betsimisaraka tribe and Ravalomanana comes from the highland Merina tribe.

After the end of the 2002 political crisis, President Ravalomanana began many reform projects, forcefully advocating "rapid and durable development" and the launching of a battle against corruption. December 2002 legislative elections gave his newly formed TIM (*Tiako-i-Madagasikara*--I Love Madagascar) Party a commanding majority in the National Assembly. November 2003 municipal elections were conducted freely, returning a majority of supporters of the president, but also significant numbers of independent and regional opposition figures.

Following the crisis of 2002, the President replaced provincial governors with appointed PDSs (Presidents des Delegations Speciales). This effectively put an end to the "autonomous provinces," although they nominally remained in place because they were included in the constitution. Subsequent legislation established a structure of 22 regions to decentralize administration. In September 2004, the government named 22 Regional Chiefs, reporting directly to the President, to implement its decentralization plans. Rumors about the dissolution of the autonomous provinces had been around for some time, and on April 4, 2007 a constitutional referendum was held, in which the majority of the voters backed a revised constitution without any provinces. The new regions have become the highest level of subdivision.

On March 17, 2009, President Ravalomanana stepped down, handing the government over to the military, which in turn conferred the presidency on opposition leader Andry Rajoelina. Rajoelina has declared himself "President of the High Transitional Authority" and pledged to hold presidential elections by October 2010, following a constitutional referendum and revision of the electoral code. The United States has condemned the unconstitutional and undemocratic change of power in Madagascar. We consider the recent series of events a military coup d'état.

ECONOMY

Rank	130th (IMF); 133rd (CIA); 131st (WB)
Currency	1 Malagasy ariary (MGA) = 5 Iraimbilanja
Fiscal year	calendar year
Trade organisations	WTO
	Statistics
GDP	USD $10.117 billion
GDP growth	1.9%
GDP per capita	USD $ 451
GDP by sector	agriculture(26%), industry(15,9%), services(58,1%)
Inflation (CPI)	9.2%
Gini coefficient	47.5 List of countries by income equality
Labour force	9.504 million
Unemployment	5.9%
Main industries	meat processing, soap, breweries, tanneries, sugar, textiles, glassware, cement, automobile

	assembly plant, paper, petroleum, tourism,
Ease-of-doing-business rank	142nd
	External
Exports	$640.7 million
Export goods	coffee, vanilla, shellfish, sugar, cotton cloth, clothing, chromite, petroleum products
Main export partners	France 23.1% China 6.5% United States 6.5% Singapore 5.8% Canada 5.4% India 5.3% Germany 5.3% Indonesia 5.2% South Africa 4.4%
Imports	$2.755 billion
Import goods	capital goods, petroleum, consumer goods, food
Main import partners	China 17.2% France 12.1% South Africa 5.3% Bahrain 5.1% India 5.0% Mauritius 4.7% Kuwait 4.4%
	Public finances
Public debt	$3.127 billion
Revenues	$1.758 billion
Expenses	$1.929 billion
Economic aid	recipient: $838 million

Agriculture, including fishing and forestry, is the mainstay of the Madagascar economy and the country has a great potential for growth in the sector. In 2009, agriculture accounted for 24% of Gross Domestic Product (GDP), while commerce and services accounted for 55%. Agriculture employs more than 70% of the labour force and provides livelihoods to the vast majority of about 20 million inhabitants, contributing more than 70% to export earnings, mostly through the export of seafood (mainly shrimp), vanilla, coffee, cacao, litchi, pepper, cotton, tobacco, groundnut, sisal, clove and ylang-ylang. Industry features textile manufacturing and the processing of agricultural products. Growth in output in 1992–97 averaged less than the growth rate of the population. Growth has been held back by a decline in world coffee demand, and the erratic commitment of the government to economic reform. Formidable obstacles stand in the way of Madagascar's realizing its considerable growth potential; the extent of government reforms, outside financial aid, and foreign investment will be key determinants.

Madagascar is an island endowed with a tropical climate along the coasts, a moderate climate in the highlands and an arid climate in the south. The diversity of its ecology and climate makes it possible to grow temperate crops such as apples, pears, plums, grapes and citrus fruits and tropical products such as mangoes and lychees, as well as a wide variety of other crops including coffee, cloves, sisal, maize, tubers and various spices.

RESOURCES

Madagascar's sources of growth are tourism; textile and light manufacturing exports (notably through the EPZs); agricultural products and mining. Madagascar was the world's leading producer of vanilla until 1986 and is still one of the top producers, accounting for about one quarter of the world's export market. Tourism targets the niche eco-tourism market, capitalizing on Madagascar's unique biodiversity, unspoiled natural habitats, national parks and lemur species. Exports from the EPZs, located around Antananarivo and Antsirabe, consist the most part of garment manufacture, targeting the US market under AGOA and the European markets under the Everything But Arms (EBA) agreement. Agricultural exports consist of low-volume high-value products like vanilla, lychees and essential oils. Madagascar has the largest cinnamon market in Africa. Madagascar also is a large exporter of coffee.

MINING

A small but growing part of the economy is based on mining of ilmenite, with investments emerging in recent years, particularly near Tulear and Fort Dauphin. Mining corporation Rio Tinto Group started production at its Fort Dauphin mine in January 2009, following several years of infrastructure preparation. The mining project is highly controversial, with Friends of the Earth and other environmental organizations filing reports to detail their concerns about effects on the local environment and communities. Gemstone mining is also an important part of Madagascar's economy.

Several major projects are underway in the mining and oil and gas sectors that, if successful, will give a significant boost. In the mining sector, these include the development of coal at Sakoa and nickel near Tamatave. The Ambatovy nickel mine (Sherrit International 40%, Sumitomo 27.5%, Korea Resources 27.5%, SNC Lavelin 5%) is a huge operation having cost $4.76m to date and is due to start production in 2011. In oil, Madagascar Oil is developing the massive onshore heavy oil field at Tsimiroro and ultra heavy oil field at Bemolanga.

Structural reforms began in the late 1980s, initially under pressure from international financial institutions. An initial privatization program (1988-1993) and the development of an export processing zone (EPZ) regime in the early 1990s were key milestones in this effort. A period of significant stagnation from 1991-96 was followed by 5 years of solid economic growth and accelerating foreign investment, driven by a second wave of privatizations and EPZ development. Although structural reforms advanced, governance remained weak and perceived corruption in Madagascar was extremely high. During the period of solid growth from 1997 through 2001, poverty levels remained stubbornly high, especially in rural areas. A six-month political crisis triggered by a dispute over the outcome of the presidential elections held in December 2001 virtually halted economic activity in much of the country in the first half of 2002. Real GDP dropped 12.7% for the year 2002, inflows of foreign investment dropped sharply, and the crisis tarnished Madagascar's budding reputation as an African Growth and Opportunity Act (AGOA) standout and a promising place to invest. Following resolution of the crisis, the economy rebounded with GDP growth of over 9% in 2003. Currency depreciation and rising inflation hampered economic performance in 2004-2005; by 2006 inflation had abated somewhat (to 11%) but growth remained sluggish (4.7% est.)

Following the 2002 political crisis, the government attempted to set a new course and build confidence in coordination with international financial institutions and the donor community. Madagascar developed a recovery plan in collaboration with the private sector and donors and presented it at a "Friends of Madagascar" conference organized by the World Bank in Paris in July 2002. Donor countries demonstrated their confidence in the new government by pledging $1 billion in assistance over five years. The Malagasy Government identified road infrastructure as its principal priority and underlined its commitment to public-private partnership by establishing a joint public-private sector steering committee.

In 2000, Madagascar embarked on the preparation of a Poverty Reduction Strategy Paper (PRSP) under the Heavily Indebted Poor Countries (HIPC) Initiative. The boards of the International Monetary Fund (IMF) and World Bank agreed in December 2000 that the country had reached the decision point for debt relief under the HIPC Initiative and defined a set of conditions for Madagascar to reach the completion point. In October 2004, the boards of the IMF and the World Bank determined that Madagascar had reached the completion point under the enhanced HIPC Initiative.

The Madagascar-U.S. Business Council was formed in Madagascar in 2002. The U.S.-Madagascar Business Council was formed in the United States in May 2003, and the two organizations continue to explore ways to work for the benefit of both groups. An American Chamber of Commerce was launched at the end of 2008, with plans to begin activity in early 2009.

Madagascar's ongoing political crisis continues to negatively impact key macroeconomic indicators and the business sector.

FOREIGN RELATIONS

Madagascar, which has historically been perceived as on the margin of mainstream African affairs, eagerly rejoined the African Union (AU) in July 2003 after a 14-month hiatus triggered by the 2002 political crisis, and joined the Southern African Development Community (SADC) in 2006. From 1978 until 1991, then-President Ratsiraka emphasized independence and nonalignment and followed an "all points" policy stressing ties with socialist and radical regimes, including North Korea, Cuba, Libya, and Iran. Taking office in 1993, President Albert Zafy expressed his desire for diplomatic relations with all countries. Early in his tenure, he established formal ties with South Korea and sent emissaries to Morocco.

Starting in 1997, globalization encouraged the government and President Ratsiraka to adhere to market-oriented policies and to engage world markets. External relations reflect this trend, although Madagascar's physical isolation and strong traditional insular orientation have limited its activity in regional economic organizations and relations with its East African neighbors. During his term, President Ravalomanana welcomed relations with all countries interested in helping Madagascar to develop. He consciously sought to strengthen relations with Anglophone countries as a means of balancing traditional strong French influence.

Following the 2009 coup d'état, Madagascar was suspended from participating in AU and SADC activities until constitutional order is restored. Several donors in Madagascar, including the U.S., have suspended assistance programs to the Government of Madagascar. The AU formed an International Contact Group to coordinate international community action to ensure a return to constitutional rule as quickly as possible.

U.S.-MALAGASY RELATIONS

Relations with the United States date to the middle 1800s. The two countries concluded a commercial convention in 1867 and a treaty of peace, friendship, and commerce in 1881. Traditionally warm relations suffered considerably during the 1970s, when Madagascar expelled the U.S. ambassador, closed a NASA tracking station, and nationalized two U.S. oil companies. In 1980, relations at the ambassadorial level were restored.

Throughout the troubled period, commercial and cultural relations remained active. In 1990, Madagascar was designated as a priority aid recipient, and assistance increased from $15 million in 1989 to $40 million in 1993. Recent U.S. assistance has contributed to a population census and family planning programs; conservation of Madagascar's remarkable biodiversity, private sector development, agriculture, democracy and governance initiatives; and media training. Madagascar became the very first country with a Millennium Challenge Account compact when it signed an agreement worth $110 million in April 2006, although the compact has been terminated due to the recent political crisis. The Ravalomanana government was especially positive about ties with the United States.

The United States considers the recent series of events in Madagascar a military coup d'état, and as a result has suspended all assistance programs that directly benefit the government as well as all non-humanitarian assistance to Madagascar. The United States' intent is to support international efforts led by the AU to ensure that a credible electoral process takes place as soon as possible, organized by an independent entity.

U.S. Embassy Officials
Ambassador--R. Niels Marquardt
Deputy Chief of Mission--Eric Stromayer
USAID Director--Rudolph Thomas
Defense Attaché--CDR John Ries
Public Affairs Officer--Rodney Ford
Consular Officer--Melanie Rubenstein
Economic/Commercial Section Chief--Dovie Holland
Political Officer--Jeff Hulse
Management Officer--Steve Dodson
Peace Corps Director--Steve Wisecarver

The U.S. Embassy in Madagascar is located at 14, rue Rainitovo, Antsahavola, Antananarivo (tel. 261-20-22-212-57, 033-44-22-000; fax 261-20-345-39. The postal address is Ambassader Americaine, B.P. 620, Antananarivo, Madagascar.

TRAVEL AND BUSINESS INFORMATION

The U.S. Department of State's Consular Information Program advises Americans traveling and residing abroad through Country Specific Information, Travel Alerts, and Travel Warnings. **Country Specific Information** exists for all countries and includes information on entry and exit requirements, currency regulations, health conditions, safety and security, crime, political disturbances, and the addresses of the U.S. embassies and consulates abroad. **Travel Alerts** are issued to disseminate information quickly about terrorist threats and other relatively short-term conditions overseas that pose significant risks to the security of American travelers. **Travel Warnings** are issued when the State Department recommends that Americans avoid travel to a certain country because the situation is dangerous or unstable.

For the latest security information, Americans living and traveling abroad should regularly monitor the Department's Bureau of Consular Affairs Internet web site at http://www.travel.state.gov, where the current Worldwide Caution, Travel Alerts, and Travel Warnings can be found. Consular Affairs Publications, which contain information on obtaining passports and planning a safe trip abroad, are also available at http://www.travel.state.gov. For additional information on international travel, see http://www.usa.gov/Citizen/Topics/Travel/International.shtml.

The Department of State encourages all U.S. citizens traveling or residing abroad to register via the State Department's travel registration website or at the nearest U.S. embassy or consulate abroad. Registration will make your presence and whereabouts known in case it is necessary to contact you in an emergency and will enable you to receive up-to-date information on security conditions.

Emergency information concerning Americans traveling abroad may be obtained by calling 1-888-407-4747 toll free in the U.S. and Canada or the regular toll line 1-202-501-4444 for callers outside the U.S. and Canada.

The National Passport Information Center (NPIC) is the U.S. Department of State's single, centralized public contact center for U.S. passport information. Telephone: 1-877-4-USA-PPT (1-877-487-2778); TDD/TTY: 1-888-874-7793. Passport information is available 24 hours, 7 days a week. You may speak with a representative Monday-Friday, 8 a.m. to 10 p.m., Eastern Time, excluding federal holidays.

Travelers can check the latest health information with the U.S. Centers for Disease Control and Prevention in Atlanta, Georgia. A hotline at 800-CDC-INFO (800-232-4636) and a web site at http://wwwn.cdc.gov/travel/default.aspx give the most recent health advisories, immunization recommendations or requirements, and advice on food and drinking water safety for regions and countries

PRACTICAL INFORMATION FOR BUSINESS AND INVESTMENTS[1]

STARTING BUSINESS IN MADAGASAR

MARKET OVERVIEW

An island in the Western Indian Ocean with a population of around 22 million, Madagascar ranks among the poorest countries in the world. Almost 80 percent of the population lives in poverty.

In March 2009, elected President Marc Ravalomanana was ousted by the former mayor of Antananarivo, Andry Rajoelina, in a coup supported by the army. The international community does not recognize the de facto transition regime that has been in power since that time. Most donors suspended their non-humanitarian aid programs, and the USG terminated the Millennium Challenge Account (MCA) program on May 19, 2009. On December 23, 2009, the country's eligibility under the African Growth and Opportunity Act (AGOA) was also suspended as the country no longer met the criteria regarding political pluralism and rule of law.

The Transitional Independent National Electoral Commission (CENI-T), in collaboration with the United Nations, the Southern African Development Community (SADC), and de facto Malagasy authorities, has made preparations to hold presidential and legislative elections in mid-2013. However, as of the completion of this report, it remains unclear whether these elections will take place as scheduled.

In October 2012, the World Bank noted that due to the three and half years of political crisis, the economy has severely stalled, poverty has sharply increased, and social outcomes have worsened. In its most recent projections, it estimated Madagascar's 2012 inflation rate at 8.5% and its growth rate of 2.5%

State divestiture from public enterprises has been a cornerstone of government policy for the two last decades, although the water and energy utility company, two large insurance companies, and the national airline still belong to the Malagasy state.

Combating corruption was a stated priority of the Ravalomanana administration. In 2003, the President created the Anti-Corruption Council; and in September 2004, the Independent Anti-Corruption Office (BIANCO), began operations. Official corruption has risen since the unconstitutional change of government in March 2009.

On July 19, 2008, the previous administration created the Malagasy Financial Intelligence Service (SAMIFIN), a financial intelligence unit in charge of combating money laundering. In 2012, SAMIFIN received 61 suspicious transaction reports and referred 23 cases to public prosecutors.

Despite the political crisis Rio Tinto continued to export ilmenite in 2012, and Ambatovy (a joint venture of Sherritt, SNC Lavalin, Kores, and Sumitomo) started exporting nickel on November 8, 2012.

MARKET CHALLENGES

[1] US Governmetn Materials

In general, there are no specific barriers to market entry, but direct marketing for American-made products is difficult. The Malagasy consumer is unaccustomed to Western marketing styles. In addition, French language nuances may not be as evident to an American businessperson. The Embassy encourages U.S. operators to market to local distributors and agents.

MARKET OPPORTUNITIES

The best prospects for future U.S. sales and investments are in the energy, oil exploration, and mining sectors. There are under-exploited opportunities in consulting and engineering.

The country has commercially significant reserves of several minerals, including rare earths, uranium, coal, chromites, graphite, and mica. Gold and significant quantities of various precious and semi-precious stones—ruby, sapphire, and emerald—are also found in the country.

Madagascar's rich biodiversity and high level of endemic plants and animals are the basis for eco-tourism development and might attract foreign investors, along with potential for development of beach resorts.

Despite Madagascar's poverty, the island's unique natural environment, its wide variety of resources, its competitive labor force, and its location on the crossroads between Asia and Africa offer potential long-term investment opportunities, following the resolution of the current political crisis. However, investors should note that periodic political instability, the lack of a level playing field in particular sectors, an unreliable legal system, rampant corruption at the highest levels, and a lack of transparency in contracting and regulatory decisions can make doing business in Madagascar challenging.

MARKET ENTRY STRATEGY

The use of distributors, particularly with prior experience in distributing imported goods, is highly recommended. Local agents have contacts to develop a customer base and can easily communicate in Malagasy and/or in French. Partners can be found by obtaining a list of importers from the Embassy Commercial Section or by contacting business groups and market survey firms (see at Chapter 9).

SELLING U.S. PRODUCTS AND SERVICES

USING AN AGENT OR DISTRIBUTOR

For new American operators, the use of agents and distributors, particularly those with prior experience in distributing imported products is highly recommended. Local agents have contacts to develop a customer base and can easily communicate in Malagasy and/or French. The Embassy recommends that U.S. firms visit Madagascar and negotiate a distribution contract face-to-face in order to develop the personal relationships that facilitate doing business in the country.

ESTABLISHING AN OFFICE

In May 2006, the Government of Madagascar (GOM) established an investment promotion office: the Economic Development Board of Madagascar (EDBM). It is a one-stop shop for investment and business development to facilitate company registration procedures and to assist local and foreign investors. Now it takes as little as a week to register a company, whereas in the past it took at least one month.

Office space can be found through a handful of real estate agents, advertisements in local papers, or word of mouth. Landlords will rent to new companies even if they have not obtained all their operating permits. Office furniture can be obtained locally at reasonable prices and telephone services—fixed or mobile—are available in the main towns. There are increasing numbers of multilingual, qualified secretaries and administrative assistants interested in working with foreign businesses.

FRANCHISING

A number of Malagasy businesspersons have expressed interest in establishing franchises of U.S. businesses in Madagascar, particularly fast food chains such as McDonalds and Kentucky Fried Chicken. However they have been unsuccessful due to the high fees and the lack of local consumer purchasing power. A number of leading U.S. products and services are sold through distributorships, including automotive and machinery (Caterpillar, Ford, General Motors); communications and information technology (Apple, AT&T, Cisco, Compaq, Dell, HP, Motorola, NCR, Oracle, Packard Bell, and Sun Microsystems); Coca-Cola, and Kodak films.

DIRECT MARKETING

Although there are exceptions, direct marketing for U.S.-made products is difficult. Therefore, the Embassy encourages U.S. businesspersons to negotiate with local distributors and agents.

JOINT VENTURES/LICENSING

Joint ventures with local companies are not required, but are generally recommended. The benefit of joint ventures is that the local partners have knowledge and experience in the country and can navigate complex bureaucratic administrative procedures. The drawback is that a local partner will likely be a minority shareholder in capital terms and must be carefully screened through independent references and past business history.

In the domain of oil exploration, companies must negotiate production sharing contracts with the government's Office of National Mines and Strategic Industries (OMNIS): http://omnis.mg/.

There are only a few licensing ventures, the most prominent being Coca-Cola with Star Brewery.

SELLING TO GOVERNMENT

As part of its liberalization strategy, the de facto GOM frequently advertises calls for international bids to supply government-funded projects in official and local newspapers. These bids are opened publicly and tend not to be contested. The most frequent opportunities are in road construction, supply of computers, consulting, engineering, etc.

DISTRIBUTION AND SALES CHANNELS

Imported goods can enter Madagascar via air at Ivato international airport in Antananarivo or via sea at the ports of Tamatave, Majunga, Antsiranana, Tulear and Fort Dauphin. Some 90 percent of containerized imports and exports transit the country's largest port, at Tamatave. Products are then distributed by road, sea or rail throughout the country. Distribution is usually handled by the importing company or by wholesalers and retailers. Roads are poor in much of the country; some areas cannot be accessed by road during the rainy season (December-March).

SELLING FACTORS/TECHNIQUES

The purchasing power of the average Malagasy is very low, so most Malagasy can only afford immediate necessities. When selling, there is no requirement to translate labels into Malagasy. Retailers and sales clerks respond to customers' needs and process sales, but there is only a dawning awareness of service or sales techniques common in the United States or Europe.

ELECTRONIC COMMERCE

E-Commerce is beginning to be used in the country. Payment by credit cards (Visa and, in limited circumstances, MasterCard) is accepted in large supermarkets and hotels.

Each gas distributor has its own payment card. Since 2010, a few department stores began accepting payment through mobile phones. Mobile banking, such as the payment of air ticket through mobile phone, is widely used, although no legal framework is in place to regulate it.

TRADE PROMOTION AND ADVERTISING

Marketing is a relatively new industry to Madagascar. Avenues of advertising include billboards, posters, newspapers, radio and television. Prominent campaigns have European influence and often link the product with leisure activities or personal enjoyment. The quality of advertising campaigns varies and appears to depend on the budget of the advertiser. It is possible to pay a newspaper for a full-page article/advertisement, or television stations to broadcast an info/ad program.

Local fair authorities/organizations

Premiere Ligne
13, rue Ratsimilaho, Antaninarenina
Antananarivo 101 – Madagascar
Tel: (261 20) 22 212 40
Fax: (261 20) 22 212 41
Website: http://www.siit-technopole.mg/ or http://www.foire-de-madagascar.mg/
E-mail: siit-technopole@moov.mg or f-i-m@moov.mg
Contact: Mr. Michel Raharimanana

Madavision
Lot VP pres 27 A Bis, Ambohimiandra
Antananarivo 101 – Madagascar
Tel: (261 20) 22 564 41
E-mail: contact@grandebraderie.com
Contact: Mrs. Harilala Ramanantsoa

Synergie Communication
43 rue de Russie Isoraka
Antananarivo 101 – Madagascar
Tel: (261 20) 22 618 97
E-mail: synergy@moov.mg

Daily newspapers:

L' Express de Madagascar
P.O. Box 171
Antananarivo 101 – Madagascar
Tel: (261 20) 22 203 10
Fax: (261 20) 22 213 83
Website: http://www.lexpressmada.com/
E-mail: lexpress@malagasy.com

Midi Madagasikara
P.O. Box 1414
Antananarivo 101 – Madagascar
Tel: (261 20) 22 300 38
Fax: (261 20) 22 273 51
Website: http://www.mid-madagasikara.mg/
E-mail: midi@moov.mg

Madagascar Tribune
P.O. Box 659
Antananarivo 101 – Madagascar
Tel: (261 20) 22 226 35
Fax: (261 20) 22 2222 54
Website: http://www.madagascar-tribune.com/
E-mail: tribune@moov.mg

La Gazette de la Grande Ile
P.O. Box 8678
Antananarivo 101 – Madagascar
Tel: (261 20) 22 613 77
Fax; (261 20) 22 651 88
Website: http://www.lagazette-dgi.com/
E-mail: administration@lagazzette-dgi.com

Les Nouvelles
P.O. Box 194
Antananarivo 101 – Madagascar
Tel: (261 20) 22 354 33
Website: http://www.les-nouvelles.com/
E-mail: redaction@les-nouvelles.com

Le Courrier
Immeuble SME, Ankorondrano
Antananarivo 101 – Madagascar
Tel: (261 20) 22 378 95
Website: http://www.courriermada.com/
E-mail: dirpublc@blueline.mg

Madagascar Matin
P.O. Box 194
Antananarivo 101 – Madagascar
Tel: (261 20) 26 295 21
E-mail: madagascarmatin@gmail.com

L'Observateur
Lot II M 85 bis Antsakaviro
Antananarivo 101 – Madagascar
Tel: (261 20) 22 216 69
E-mail: lobservateur@gmail.com

Business Journals:

Revue de l'Ocean Indien (ROI)
P.O. Box 46
Antananarivo 101 – Madagascar
Tel: (261 20) 22 225 36
Fax: (261 20) 22 345 34
E-mail: roi@moov.mg

Television Stations:

Television Malagasy (TVM) (state)
Anosy
Antananarivo 101 – Madagascar
Tel: (261 20) 22 208 97
Fax: (261 20) 22 344 21

RTA
P.O. Box 7547
Antananarivo 101 – Madagascar
Tel: (261 20) 22 627 76
Fax: (261 20) 22 558 80
Website: http://www.rta.mg/
E-mail: flash@rts.mg

TVPLUS
Anosizato
Antananarivo 101 – Madagascar
Tel/Fax: (261 20) 22 676 73

MATV
B.P.: 1414. Ankorondrano, Antananarivo, Madagasikara
Tel: (261 20) 22 364 69/70
Fax: (261 20) 22 671 27
http://www.matvonline.tv/

TELERECORD
P.O. Box 7522
Antananarivo 101 – Madagascar
Tel: (261 20) 22 295 32
Fax: (261 20) 22 664 68
Website: http://www.rtv-record.com/
E-mail: rtv.record@iris.mg

VIVA Television
Tana Water Front, Ambodivona
Antananarivo 101 – Madagascar

Tel: (261 20) 22 567 88
Fax: (261 20) 22 684 95

PRICING

Pricing of imported products depends on import duties, which generally range from 0 to 20 percent. Since 2008, a value added tax (VAT) of 20 percent has been added onto the retail price, and profit margins on products tend to be around 7 to 10 percent.

SALES SERVICE/CUSTOMER SUPPORT

The concept of sales service and customer support is relatively new to Madagascar and is limited primarily to distributors of vehicles, computers and electronic equipment. Retailers of most consumer goods rarely accept returns of defective products. To protect consumers' rights, two private consumer organizations were created, but their actions have reportedly so far been limited.

Contacts for local IPR registration and enforcement:

OMAPI, *Office Malgache de la Propriété Industrielle* (Malagasy Office for Industrial Property); e-mail: omapi@moov.mg

OMDA, *Office Malgache des Dorits d'Auteurs* (Malagasy Office for Copyrights); e-mail: omda@moov.mg

PROTECTING INTELLECTUAL PROPERTY

Several general principles are important for effective management of intellectual property ("IP") rights in Madagascar. First, it is important to have an overall strategy to protect your IP. Second, IP is protected differently in Madagascar than in the United States. Third, rights must be registered and enforced in Madagascar, under local laws. Your U.S. trademark and patent registrations will not protect you in Madagascar. There is no such thing as an "international copyright" that will automatically protect an author's writings throughout the entire world. Protection against unauthorized use in a particular country depends, basically, on the national laws of that country. However, most countries do offer copyright protection to foreign works under certain conditions, and these conditions have been greatly simplified by international copyright treaties and conventions.

Registration of patents and trademarks is on a first-in-time, first-in-right basis, so you should consider applying for trademark and patent protection even before selling your products or services in the Madagascar market. It is vital that companies understand that intellectual property is primarily a private right and that the U.S. Government generally cannot enforce rights for private individuals in Madagascar. It is the responsibility of the rights' holders to register, protect, and enforce their rights where relevant, retaining their own counsel and advisors. Companies may wish to seek advice from local attorneys or IP consultants who are experts in Madagascar law. The U.S. Commercial Service (http://www.trade.gov/cs/) can provide a list of local lawyers upon request.

While the U.S. Government stands ready to assist, there is little we can do if the rights' holders have not taken these fundamental steps necessary to securing and enforcing their IP in a timely fashion. Moreover, in many countries, rights' holders who delay enforcing their rights on a mistaken belief that the U.S. Government can provide a political resolution to a legal problem may find that their rights have been eroded or abrogated due to legal doctrines such as statutes of limitations, laches, estoppel, or unreasonable delay in prosecuting a law suit. In no instance should U.S. Government advice be seen as a substitute for the obligation of a rights holder to promptly pursue its case.

It is always advisable to conduct due diligence on potential partners. Negotiate from the position of your partner and give your partner clear incentives to honor the contract. A good partner is an important ally in protecting IP rights. Consider carefully, however, whether to permit your partner to register your IP rights on your behalf. Doing so may create a risk that your partner will list itself as the IP owner and fail to transfer the rights should the partnership end. Keep an eye on your cost structure and reduce the margins (and the incentive) of would-be bad actors. Projects and sales in Madagascar require constant attention. Work with legal counsel familiar with Madagascar laws to create a solid contract that includes non-compete clauses, and confidentiality/non-disclosure provisions.

It is also recommended that small and medium-size companies understand the importance of working together with trade associations and organizations to support efforts to protect IP and stop counterfeiting. There are a number of these organizations, both Madagascar or U.S.-based. These include:

The U.S. Chamber and local American Chambers of Commerce
National Association of Manufacturers (NAM)
International Intellectual Property Alliance (IIPA)
International Trademark Association (INTA)
The Coalition Against Counterfeiting and Piracy
International Anti-Counterfeiting Coalition (IACC)
Pharmaceutical Research and Manufacturers of America (PhRMA)
Biotechnology Industry Organization (BIO)

IP RESOURCES

A wealth of information on protecting IP is freely available to U.S. rights' holders. Some excellent resources for companies regarding intellectual property include the following:

For information about patent, trademark, or copyright issues—including enforcement issues in the US and other countries—call the STOP! Hotline: **1-866-999-HALT** or register athttp://www.stopfakes.gov/.

For more information about registering trademarks and patents (both in the United States as well as in foreign countries), contact the U.S. Patent and Trademark Office (USPTO) at: **1-800-786-9199**.

For more information about registering for copyright protection in the United States, contact the U.S. Copyright Office at: **1-202-707-5959**.

For more information about how to evaluate, protect, and enforce intellectual property rights and how these rights may be important for businesses, a free online training program is available athttp://www.stopfakes.gov/.

For U.S. small and medium-size companies, the Department of Commerce offers an "International Intellectual Property Rights (IPR) Advisory Program" available through the

American Bar Association that provides a free, one-hour consultation with a volunteer attorney knowledgeable in both industry IPR issues and a particular country. Expertise is now available for **Angola, Argentina, Brazil, China, Colombia, Egypt, Ghana, India, Indonesia, Kenya, Mexico, Mozambique, Nigeria, Russia, Saudi Arabia, Senegal, South Africa, Thailand, Turkey, and Vietnam**. For details and to register, visit: http://www.stopfakes.gov/business-tools/international-ip-advisory-program orhttp://www.abanet.org/intlaw/intlproj/iprprogram_consultation.html

For information on obtaining and enforcing intellectual property rights and market-specific IP Toolkits visit: http://www.stopfakes.gov/ This site is linked to the USPTO website for registering trademarks and patents (both in the United States as well as in foreign countries), the U.S. Customs & Border Protection website to record registered trademarks and copyrighted works (to assist customs in blocking imports of IP-infringing products), and allows you to register for Webinars on protecting IP.

The U.S. Department of Commerce has positioned IP attachés in key markets around the world.

DUE DILIGENCE

Accountants commonly perform due diligence in Madagascar, usually in areas of investment, joint venture/partnership, and loans.

LEADING SECTORS FOR U.S. EXPORT AND INVESTMENT

ARTICLES OF IRON AND STEEL

Unit: USD thousands

	2011	2012	2013(estimated)	2014(estimated)
Total Market Size	n/a	n/a	n/a	n/a
Total Imports	169,593,580	119,299,908	n/a	
Imports from the United States	1,387,900	721,000	33,000 (Jan-Feb)	
Exchange Rate: 1 USD	2,025	2,194	2,214 (Jan–Feb)	

Products covered are within HTS Chapter 72 iron and steel products (such as stainless steel, bars, rods, wire of alloy steel) and HTS Chapter 73 articles of iron or steel (such as wires, ropes, cables, tubes and pipes).

SUB-SECTOR BEST PROSPECTS AND OPPORTUNITIES

Given Madagascar's total imports of USD 119 million in 2012 and considering the low U.S. market share, U.S. exporters can increase their sales in this area through the establishment of a sales agent or by negotiating with a well-known importer or distributor. The main sources of imports include India, China, Malaysia and South Africa.

Madagascar possesses several iron ore deposits: The Soalala deposit (the most significant), estimated at 360 million tons at a grade of 35% iron, has been granted to the China's Wuhan Iron and Steel Company (WISCO). However, there are still two important deposits that can be exploited: the Betioky deposit, with 30 million tons of ore at 24% iron and 130 million tons of ore at between 10% and 14% iron; and the Bekisopa deposit, which has around 10 million tons of ore at a grade of 60% iron and 140 million tons at a grade of 10% to 14% iron. Small iron deposits also exist throughout the country. After new elections, should the Ministry of Mines conduct a new international solicitation for licenses on these iron deposits, the Commercial Section would notify the Department of Commerce and potential U.S. investors.

PLASTICS AND ARTICLES THEREOF

Unit: USD thousands

	2011	2012	2013(estimated)	2014(estimated)
Total Market Size	n/a	n/a	n/a	
Total Local Production	0	0	0	
Total Exports	0	0	0	
Total Imports	85,092,839	78,319,963	n/a	
Imports from the United States	404,600	1,032,300	98,800 (Jan-Feb)	
Exchange Rate: 1 USD	2,025	2,194	2,214 (Jan-Feb)	

Products covered are within HTS Chapter 39: plastics and articles thereof including articles of polymers and resins; tubes, pipes and hoses of plastics; cellulose and its chemical derivatives in primary forms.

Madagascar has approximately 10 companies processing plastic products, such as tubes, pipes, plates, buckets and bags. The raw materials are mainly imported from South Africa, China, the Republic of Korea, France, and India.

SUB-SECTOR BEST PROSPECTS AND OPPORTUNITIES

Considering the significant needs of the Malagasy market in plastics products (USD 78 million, it is obvious that the U.S. plastics industry might still uncover a huge market in Madagascar. To enter the market, U.S. products must be very competitive, because Asian suppliers have good trade links and usually sell at a low price. The best way to enter the market would be through an agent distributor or a well-known importer who has a good distribution nationwide.

VEGETABLE OIL

Unit: USD thousands

	2011	2012	2013 (estimated)	2014(estimated)
Total Imports	42,320,000	45,250,000	n/a	n/a
Imports from the United States	5,992,800	3,610,800	0	n/a
Exchange Rate: 1 USD	2,025	2,194	2,214 (Jan-Feb)	

Madagascar imports nearly 100 percent of its vegetable oil. There are small artisanal units that process oil from peanuts, but they do not meet the regular standards. Data on market size and production are not available.

SUB-SECTOR BEST PROSPECTS AND OPPORTUNITIES

In 2012, Madagascar imported soybean oil (HTS 1507) and fixed vegetable fats and oils (HTS 1515) from the United States for a total value of USD 3,610,800. Since 1995, imports of soybean oil from the United States have been funded by the Food for Peace Program (Public Law 480) managed by the United States Agency for International Development (USAID) or by the U.S. Department of Agriculture. With total imports of USD 45 million in 2012, the United States still has a significant opportunity in the Malagasy market. Madagascar imports refined vegetable oil from various sources, such as Egypt, France, Italy, China, Indonesia, Malaysia and even Brazil and Argentina. The best way to enter the market would be through an agent distributor or by contacting business associations (see Chapter 9).

TRADE REGULATIONS, CUSTOMS AND STANDARDS

IMPORT TARIFFS

Custom duties range from 5% to 20%. Based on the 2013 budget law, ovens, lamps and calculators using solar energy are exempt from customs duties. Likewise, prepared animal fodder and residues and waste from the food industries are exempt both from VAT and custom duties. Custom duties for plates, sheets, film, foil and strip have been reduced from 10 to 5 percent. Custom duties for paper, paperboard, and articles of paper have been reduced from 10 percent to 5 percent.

In compliance with the "UNESCO Florence Agreement on the Importation of Educational, Scientific and Cultural Materials," printed books, brochures, newspapers, journals and periodicals are exempted from custom duties and VAT.

VAT is fixed at 20% for all goods except rice, agricultural equipment, agricultural inputs (seeds, fertilizers, animal food and vitamins), newspapers, magazines, and sports equipment, which are all exempt.

TRADE BARRIERS

Like many developing countries, Madagascar collects a significant share of government revenue through customs duties, import taxes and VAT on imports. Although they have been lowered recently, tax and customs duty rates are still relatively high. Madagascar does not have significant formal non-tariff barriers to trade.

IMPORT REQUIREMENTS AND DOCUMENTATION

The following documents are required for imports:

BSC (*Bordereau de Suivi des Cargaisons*, cargo follow-up document)

Commercial invoice

Bill of lading or Air Way Bill

Packing list

Import declaration

Certificate of origin

EXPORT REQUIREMENTS AND DOCUMENTATION

Most exports from Madagascar have been liberalized. However, since 2010, a special export permit is required for rice, due to the shortage of local production.

In addition, the Convention on International Trade in Endangered Species (CITES), of which Madagascar and the United States are members, prohibits or restricts international trade in some protected plant and animal species.

The CITES Appendix I lists species that are the most endangered among CITES-listed animals and plants. They are threatened with extinction, and CITES prohibits international trade in specimens of these species except when the purpose of the import is not commercial.

For Madagascar, Appendix I includes most types of lemurs, rosewood, the Malagasy tree boa, radiated tortoises, and the Madagascar Angulated Tortoise.

Appendix II lists species that are not necessarily now threatened with extinction but that may become so unless trade is closely controlled. It also includes so-called "look-alike species", i.e., species of which the specimens in trade look like those of species listed for conservation reasons. International trade in specimens of Appendix-II species may be authorized by the granting of an export permit or re-export certificate. No import permit is necessary for these species under CITES (although a permit is needed in some countries that have taken stricter measures than CITES requires).

For Madagascar, crocodiles, the Malagasy big-headed tortoise, and the Malagasy big-headed turtle are included in Appendix II.

Appendix III is a list of species included at the request of a Party that already regulates trade in the species and that needs the cooperation of other countries to prevent unsustainable or illegal exploitation (see Article II, paragraph 3, of the Convention). International trade in specimens of species listed in this Appendix is allowed only on presentation of the appropriate permits or certificates. (See Article V of the Convention)

The ploughshare tortoise, ebony, numerous chameleon species, and many orchids species are included Appendix III.

Exporters are obliged to repatriate their foreign exchange earnings within 180 days following shipment.

These lists are not intended to be inclusive of all species on the list of CITES protected animals and plants in Madagascar. To verify whether you need a permit according to the CITES accord to export a plant or animal from Madagascar, please first check the following website. http://www.cites.org/eng/app/appendices.php

Then, the following documents are required for exports:

Commercial invoice

Bill of lading or Air Way Bill

Certificate of origin (under GSP regime, JADE Act)

Phytosanitary certificate, if required

Packing list

Export declaration

Customs declaration

Quality certificate, if required

U.S. EXPORT CONTROLS

There are no U.S. export controls specifically related to Madagascar. However, companies should ensure that imports of flora or fauna from Madagascar to the United States adhere to the provisions of the Lacey Act, which does not allow the import, export, transport, sale, receipt or purchase of plant materials taken, possessed, transported, or sold in violation of U.S. or foreign laws. American law enforcement officials took action in 2010 against companies that imported rosewood that had been illegally felled in Madagascar.

TEMPORARY ENTRY

Personal effects of diplomatic corps and international organizations are not subject to import taxes upon entry, but if personnel sell their effects before leaving the country, they must pay the import duties. Madagascar has a temporary admission regime under which certain items may enter duty free for up to 12 months. These items include imported goods that are expected to be re-exported (as is or after transformation); goods subject to experiment, repairs, and testing; goods exhibited during an international trade fair; and equipment used in public works.

LABELING AND MARKING REQUIREMENTS

For each certified product, labeling and marking are required on the packaging of the product before sale or export. All perishable foods must bear a label, in French or English, indicating the origin, the sell-by or use-by date, the ingredients, the method of storage, the manufacturer's name and registration number where appropriate, and the intended use. Use of the metric system is compulsory in Madagascar.

For further information, the point of contact is:
Bureau National des Normes (BNM)
P.O. Box 1316
Antananarivo 101 – Madagascar
Tel: (261 20) 22 279 70
E-mail: bnm@moov.mg

PROHIBITED AND RESTRICTED IMPORTS

Imports into Madagascar are liberalized and no longer require any import license, except for a few categories of items which are considered by the GOM as strategic and which are specially regulated. The importations of radioactive waste from nuclear power stations, pornographic materials, counterfeit branded products, pirated goods and goods bearing false indications of origin are prohibited. The importation of products such as arms, explosives and narcotic drugs is subject to prior authorization. The same applies to imports of diamonds, gemstones, gold and platinum jewelry, and vanilla. Madagascar also maintains a special regime for imports of leaf tobacco. An import license is required for lubricants. In addition, Madagascar applies prohibitions and licenses under multilateral environmental agreements to which it is party.

CUSTOMS REGULATIONS AND CONTACT INFORMATION

Madagascar is a member of the World Customs Organization (WCO). Since November 2000, the Malagasy customs authorities have implemented the "transactional value" definition of the WCO. Customs duties are valued based on Cargo, Insurance and Freight (CIF).

Customs contact information:
Mr. Vola Razafindramiandra Ramiandrasoa
Director General of Customs
Ministry of Finance, Budget and Economy
Antaninarenina, Antananarivo 101
Madagascar
Tel: (261 20) 22 229 16
Fax: (261 20) 22 646 80

EXPORT STANDARDS

Madagascar's Standards Office (*Le Bureau de Normes de Madagascar*, BNM), is the official body in charge of standards and conformity assessment in Madagascar. BNM's objective is to draft and publish national standards, manage national trademark conformity and apply national standards. BNM also represents Madagascar at regional and international standards organizations such as the ISO (International Organization for Standardization), the CEI (Cycle Engineers' Institute), the OIML (International Organization of Legal Metrology), and the Codex Alimentarius. When developing standards, BNM follows international standards, mainly those established by ISO.

PRONABIO (*Produits Naturels et Biologiques)*, a local organization, has developed its own standards, called "NATIORA" to certify its natural goods such as vegetables, spices, and essential oils.

STANDARDS ORGANIZATIONS

The main national testing laboratories are:

The National Laboratory of Public Works and Building (*Laboratoire National des Travaux Publics et du Batiment*, LNTPB), which develops standards in construction and engineering materials.

The National Institute and Laboratory of Nuclear Sciences and Technogy (*Laboratoire de l'Institut National des Sciences et Techniques Nucléaires*, LINSTN). Other national laboratories test for conformity with international standards, as highlighted in the next section.

NIST NOTIFY U.S. SERVICE

Member countries of the World Trade Organization (WTO) are required under the Agreement on Technical Barriers to Trade (TBT Agreement) to report to the WTO all proposed technical regulations that could affect trade with other Member countries. **Notify U.S.** is a free, web-based e-mail subscription service that offers an opportunity to review and comment on proposed foreign technical regulations that can affect your access to international markets. Register online at:http://www.nist.gov/notifyus/%0d

CONFORMITY ASSESSMENT

The BNM and the following testing laboratories ensure conformity assessment in Madagascar.

National Laboratory of Public Works and Building (*Laboratoire National des Travaux Publics et du Bâtiment*, LNTPB): certification of construction materials (cement, iron, etc); study of road materials; study of soil in view of construction stability assessment; control of construction; description of maintenance works;; training of engineers.

Antananarivo Laboratory of Chemistry and Microbiology (*Laboratoire de Chimie et de Microbiologie d'Antananarivo*, LCMA): quality control of food and agricultural goods, classification and conformity assessment. Standards used are AFNOR, ISO, and the Codex Alimentarius.

Chemistry Laboratory of Tamatave (*Laboratoire de Chimie de Tamatave*, LCT): quality control of agricultural goods such as coffee, vanilla, cloves, litchi, pepper, and essential oils; classification and conformity assessment. Standards used are AFNOR and ISO.

Laboratory of Legal Metrology (*Laboratoire de Métrologie Légale*, LML): control and standardization of measuring equipment in the commercial and industrial sector. LML reports to the Ministry of Trade.

Laboratory of the National Center of Research for the Environment (*Laboratoire du Centre National de Recherche pour l'Environnement*, LCNRE): analysis of environmental samples; monitoring of impacts of industrial activities of environment; scientific support to the industrial sector; control and analysis in the nutritional and food sector; scientific support to the private sector in product quality (shrimp, lobster, agricultural goods, etc).

Laboratory of Biochemical Nutrition for the Department of Zootechnics and Veterinary Research (*Laboratoire de Biochimie Nutrition du Département de Recherche Zootechniques et Vétérinaires*, LBN): chemical and microbiological analysis of raw materials for animal food.

Laboratory of the National Center of Industrial and Technological Research (*Laboratoire du Centre National de Recherches Industrielles et Technologiques*, CNRIT): conformity assessment in the following sectors: water, various chemical products, construction materials, civil engineering, and electronics. Technical support to enterprises.

Laboratory for the Control of Pesticides (*Laboratoire de Contrôle des Pesticides*, LCP): control of agro-pharmaceutical products and pesticides (local or imported).

Laboratory of Microbiology, Water, and Consumables (*Laboratoire de Microbiologie, des Eaux et des Denrées Alimentaires de l'Institut Pasteur de Madagascar*): bacteriological analysis of food, water, and medicines.

National Laboratory of the Minister of Mines (*Laboratoire National des Mines du Ministère de Mines*, LNM): certification of jewelry and precious stones for exports; LNM belongs to the Ministry of Mines.

National Laboratory of Research in Telecommunications (*Laboratoire National de Recherches en Télécommunications*, LNRT): verification, inspection and certification of telecommunications equipment.

National Institute and Laboratory of Nuclear Sciences and Technogy (*Laboratoire de l'Institut National des Sciences et Techniques Nucléaires*, LINSTN): standardization of ionizing radiation detection apparatus; radioactivity control of food and metallic waste; analysis of geological samples; detection of heavy metal; control of heavy metal in seafood and meat; quantitative/qualitative analysis of atomic elements in powder, solid, and liquid samples.

PRODUCT CERTIFICATION

Vanilla, coffee, meat, seafood, and mining products should be certified before export. A few forestry products (under CITES regulations) should be certified before export (see Chapter 5 for further details). There are no mutual recognition agreements (MRAs) with U.S. organizations.

ACCREDITATION

Accreditation body and contact information:
BNM
P.O. Box 1316
Antananarivo 101 – Madagascar
Tel: (261 20) 22 279 70
E-mail: bnm@moov.mg

Accreditation is primarily required in the construction sector. American companies should work with Malagasy importers to accredit all imported materials in the construction sector (such as cement, iron, etc) in order to avoid potential penalties.

The National Laboratory of Public Works and Building (*Laboratoire National des Travaux Publics et du Batiment*, LNTPB) provides accreditation of these materials.

PUBLICATION OF TECHNICAL REGULATIONS

Technical regulations and standards developed by the different laboratories are published in the National Gazette of the Republic of Madagascar if required by law. U.S. or foreign entities can approach the different laboratories or related departments to comment on final regulations.

LABELING AND MARKING

For each certified product, labeling and marking are required on the packaging of the product before sale or export. All perishable foods must bear a label, in French or English, indicating the origin, the sell-by or use-by date, the ingredients, the method of storage, the name of the manufacturer together with his registration number where appropriate, and the intended use. Use of the metric system is compulsory in Madagascar.

TRADE AGREEMENTS

Madagascar is a signatory to the following regional and international agreements:

1964: United Nations Convention on Trade and Development (UNCTAD)

1992: Indian Ocean Commission (COI). Since 1998, elimination of tariffs on goods originating from the COI countries.

1993: Common Market for East and Southern Africa (COMESA). Free Trade Area since 2000

1995: World Trade Organization (WTO)

2000: Cotonou Agreementhttp://ec.europa.eu/europeaid/where/acp/overview/cotonou-agreement/

2005: Southern African Development Community (SADC). Free Trade Area since 2008

2009: Interim Economic Partnership Agreement with the European Union.

INVESTMENT CLIMATE

OPENNESS TO FOREIGN INVESTMENT

Officially, the de facto GOM welcomes foreign investment. However, political turmoil; weakness in the judicial system and the banking sector; the high cost and low quality of electric power; corruption; a lack of transparency in decision-making; limited road, rail and port infrastructure; and the high cost of air transport make investing in Madagascar a challenge. According to the Economic Development Board of Madagascar (EDBM), few foreign investors showed interest in investment during 2012, though there was no available data on the real flow of foreign direct investment (FDI).

Prior to a March 2009 coup d'état, the Bretton Woods institutions had generally endorsed the government's macro-economic regime, although they questioned certain non-transparent budget and tax decisions in late 2008. Effective March 17, 2009, the World Bank's operations in Madagascar have been guided by its Operation Policy (OP) 7.30 for dealing with de facto governments, and no fund withdrawal requests have been processed since that date, except those dealing with nutrition, HIV/AIDS, food security, and environmental protection.

As a result of the coup, the USG terminated the Millennium Challenge Account (MCA) program on May 19, 2009 and AGOA eligibility on December 23, 2009, as the country no longer met the criteria regarding rule of law, good governance, and political pluralism. On October 26, 2012, the Board of the Extractive Industries Transparency Initiative (EITI) extended Madagascar's suspension from the EITI due to the African Union's continued non-recognition of the government.

Since April 2009, the African Union and SADC have engaged in mediation efforts with the regime, ousted President Ravalomanana, and other key opposition leaders. Since the September 2011 signing of SADC's Roadmap for Ending the Crisis in Madagascar, a consensus Prime Minister, an expanded Cabinet, a new parliament, and a transitional independent national electoral commission (CENI-T) have been appointed. Key provisions of the Roadmap remain unfulfilled, however, including those calling for the return of all political exiles and for respect for human rights and media freedom. The prospects for elections in 2013 look uncertain as of the drafting of this report.

There is no law or regulation authorizing private firms to adopt articles of incorporation or association that limit or prohibit foreign investment, participation or control. Furthermore, there is no official or private practice to restrict foreign investment, participation, or control of domestic enterprises. There is no mandatory screening of foreign investment, and there is no discrimination against foreign investors at the time of the initial investment or after the investment is made, such as through special tax treatment, access to licenses, approvals, or procurement.

A prohibition on land ownership by foreigners impedes access to real property. If foreign nationals own a company that is registered in Madagascar, they can obtain long-term leases (99-year expiration). The system of long-term leases was established in 2008 following the adoption of investment law 2007-036 to address the issue, but there have been long delays and few successes so far in the approval of land leases for foreigners. The new investment law grants land and properties to companies registered in Madagascar under certain conditions fixed by EDBM, which issues authorization documents.

In its October 2012 economic update, the World Bank noted that due to the three and half years of political crisis, the economy has severely stalled, poverty has sharply increased, and social outcomes have worsened. Most recent projections anticipated an inflation rate of 8.5% and a growth rate of 2.5% in 2012.

Increasing corruption by officials and direct supporters of de facto President Andry Rajoelina have progressively deterred major foreign investment in Madagascar and discouraged the companies already invested in the country.

The judicial system does not function independently of the de facto government. In some sectors, such as extractive industries, bureaucratic bodies intended to govern the sector have been dismantled by the de facto government.

Measure	Year	Index/Ranking
TI Corruption Index	2012	32/100
Heritage Economic Freedom	2012	62.4/81
World Bank Doing Business	2013	142 out of 185 countries

CONVERSION AND TRANSFER POLICIES

In 1998, the GOM lifted all restrictions on current payment and transfers and accepted the obligations of Article VIII of the IMF Articles of Agreement, which provides for the complete elimination of exchange controls. There are no restrictions on converting or transferring funds associated with foreign investment, including remittances of investment capital, earnings, loan repayments, lease payments into a freely usable currency and at a legal market clearing rate. There are no plans to change remittance policies that have tightened or relaxed access to foreign exchange for investment remittances. When delays occur in conversion or funds transfer, they are due to temporary shortages of foreign exchange. There is no limitation on the inflow or outflow of funds for remittances of profits, debt service, capital, and returns on intellectual property or imported inputs. There are no surrender requirements for profits earned overseas.

Exporters and foreign investors may maintain bank accounts in foreign currencies. Madagascar uses exchange rate policy to counter underlying currency market pressures and keep commodity prices stable.

EXPROPRIATION AND COMPENSATION

There are no recent cases of expropriation actions by the GOM. However, local investors fear that the de facto government will return to monopoly policies or attempt to nationalize key sectors (particularly telecommunications and mining). There are no laws that force local ownership.

DISPUTE SETTLEMENT

Madagascar's legal system is based on French civil law, and its provisions contain adequate protections for private property rights. Malagasy commercial law consists largely of the Code of Commerce and annexed laws, which are reportedly applied in a non-discriminatory manner. Madagascar has a written bankruptcy law, created in 1996 and currently included in the Code of Commerce. The Malagasy judicial system is slow and complex and has a reputation for opacity and corruption. In the past, U.S. assistance has supported the development of alternative dispute resolution systems to provide more rapid, more transparent, and less costly resolution of commercial disputes.

Under the privatization law, the GOM accepts binding international arbitration of investment disputes between foreign investors and the state. The courts in theory recognize and enforce foreign arbitral awards and international arbitration is accepted as a means for settling investment disputes between private parties. The Malagasy Arbitration and Mediation Center (known by its French acronym, CAMM) was created in 2000 as a private organization to promote and facilitate the use of arbitration to resolve commercial disputes and to lessen reliance on a court system that is, at a minimum, overburdened. As a result, many private contracts now include arbitration clauses.

Madagascar is a signatory to the International Center for the Settlement of Investment Disputes (ICSID) Convention, as well as the New York Convention of 1958 on the Recognition and Enforcement of Foreign Arbitral Awards. Madagascar has been a member of the Multilateral Investment Guarantee Agency (MIGA) since 1989.

PERFORMANCE REQUIREMENTS AND INCENTIVES

As a signatory of the WTO Agreement, Madagascar is bound by the WTO Trade Related Investment Measures (TRIMS). Performance requirements are not imposed as conditions for establishing or maintaining investments, except in the Export Processing Zones (EPZ) regime, under which firms must export 95 percent of output to qualify for EPZ investment incentives. Foreign or local investors can benefit from tax exemptions provided that their EPZ projects fall into the following categories: (1) investment in export-oriented manufacturing industries; (2) development or management of industrial free zones; or (3) provision of services to EPZ companies.

The EPZ law approved in December 2007 granted the following advantages and tax incentives to EPZ companies: (1) the EDBM is in charge of EPZ companies' approval and has to deliver an eligibility certificate within 20 days of deposit of file; (2) 15 years tax exemption for EPZ companies; (3) no VAT or customs duties on imports of raw materials; (4) no registration taxes; (5) no customs tax on exported goods; (6) income tax on expatriation not exceeding 30 percent of the taxable basis; and (7) free access to foreign currency deposited in the company's foreign currency bank account.

There is no requirement restricting the mobility of foreign investors. The regime for visas, residence, and work permits is neither discriminatory nor excessively onerous. Since the creation of the EDBM, processing of residence and work permits has been streamlined.

There is no requirement that investors purchase from local sources, or export a certain percentage of output (except for EPZ companies), or only have access to foreign exchange in relation to their exports. There is no requirement that nationals own shares of foreign companies, that the share of foreign equity is reduced over time, or that technology is transferred on certain terms. There are no government-imposed conditions on permission to invest (although investors must apply for such permission), including location in a specific geographical area, specific percentage of local content or local equity, substitution for imports, export requirements or targets, employment of host country nationals, or technology transfer. Investors are not required to disclose proprietary information to the government as part of the regulatory approval process. U.S. and other foreign firms are able to participate in government-financed and/or subsidized research and development programs on a national treatment basis. There are officially no discriminatory or preferential export or import policies that would affect foreign investors, nor discriminatory tariff or non-tariff barriers. In April 2011 and again in January 2013, the de facto regime rejected market-based economic principles by imposing a fixed retail price on fuel distributors.

RIGHT TO PRIVATE OWNERSHIP AND ESTABLISHMENT

Foreign and domestic private entities may establish and own business enterprises and engage in all forms of remunerative activity. They may freely establish, acquire, and dispose of interests in business enterprises. The government remains a minority shareholder in some privatized companies, such as in the Malagasy Telecommunications Company (Telma), and continues to own Air Madagascar, but competitive equality is the official standard applied to all private enterprises with respect to access to markets, credit, and other business operations such as licenses and supplies.

PROTECTION OF PROPERTY RIGHTS

Secured interests in property are recognized, but not entirely enforced in the country. Banks and insurance companies use mortgages on commercial property to guarantee loans.

A prohibition on land ownership by foreigners impedes access to real property, and the entire issue remains highly controversial and problematic on a cultural level despite legal advances. A system of long-term leases—up to 99 years—was established in 2008 following the adoption of investment law 2007-036 to address the issue, but there have been long delays and few successes so far in the approval of land leases for foreigners. The new investment law grants land and properties to companies registered in Madagascar under certain conditions fixed by EDBM, which issues authorization documents. In addition, MCA's contribution to the land tenure issue improved the land rights process prior to early termination of the program in late 2009 due to the political crisis.

Madagascar is a member of the World Intellectual Property Organization (WIPO) and is a signatory to the WTO TRIPS agreement on trade related aspects of intellectual property. Two government offices share responsibility for the protection of intellectual property rights: the Malagasy Office for Industrial Property (OMAPI) and the Malagasy Copyright Office (OMDA).

Protection of intellectual property rights is uneven. Officially, authorities protect against infringement, but in reality, enforcement capacity is quite limited due to resource constraints, absence of political will, and weakness of the judicial system. Major brands are generally respected, but pirated copies of movie DVDs, music CDs and tapes, electronic equipment and spare parts are sold openly. Some television stations regularly show pirated copies of first-run U.S. and European movies. Madagascar has not yet signed the WIPO Internet treaties.

TRANSPARENCY OF REGULATORY SYSTEM

Excessive complexities and inconsistently applied regulations impede investment and can be a breeding ground for corrupt practices. The lack of transparency in government regulatory decisions has generated numerous complaints from investors. Although regulatory decisions can impede start-up in particular industries, the normal business registration process has been streamlined by EDBM and generally takes less than two weeks.

Some investors, especially in the mining sector, have encountered difficulty and/or delays in obtaining necessary operating permits as a result of irregularities in the regulatory system. Ambatovy, a USD 6 billion laterite nickel mining project that represents the largest foreign direct investment in Madagascar, faced significant obstacles and political interference before obtaining a temporary, six-month operating permit from the de facto regime.

Tax, labor, environment, health, and safety standards are generally not used to impede foreign investment. Bureaucratic procedures and red tape are often sources of corruption. There are no informal regulatory processes managed by non-governmental organizations or private sector associations. Proposed laws and regulations are not published in draft form for public comment. The only opportunity for comment on proposed laws and regulations is at the parliamentary level.

Accounting systems are transparent and consistent with international norms, and there are no private sector and/or government/authority efforts to restrict foreign participation in industry standard-setting consortia or organizations.

EFFICIENT CAPITAL MARKETS AND PORTFOLIO INVESTMENT

In spite of the general underdevelopment of the banking system, banks are free to support the flow of resources in the product and factors markets. The assets of the country's largest bank total an estimated USD 400 million. Credit is usually allocated on market terms, and the private sector/foreign investors can obtain credit on the local market. However, many of the EPZ companies use the services of banks in neighboring Mauritius, where the sector is more developed.

Within Malagasy law, there is an effective regulatory system established to encourage and facilitate portfolio investment. There are no cross-shareholding arrangements used by private firms to restrict foreign investment through mergers and acquisitions. There are no visible private sector and/or government efforts to restrict foreign participation in industry or control of domestic enterprises.

COMPETITION FROM STATE OWNED ENTERPRISES

Private enterprises are allowed to compete with public enterprises under the same terms and conditions with respect to access to markets, credit, and other business operations, such as licenses and supplies. The main SOEs are the National Malagasy Airline (Air Madagascar) and the Malagasy Water and Energy Company (*Jiro Sy Rano Malagasy*, or JIRAMA). SOEs have boards of directors for which seats are specifically allocated to senior government officials, private operators, or politically affiliated individuals.

A sovereign wealth fund (SWF) or asset management bureau (AMB) does not exist in the country.

SOEs are required by law to publish an annual report, and they are also required to submit their books to independent audit.

CORPORATE SOCIAL RESPONSIBILITY

There is a lack of general awareness of corporate social responsibility (CSR) among producers and consumers, but CSR principles are applied by several large, formal sector companies. Although those companies do not follow the OECD Guidelines for Multinational Enterprises, public opinion is favorable regarding those firms who pursue CSR.

POLITICAL VIOLENCE

As in 2009 and 2010, Madagascar experienced political violence and civil unrest in 2012. The ongoing political crisis continues to create the conditions for possible future instability. At various times, small improvised explosive devices have been detonated in the capital, but have caused only superficial damage. A 2012 military operation against alleged cattle rustlers in the south led to numerous accusations of human rights violations against the de facto regime. The army put down an attempted mutiny at a military base near the capital in July 2012. Street demonstrations are forbidden by the de facto regime, but opposition political gatherings are permitted indoors.

Public safety remains fairly adequate, although petty crimes have increased as the economic and political crisis has worn on. Standard warnings to guard against street crime and theft from vehicles, and to minimize or avoid nighttime road travel, apply, particularly in rural areas.

Kidnappings targeting business leaders (usually, but not always, of Indo-Pakistani heritage) have recently increased in frequency and have begun demanding higher ransoms. Madagascar is not a xenophobic country in general, but anti-foreigner rhetoric sometimes surges as a consequence of political manipulation. In May 2013, demonstrations against international organizations occurred in the capital, and some foreign diplomats received threatening phone messages. Madagascar, being an island, has no belligerent neighbors.

CORRUPTION

Corruption, including official solicitation at high levels of government, raises the costs and risks of doing business. Corruption has a corrosive impact on both market opportunities overseas for U.S. companies and the broader business climate. It also deters international investment, stifles economic growth and development, distorts prices, and undermines the rule of law.

It is important for U.S. companies, irrespective of their size, to assess the business climate in the relevant market in which they will be operating or investing, and to have an effective compliance program or measures to prevent and detect corruption, including foreign bribery. U.S. individuals and firms operating or investing in foreign markets should take the time to become familiar with the relevant anticorruption laws of both the foreign country and the United States in order to properly comply with them, and where appropriate, they should seek the advice of legal counsel.

The U.S. Government seeks to level the global playing field for U.S. businesses by encouraging other countries to take steps to criminalize their own companies' acts of corruption, including bribery of foreign public officials, by requiring them to uphold their obligations under relevant international conventions. A U.S. firm that believes a competitor is seeking to use bribery of a foreign public official to secure a contract should bring this to the attention of appropriate U.S. agencies, as noted below.

U.S. Foreign Corrupt Practices Act: In 1977, the United States enacted the Foreign Corrupt Practices Act (FCPA), which makes it unlawful for a U.S. person, and certain foreign issuers of securities, to make a corrupt payment to foreign public officials for the purpose of obtaining or retaining business for or with, or directing business to, any person. The FCPA also applies to foreign firms and persons who take any act in furtherance of such a corrupt payment while in the United States. For more detailed information on the FCPA, see the FCPA Lay-Person's Guide at:http://www.justice.gov/criminal/fraud/

Other Instruments: It is U.S. Government policy to promote good governance, including host country implementation and enforcement of anti-corruption laws and policies pursuant to their obligations under international agreements. Since enactment of the FCPA, the United States has been instrumental to the expansion of the international framework to fight corruption. Several significant components of this framework are the OECD Convention on Combating Bribery of Foreign Public Officials in International Business Transactions (OECD Antibribery Convention), the United Nations Convention against Corruption (UN Convention), the Inter-American Convention against Corruption (OAS Convention), the Council of Europe Criminal and Civil Law Conventions, and a growing list of U.S. free trade agreements

OECD Antibribery Convention: The OECD Antibribery Convention (http://www.oecd.org/daf/anti-bribery/oecdantibriberyconvention.htm) entered into force in February 1999. As of November 2012, there are 40 parties to the Convention including the United States (seehttp://www.oecd.org/daf/anti-bribery/antibriberyconventionratification.pdf). Major exporters China and India are not parties, although the U.S. Government strongly endorses their eventual accession to the Convention. The Convention obligates the Parties to criminalize bribery of foreign public officials in the conduct of international business. The United States meets its international obligations under the OECD Antibribery Convention through the U.S. FCPA.

Madagascar is not a party to the OECD Convention.

UN Convention: The UN Anticorruption Convention entered into force on December 14, 2005, and there are 167 parties to it as of May 2013 (seehttp://www.unodc.org/unodc/en/treaties/CAC/signatories.html). The UN Convention is the first global comprehensive international anticorruption agreement. The UN Convention requires countries to establish criminal and other offences to cover a wide range of acts of corruption. The UN Convention goes beyond previous anticorruption instruments, covering a broad range of issues ranging from basic forms of corruption such as bribery and solicitation, embezzlement, trading in influence to the concealment and laundering of the proceeds of corruption. The Convention contains transnational business bribery provisions that are functionally similar to those in the OECD Antibribery Convention and contains provisions on private sector auditing and books and records requirements. Other provisions address matters such as prevention, international cooperation, and asset recovery.

Madagascar is a party to the UN Convention, but the de facto government does not currently observe many of its provisions in practice.

OAS Convention: In 1996, the Member States of the Organization of American States (OAS) adopted the first international anticorruption legal instrument, the Inter-American Convention against Corruption (OAS Convention), which entered into force in March 1997. The OAS Convention, among other things, establishes a set of preventive measures against corruption, provides for the criminalization of certain acts of corruption, including transnational bribery and illicit enrichment, and contains a series of provisions to strengthen the cooperation between its States Parties in areas such as mutual legal assistance and technical cooperation. As of June 2013, the OAS Convention has 34 parties (seehttp://www.oas.org/juridico/english/Sigs/b-58.html)

Madagascar is not a party to the OAS Convention.

Council of Europe Criminal Law and Civil Law Conventions: Many European countries are parties to either the Council of Europe (CoE) Criminal Law Convention on Corruption, the Civil Law Convention, or both. The Criminal Law Convention requires criminalization of a wide range of national and transnational conduct, including bribery, money-laundering, and account offenses. It also incorporates provisions on liability of legal persons and witness protection. The Civil Law Convention includes provisions on compensation for damage relating to corrupt acts, whistleblower protection, and validity of contracts, inter alia. The Group of States against Corruption (GRECO) was established in 1999 by the CoE to monitor compliance with these and related anti-corruption standards. Currently, GRECO comprises 49 member States (48 European countries and the United States). As of June 2013, the Criminal Law Convention has 47 parties (see http://conventions.coe.int/Treaty/en/Treaties/Html/173-1.htm) and the Civil Law Convention has 34
(see http://conventions.coe.int/Treaty/Commun/ChercheSig.asp?NT=174&CM=&DF=&CL=ENG.)

Madagascar is not a party to the Council of Europe Conventions.

Free Trade Agreements: While it is U.S. Government policy to include anticorruption provisions in free trade agreements (FTAs) that it negotiates with its trading partners, the anticorruption provisions have evolved over time. The most recent FTAs negotiated now require trading partners to criminalize "active bribery" of public officials (offering bribes to any public official must be made a criminal offense, both domestically and trans-nationally) as well as domestic "passive bribery" (solicitation of a bribe by a domestic official). All U.S. FTAs may be found at the U.S. Trade Representative website: http://www.ustr.gov/trade-agreements/free-trade-agreements.

Madagascar does not have an FTA with the United States.

Local Laws: U.S. firms should familiarize themselves with local anticorruption laws, and, where appropriate, seek legal counsel.

While the U.S. Department of Commerce cannot provide legal advice on local laws, the Department's U.S. and Foreign Commercial Service can provide assistance with navigating the host country's legal system and obtaining a list of local legal counsel.

Assistance for U.S. Businesses: The U.S. Department of Commerce offers several services to aid U.S. businesses seeking to address business-related corruption issues. For example, the U.S. and Foreign Commercial Service can provide services that may assist U.S. companies in conducting their due diligence as part of the company's overarching compliance program when choosing business partners or agents overseas. The U.S. Foreign and Commercial Service can be reached directly through its offices in every major U.S. and foreign city, or through its website at www.trade.gov/cs.

The Departments of Commerce and State provide worldwide support for qualified U.S. companies bidding on foreign government contracts through the Commerce Department's Advocacy Center and State's Office of Commercial and Business Affairs. Problems, including alleged corruption by foreign governments or competitors, encountered by U.S. companies in seeking such foreign business opportunities can be brought to the attention of appropriate U.S. government officials, including local embassy personnel and through the Department of Commerce Trade Compliance Center "Report A Trade Barrier" website attcc.export.gov/Report_a_Barrier/index.asp.

Guidance on the U.S. FCPA: The Department of Justice's (DOJ) FCPA Opinion Procedure enables U.S. firms and individuals to request a statement of the Justice Department's present enforcement intentions under the anti-bribery provisions of the FCPA regarding any proposed business conduct. The details of the opinion procedure are available on DOJ's Fraud Section website at www.justice.gov/criminal/fraud/fcpa. Although the Department of Commerce has no enforcement role with respect to the FCPA, it supplies general guidance to U.S. exporters who have questions about the FCPA and about international developments concerning the FCPA. For further information, see the website of the Office of the Chief Counsel for International Counsel, U.S. Department of Commerce, athttp://www.ogc.doc.gov/trans_anti_bribery.html. More general information on the FCPA is available at the websites listed below.

Exporters and investors should be aware that generally all countries prohibit the bribery of their public officials, and prohibit their officials from soliciting bribes under domestic laws. Most countries are required to criminalize such bribery and other acts of corruption by virtue of being parties to various international conventions discussed above.

In 2012, Transparency International ranked Madagascar 118th out of 175 countries surveyed, with a score of 32/100 on the Corruption Perception Index (CPI), indicating a severe corruption problem. While giving or accepting a bribe is a criminal act and is subject to trial by court, complicated administrative procedures introduce delays and uncertainties increasing possibilities for corruption. Corruption is most pervasive in the following areas: the de facto Presidency's office, judiciary, police, tax, customs, land, trade, mining, industry, environment, education, and health. BIANCO is the agency formally responsible for combating corruption, but its efforts have been limited by the de facto government. Transparency International has an office in the country. Corruption at high levels exists in nearly all sectors.

Smuggling of precious stones, hardwood, and animals increasingly drains Madagascar's natural resources and breeds criminality. In April 2010, the de facto regime adopted a decree to prohibit all exports of rosewood and precious timber. Despite this ban, containers of rosewood continue to be shipped. In September 2011, the de facto regime decided to include rosewood in Annex III of CITES. However, despite the fact that this provision was introduced by the de facto government, it has been regularly violated since that time by public officials and private entities.

Madagascar created a Financial Intelligence Unit (SAMIFIN) in mid-2008 to carry out research and financial analysis related to money laundering. In 2012, SAMIFIN received 61 suspicious transaction reports and referred 23 cases to public prosecutors.

Madagascar has signed and ratified the UN Anticorruption Convention and the African Union Convention against Corruption. It has not yet signed the Convention on Combating Bribery of Foreign Public Officials in International Business Transactions.

There is no requirement for companies to establish internal codes of conduct that, inter alia, prohibit bribery of public officials. However, some foreign companies have begun to orient their internal controls and ethics and compliance programs to prevent bribery.

ANTI-CORRUPTION RESOURCES

Some useful resources for individuals and companies regarding combating corruption in global markets include the following:

Information about the U.S. Foreign Corrupt Practices Act (FCPA), including a "Lay-Person's Guide to the FCPA" is available at the U.S. Department of Justice's website at:http://www.justice.gov/criminal/fraud/fcpa.
Information about the OECD Antibribery Convention including links to national implementing legislation and country monitoring reports is available at: http://www.oecd.org/daf/anti-bribery/. See also new Antibribery Recommendation and Good Practice Guidance Annex for companies: http://www.oecd.org/dataoecd/11/40/44176910.pdf.
General information about anticorruption initiatives, such as the OECD Convention and the FCPA, including translations of the statute into several languages, is available at the Department of Commerce Office of the Chief Counsel for International Commerce website:http://www.ogc.doc.gov/trans_anti_bribery.html.
Transparency International (TI) publishes an annual Corruption Perceptions Index (CPI). The CPI measures the perceived level of public-sector corruption in 180 countries and territories around the world. The latest CPI is available at:http://cpi.transparency.org/cpi2012/. TI also publishes an annual*Global Corruption Report* which provides a systematic evaluation of the state of corruption around the world. It includes an in-depth analysis of a focal theme, a series of country reports that document major corruption related events and developments from all continents and an overview of the latest research findings on anti-corruption diagnostics and tools. Seehttp://www.transparency.org/whatwedo/publications/doc/gcr/
The World Bank Institute publishes Worldwide Governance Indicators (WGI). These indicators assess six dimensions of governance in 213 countries, including Voice and Accountability, Political Stability and Absence of Violence, Government Effectiveness, Regulatory Quality, Rule of Law and Control of Corruption. See http://info.worldbank.org/governance/wgi/index.asp. The World Bank Business Environment and Enterprise Performance Surveys may also be of interest and are available at: http://data.worldbank.org/data-catalog/BEEPS.
The World Economic Forum publishes the *Global Enabling Trade Report*, which presents the rankings of the Enabling Trade Index, and includes an assessment of the transparency of border administration (focused on bribe payments and corruption) and a separate segment on corruption and the regulatory environment. Seehttp://www.weforum.org/s?s=global+enabling+trade+report.
Additional country information related to corruption can be found in the U.S. Department of State's annual *Human Rights Report*available at http://www.state.gov/g/drl/rls/hrrpt/.
Global Integrity, a nonprofit organization, publishes its annual *Global Integrity Report*, which provides indicators for 31 countries with respect to governance and anti-corruption. The report highlights the strengths and weaknesses of national level anti-corruption systems. The report is available at: http://report.globalintegrity.org/.

BILATERAL INVESTMENT AGREEMENTS

According to the International Center for the Settlement of Investment Disputes (ICSID) and the United Nations Conference on Trade and Development (UNCTAD), Madagascar has concluded bilateral investment agreements with Belgium, Canada, China, France, Germany, Mauritius, Norway, Sweden, and Thailand. Madagascar has also signed double taxation treaties with France and Mauritius. As the Malagasy government had expressed interest in negotiating a bilateral investment treaty with the United States, initial discussions began in late 2008, but stalled due to the unconstitutional change of government in March 2009.

OPIC AND OTHER INVESTMENT INSURANCE PROGRAMS

On March 31, 1998, the Overseas Private Investment Corporation (OPIC) and Madagascar signed a bilateral Investment Incentive Agreement, which updated the previous agreement of 1963. Madagascar is a member of the MIGA. The average daily exchange rate in 2012 was 2,188 Ariary per one U.S. dollar.

LABOR

Madagascar has a significant pool of available labor, due to the combined impacts of unemployment and underemployment. Private sector wages have been relatively stable and are below those in most competitor countries; indeed, this fact, combined with the high quality of much Malagasy labor, may constitute the country's strongest attraction for foreign investors. The minimum wage for the non-agricultural private sector in 2011 was approximately 45 USD per month (91,000 Ariary). The Constitution and Labor Code grant workers in the private and public sectors the right to establish and join labor unions and to bargain collectively. The National Labor Code and implementing legislation prescribe working conditions, wages, and standards for worksite safety. Madagascar is a member of the International Labor Organization (ILO) and adheres to the ILO convention protecting workers rights.

FOREIGN-TRADE ZONES/FREE PORTS

The incentives available in the EPZ are described in "Performance Requirements/Incentives." There is no distinction between foreign and domestically owned firms, in terms of eligibility for EPZ treatment, which has been granted by the EDBM since December 2007.

FOREIGN DIRECT INVESTMENT STATISTICS

During 2012, QMM/Rio Tinto continued its mining and exportation of ilmenite and related products. Ambatovy concluded its construction of the nickel and cobalt mine and began exploitation/exportation. As the two companies are the largest contributors of foreign direct investment (FDI) in the country, and with the Ambatovy project's investment phase coming to an end, foreign exchange inflows fell in comparison to 2011.

According to the Central Bank of Madagascar, FDI inflows for 2011 amounted to USD 940.8 million, and during the first quarter of 2012, it amounted to USD 256.6 million.

FDI inflows and stocks during the past three years (in USD)

	2009	2010	2011	2012 (First quarter)
FDI inflows	1,294,699,549	807,984,845	940,799,278	256,581,621
FDI stock	3,944,971,013	4,499,344,642	n.a	n.a

Source: Central Bank of Madagascar

	2009	2010	2011 (First Semester)
Extractive activities	1,058,167,950	695,275,196	308,726,655

Agriculture	7,233,929	(429,435)	(622,203.79)
Fishing and fish farming	9,616,269	17,739,742	(17,757,498.54)
Manufacturing	50,934,020	21,216,118	8,103,463
Gas, electricity, water production and distribution	132,920	117,583	(9,876)
Construction and public works	16,318,518	27,402,022	33,821,220
Commerce	15,812,398	9,406,664	5,950,440
Hotels and restaurants	19,166,079	18,455,467	(444,431)
Transportation	5,567,314	1,457,011	(7,244,229)
Finance	30,510,312	29,344,703	53,470,020
Real estate and services to enterprises	3,864,912	5,367,933	1,491,313
Oil distribution	33,424,333	29,753,689	25,139,995.85
Telecommunication	43,868,797	8,435,324	(24,300,514.55)
Others	81,797	(35,786)	(24,690.63)
Total	1,294,699,549	863,506,232	386,299,665

TRADE AND PROJECT FINANCING

METHODS OF PAYMENT

Methods of payment are usually through banks by open account, letter of credit, cash in advance, or by documentary collection. The banking system consists of eight commercial banks. European banking institutions hold a controlling interest in four banks: the Banque Malgache de l'Ocean Indien (BMOI), BNI-Crédit Agricole (BNI-CA), BTM-BOA, and BFV-SG. The Union Commercial Bank (UCB) and State Bank of Mauritius (SBM) are branches of Mauritian parent companies of the same name. The Hong-Kong group Gahood Holding International, Ltd., owns 70 percent of the shares of BICM bank. The German group Access Holding owns the Access Bank Madagascar. For those banks, financial statements are in compliance with international standards, and audits are performed both by local and internationally recognized firms. A new bank, Banque Gabonaise et Francaise Internationale (BGFI) became operational in 2010.

Thanks to MCA's contribution in 2008, the central bank adopted a new automated payment and clearing system for the banking sector in October 2009. The new system is aimed at streamlining the payment and compensation procedures, reducing costs and improving confidence in the payment instruments.

HOW DOES THE BANKING SYSTEM OPERATE?

Madagascar has relatively rudimentary financial markets and a very low rate of bank penetration. High interest rates, stringent requirements for collateral and guarantees, limited competition among banks, and reluctance to finance foreign trade or working capital even when secured by letters of credit make financing very expensive and difficult to access. The difficulty of increasing working capital through bank borrowing is a severe constraint on local firms' ability to expand. Banks maintain that many prospective borrowers lack reliable and transparent balance sheets and that long-term financing is difficult because they lack a long-term deposit policy. A substantial portion of domestic credit is effectively extended to the public sector because banks invest surplus funds in largely risk-free government treasury bills (*bons de trésor*). Only well-known and significant operators can get credit in Madagascar. The credit granted is mainly for the purchase of traditional agricultural products such as vanilla, coffee, and cloves. In case of pre-financing by foreign importers, local exporters still have to pay high interest rates to their banks. Generally speaking, the financing possibilities that are available to local firms are quite limited.

FOREIGN-EXCHANGE CONTROLS

Since May 1994, an inter-bank foreign exchange market (MID) has set daily the rate of the Malagasy currency (MGA). At the end of July 2005, the organization and the operation of the inter-bank foreign exchange market were improved by the adoption of a continuous system of quotation of the two main currencies of reference, the U.S. dollar and the Euro. Since 1996, the GOM has lifted all restrictions on current payment and transfers and has accepted the obligations of Article VII of the IMF Articles of Agreement to abolish exchange controls. However, on July 11, 2004, following a significant depreciation of the Malagasy currency, the GOM adopted a law stating that residents are not authorized to transfer foreign currency to another foreign currency bank account except within the MID. However, between EPZ companies, foreign currency transfers are allowed.

U.S. BANKS AND LOCAL CORRESPONDENT BANKS

BMOI:

BNP Paribas/New York

BNI-CA:

Deutsche Bank Trust Company America/New York

JPMorgan Chase/New York

BTM-BOA:

Citibank/New York

Deutsche Bank Trust Company America/New York

UCB: Citibank/New York

BFV-SG:

Société Générale/New York

SBM:

Citibank/New York

PROJECT FINANCING

The GOM supports the establishment of credit unions and other suitable credit facilities and encourages creditors and donors to harmonize their efforts in this field. The World Bank, the

European Union, the U.S. Trade and Development Agency (USTDA), and the African Development Bank have funded many infrastructure and other development projects.

In March 1998, an agreement was signed between OPIC and the GOM to facilitate U.S. investment in the country.

In June 2004, the International Finance Corporation (IFC) of the World Bank created an SME (Small and Medium Enterprise) Solution Center to address credit access of local SMEs. Between 2005 and 2009, the GOM, with financing from an MCA compact, implemented banking sector reform and promoted access to microcredit.

WEB RESOURCES

Export-Import Bank of the United States: http://www.exim.gov/
Country Limitation Schedule:http://www.exim.gov/tools/country/country_limits.html
OPIC: http://www.opic.gov/
U.S. Trade and Development Agency: http://www.ustda.gov/
SBA's Office of International Trade: http://www.sba.gov/oit/
USDA Commodity Credit Corporation:http://www.fsa.usda.gov/ccc/default.htm
U.S. Agency for International Development: http://www.usaid.gov/
Multilateral Development Banks web resources:
World Bank: http://www.worldbank.org/madagascar
IFAD (agribusiness promotion): http://www.ifad.org/french/operations/pf/mdg/index.htm
UNIDO (industry): http://www.unido.org/office/madagascar
African Development Bank: http://afdb.org/en/countries/southern-africa/madagascar

BUSINESS TRAVEL

BUSINESS CUSTOMS

Laws and common business practices are based on the European, particularly French, business style.

TRAVEL ADVISORY

For further information about visa requirements and travel information, the following State Department web site is available: http://travel.state.gov/

VISA REQUIREMENTS

A visa is required for entry into Madagascar and can be obtained at the airport for stays of less than 30 days. See U.S. Department of State and GOM's websites for visa information.

U.S. companies that require travel of foreign businesspersons to the United States should be advised that security evaluations are handled via an interagency process. Visa applicants should go to the following links.

Department of State Visa website: http://travel.state.gov/visa/

U.S. Embassy Antananarivo Visa website:http://www.antananarivo.usembassy.gov/non-immigrant_visas.html

TELECOMMUNICATIONS

Internet is accessible in hotels and at cyber cafes of major towns. There are three cellular phone companies: Airtel, Orange and Telma, which use the GSM system.

TRANSPORTATION

Air transportation is the best way to get to the country. Maritime transport is mainly used for local transportation around the island, and to the Indian Ocean Islands (Mauritius, Seychelles, Comoros, and Reunion). Visitors to the capital city of Antananarivo or other cities can easily find taxis. Taxi fares are relatively low, but taxis typically do not meet U.S. safety standards.

Railway transport is available, but with limited connections.

Rental cars are available but can be quite expensive depending on the vehicle type, and non-residents are usually required to hire a chauffeur.

Commercial air service is available to major cities and resorts in the country. Private air charters can be arranged to various destinations.

International express delivery is now available from FedEx, UPS, DHL, and TNT.

LANGUAGE

Malagasy is the official language, along with French and English. However, English is not widely spoken. French is the common language of business.

HEALTH

Visitors to Madagascar are advised to obtain vaccinations against polio, hepatitis A and B, tetanus, diphtheria, typhoid, and those who will be working in the rural areas, rabies. Malaria medication is not necessary in Antananarivo but should be taken if traveling to other (lower elevation) areas of the island. Visitors are strongly urged to purchase medevac insurance prior to arrival. Local hospitals do not conform to U.S. standards, especially for emergency care, and evacuation to South Africa or Mauritius is expensive. In the event of a medical emergency, visitors should ask to be taken to the Polyclinique Ilafy and should notify the Embassy Consular Section at: http://www.antananarivo.usembassy.gov.

LOCAL TIME, BUSINESS HOURS, AND HOLIDAYS

The Malagasy Time Zone is Greenwich plus three. When it is noon EST in Washington, it is 8 p.m. in Madagascar. The typical hours of business are from 8:30 a.m. to 5 p.m., with a lunch break between noon and 1 p.m.

Holiday schedule:
Friday March 29 Day Commemorating Martyrs
Monday April 1 Easter Monday
Wednesday May 1 Labor Day
Thursday May 9 Ascension Day
Monday May 20 Pentecost Monday
Wednesday June 26Independence Day

Thursday August 15 Assumption Day
Friday November 1 All Saints Day
Wednesday December 25 Christmas Day

Note: The GOM sometimes declares an additional "bridge" holiday on the Friday following a Thursday holiday.

TEMPORARY ENTRY OF MATERIALS AND PERSONAL BELONGINGS

When not imported for sale, goods may be admitted into the country without the payment of duty.

CONTACTS

GOVERNMENT AGENCIES

EDBM (Economic Development Board of Madagascar)
Immeuble EDBM, Antaninarenina
Antananarivo 101 – Madagascar
Tel: (261 20) 22 670 40
Fax: (261 20) 22 661 05
Website: http://www.edbm.gov.mg/
E-mail: edbm@edbm.mg

Presidency's Office
P.O. Box 955, Ambohitsirohitra
Antananarivo 101 – Madagascar
Tel: (261 20) 22 547 03
Fax: (261 20) 22 562 52
Website: http://www.hat.gov.mg/

Prime Minister's Office
P.O. Box 248
Antananarivo 101 – Madagascar
Tel: (261 20) 22 246 04
Fax: (261 20) 22 548 40
Website: http://www.madagascar.gov.mg/ orhttp://www.primature.gov.mg/

Ministry of Finance and Budget
P.O. Box 61
Antananarivo 101 – Madagascar
Tel: (261 20) 22 336 30
Fax: (261 20) 22 345 30
Website: http://www.mefb.gov.mg/

Ministry of Economy and Industry
P.O. Box 527
Antananarivo 101 – Madagascar
Tel: (261 20) 22 291 28
Website: http://www.mei.gov.mg/

Ministry of Energy
P.O. Box 257
Antananarivo 101 – Madagascar

Tel: (261 20) 34 83 701 79
Websites: http://www.energy.gov.mg/

Ministry of Mining
Ampandrianomby
Antananarivo 101 – Madagascar
Tel: (261 20) 32 03 110 20
Website: http://www.mines.gov.mg/

Ministry of Hydrocarbons
Ampandrianomby
Antananarivo 101 – Madagascar
Tel: (261 20) 34 20 088 28

Ministry of Agriculture
P.O. Box 842
Antananarivo 101 – Madagascar
Tel: (261 20) 22 247 10
Fax: (261 20) 22 265 61
Website: http://www.maep.gov.mg/

Ministry of Transportation
P.O. Box 4139
Antananarivo 101 – Madagascar
Tel: (261 20) 22 246 04
Fax: (261 20) 22 356 26
Website: http://www.mtpm.gov.mg/; http://www.transport.gov.mg/

Ministry of Public Works
P.O. Box 295
Antananarivo 101 – Madagascar
Tel: (261 20) 22 232 15
Fax: (261 20) 22 208 90
Website: http://www.mtpm.gov.mg/

Ministry of Telecommunications and Post
Antaninarenina
Antananarivo 101 – Madagascar
Tel: (261 20) 22 232 67
Fax: (261 20) 358 94
Website: http://www.mtpc.gov.mg/

Ministry of Environment and Forestry
Antsahavola
Antananarivo 101 – Madagascar
Tel: (261 20) 22 668 05
Fax: (261 20) 22 345 10
Website: http://www.meeft.mg/

Ministry of Tourism
Tsimbazaza
Antananarivo 101 – Madagascar
Tel: (261 20) 22 668 05
Fax: (261 20) 22 354 10

Website: http://www.mtoura.gov.mg/

Central Bank of Madagascar
P.O. Box 550
Antananarivo 101 – Madagascar
Tel: (261 20) 22 217 51
Fax: (261 20) 22 345 32
Website: http://www.banque-centrale.mg/

Madagascar Embassy in the United States of America
2374 Massachusetts Avenue
Washington D.C 20008
USA
Tel: 202 265 55 25
Fax: 202 265 30 34
E-mail: Malagasy@embassy.org

COUNTRY BUSINESS ASOCIATIONS

American Chamber of Commerce in Madagascar (AmCham)
Bâtiment C1
Village des Jeux, Ankorondrano
Antananarivo 101 – Madagascar
E-mail: executivesecretary@amcham-mada.mg
Website: http://www.amcham-mada.mg/
Tel: (261 20) 32 02 814 39

Chambre de Commerce, d'Industrie d'Antananarivo
P.O. Box 166
Antananarivo 101 – Madagascar
Tel: (261 20) 22 202 11
Fax: (261 20) 22 202 13
Website: http://www.tana-cciaa.org/

FIVMPAMA (Association of Malagasy Businessmen)
12, rue Rainizanabolona, Antanimena
Antananarivo 101 – Madagascar
Tel: (261 20) 22 690 78
Fax: (261 20) 22 320 56
E-mail: fivmpama@moov.mg

GEM (Group of Enterprises of Madagascar)
P.O. Box 1695
Antananarivo 101 – Madagascar
Tel: (261 20) 22 238 41
Fax: (261 20) 22 219 65
Website: http://www.gem-madagascar.com/
E-mail: gem@iris.mg

SIM (Union of Industries of Madagascar)
Immeuble Holcim, Tsaralalana
Antananarivo 101 – Madagascar
Tel: (261 20) 240 07

Fax: (261 20) 22 225 18
Website: http://www.sindusmad.com/
E-mail: mailto:syndusmad@moov.mg or de@sym.mg

GEFP (Group of Export Processing Zone companies)
Village E2 – Village des Jeux
Ankorondrano
Antananarivo 101 – Madagascar
Tel: (261 20) 22 380 50
Fax: (261 20) 22 403 73
Website: http://www.gefpmg.com/
E-mail: mailto:gefpmg@moov.mg

Chambre des Mines de Madagascar (Mining Chamber)
QMM Rio Tinto, Villa 3H, Lot IIJ 169, Ivandry, Antananarivo
Madagascar
Tel: (261 20) 32 07 632 21
Contact: Mr. Willy Ranjatoelina, Executive Secretary
E-mail: rwr@blueline.mg
http://chambredesminesdemadagascar.com/en/content/home

COUNTRY MARKET RESEARCH FIRMS

GAMA Consult
Immeuble ARO
Antsahavola
Antananarivo 101 – Madagascar
Tel: (261 20) 22 238 52
Fax: (261 20) 22 238 88
Website: http://www.gamaconsult.com/
E-mail: gamaconsult@moov.mg

FTHM Conseils
Immeuble ARO
Antsahavola
Antananarivo 101 – Madagascar
Tel: (261 20) 22 631 87
Fax: (261 20) 22 337 20
E-mail: fthm@moov.mg

ATW Consultants de Madagascar
Lot II Y 9F, Antanimora
Antananarivo 101 – Madagascar
Tel/Fax: (261 20) 22 345 98
E-mail: atw@moov.mg

R Conseil
P.O. Box 8301
Antananarivo 101 – Madagascar
Tel: (261 20) 22 432 79
Fax: (261 20) 289 97
E-mail: rconseil@moov.mg

USEFUL WEBSITES

Presidency: http://www.presidency.gov.mg/
Government: http://www.madagascar.gov.mg/
Data bank: http://www.instat.mg/
Tourism: http://www.tourisme-madagascar.com/
Investment: http://www.edbm.gov.mg/ or http://www.bni.mg/
General/Economy: http://www.madagascar-contacts.com/
General
information: http://www.sobika.com/ orhttp://www.madagate.com/ or http://www.moov.mg/

OMNIS is a good source for potential investors in the oil, coal and uranium sectors: http://www.omnis.mg/

The Governance Project for Mineral Resources (PGRM) is a good source for potential investors in the mining sector: http://www.pgrm.mg/

MARKET RESEARCH

To view market research reports produced by the U.S. Commercial Service, please go to the following website:http://www.export.gov/mrktresearch/index.asp and click on Country and Industry Market Reports.

Please note that these reports are only available to U.S. citizens and U.S.companies. Registration to the site is required, and is free.

TRADE EVENTS

Please click on the link below for information on upcoming trade events.
http://www.export.gov/tradeevents/index.asp

TRADE AND INVESTMENT REGIMES

The results of Madagascar's presidential election of December 2001 provoked a socio-political crisis which ended in July 2002. Though of short duration, the crisis seriously affected the country's economic performance (Chapter I(2)). A new Constitution was adopted by referendum on 4 April 2007.[2] The main change concerns the organization of the territory of Madagascar, following the replacement of the six provinces by 22 regions, subdivided into communes. In principle, they enjoy administrative and financial autonomy, which will be introduced gradually. Madagascar also now has three official languages: Malagasy, French and English.

Executive power is exercised by the President of the Republic and the Government. The President of the Republic is elected by direct universal suffrage for a term of five years, renewable once only; the most recent presidential election was held in December 2006. The Government is composed of the Prime Minister and his cabinet; the current Government was sworn in on 25 January 2007. The Government Council, which is mainly responsible for legislative initiatives, is headed by the Prime Minister. The ministries prepare draft legislation in their respective areas of competence for submission to the Council. Improvement of the business environment is a State priority, (section (2) below), but the Committee for the Reform of Business Law (*Comité pour la réforme du droit des affaires* – CRDA), which is meant to coordinate legislative proposals in this area, suffers from a lack of financial resources.[3] The Parliament exercises legislative power. To be adopted, draft laws must be approved by each of the two chambers of the Parliament (the Senate and National Assembly).[4] The President of the Republic promulgates the draft laws that have been passed by the Parliament.[5] Laws are then published in the *Journal officiel de la république* (Official Journal of the Republic), which is available only as a printed document.

The President of the Republic signs international treaties and agreements and promulgates them after ratification by the Parliament[6]; this was the case with the WTO Agreement (section (iii)). Under the Constitution, international treaties and agreements, upon ratification, take precedence over laws, subject to implementation by the other parties to the treaty or agreement concerned. They are applicable as law in Madagascar as soon as they are ratified and are automatically binding. Under this monist system, the WTO Agreement may be invoked directly in domestic courts, although this has never yet happened. In hierarchical terms, ratified international treaties and agreements are followed in importance by the Constitution, laws, ordinances[7], decrees and orders. The main trade-related laws, ordinances and regulations are set out in Table II.1.

[2] Law 2007-001 of 27 April 2007. Consulted online at: http://www.madagascar-presidency.gov.mg/index.php/item/449.
[3] "Madagascar: Bilan commun pays CCA", July 2003. Consulted online at: http://www.undg.org/archive_docs/5452-Madagascar_CCA.pdf [21 December 2007].
[4] The National Assembly has 121 seats and the Senate 90. Deputies are elected by direct universal suffrage for a term of five years; the last (early) legislative elections took place on 23 September 2007. The next Senate elections will be held in 2008. The Senate represents the decentralized territorial authorities.
[5] According to article 58 of the 2007 Constitution, the President of the Republic shall promulgate laws within three weeks following their transmission by the National Assembly. Prior to the expiration of that deadline, the President of the Republic may submit a request to Parliament, which cannot be refused, to reconsider the law or some of the articles thereof.
[6] Title IV of the 2007 Constitution.
[7] Under Article 99 of the 2007 Constitution, the Parliament, by an absolute majority of votes, may authorize the President of the Republic to take measures by ordinance which normally require legislation. Ordinances are adopted by the Council of Ministers and enter into force upon publication in the Official Journal of the Republic.

Table II.1 Madagascar's principal trade-related laws and regulations

Sector	Instrument/Law
Customs legislation	Customs Code 2006, Customs Tariff 2007
Status of trader	Commercial Code
Value added tax, excise duties and customs border levies	Tax Code (2006 edition) and Finance Laws of 2006 and 2007
Import prohibitions and licences	Decree No. 92-993 of 2 December 1992
Technical standards and regulations	Law No. 97-024 of 14 August 1997
Sanitary measures	Ordinance No. 62-072 of 29 September 1962
Phytosanitary measures	Ordinance No. 86-013 of 17 September 1986
Investment	Law No. 96-015 of 13 September 1996
Industrial free zone regime	Law No. 89-027 of 29 December 1989, as supplemented and amended by Law No. 91-020 of 12 August 1991
Large-scale investment in mining	Law No. 2005-024 of 17 November 2005
Procedures and regulations for the establishment of private commercial enterprises	Law No. 2003-036 of 30 January 2004
Protection of industrial property	Ordinance No. 89-019 of 31 July 1989
Protection of copyright and related rights	Law No. 94-036 of 9 December 1994
Competition	Law No. 2005-020 of 17 July 2005
Privatization of State-owned enterprises	Law No. 96-011 of 13 August 1996
Government procurement	Law No. 2004-009 of 26 July 2004
Environment	Law No. 90-033 of 21 December 1990
Forests	Law No. 97-017 of 8 August 1997
Fisheries and aquaculture	Ordinance No. 93-022 of 4 May 1993
Mining Code	Law No. 99-022 of 19 August 1999
Hydrocarbons (prospecting, exploration and exploitation)	Law No. 96-018 of 4 September 1996
Hydrocarbons (downstream activities)	Law No. 99-010 of 17 April 1999
Electricity	Law No. 98-032 of 22 December 1998
Water	Law No. 98-029 of 20 January 1999
Land transport	Law No. 2004-53 of 28 January 2005
Maritime transport	Law No. 99-028 of 3 February 2000
Civil aviation	Law No. 2004-027 of 9 September 2004
Telecommunications	Law No. 96-034 of 13 December 1996, as supplemented and amended by Law No. 2005-023 of 17 October 2005
Tourism	Law No. 95-017 of 25 July 1995
Foreign exchange regime	Law No. 2006-08 of 13 July 2006
Banking services (credit institutions)	Law No. 95-030 of 22 February 1996
Banking services (microfinance institutions)	Law No. 2005-016 of 29 September 2005
Insurance	Law No. 99-013 of 2 August 1999

Source: Malagasy authorities.

Judicial authority is vested in the Supreme Court, the courts of appeal and the lower courts attached to them, as well as the High Court of Justice. The commercial courts are empowered to deal with trade disputes; various mechanisms are provided for the settlement of disputes between foreign investors and the State (section (4) below). Judges are appointed by the Judicial Service Commission, presided over by the President of the Republic. The Constitutional Court rules on the constitutionality of treaties, ordinances and organic laws; conflicts of jurisdiction; and disputes relating to referendums and presidential, legislative and Senate elections. The development partners support a number of projects aimed at capacity building for judges and improving the functioning of Madagascar's judicial system.

The main function of the Ministry of the Economy, Planning, the Private Sector and Trade hereinafter the "Ministry in charge of trade" is to formulate and implement trade policy, including WTO-related matters, and all bilateral or plurilateral trade agreements. Madagascar has not established an interministerial committee to follow up trade negotiations. However, a National Trade Policy Development Forum involves the private sector, on an ad hoc basis, in follow-up to trade policy issues (for example, establishment of the list of sensitive products in the context of the negotiations for an Economic Partnership Agreement (EPA) with the European Union (EU)). The Ministry of Industry, in collaboration with the Economic Development Board of Madagascar (EDBM), is responsible for investment policy, including the industrial free zone (IFZ) (section 4)). Other ministries are also involved in formulating and implementing trade policy, including the Ministry of Finance and those responsible for sectoral matters.

A number of employers' and trade union organizations contribute to the elaboration of trade policy in Madagascar on an ad hoc basis. They include the *Syndicat des industries de Madagascar* – SIM (Industrial Trade Union of Madagascar), the *Groupement du patronat malgache* – FIV.MPA.MA (Madagascar Employers Group), the Chamber of Commerce, Industry and Handicrafts, the Chamber of Agriculture, the *Groupement des entreprises de Madagascar* – GEM (Madagascar Enterprises Group) and the *Groupement des entreprises franches et partenaires* – GEFP (Group of Free Enterprises and Partners). However, there is no permanent structure for public-private dialogue and the State mainly uses ad hoc consultation mechanisms. No national body is responsible for evaluating Madagascar's trade policy, but impact studies may be carried out (for example, concerning the EPA with the EU).

POLICY OBJECTIVES

Madagascar's economic and social development strategy for the period 2007-2011, as set out in the Madagascar Action Plan (MAP)[8], is aimed at achieving the Millennium Development Goals (MDGs) and is inspired by the national vision "Madagascar *Naturellement*". The MAP follows on from the "Poverty Reduction Strategy Paper" (PRSP)[9] adopted in July 2003. The major objective of the MAP is to raise Madagascar from 146th place (out of 177 countries) in the 2005 UNDP ranking to 100th place in 2012[10], by reducing the proportion of the population living on less than US$2 per day from 85 per cent in 2003 to 50 per cent in 2012, and by raising the real annual average economic growth rate from 4.6 per cent in 2005 to 7-10 per cent by 2012. In order to achieve strong economic growth, the State is counting on the emergence of a "thriving private sector in the areas of trade and investment at the national, regional and international levels". Madagascar has drawn up a macroeconomic and structural reform programme for the period 2006-2008, supported by an IMF Poverty Reduction and Growth Facility (PRGF) (Chapter I(2)); Madagascar receives support from its development partners.

Since its first TPR, Madagascar has reviewed its trade policy and its investment regime; new frameworks for investment and for the industrial free zone (IFZ) are planned for 2008. The State is relying on the development of agriculture, mining and tourism to accelerate economic growth, and it encourages both local and foreign direct investment. The State is seeking to strengthen the private sector and improve the international competitiveness of Malagasy goods and services,

[8] IMF (2007a).
[9] IMF (2003).
[10] UNDP (2006).

in particular by dismantling the numerous supply-side constraints. It is also endeavouring to take better advantage of trade integration opportunities at the multilateral, regional and bilateral levels.

The authorities are aware of the need to improve the business environment.[11] One important aspect of such improvement consists in advancing the rule of law and good governance, inasmuch as the NGO Transparency International considers Madagascar to have a corruption problem.[12] Noteworthy among the measures taken in this regard are the stepping up of action to combat corruption[13], *inter alia* through the establishment of the *Bureau indépendant anti-corruption* – BIANCO (Independent Anti-Corruption Bureau), which is responsible for implementing the national anti-corruption strategy.[14] In 2005, the BIANCO found that "corruption is still rife in all sectors and this problem is compounded by multiple functional shortcomings in the public services".[15] The BIANCO is finding it difficult to obtain periodic declarations of personal assets, although these are compulsory for persons in high office (except for the President of the Republic).[16] The authorities are planning to join the Extractive Industries Transparency Initiative (EITI).[17]

TRADE AGREEMENTS AND ARRANGEMENTS

WTO

Madagascar signed the Marrakesh Agreement on 15 April 1994 and became a WTO Member on 17 November 1995, following ratification by its Parliament.[18] It is recognized as a least developed country (LDC). It is not a party to any plurilateral agreement or to any of the protocols and agreements concluded under WTO auspices. Madagascar grants most-favoured-nation (MFN) treatment to all its trading partners.

The concessions made by Madagascar during the Uruguay Round are contained in Schedule LI for goods (Chapter III(2)(iv)(a)), and document GATS/SC/51 with regard to services (Chapter IV(5)). Since its first TPR in 2001, Madagascar has made progress in the implementation of WTO agreements (Chapter III). It maintains a mission in Geneva, but inadequate human resources are a continuing obstacle to its participation in day-to-day WTO activities. Since 1995, Madagascar has participated in four WTO dispute settlement proceedings as a third party.[19] It participates in the WTO Ministerial Conferences[20], and generally supports the positions of the LDCs, the African Group, the ACP countries and the Group of 77 Developing Countries on questions relating to multilateral obligations and the strengthening of technical cooperation activities.

---

[11] Madagascar is ranked 149th out of 175 countries in the World Bank Doing Business Index, World Bank (undated).
[12] Madagascar is ranked 86th out of 163 countries in the Corruption Perceptions Index 2006. Consulted at: http://www.transparency.org/policy_research/surveys_indices/cpi [11 August 2007].
[13] Law No. 2004-030 of 29 July 2004.
[14] Information on the BIANCO consulted online at: http://www.bianco-mg.org [11 August 2007].
[15] BIANCO (2006).
[16] Decree No. 2004-983 of 12 October 2004.
[17] *Les Nouvelles*, "Les revenus des industries d'extraction sur le tapis de la transparence", 18 October 2006. Consulted online at: http://www.pgrm.mg/index.php?option=com_content&task=view&id=167& Itemid=20 [11 August 2007].
[18] Law No. 95-008 of 10 July 1995.
[19] European Communities – Regime for the Importation, Sale and Distribution of Bananas (DS27); European Communities – Export Subsidies on Sugar (DS265); European Communities – Export Subsidies on Sugar (DS266); European Communities – Export Subsidies on Sugar (DS283).
[20] WTO documents WT/MIN(96)/ST/119 of 12 December 1996, WT/MIN(99)/ST/66 of 1 December 1999, WT/MIN(01)/ST/88 of 11 November 2001, WT/MIN(03)/ST/52 of 11 September 2003 and WT/MIN(05)/ST/72 of 15 December 2005.

Madagascar is eligible for the trade policy courses and has benefited from several other types of technical assistance offered by the WTO. Nonetheless, technical assistance is still necessary (Annex II.1), as some problems that were noted during the first TPR in 2001 appear to persist in 2007. Exemptions from the principle of national treatment have been noted in the application of excise duties (Chapter III(2)(iv)(d)). Madagascar is still having difficulty in updating its WTO notifications (Table II.2), including the Integrated Database (IDB) since June 2005.[21] Capacity building in the areas of customs valuation and technical barriers to trade would also be desirable.

Table II.2 Status of WTO notifications

Agreement	WTO document	Content
Marrakesh Agreement	WT/Let/112 of 30 September 1996	Delay in the application of the Agreement on Customs Valuation until 17 November 2000; and reservations under paragraphs 3 and 4 of Annex III
Agreement on Agriculture	G/AG/N/MDG/1 of 11 October 2000	No export subsidies, 1995-1999
	G/AG/N/MDG/2 of 11 October 2000	No domestic support measures, 1995-1999
III. Enabling Clause of the GATT 1994	WT/COMTD/N/3 of 29 June 1995	Common Market for Eastern and Southern Africa (COMESA)
IV. Article XXIV of the GATT 1994	WT/REG176/N/1 of 9 August 2004, WT/REG176/N/1/Rev.1 of 27 August 2004	Southern African Development Community (SADC)
	WT/REG176/1 of 8 October 2004, WT/REG176/2 of 8 October 2004, WT/REG176/2/Rev.1 of 19 November 2004	Protocol on Trade in the Southern African Development Community (SADC); and revision[a]
Agreement on Implementation of Article VI of the GATT 1994	G/ADP/N/1/MDG/1 of 11 May 2001	No legislation
Agreement on Implementation of Article VII of the GATT 1994	WT/Let/112 of 30 September 1996	Reservations
	G/C/W/259 of 9 April 2001 and G/C/W/259/Rev. 1 of 12 April 2001	Request for waiver in order to maintain minimum values[b]
Agreement on Preshipment Inspection	G/PSI/N/1/Add.4 of 9 October 1996	Domestic legislation
Agreement on Import Licensing Procedures	G/LIC/N/3/MDG/1 of 9 September 2002	Description of procedures
	G/LIC/N/3/MDG/2 of 21 June 2005	Description of new procedures
Agreement on Subsidies and Countervailing Measures, and Article XVI:1 of the GATT 1994	G/SCM/N/95/MDG of 16 July 2003	No prescribed measures
	G/SCM/N/95/MDG/Suppl.1 of 21 October 2004	No prescribed measures

[21] WTO document G/MA/IDB/2/Rev.25 of 26 March 2007.

Agreement	WTO document	Content
Agreement on Safeguards	G/SG/N/1/MDG/1 of 16 May 2001	No legislation
Agreement on Trade-Related Investment Measures	G/TRIMS/N/2/Rev.8 of 19 July 2001	Industrial Free Zone regime

a File reviewed by Members (WTO documents WT/REG176/3 of 22 December 2004, WT/REG176/4 of 12 March 2007, WT/REG176/5 of 2 May 2007, WT/REG176/M/1 of 12 June 2007, WT/REG176/6 of 3 July 2007).

b Agreed by Decision of 18 July 2001 (WTO document WT/L/408 of 26 July 2001).

Source: WTO Secretariat.

REGIONAL AGREEMENTS

AFRICAN UNION[22]

Madagascar is a founding member of the African Union, the successor to the Organization of African Unity (OAU).[23] Eventually, the African Union will be an economic and monetary union whose component institutions will be the Conference of Heads of State and Government (already established), the Council of Ministers (established), the Peace and Security Council (established), the Commission (established), the Pan-African Parliament (established), together with a Central Bank, a Monetary Fund, an African Investment Bank, a Court of Justice, an Economic, Social and Cultural Council (statutes already prepared), and technical committees.

The African Economic Community (AEC) was founded in June 1991 under the auspices of the OAU, now the AU, under the terms of the Treaty of Abuja. This treaty provides for the creation of an African common market in six stages spread over 34 years. The integration process is based on the coordination and harmonization of tariff and non-tariff measures, between various trade and subregional groups (known as Regional Economic Communities (RECs)), with a view to establishing a continent-wide customs union. Madagascar belongs to two of the seven RECs recognized by the African Union, namely the Common Market for Eastern and Southern Africa (section (b) below) and the Southern African Development Community (SADC) (section (c) below).

The New Partnership for Africa's Development (NEPAD), adopted at the Lusaka (Zambia) Summit, is an AU programme with a Secretariat based in South Africa. Its objectives include the development of appropriate infrastructures to support the process of regional integration.[24] The

[22] Information on the African Union was gathered from: http://www.africa-union.org [12 August 2007].
[23] The Charter establishing the OAU was signed on 25 May 1963. The Constitutive Act of the African Union was adopted at the summit held in July 2000 in Lomé (Togo). The African Union, which has replaced the OAU, was proclaimed on 11 July 2001 in Lusaka, Zambia, following ratification of the Constitutive Act by more than 44 of the OAU's 53 member States. The African Union was launched by the Durban Summit of 9 July 2002.
[24] NEPAD (2006).

European Union (EU) launched a partnership on infrastructure in 2006, with €5.6 billion in financing from the tenth European Development Fund (EDF, 2008-2013).[25]

COMMON MARKET FOR EASTERN AND SOUTHERN AFRICAN (COMESA)[26]

Madagascar is a founding member of COMESA[27], which has as its main objective the establishment of a common market, together with a monetary union (in 2025), with a view to achieving the continent-wide integration provided for by the African Union (section (a) above). The COMESA treaty was notified to the WTO under the Enabling Clause of the GATT 1994[28], but has not yet been the subject of detailed examination by Members.

COMESA's institutional framework comprises the Conference of Heads of State and Government (already established), the Council of Ministers (established), the Secretariat (established in Lusaka, Zambia), a Court of Justice (established), a Committee of Governors of Central Banks (established), an Intergovernmental Committee (established), a Consultative Committee (not yet established), and technical committees (e.g. on trade and customs matters) (established). The Trade and Development Bank for Eastern and Southern Africa (PTA Bank) finances foreign trade transactions and projects by public or private investors resident in one of the member States. The African Trade Insurance Agency (ATI) provides cover against political risks for investors. The PTA Reinsurance Company (PTA-RE) helps to promote insurance and reinsurance in the region.

Under the COMESA programme, the free trade area (FTA) was established on 1 November 2000. Its guiding principle is the exchange of preferences on originating products (Chapter III(2)(x)), on a reciprocal basis. Djibouti, Egypt, Kenya[29], Madagascar (Chapter III(2)(x)), Malawi, Mauritius, Sudan, Zambia and Zimbabwe eliminated their customs duties (on a reciprocal basis) on originating products on the agreed date; they were joined by Burundi and Rwanda on 1 January 2004. In order to facilitate their trade integration, the COMESA member countries adopted the Harmonized System (HS) 2002, the Automated System for Customs Data (ASYCUDA) and EUROTRACE. The customs union was to have entered into force at the end of 2004, but this project has been postponed until December 2008. The common external tariff (CET) rates that have been adopted are: zero per cent for raw materials and capital goods; 10 per cent for intermediate products; 25 per cent for finished goods. However, the member countries' product classifications have not yet been harmonized. Nor do members have an agenda for harmonizing domestic taxes on products, but the COMESA Secretariat identifies non-tariff barriers (e.g. non-recognition of certificates of origin) and is undertaking missions to promote awareness in the countries concerned.

The other stages in the establishment of a common market concern the free movement of persons, capital and services. The Protocol on the free movement of persons should lead in the first instance to the abolition of the compulsory visa in 2000. Madagascar has not yet signed the

[25] European Commission, press release IP/06/986, 13 July 2006. Consulted at: http//europa.eu/rapid/pressReleasesAction.do?reference=IP/06/986/&forma=HTML&aged=1&langage=EN&.guiLangage=fr [12 August 2007].
[26] Information on COMESA was consulted at: http://www.comesa.int/ [12 August 2007].
[27] The treaty establishing COMESA was signed in 1993. The members of COMESA are: Burundi, Comoros, Democratic Republic of the Congo, Djibouti, Egypt, Eritrea, Ethiopia, Kenya, Madagascar, Malawi, Mauritius, Rwanda, Seychelles, Sudan, Swaziland, Uganda, Zambia and Zimbabwe. Lesotho and Mozambique (1997), Tanzania (1999) and Namibia (2004) have left COMESA, and Angola suspended its participation because of duplication between COMESA and the SADC (section (c)) in the region.
[28] WTO document WT/COMTD/N/3 of 29 June 1995.
[29] In order to protect its domestic industry, Kenya has been authorized to apply a non-preferential tariff on sugar from other COMESA members, until 28 February 2008.

Protocol; however, a 90-day visa is issued on arrival to nationals of COMESA member countries. COMESA was made a common investment zone in 2003, and the regional investment agency established in Cairo, Egypt, has consultative links with the national investment promotion agencies.

The establishment of a monetary union in 2025 has been an objective (of the PTA) since 1992, an objective which was revived in 1999. Until 2000, it was planned that member States with significant cross-border trade should introduce limited convertibility of their currencies. Between 2000 and 2024, it was planned to establish a single currency and to achieve macroeconomic convergence in order to support monetary union. Since 2006, the COMESA member countries have been studying the possibility of establishing a monetary institute to lay the groundwork for monetary union.

The members of COMESA are continuing negotiations with the EU for the conclusion of an Economic Partnership Agreement (EPA) by the end of 2008 (section (e) below); Madagascar is a member of the Eastern and Southern Africa Group (AFOA)[30] (section (e) below). COMESA and the United States consult regularly on matters relating to the promotion of trade and bilateral investment through the Trade and Investment Council set up under an agreement of 29 October 2001 (section (f) below).[31]

SOUTHERN AFRICAN DEVELOPMENT COMMUNITY (SADC)[32]

Established in 1992, the SADC succeeded the Southern African Development Coordination Conference (SADCC).[33] Madagascar has been an SADC member since 18 August 2005. The initial objective of the SADC is to establish a free trade area in 2008; this project has been notified to the WTO under Article XXIV of the GATT 1994[34], and was considered by the Members at their meeting on 15-16 May 2007.[35] In October 2006, the SADC undertook to establish a customs union in 2010, a common market in 2015 and a monetary union in 2016. A further aim of the SADC is to contribute to the maintenance of peace and security in the region, and the SADC Brigade was recently established for that purpose.

The institutional framework of the SADC comprises the Conference of Heads of State and Government (already established), the Council of Ministers (established), the Secretariat (established in Gabarone, Botswana), a Court (established in Windhoek and operational since October 2006) and technical committees of Ministers (for example, the already established Council of Ministers responsible for trade matters (CMT)).

---

[30] Burundi, Comoros, Democratic Republic of the Congo, Djibouti, Eritria, Ethiopia, Kenya, Madagascar, Malawi, Mauritius, Rwanda, Seychelles, Sudan, Uganda, Zambia and Zimbabwe. The COMESA members not involved in the AFOA are Djibouti, Egypt and Swaziland, which, for negotiating purposes, are included in other groups.

[31] Agreement between the Government of the United States of America and the Common Market of Southern and Eastern Africa concerning the development of trade and investment relations. Consulted at: www.ustr.gov/assets/Trade_Agreements/TIFA/asset_upload_file563_7723.pdf [13 August 2007].

[32] Web portal of the SADC: http://www.sadc.int/ [13 August 2007].

[33] The members of the SADC are: Angola, Botswana, Democratic Republic of the Congo, Lesotho, Madagascar, Malawi, Mauritius, Mozambique, Namibia, South Africa, Swaziland, Tanzania, Zambia and Zimbabwe. The five members of the Southern African Customs Union (SACU) are members of the SADC. The Seychelles left the Community in 2002.

[34] WTO documents WT/REG176/N/1 of 9 August 2004, WT/REG176/N/1/Rev.1 of 27 August 2004, WT/REG176/1 of 8 October 2004, WT/REG176/2 of 8 October 2004, and WT/REG/176/2/Rev. 1 of 19 November 2004.

[35] WTO document WT/REG176/M/1 of 12 June 2007.

The Protocol on Trade (and the amendment thereto)[36], which has been implemented since 1 September 2000, is aimed at establishing a free trade area from 2008; Madagascar deposited its instruments of ratification on 21 February 2006.[37] Each of the member States presents its tariff reduction scheme for approval; Madagascar's scheme was endorsed at the Extraordinary Summit of Heads of State and Government of the SADC held in October 2006. Each scheme is based on three main categories of product: those in category A (mainly capital goods) are liberalized as from the first year; products in category B (e.g. goods that constitute major sources of customs revenue) are to be liberalized gradually by 2008; and products in category C (which are deemed sensitive by member States and may not exceed 15 per cent of each member's total merchandise trade) are to be liberalized by 2012.[38] Sugar is not included in the free trade regime and is the subject of special treatment; Madagascar supports such treatment in order to revive its sugar subsector (Chapter IV(2)(iii)). SADC rules of origin are negotiated on a product-by-product basis (Chapter III(2)(iii)).

In order to facilitate their trade integration, the member countries of the SADC have harmonized the various documents required for import and export, including the certificate of origin. The member States are also examining non-tariff barriers to trade between SADC member countries. The SADC has adopted a memorandum of understanding on standardization, quality, accreditation and metrology. However, the harmonization of internal taxes is not yet envisaged.

In the context of the liberalization of trade in services, a protocol on services was drawn up and adopted in June 2007. The SADC has also concluded a protocol on finance and investment (already signed by Madagascar), and a protocol on facilitation of the movement of persons; none of these protocols has yet come into force.

Some SADC member countries are continuing negotiations with the EU with a view to concluding an economic partnership agreement (EPA) by the end of 2008 (section (e) below); Madagascar belongs to the AFOA group (section (b) above).

INDIAN OCEAN COMMISSION (COI)[39]

Madagascar is a founding member of the COI which was established in 1984 by the Victoria Agreement, with a secretariat based in Quatre Bornes (Mauritius).[40] Since 1998, Madagascar has eliminated tariffs on goods originating from the COI countries. Since adopting new guidelines at the third Summit of Heads of State and Government in July 2005, the COI's mandate has been to encourage intra-regional trade and to defend the island interests of its members. "The COI today constitutes a leading circle of cooperation designed to facilitate integration of the south-

[36] The Protocol was signed on 24 August 1996 and entered into force on 25 January 2000, while the amendment entered into force on 7 August 2000. The SADC members that have acceded to the Protocol are: Angola, Botswana, Lesotho, Madagascar, Malawi, Mauritius, Mozambique, Namibia, South Africa, Swaziland, Tanzania, Zambia and Zimbabwe (the Democratic Republic of the Congo is not a signatory). The five members of the Southern African Customs Union (SACU) are parties to the Protocol. Angola has not yet submitted its offer for tariff reduction to the members of the SADC. For further details concerning this instrument, see the Secretariat report contained in WTO document WT/REG176/4 of 12 March 2007.

[37] According to the authorities, Madagascar has signed and ratified the Protocol on Immunities and Privileges, the Protocol on the Tribunal, the Protocol on Education and Training, the Protocol on Health, and the Protocol against corruption.

[38] In addition, a fourth category (E) covers products ineligible for preferential treatment under the general and security exceptions provided for in Articles 9 and 10 of the Protocol.

[39] Information on the COI was consulted on its web portal: http://www.coi-ioc.org/ [13 August 2007].

[40] The members of the COI are: Comoros, Réunion (France), Madagascar, Mauritius and the Seychelles.

west Indian Ocean islands into broader regional groupings and, thus, help them to adjust to the globalization process".[41]

RELATIONS WITH THE EUROPEAN UNION (EU)

Madagascar is one of the 79 ACP countries with which the EU signed the Cotonou Agreement, which provisionally entered into force on 1 March 2000.[42] The trade provisions are one of the mechanisms for cooperation between the ACP countries and the EU, whereby the latter grants duty-free admission to non-agricultural products and the majority of processed agricultural products originating in 78 ACP countries (excluding South Africa) on a non-reciprocal basis. Madagascar is one of the countries that have benefited, under the Agreement, from the provisions of the protocols on sugar[43], bananas and bovine meat.

The Members of the WTO have granted the EU a waiver from its obligations under Article I:1 of the GATT 1994 (on MFN treatment) for the period extending from 1 March 2000 to 31 December 2007, at which date new trading arrangements consistent with WTO rules must be concluded between the two parties.[44] In accordance with the Cotonou Agreement, these arrangements will take the form of economic partnership agreements (EPAs) between the EU and various ACP regional groupings; Madagascar belongs to the AFOA group (section (b) above). However, as the parties concerned were unable to finalize any formal agreement by 31 December 2007, they signed an Interim Agreement on Market Access, Economic Cooperation and Development, and Fisheries.[45] The Interim Agreement entered into force on 1 January 2008, but the negotiations will continue until the full agreement is concluded by 31 December 2008.

Madagascar has submitted a tariff offer in collaboration with the Comoros, Seychelles and Mauritius (CMMS subgroup). The offer relates to a tariff reduction spread over 15 years. The EU's market access offer relates to duty-free and quota-free imports of all products, with the exception of rice and sugar (with continued implementation of the Protocol on Sugar until 30 September 2009, followed by a transition period until 30 September 2015).

According to the authorities, Malagasy economic operators use preferences granted under the Cotonou Agreement, but not those granted to LDCs (including Madagascar) under the

---

[41] COI Press Release, 23rd Session of the COI Council. Consulted online at: http://www.coi-ioc.org/fileadmin/multimedia_francais/centre_medias/communiques_de_presse/downloads/COMMUNIQUE_DE_PRESSE-23emeConseil.pdf [14 August 2007].

[42] The Agreement was signed on 23 June 2000 at Cotonou, in Benin, and officially entered into force on 1 April 2003 after its ratification. The Agreement replaced the Lomé Convention, in effect since 1975, the fourth extension of which expired at the end of February 2000.

[43] The European Union undertook to purchase some 1.4 million tonnes of sugar, at the guaranteed Community price, from countries that are signatories to Protocol No. 8 on Sugar under the Cotonou Agreement (Barbados, Belize, Republic of the Congo, Fiji, Guyana, Côte d'Ivoire, Jamaica, Kenya, Madagascar, Malawi, Mauritius, Suriname, St. Kitts and Nevis, Swaziland, Tanzania, Trinidad and Tobago, Uganda, Zimbabwe and Zambia); the bilateral agreement between the EU and India contains identical provisions. The new market organization for sugar came into force on 1 July 2006 and provides for a 36 per cent cumulative reduction in the price of sugar on the European market between 2006 and 2009 (WTO document WT/TPR/S/177/Rev.1 of 15 May 2007).

[44] WTO document WT/MIN(01)/15 of 14 November 2001.

[45] The Interim Agreement between the EU, on the one hand, and the Comoros and Madagascar, on the other, was signed on 11 December 2007. European Commission, Trade DG, "Update: Interim Economic Partnership Agreements". Consulted online at: http://trade.ec.europa.eu/doclib/docs/2007/november/tradoc_136959.pdf [21 December 2007].

"Everything but Arms" (EBA) initiative of the EU[46], since the rules of origin under the Cotonou Agreement are considered more favourable to them.

Madagascar exports sugar to the EU under three types of preferential quota: a quota of 10,760 tonnes under the Sugar Protocol of the ACP-EU Agreement, which has been extended under the Interim Agreement; a quota of 2,500 tonnes under the special preferential sugar regime (SPS); and a quota of 5,000 tonnes under the EBA initiative. The enterprises active in the sector nevertheless focus on only the first of these quotas, given inadequate production levels (Chapter IV(2)(iii)).

RELATIONS WITH THE UNITED STATES OF AMERICA

Madagascar is one of the 37 countries eligible for the programme set up by the United States under the African Growth and Opportunity Act (AGOA)[47]; Madagascar is also eligible for United States preferences under the Generalized System of Preferences (GSP), but they are not used by Malagasy economic operators. The AGOA beneficiary countries are granted duty-free and quota-free access to the US market until 2015 for a range of products, including selected agricultural and textile products (except for wearing apparel). As regards wearing apparel, Madagascar has been eligible, since 1 March 2002, for the special provision on the inclusion of fabrics from third countries, which will remain in force until 30 September 2012[48]; the authorities report 21.4 million kilograms of Malagasy textile exports under the AGOA in 2006, for a total value of US$195 million, roughly double the 2001 level. As a member of COMESA (section (b) above), Madagascar qualifies for the AGOA Linkage in COMESA (ALINC) programme.[49] Madagascar is also granted preferential access for its sugar exports within the limits of a quota, which is not filled, however, because of low Malagasy sugar output (Chapter IV(2)(iii)).

OTHER TRADE AGREEMENTS AND ARRANGEMENTS

Many countries extend (non-reciprocal) preferential tariff treatment to goods originating in Madagascar under the Generalized System of Preferences (GSP). The authorities state that China has granted zero-rate Special Preferential Customs Tariff (SPCT) treatment for 187 products since early 2005.

INVESTMENT

The general framework for investment in Madagascar did not change substantially between the country's first TPR in 2001 and the end of December 2007. This general framework comprises domestic legislation establishing the general principles governing the reception and protection of foreign investment[50], supplemented by specific frameworks for large-scale mining investments[51],

[46] Under this initiative, the EU has since 2001 granted duty-free access, without any quantitative restriction, to products originating from the LDCs (except for arms and ammunition). However, temporary exceptions are provided for rice and sugar (until the end of 2009). The exception has ended for bananas, for which imports into the EU from eligible LDCs have been exempt from customs duties since 1 January 2006 (WTO document WT/TPR/S/177/Rev.1 of 15 May 2007).
[47] USTR (2007).
[48] Madagascar also benefits from the provision on handmade ("category 9") products.
[49] Programme of assistance introduced to stimulate exports from the COMESA countries to the United States. Consulted online at: http://www.addistribune.com/Archives/2002/09/06-09-02/AGOA.htm [14 August 2007].
[50] Law No. 96-015 of 13 September 1996 (under revision for 2008).
[51] Law No. 2005-024 of 17 November 2005.

and the industrial free zone (IFZ) regime.[52] The authorities have indicated that the investment and IFZ regimes are due to be modified from 2008 onwards. Under this domestic legislation, Madagascar offers the customary guarantees for foreign direct investors in respect of security of capital and investment, freedom to transfer capital contributions, compensation for expropriation, and equality of treatment. Legal and natural persons may establish businesses in all areas of activity and hold 100 per cent of a firm's capital (with the exception of certain activities such as fixed telecommunications (until June 2008), postal services, transport and distribution of electric power, and certain transport, airport and port services (Chapter III(4)(iii)). Under the foreign exchange regime in force, foreign direct investment is not subject to declaration, prior authorization or control, and non-residents may undertake capital transactions.[53]

Madagascar has signed bilateral agreements on investment promotion and protection with: France (in force since 2005), Mauritius (2006), the OPEC Fund (2006), the Belgium-Luxembourg Economic Union (2006), China (2006), Germany (2007) and South Africa (2007). Agreements with Thailand, Switzerland, the Republic of Guinea, Morocco and the Netherlands are in the process of being finalized. Existing tax treaties with France (1984) and Mauritius (1996) are designed to prevent double taxation of nationals resident in one or the other of the partner countries. The Cotonou ACP-EU Agreement provides for the protection of European investments in the ACP countries (Articles 260, 261 and 262); this topic should in principle also be covered by the Economic Partnership Agreement (section (3)(ii)(e)).

Madagascar's bilateral agreements on the promotion and protection of investment provide for: national treatment and most-favoured-nation treatment (on a reciprocal basis) for investors from other contracting parties; compensation for expropriation; freedom to transfer funds earned from investment activities; and dispute settlement. On the latter point, Madagascar offers foreign investors a choice between referral to a national arbitration body or court, on the one hand, and arbitration by the International Centre for Settlement of Investment Disputes (ICSID), on the other. Madagascar's membership, since 1989, of the Multilateral Investment Guarantee Agency (MIGA) also offers investors the possibility of guarantees against non-commercial risks. Cover against political risk is also available to investors through the African Trade Insurance Agency (ATI), of which Madagascar is also a member.

Since the first TPR of Madagascar, a new legal framework inspired by the OHADA Uniform Act on Trading Companies has been made applicable to trading companies set up in Madagascar.[54] Since 2003, private land acquisition by foreign investors is permitted, provided that the foreign exchange input amounts to US$500,000 or more.[55] Under this provision, foreigners may acquire land with a maximum surface area of: 10,000 m^2 for an activity in the banking or insurance sector; 15,000 m^2 for real estate activities; 25,000 m^2 for tourist activities; and 5,000 m^2 for any other activity. A waiver may be requested with regard to the maximum surface area in the case of a foreign exchange input higher than the required minimum. Authorization from the Government Council is required. Although the acquisition of State land continues to be reserved to nationals, access to such land by foreigners is facilitated by the granting of long leases (ranging from 18 to 99 years).[56]

At the institutional level, the main innovation since the first TPR of Madagascar in 2001 concerns the establishment of a Single Window for investment and the development of enterprises

[52] Law No. 89-027 of 29 December 1989, as supplemented and amended by Law No. 91-020 of 12 August 1991.
[53] Law No. 2006-008 of 13 July 2006.
[54] Law No. 2003-036 of 30 January 2004.
[55] Law No. 2003-028 of 27 August 2003.
[56] Law No. 96-016 of 13 August 1996.

(*Guichet unique des investissements et de développement des entreprises* – GUIDE)[57], which has been operational since 2004. The GUIDE groups together the services concerned by company formation formalities, which may be carried out for promoters within four days, without costs. The GUIDE receives the files containing applications for access to land[58], authorizations for recruitment of foreign workers[59], authorizations for tourism establishments, or for approval under the industrial free zone (IFZ) regime. The GUIDE processes these files and issues the documents requested. The GUIDE is currently integrated into the Economic Development Board of Madagascar (EDBM)[60], which started operating in March 2007. The EDBM is responsible for Madagascar's investment policy and for promoting Madagascar as a destination.

Under the ordinary law regime, any investment for the establishment of an enterprise is subject to a "capital inflow duty" (*droit sur les apports* – DA), which is determined in the light of the amount of the investment[61], a professional tax[62], miscellaneous duties and charges on the purchase of buildings (by Malagasy companies) or on the long-term rental of buildings (by foreign companies). Enterprises are subject to the company profits tax (IBS), set at 30 per cent with a minimum leviable amount[63]; this rate is set at 45 per cent for foreign companies whose registered offices are not in Madagascar, except where they perform public works contracts. Microfinance institutions are granted fiscal incentives under the ordinary law regime in order to stimulate the supply of their services (Chapter IV(5)(iv)).[64]

Madagascar offers two special tax regimes for investors, one for large-scale mining investments (Chapter IV(3)(i)), the other for enterprises established in the industrial free zone (IFZ).[65] The latter regime is available to companies whose activities are mainly export-oriented, or which sell directly to enterprises eligible for the IFZ regime. In the case of the former, exports must account for at least 95 per cent of their sales; 5 per cent may be sold on the domestic market, subject to the payment of ordinary import duties and taxes. In practice, these are free points (isolated free enterprises not located in a defined geographical area). The method of financing investment projects constitutes one of the conditions of eligibility for the free zone regime: for enterprises wholly owned by non-resident foreigners, all start-up investment costs (including the initial working capital) must be covered by foreign exchange inflows; in the case of associations between foreigners and nationals, any foreign exchange investment (including the initial working capital) must be covered by foreign exchange financing; and if the capital is wholly owned by residents, any investment financing scheme is acceptable.

[57] Decree No. 2003-938 of 9 September 2003.
[58] For example, http://www.tana-cciaa.org/download.php?cat=invest&file=dd529608eaab.pdf.
[59] Order No. 18638/05 of 1 December 2005.
[60] Decree No. 2006-382 of 31 May 2006. Information on the EDBM was obtained from the web portal: http://www.edbm.gov.mg/ [14 August 2007].
[61] The duty (levy charged by the State) amounts to 1 per cent for the first bracket (up to MGA 10 million), 0.5 per cent for the second bracket (between MGA 10 million and MGA 100 million), and 0.1 per cent for the third bracket (amounts in excess of MGA 1,000 million).
[62] According to the authorities, this provision is repealed by the 2008 Finance Law.
[63] Article 01.01.16 of the General Tax Code (2006 edition). The minimum leviable amount is: MGA 100,000, increased by 0.5 per cent of the annual turnover for enterprises in the manufacturing, handicrafts, agriculture, mining, transport, tourism and hotel sectors; MGA 300,000, increased by 0.5 per cent of the annual turnover for other enterprises. The IBS reductions provided for newly established enterprises are no longer available as from fiscal year 2007.
[64] These are exempt from the IBS of 30 per cent and from the minimum flat-rate tax over the first five fiscal years and, in the case of those that are not mutual institutions, an additional 50 per cent reduction on the IBS is applied up to the 10th fiscal year.
[65] Law No. 89-027 of 29 December 1989, as supplemented and amended by Law No. 91-020 of 12 August 1991. This regime has been notified by Madagascar to the WTO under the Agreement on Trade-Related Investment Measures (WTO document G/TRIMS/N/2/Rev.8 of 19 July 2001).

Compared to the ordinary law regime, the IFZ regime offers important advantages (Table II.3). Ordinary law enterprises which supply free enterprises are subject to VAT, but the latter may apply for reimbursement thereof within 60 days following the final export of finished goods. Investors may open foreign exchange accounts for their repatriated export earnings. Project promoters wishing to obtain the status of free enterprise must file their applications with the EDBM or the Directorate for the Support of Industrial and Handicrafts Development (DADIA) within the Ministry of Industry. Each application file follows a lengthy procedure leading up to approval or rejection (file to be corrected or redrafted) by the interministerial technical committee to which it is submitted. Free enterprise status is conferred by final decree signed by the Secretary-General of the Government and the promoter is so notified.

Table II.3

Fiscal regulations under the industrial free zone regime, December 2007

	Fiscal regulation
1 – Enterprises	
(a) Company profits tax (IBS)	
Promotion/exploitation enterprise (EPE)	Exempt for 15 years, thereafter liable to IBS at 10 per cent
Industrial processing enterprise (EIT)	Exempt for 5 years, thereafter liable to IBS at 10 per cent
Intensive basic production enterprise (EPIB)	Exempt for 5 years, thereafter liable to IBS at 10 per cent
Service enterprise (ES)	Exempt for 2 years, thereafter liable to IBS at 10 per cent
(b) Professional tax	Exempt
2 – Persons	
(a) Taxes on distributed dividends	10 per cent without grace period
(b) Taxes on salaries	Maximum of 35 per cent of the taxable base (for expatriates)
3 – Goods	
(a) Customs duty and import tax	Exempt
(b) Value-added tax	General principle: all VAT payments to be the subject of automatic reimbursement
(c) Export duties and taxes	Exempt
(d) Excise duty	Exempt

Source: Malagasy authorities

ANNEX II.1: TRADE-RELATED TECHNICAL ASSISTANCE

With the support of the international community, Madagascar has since 2002 been implementing an economic and structural reform programme. The Madagascar Action Plan (MAP) reflects the Government's commitment to attain rapid economic growth and reduce poverty. To that end, in the context of this second Trade Policy Review (TPR), the authorities expect to mobilize trade-related technical assistance in order to achieve the various objectives, including those defined in the MAP. Madagascar already participates in the Integrated Framework (IF)[66], and also wishes to join the JITAP[67] (Joint Integrated Technical Assistance Programme).

[66] Consulted at: http://www.integratedframework.org.
[67] Consulted at: http://www.jitap.org.

Madagascar has benefited from a large number of actions undertaken by the WTO and by other international organizations such as the United Nations Conference on Trade and Development (UNCTAD), the International Trade Centre (ITC), the United Nations Development Programme (UNDP), the World Bank (WB), the International Monetary Fund (IMF), to support the development of its international trade. Those actions worthy of special mention include the participation of Malagasy officials in 120 seminars, workshops, courses, missions and other WTO activities between the first TPR in 2001 and May 2007. In 2007, a Malagasy official attended the Netherlands training programme administered by the WTO. In terms of support infrastructure, Madagascar has benefited from a reference centre set up on the premises of the Ministry of Trade; however, some of the Centre's equipment needs to be replaced in order to enable civil servants and other users to receive timely information on the multilateral trading system.

Madagascar currently has trade-related technical assistance needs in various areas, namely: implementation of trade-related agreements; participation in the regular activities of the WTO; capacity-building for participation in trade negotiations; formulation of trade policy; supply-side constraints; and the integration of trade and development policies.

IMPLEMENTATION OF AGREEMENTS, TRAINING AND POLICY FORMULATION

The implementation issues of most concern to Madagascar are those relating to WTO rules such as anti-dumping, countervailing and safeguard measures; trade-related aspects of intellectual property rights (TRIPS); sanitary and phytosanitary measures (SPS); technical barriers to trade (TBT); customs valuation; trade negotiation techniques; establishment of the necessary institutional structures; harmonization of domestic laws and regulations with WTO principles and rules; notifications; and dispute settlement.

As regards rules, the Government of Madagascar wishes to establish a national authority responsible for remedial measures. Madagascar currently has no legislation in the area of anti-dumping and countervailing duties or safeguard measures. It wishes to strengthen national capacity in respect of geographical indications. Madagascar is experiencing a great deal of difficulty in complying with sanitary and phytosanitary measures and international technical regulations, particularly those required for its exports of agricultural products, mainly plants, fresh fruit and vegetables, meat and other food products. Moreover, information on these regulations is still not disseminated widely enough in Madagascar. These problems limit the potential for access to the different regional and international markets, and Madagascar needs support in the preparation, finalization and implementation of projects under the Standards and Trade Development Facility (STDF).

Madagascar would need capacity-building and technical assistance to align certain domestic laws with WTO rules. Customs officials and economic operators encounter difficulties with certain implementation aspects of the Agreement on Customs Valuation; technical assistance in this area is requested. Training for the main actors in the private sector, academics, parliamentarians and the media is requested to make them aware of the obligations and benefits generated by the multilateral trading system. Madagascar is having difficulty in honouring its notification obligations; training in this field appears to be necessary.

Madagascar wishes to build capacity in order to participate efficiently in the negotiations under way at the multilateral, regional and bilateral levels. The dispute settlement mechanism is another area in which Madagascar would have liked to acquire proficiency so as to be prepared for any trade disputes.

SUPPLY-SIDE CONSTRAINTS

Supply-side constraints are among the main factors limiting the expansion of Madagascar's external trade. The Government has already sought to develop infrastructure, and technical assistance could help strengthen those efforts. In this connection, Madagascar wishes to receive support for the development of a multimodal transport system, through the rehabilitation of ports and roads and the promotion of air transport in order to reduce the associated costs. Operational support for customs administration (extension of the ASYCUDA++ system) is also desirable.

Agriculture is a key sector for Madagascar, but output is low. The low yields from agricultural production have an impact on the domestic economy. Indeed, Madagascar continues to be incapable of fulfilling its supply commitments: it is known as a "sample country". Continued efforts by the World Bank and other international organizations will be necessary to increase production and both horizontal and vertical diversification. Madagascar's exports have suffered from preference erosion and from declining prices for basic commodities on the international market, particularly vanilla. This reflects the lack of competitiveness of such products, and solutions need to be found to this problem.

Malagasy enterprises, including free zone enterprises, experience difficulties of access to credit and inputs, including electricity, water and telecommunications, and also suffer the adverse effects of poor governance. The efforts undertaken by the State remain inadequate. Funding for economic activities by the banking system does not appear to be on a sufficiently large scale to provide support for small and medium-sized enterprises planning long-term (high-risk) investments. The extension of microfinance in rural areas is a solution which might make it possible to cross the self-sufficiency threshold in agricultural activity. The improvement of supply in the services sector, and more particularly in the fields of transport, telecommunications and tourism, is also desirable.

ONGOING INTEGRATION OF TRAINING AGREEMENTS AND POLICY FORMULATION

After developing a number of programmes under the "Madagascar *Naturellement*" vision and/or the Poverty Reduction Strategy Paper (PRSP), Madagascar is currently entering the phase of implementation of the MAP with a view to accelerating and better coordinating its development process. However, none of these documents pays sufficient attention to trade. The results of Madagascar's second TPR could be exploited for this purpose.

For poverty reduction purposes, emphasis could be placed on improving marketing channels in areas of activity of particular interest to the most vulnerable social groups, and on facilitating their access to the means of production and improving their productivity.

In overall terms, action to deal with the trade aspects should facilitate fulfilment of the main objectives of the MAP.

TRADE POLICIES AND PRACTICES BY MEASURE

Since its last trade policy review (TPR) in 2001, Madagascar has made further progress with the liberalization of its trade regime. In 2005, Madagascar eliminated other import taxes collected at the customs cordon. With the exception of petroleum products, all Malagasy tariff rates are *ad valorem*; in 2008, the simple average rate is 13 per cent, 3 points lower than in 2000. Madagascar has bound all its agricultural lines and several non-agricultural lines, which together account for 29 per cent of all tariff lines. VAT and, where appropriate, excise duties are also levied, but the imposition of the latter does not comply with the principle of national treatment as imported alcoholic beverages and tobacco products are more heavily taxed than their local substitutes.

Madagascar has made progress with the simplification and computerization of its customs procedures. Pre-shipment inspection ceased to be compulsory in April 2007, but use of the GasyNet customs data processing system is mandatory, the corresponding charges amounting to 0.5 per cent of the c.i.f. value of the goods. Madagascar has moved ahead with the implementation of the WTO Valuation Agreement; it is requesting technical assistance to build capacity in this area. Trade facilitation measures have been adopted. However, many duty concessions are granted on a discretionary basis, which is adversely affecting customs receipts and contributing to the problem of transparency and governance. The exportation of rough and semi-finished wood has been prohibited since July 2007.

There has been considerable progress with standardization, which was just beginning in 2001. To satisfy the quality requirements of the international markets, Madagascar has proceeded with the standardization of agricultural products with a high export potential. Madagascar is one of the countries with businesses that comply with the European Union's sanitary standards for fishery product imports. Madagascar also applies sanitary and phytosanitary controls at the customs cordon; however, the measures taken have not been notified to the WTO. Madagascar has no contingency trade measure legislation.

Competition on the Malagasy market continues to be hampered by the small number of suppliers and the strong State presence in the national economy, with the State holding shares in numerous enterprises. Since Madagascar's first TPR, the State has withdrawn from several key sectors (fixed telephony, cotton lint, northern rail network), but still has stakes in others. One priority for 2007 concerns the reorganization of the historical operator JIRAMA, to improve the country's electricity supply. The restructuring of port, airport and air and rail transport services in the south of the country is also on the agenda. Moreover, Madagascar has liberalized the prices of most goods and services, with only a few exceptions: for example, administrative price controls are applied to medicinal products, while the price of rice, the staple food, is monitored; petroleum product prices were liberalized in 2004. The progressive implementation of the new government procurement regime is expected to lead to improvements.

The Malagasy industrial and artistic property regime has been harmonized with certain provisions of the WTO's TRIPS Agreement. The efforts begun since Madagascar's first TPR to ensure respect for intellectual property rights, and in particular to combat piracy and counterfeiting, are continuing.

MEASURES DIRECTLY AFFECTING IMPORTS

REGISTRATION

To be a trader in Madagascar it is necessary to enrol in the trade and companies register[68], to obtain a tax registration number from the Tax Administration Service[69], and to pay the occupational tax (abolished, in principle, by the 2008 Finance Law).[70] These requirements are the same for natural and legal persons, whether of Malagasy or foreign nationality.

[68] Laws No. 99-018 of 2 August 1999 and No. 99-025 of 19 August 1999.
[69] Title 5, Book 3 of General Tax Code (2006 edition).
[70] Title 1, Book 2 of General Tax Code (2006 edition).

CUSTOMS PROCEDURES[71]

Madagascar applies its Customs Code (1960)[72] as amended by successive finance laws. In 2007, the customs procedures in force were: release for home consumption; exportation; the economic procedures, i.e. temporary admission for inward processing or for free zone enterprises; national road transit with a view to release for home consumption; and customs warehousing. According to the authorities, in 2006, about 20 per cent of import operations came under the temporary admission for free zone enterprises regime.

The rules established by the WTO's Customs Valuation Agreement are incorporated in Madagascar's Customs Code (2007) but are understood to have been in use since 17 November 2000.[73] Madagascar requested and obtained a waiver from WTO Members to maintain minimum values for the customs valuation of used goods until 17 November 2003.[74] Moreover, Madagascar maintains a reservation concerning the order of the methods to be used if the transaction value is rejected (Chapter II (3)(i)).[75] However, in view of the difficulties experienced by the Customs Administration in effectively implementing the Agreement, Madagascar is requesting technical assistance in order to build national capacity in this area (Annex II.1).

In March 2007, Madagascar ceased relying on the pre-shipment inspection services provided since 25 February 2002 by the *Société générale de surveillance* (SGS).[76] On 2 April 2007, the government rolled out the GasyNet (modeled on the Tradenet developed during the 1990s by the Port of Singapore)[77], within the framework of an agreement of 4 May 2006 between the State and SGS. GasyNet is the exclusive provider of services for enabling registered operators to complete all import and export formalities at a single window. To this end, a new requirement for all cargoes being shipped to Madagascar is the *Bordereau de suivi des cargaisons* – BSC (Cargo Tracker Note)[78], which can be opened online[79], and must be duly validated by GasyNet. GasyNet's charges (PGN) are fixed by regulation at 0.5 per cent of the c.i.f. value of the goods imported or exported, or at flat-rate levels for goods with an f.o.b. value of less than the equivalent of €25,000 in MGA.[80] The charges for GasyNet's services include a flat-rate levy in

[71] Madagascar is a member of the World Customs Organization (WCO) and has ratified the Revised Kyoto Convention (Law No. 2006-024 of 17 July 2006). In principle, all the customs texts are available online on the web site: http://www.mefb.gov.mg/ [26 August 2007].
[72] Ordinance No. 60-084 of 18 August 1960.
[73] Section IV, Chapter V of the Customs Code (2007 edition).
[74] The waiver was granted by a Decision of 18 July 2001 (WTO document WT/L/408 of 26 July 2001).
[75] If the value declared by the importer is rejected, the WTO Agreement provides for the use of one of the following methods: transaction value of identical goods (Article 2); transaction value of similar goods (Article 3); deductive value (Article 5); constructed value (Article 6); fallback method (Article 7). These valuation methods must be used in the order listed. However, Article 4 of the Agreement states that the importer may request the order of application of Articles 5 and 6 to be reversed. In its notification to the WTO (WTO document WT/Let/112 of 30 September 1996) Madagascar pointed out that it reserved the right to decide that the provisions of Article 4 of the Agreement should apply only when the customs authorities agreed to the importer's request to reverse the order of application of Articles 5 and 6. Madagascar also noted that paragraph 2 of Article 5 of the Agreement would be applied whether or not the importer so requested.
[76] The reports issued by SGS for 2006 are being audited by independent auditors.
[77] Total investment for GasyNet is estimated at €15 million, with roll-out being spread over one year.
[78] Decision No. 01/MFB/SG/DGD of 23 March 2007.
[79] Consulted at: www.bscmg.sgs.com.
[80] Order No. 8426/2007 of 4 June 2007. The sums are: 10 euros, for an f.o.b. value of less than 1,000 euros (i.e. at least 1 per cent); 25 euros, for an f.o.b. value of between 1,000 and 2,500 euros (exclusive); 75 euros, for an f.o.b. value of between 2,500 and 10,000 euros (exclusive); 145 euros, for an f.o.b. value of between 10,000 and 25,000 euros (exclusive). The authorities point out that exports by Industrial Free Zone (ZFI) enterprises are subject to a rate of 0.5 per cent of the value added in the ZFI and not of the customs value.

favour of the Customs Administration for additional work and capacity building, which GasyNet pays to the Treasury. SGS holds 70 per cent of GasyNet's capital and the State 30 per cent.

Madagascar classifies imports into two categories: commercial and non-commercial.[81] The customs import formalities for commercial goods must be completed by an approved forwarding agent.[82] A single administrative document (DAU) must be filed for each commercial transaction, in one of the customs offices computerized on the basis of ASYCUDA++ (this applies to the 11 most important offices). Almost the entire volume and value of customs import transactions is computerized, as is 91 per cent of the volume and 89 per cent of the value of exports. The DAU must be accompanied by the usual documents: original invoice; transport documents; insurance; phytosanitary certificate for products of plant origin; sanitary certificate for products of animal origin; certificate of origin; and the documents in support of any request for exemption from customs duties or taxes. After registering the DAU, the Customs Administration will, if it thinks fit, inspect some or all of the goods declared.

There are trade facilitation measures in place. The green channel allows for the automatic assessment of duties and taxes following the registration of the DAU, and the immediate release of the goods after the statutory check on the payment of duties and taxes. This channel is available to those importers who are deemed to be reliable, that is to say, with no record of major infringements, and for goods subject to special measures. The minimum clearance time in the offices with ASYCUDA++ computerization is 12 hours. The GasyNet data enable a more thorough risk analysis to be carried out, with a view to identifying the channel appropriate for the importer, which makes customs controls more efficient.

In the course of the clearance procedure, the decisions of the Customs Administration concerning the tariff classification, origin and value of goods declared may form the subject of an appeal by the declarant to the *Commission de conciliation et d'expertise douanière* – CCED (Conciliation and Customs Appraisal Commission).[83] In the second instance, the declarant may appeal the decision of the CCED to the competent court.

RULES OF ORIGIN

Madagascar does not have any national rules of origin for non-preferential purposes. Madagascar is a member of the COMESA (Chapter II (3)(b)) and SADC (Chapter II (3)(c)) free trade areas and, in principle, uses their rules of origin for defining products originating in the respective area. COMESA and SADC have each developed model certificates attesting to the origin of the goods concerned.

COMESA origin may be conferred on products shipped directly from one Member State to another if those products are: (a) wholly obtained in the COMESA Member State[84]; or (b) wholly or partially manufactured in the Member State from materials imported from outside the Member States, or of indeterminate origin, in accordance with a manufacturing process that involves a substantial transformation, defined as: (i) a c.i.f. of the imported materials not exceeding 60 per cent of the total cost of the materials used in the production of the goods; or (ii) a value added resulting from the production process that accounts for at least 35 per cent of the ex-factory cost

[81] Decision of Director-General of Customs No. 051 of 24 January 2003. The importation of more than two vehicles (at a time) per person is treated as a commercial operation.
[82] Order No. 7298/2002 of 20 November 2002. Approval is granted by the Ministry responsible for customs, in consultation with the Director-General of Customs. A permanent bond of MGA 10 million is required to practise the profession.
[83] Article 111 of Customs Code (2007 edition).
[84] For example, minerals extracted from the soil or seabed and products of agriculture, fishing or hunting, or manufactured wholly from these products, without imported inputs.

of the goods; or (iii) inclusion in a list drawn up by the COMESA Council of goods of particular importance for the economic development of the Member States and incorporating at least 25 per cent of value added.[85]

According to Annex I to the SDAC Trade Protocol on rules of origin, the basic requirements for goods to be regarded as "originating" are as follows: (a) the product must have been wholly obtained in one of the Parties[86]; or (b) the non-originating materials incorporated in the product must have undergone "sufficient working or processing" in accordance with the conditions set out in Appendix I of Annex I; or (c) the value of all non-originating materials must not exceed 10 per cent of the ex-works price of the good (tolerance rule). There is no regime-wide rule of origin but Appendix I of Annex I lists the specific criteria (mostly with respect to HS tariff headings (at various levels)) that non-originating materials must meet for a final good to acquire originating status.[87]

CUSTOMS LEVIES

Goods imported into Madagascar are subject to various entry duties and taxes[88], fixed annually by the Finance Law. In 2005, Madagascar simplified the structure of its duties and taxes, in particular by abolishing the statistical tax on imports (TSI) and the import tax. Thus, apart from the tariff, Madagascar has not applied any other entry duties or taxes since that date. The taxable base for the tariff is the c.i.f. value. In 2006, customs revenue collected on imports amounted to approximately MGA 628.9 billion (Table III.1), about twice the total for 2000. In 2006, customs revenue from imports was mainly composed of: tariff (22 per cent); VAT at 18 per cent (42 per cent); tax on petroleum products (36 per cent); and excise duty (0.5 per cent). Numerous tariff concessions are granted on a discretionary basis, which explains the relatively small contribution of the tariff to total customs revenue in 2006.

Table III.1 Itemized customs revenue from imports, (in billions of MGA)

	2000	2001	2002	2003	2004	2005	2006
Customs tariff	25.4	23.3	16.7	26.3	29.2	112.2	138.6
Import tax	50.1	46.3	32.0	53.1	77.5	n.a.	n.a.
VAT	140.0	144.5	91.5	156.2	186.1	213.5	262.6
Taxes on petroleum products	79.5	54.4	51.0	73.3	136.5	154.5	223.6
Excise duty	12.0	10.6	7.9	14.4	10.6	10.5	3.3
Statistical tax on imports (TSI)	8.1	10.2	9.3	17.5	3.7	n.a.	n.a.
Other	2.8	1.2	0.4	1.9	1.6	0.6	0.7
Total	317.9	290.5	208.8	342.6	445.2	491.3	628.9

MFN TARIFF APPLIED

[85] Value added is defined as the difference between the ex-factory cost of the finished product and the c.i.f. value of the materials imported from outside the member States which enter into its production.
[86] Article 4 specifies the type of goods that can be regarded as being wholly produced in the Member States. It gives a list of the products in this category and establishes the criteria that a vessel must satisfy for it to be regarded as forming part of the territory of a Member State.
[87] For further details, see the Secretariat report in WTO document WT/REG176/4 of 12 March 2007.
[88] The entry duties and taxes in force in Madagascar in 2007 have not been notified to the IDB (WTO document G/MA/IDB/2/Rev.25 of 26 March 2007).

The 2008 Malagasy tariff comprises 6,362 eight-digit lines of the 2007 version of the Harmonized Commodity Description and Coding System (HS). Most of the rates are *ad valorem* and either zero, 5 per cent, 10 per cent, or 20 per cent.[89] For 2008, the simple average of all the rates applied is 13 per cent (Chart III.1 and Table III.2), which corresponds to an average of 14.4 per cent for agricultural products (WTO definition) and 12.7 per cent for non-agricultural products (excluding petroleum products). If the ISIC (Rev. 2) definition is used, agriculture remains the most heavily protected sector with an average tariff of 13.9 per cent (Table AIII.1), followed by the manufacturing sector (13.0 per cent) and the mining sector (7.1 per cent). Agricultural products account for a large share of the expenditure of consumers, especially those on low incomes, and the heavy taxation adds to their cost.

The coefficient of variation of 0.5 indicates moderate dispersion of the tariff rates, with about 42.5 per cent of tariff lines subject to the modal rate of 20 per cent (Chart III.2). Overall, the tariff shows mixed escalation, negative from raw materials with an average level of protection of 12.3 per cent to semi-finished products (average level of protection 10.3 per cent), and then positive with an average tariff of 14.7 per cent on finished products (Table III.3).

Table III.2 MFN applied tariff structure,

		2007	2008	Uruguay Round[a]
1	Tariff lines bound (as a percentage of all tariff lines)	29.1	29.1	..
2	Tariff lines eligible for duty-free entry (as a percentage of all tariff lines)	1.8	2.0	0.1
3	Duties other than *ad valorem* (as a percentage of all tariff lines)	0.3	0.3	0.0
4	Tariff quotas (as a percentage of all tariff lines)	0	0	0.0
5	Duties other than *ad valorem* without any AVE (as a percentage of all tariff lines)	0.3	0.3	0.0
6	Simple average rate	13.0	13.0	27.6
	Agricultural products (WTO definition)[b]	14.5	14.4	30.0
	Non-agricultural products (WTO definition)[c]	12.7	12.7	25.5
	Agriculture, hunting and forestry (ISIC 1)	13.9	13.9	30.0
	Mining and quarrying (ISIC 2)	7.1	7.1	0.0
	Manufacturing (ISIC 3)	13.0	13.0	27.1
7	National tariff peaks (as a percentage of all tariff lines)[d]	0.0	0.0	0.0
8	International tariff peaks (as a percentage of all tariff lines)[e]	42.5	42.5	92.1
9	Overall standard deviation of rates applied	6.4	6.4	5.6
10	Nuisance duties (as a percentage of all tariff lines)[f]	0.0	0.0	0.0

Table III.2 (cont'd)

Note: Indicator 1 is based on all the tariff lines (in-quota and out-of-quota lines); the other indicators exclude in-quota lines. Indicators 6 to 10 are calculated on the basis of lines for which an *ad valorem* rate could not be taken into account.

Source: WTO Secretariat calculations based on data provided by the Malagasy authorities.

[89] On 19 lines (petroleum products) the rates are specific and the authorities have not provided an *ad valorem* equivalent, while six lines present in the HS 2007 have no rate in the Malagasy tariff.

A more detailed breakdown reveals that the overall tariff structure closely reflects that prevailing, in particular, in the food (including beverages and tobacco), wood and articles of wood, chemical products, and non-metallic mineral products industries (Chart III.3). In other industries, including textiles and clothing, escalation is positive. Such a tariff structure either discourages investment in certain (processing) industries because the heavy taxation of imported inputs adds to production costs, or reduces the competitiveness of certain products processed in Madagascar under a regime that provides a fairly high level of effective protection (Chapter IV(4)). Thus, the tariff structure is not of a kind likely to encourage economic diversification. It perpetuates the need for duty and tax concessions to investors, including under the Industrial Free Zone (IFZ) regime (Chapter II(4)).

Table III.3 Summary of MFN

Description	Number of lines[a]	Rate applied 2008					Imports 2006[b] (US$ million)
		Number of lines used	Simple average duty (per cent)	Range of duty (per cent)	Standard deviation (per cent)	CV	
Total	6,362	6,343	13.0	0-20	6.4	0.5	1,760.3
By WTO category[c]							
Agricultural products	897	897	14.4	0-20	6.9	0.5	235.0
Live animals and animal products	122	122	18.9	5-20	3.9	0.2	2.6
Dairy products	30	30	17.5	5-20	5.7	0.3	8.6
Coffee, tea, cocoa, sugar, etc.	177	177	16.3	5-20	5.5	0.3	78.2
Cut flowers and plants	62	62	7.8	5-20	4.8	0.6	1.0
Fruit and vegetables	181	181	19.4	0-20	2.8	0.1	3.9
Cereals	17	17	4.7	0-10	4.5	1.0	48.1
Oilseeds, fats and oils	94	94	8.7	0-20	5.7	0.7	49.7
Beverages and alcohol	56	56	20.0	20-20	0.0	0.0	9.1
Tobacco	11	11	17.3	10-20	4.7	0.3	2.2
Other agricultural products	147	147	7.0	0-20	4.3	0.6	31.5
Non-agricultural products (excluding petroleum)	5,447	5,440	12.7	0-20	6.3	0.5	1,205.4
Fish and fish products	131	131	19.1	5-20	3.4	0.2	33.2
Minerals, precious stones and metals	383	376	13.2	0-20	7.2	0.5	70.1
Metals	663	663	10.7	5-20	4.7	0.4	96.6
Chemicals and photographic products	1,025	1,025	7.6	0-20	5.5	0.7	160.5
Leather, rubber, footwear and travel articles	272	272	14.5	5-20	5.6	0.4	32.4
Wood, wood pulp, paper and furniture	334	334	14.7	0-20	6.3	0.4	89.1
Textiles and clothing	1,102	1,102	17.0	0-20	5.8	0.3	334.4
Transport equipment	195	195	10.5	0-20	4.9	0.5	114.3
Non-electrical machinery	544	544	10.4	10-20	2.1	0.2	128.2
Electrical machinery	253	253	12.4	5-20	4.4	0.4	90.6
Non-agricultural products n.e.s.	545	545	15.3	0-20	5.2	0.3	56.0

Table III.3 (cont'd)

Description	Number of lines[a]	Rate applied 2008						Imports 2006[b] (US$ million)
		Number of lines used	Simple average duty (per cent)	Range of duty (per cent)	Standard deviation (per cent)	CV		
By ISIC[d] sector								
Agriculture, hunting, forestry and fishing	374	374	13.9	0-20	7.3	0.5		20.5
Mining and quarrying	112	109	7.1	5-20	4.8	0.7		8.0
Manufacturing	5,875	5,859	13.0	0-20	6.3	0.5		1,723.4
By stage of processing								
Raw materials	756	749	12.3	0-20	7.4	0.6		118.9
Semi-finished products	2,064	2,064	10.3	0-20	6.2	0.6		503.3
Finished products	3,542	3,530	14.7	0-20	5.8	0.4		1,129.8

a This analysis is based on a reduced frequency (number of lines), since it leaves out the lines for which there is no AVE.

b Total imports exceed the sum of the sub-lines because some products, amounting to US$8.3 million, are not classified in the Harmonized System.

c There are 18 tariff lines for petroleum products that have not been taken into account.

d International Standard Industrial Classification of All Economic Activities (Rev.2). Excluding electricity, gas and water (one tariff line).

Note: CV = coefficient of variation.

Source: WTO Secretariat estimates based on data provided by the Malagasy authorities; and the Comtrade database of the United Nations Statistical Division on imports in 2006.

BINDINGS

During the Uruguay Round, Madagascar bound 29.1 per cent of its tariff lines in its Schedule of Concessions LI annexed to the GATT 1994. These bindings were made at the ceiling rate of 30 per cent and "other duties and taxes" were bound at the ceiling rate of 250 per cent for agricultural products (as defined in Annex I to the WTO Agreement on Agriculture) and for chemical products (HS Chapters 28 and 29). Some applied rates exceed certain rates bound when Madagascar was a colony.

INTERNAL TAXES

Madagascar applies VAT. The standard rate was reduced from 20 per cent to 18 per cent in 2005, then restored to 20 per cent for 2008. VAT is levied on goods for home consumption whatever their origin.[90] The taxable base for imports is the customs value plus duty and other taxes, where applicable (apart from VAT itself), whereas that for local goods is the sale price plus other taxes, where applicable.[91] Some staple goods, whether imported or produced locally, are in

[90] Title 1, Part 6, General Tax Code (2006 edition).
[91] Any enterprise with a turnover equal to or greater than a minimum threshold (for example, MGA 200 million according to the 2008 Finance Law) is subject to VAT, and those with a turnover below this threshold can opt for VAT or for the application of another system of taxation.

principle exempt from VAT.[92] In principle, exports are zero-rated (section (3)(ii)), except for deliveries to enterprises established in free zones, in which case the VAT is refundable within 60 days on proof of outright exportation from Madagascar.

In 2007, Madagascar levied excise duty on alcoholic beverages, perfumes and cosmetics, cigars, cigarettes and tobacco[93]; there was also a charge on alcoholic beverages, perfumes and cosmetics, cigars, cigarettes and tobacco.[94] A charge (but not excise duty) was levied on sugar, wheat and meslin flour, and chemical matches. In several cases, the rates in force in 2007 differed according to the origin of the product (Table III.4), for the purpose of protecting the local industry; changes are understood to have been introduced by the 2008 Finance Law. With regard to the 80 per cent excise duty on cigarettes, a 50 per cent reduction is granted if the reference price of the product does not exceed the threshold established by regulation, while cigarettes whose Malagasy tobacco content equals or exceeds the minimum laid down by regulation benefit from a further reduction of 15 per cent. The taxable base for locally manufactured products is the sale price, whereas that for imports is the c.i.f. customs value plus duty.

Table III.4 Differences between excise duties/charges applied to local and imported products

Product	Locally produced (percentage, unless otherwise indicated)	Imported (percentage)
Wheat or meslin flour	MGA 13/kg.	10
Sugar	MGA 20/kg.	10
Malt beer	53	69
Wine:		
Champagne	170	225
liqueur	154	105
other	40	69
Vermouth	154	205
Brandy	170	205
Whiskies	282	326
Rum, gin, vodka, other	170	205
Cigars	242	250
Cigarettes, tobacco	135	230

Source: Malagasy authorities.

PREFERENCES

In principle, Madagascar grants preferences to products originating in other COMESA member countries, on a basis of reciprocity (Chapter II(3)(b))[95], and to products originating in other SADC

[92] The goods in question include the following: medicinal products; pharmaceutical articles; equipment for medical use; contact lenses, spectacle lenses, and corrective lenses; day-old chicks, seed; propane gas; agricultural inputs (fertilizer, insecticides, fungicides, herbicides); newsprint; newspapers, magazines, books, brochures and printed matter.

[93] Part 3, Title 1, General Tax Code (2006 edition).

[94] Part 4, General Tax Code (2006 edition). Mobile phone communications and the reception of pay television programmes delivered locally are also subject to a charge.

[95] The tariff reduction is 100 per cent for products originating in Burundi, Comoros, Djibouti, Egypt, Libya, Kenya, Malawi, Mauritius, Rwanda, Sudan, Swaziland (up to December 2008), Zambia and Zimbabwe; 80

member countries, in accordance with an approved tariff reduction scheme (Chapter II(3)(c)). Moreover, since 1998, Madagascar has applied a duty reduction of 100 per cent to goods originating in the Indian Ocean Commission (IOC) countries.

DUTY AND TAX EXEMPTIONS AND CONCESSIONS

Madagascar admits free of customs duty and taxes goods destined for the State (for example, gifts intended for the Head of State), goods imported by diplomatic missions and international or charitable organizations, materials covered by UNESCO's Florence Agreement, and goods imported in connection with removals, small consignments, etc. Government procurement financed by external funds is exempt from VAT. Exemption from customs duties and taxes is also granted to goods imported in connection with large-scale mining investments (Chapter IV(3)(ii)); to enterprises engaged in oil prospecting and exploration activities (Chapter IV(3)(i)); and to the company QIT Madagascar Minerals (QMM)[96], under its founding convention. Special relief may also have been granted to enterprises within the context of privatization or investment before the State stopped engaging in this practice in 2006.[97]

A 35 per cent reduction in the duties and taxes applicable is granted to goods imported by Radio Nederland, under an agreement concluded with the State. Exemptions from customs duties and taxes may also be granted, by decision of the Government Council, in exceptional circumstances, in the public interest and for reasons of state; in 2006, this category, known as "category 7", gave rise to numerous exemptions from customs duties.

PROHIBITIONS, QUANTITATIVE RESTRICTIONS AND LICENCES

Madagascar maintains a regime of prohibitions, quantitative restrictions and licences which has been in place since 1992.[98] Madagascar notified the WTO of this regime in 2002[99] and of certain amendments to it in 2005.[100] In principle, any products may be freely imported or exported, except for those that are specially regulated (section (vii)).[101] The importation of radioactive waste from nuclear power stations is prohibited. The importation of such products as arms, explosives and narcotic drugs is subject to prior authorization. The same applies to imports of diamonds, gemstones, gold and platinum jewellery, and vanillin. Madagascar also maintains a special regime for imports of leaf tobacco (Chapter IV(2)(iii)). An import licence is required for lubricants. In addition, Madagascar applies prohibitions and licences under multilateral environmental agreements to which it is party.[102] The importation of counterfeit branded products, pirated goods and goods bearing false indications of origin is also prohibited (section (4)(v)).[103]

per cent for products originating in Eritrea and Uganda; 10 per cent for products originating in Ethiopia; and zero for products originating in the Democratic Republic of the Congo and Seychelles.

[96] The State holds 20 per cent of the shares and Rio Tinto 80 per cent.

[97] For example, Article 163-quater of the 2005 Finance Law provided that investments made in Madagascar, amounting to one million or more US dollars, should benefit from a reduction in, or indeed total exemption from, duties and taxes and charges as from 2005. An investment committee was set up to study the dossiers submitted with a view to obtaining this benefit.

[98] Decree No. 92-424 of 3 April 1992.

[99] WTO document G/LIC/N/3/MDG/1 of 9 September 2002.

[100] WTO document G/LIC/N/3/MDG/2 of 21 June 2005.

[101] Article 28 of Customs Code (2007 edition).

[102] Environmental Treaties and Resource Indicators (ENTRI), Country profile: Madagascar, Consulted at: http://sedac.ciesin.org/entri/countryProfile.jsp?ISO=MDG [9 September 2007].

[103] Articles 29 and 30 of Customs Code (2007 edition).

Madagascar imports almost all the medicinal and health products consumed on its territory. Under the Public Health Code, the *Agence du médicament de Madagascar* (Madagascar Medicinal Product Agency) established in 1998[104], is responsible for registering, inspecting and controlling the quality of medicinal products and for drug testing and control.[105] Before they can be marketed, pharmaceutical products must obtain an *autorisation de mise sur le marché* – AMM (marketing authorization) issued by the *Commission nationale d'enregistrement* (National Registration Commission)[106]; there were 2,834 products registered at the end of 2006. The Commission automatically registers products that have already received a marketing authorization from the European Agency for the Evaluation of Medicinal Products, or the health authorities of the United Kingdom, the United States or France[107]; the procedures for products with other origins are more onerous. The AMM is valid for five years renewable. Since 2003, the Agency has had a drug quality control laboratory (*Laboratoire de contrôle de qualité des médicaments* – LCQM) at its disposal.

Medicinal and health products are distributed either through the public health care system or through private pharmacies.[108] The public health care system and private non-profit institutions are supplied with essential generic medicinal products (in accordance with a National List of Essential Medicinal Products) exclusively by the central purchasing agency SALAMA, which purchases its products by international competitive bidding; an initial exclusivity agreement with the State ended in 2006, and was followed by a second agreement that runs until 2016.[109] A markup of 35 per cent can be applied relative to the SALAMA purchase price (see section (4)(ii)).

STANDARDIZATION, ACCREDITATION AND CERTIFICATION

Madagascar has not made any notification to the WTO concerning its standardization regime or its accreditation and certification procedures.[110] Introduced in 1997, this regime is administered by the *Bureau de normes de Madagascar* – BNM (Madagascar Bureau of Standards), which was established in 1998[111] and became operational in 2002, under the technical supervision of the Ministry of Industry.[112] The BNM is responsible for standardization. In accordance with the agenda established by its governing board, the BNM develops a preliminary draft standard. It then convenes a technical committee composed of representatives of the sector concerned for consultation on the chosen criteria. The standards drawn up are either definitive or experimental (the latter are subject to public inquiry while the definitive standards are published in the *Official Journal*). Under the Malagasy regime, some standards may become mandatory after their adoption as such by the Ministry concerned. The only mandatory standards that affect imports are those on condoms, reflector strips, and soaps and detergents.[113] The BNM arranges for the conformity of imports with these standards to be established by a committee, which examines samples and carries out conformity tests with a view to the authorization of importation. In the absence of national capacity, only conformity tests carried out by a recognized outside laboratory

---

[104] Decree No. 98-086 of 27 January 1998, amended by Decree No. 2004-086 of 27 January 2004.
[105] *Politique pharmaceutique à Madagascar.* Consulted at: http://www.remed.org/bilan2002.rtf [26 December 2007].
[106] The costs of these procedures are fixed by Interministerial Order No. 24364/2004 of 10 January 2005.
[107] U.S. Pharmacopeia Drug Quality and Information (2003).
[108] Antananarivo Economic Mission (2007).
[109] Consulted at: http://www.salama.mg.
[110] Law No. 97-024 of 14 August 1997.
[111] Decree No. 98-944 of 4 November 1998. The *Conseil national de normalisation* – CNN (National Standardization Council), created by Decree No. 99-024 of 20 January 1999, is no longer active.
[112] Information on the BNM is available on its web site: http://www.interbat.mg/ acceuilbnm.htm [14 September 2007].
[113] Fuels are also the subject of standards relating to their ingredients, established by the *Office malgache des hydrocarbures* – OMH Malagasy Hydrocarbons Office).

independent of the manufacturer of the product are considered authentic. Madagascar has established voluntary standards for construction materials, road safety and urban public transport.

Madagascar has established mandatory standards on the quality, packing and labelling of coffee[114] and vanilla[115] for export. To meet the requirements of the international markets, the BNM has proceeded to establish voluntary standards for certain products with a high export potential such as honey and litchis. Moreover, some Malagasy economic operators have obtained third party certification for their litchi and French bean production to satisfy the requirements of EU market importers.

As a corresponding member of the International Organization for Standardization, Madagascar does not take an active part in the technical and policy-making work of that organization.

SANITARY AND PHYTOSANITARY (SPS) MEASURES

Madagascar has not made any notification to the WTO concerning sanitary and phytosanitary measures; according to the authorities, the only SPS measures taken with respect to imports are based on international standards drawn up by the World Organization for Animal Health (OIE), the International Plant Protection Convention (IPPC) and the Codex Alimentarius. Madagascar forms part of the Regional Programme for Plant Protection established for the countries of the Indian Ocean.[116] Moreover, fishery products for export to EU markets are subject to specific regulations (section (3)(iv)).

The Ministry of Agriculture, Livestock and Fisheries (MAEP) is responsible for taking sanitary measures relating to animals with a view to keeping Madagascar free of diseases that do not exist there.[117] Madagascar has prohibited the importation of all live animals and meat and meat products from origins declared by the OIE to be sources of foot and mouth disease, in particular, South Africa from 2000[118] and some European origins since 2001, these latter measures having meantime been eased.[119] Since 2004, Madagascar has also taken a number of measures to prevent the outbreak of bird flu, in view of the risk associated with the migration of wild birds from Asia. These measures concern the origins identified by the OIE.[120]

A veterinary certificate is needed to import and export live animals and animal feed.[121] An application must be made to the Animal Health and Phytosanitary Directorate. At importation, the sanitary certificate of the country of origin is required for the purposes of issuing a permit. As soon as the goods in question arrive, the importer must inform the Animal Quarantine Service, which proceeds to carry out sanitary controls. These controls take the form of verification of the sanitary documents and verification or inspection of the regulated articles. Then, depending on the result of the controls, a release note for the goods may be issued. A period of quarantine is

[114] Decree No. 85-129 of 3 May 1985.
[115] Interministerial Order No. 4911/99-MCC of 12 May 1999.
[116] Consulted at: http://www.prpv.org/.
[117] Law No. 91-008 of 25 July 1991.
[118] Order No. 11.565/00 of 20 October 2000.
[119] Interministerial Order No. 3168/2001 of 16 March 2001, amended by Interministerial Order No. 9459/2001 of 23 August 2001, eased by Interministerial Order No. 11780/2001 of 3 October 2001 and Interministerial Order No. 5768/2003 of 10 April 2003. Decree No. 2004/040 of 20 January 2004 authorized the importation of 2,000 dairy cows from New Zealand in 2005 and 2006.
[120] Decree No. 2004-170 of 3 February 2004.
[121] Decree No. 2004-041 of 20 January 2004 establishes the regime applicable to the importation and exportation of animals, products and foods of animal origin, and grain, fodder and feed for animals. The requirements are listed on the web site of the Ministry of Agriculture, Livestock and Fisheries (http://www.maep.gov.mg/fr/formulaire.php?maeplink=form_animaux.htm) [14 September 2007].

normally required. The costs of the sanitary controls are borne by the Malagasy State, with the exception of those relating to detention in quarantine and sanitary monitoring at farm level.

Phytosanitary measures are administered by the Plant Quarantine Service.[122] To import live plants, seed and parts of live plants, as well as plant products, soil and growing media, and packaging made of plant material it is first necessary to obtain a phytosanitary permit, the application for which must be accompanied by the phytosanitary certificate of the country of origin of the goods.[123] As soon as the goods in question arrive, the importer must inform the Plant Quarantine Service, which proceeds to carry out phytosanitary controls. These controls take the form of verification of the phytosanitary documents and verification or inspection of the regulated articles. Then, depending on the result of the controls, a release note for the goods may be issued. A period of quarantine may be required. The costs are borne by the Malagasy State, with the exception of those relating to detention in quarantine and sanitary monitoring at farm level.

Since June 2003, the authorities have identified numerous food products that were being sold to consumers with false use-by dates.[124] To meet these concerns, in 2003, Madagascar set up, within the Ministry of Health and Family Planning (MINSANPF), a *Unité de contrôle de qualité des denrées alimentaires* – UCQDA (Food Quality Control Unit) whose responsibilities were taken over, in 2005, by the *Agence de contrôle de la sécurité sanitaire et de la qualité des denrées alimentaires* – ACSSQDA (Agency for Monitoring Food Safety and Quality). The Agency's task is to ensure that food consumed, distributed, marketed or produced in Madagascar complies with the strictest safety standards. Since 2004, certificates of fitness for consumption and conformity have been issued, establishments have been inspected and various analyses have been carried out; technical services are provided by a network of seven food testing laboratories. ACSSQDA is responsible for developing national food safety policy. The legal framework, which is currently concerned with the repression of fraud and export quality control[125], will, in principle, be supplemented in accordance with the FAO/WHO model. The National Committee of the Codex Alimentarius has been in existence since April 2005.

RULES ON PACKAGING, MARKING AND LABELLING

In Madagascar, rules on compulsory marking apply to pre-packaged foods, in accordance with the relevant Codex standard.[126] All perishable foods must bear a label, in French or English, indicating the origin, the sell-by or use-by date, the ingredients, the method of storage, the name of the manufacturer together with his registration number, where appropriate, and the intended use. The utilization of the metric system is compulsory in Madagascar.

CONTINGENCY MEASURES

[122] Law No. 86-017 of 3 November 1986 ratifying Ordinance No. 86-013 of 17 September 1986, and Implementing Decree No. 86-310 of 23 September 1986.
[123] Order No. 4736/2002 of 7 October 2002. The practical information on the importation of plants was consulted at: http://www.prpv.org/index.php/fr/reglementation/importer_exporter_des_vegetaux/importer_exporter_a_madagascar/informations_pratiques [14 September 2007].
[124] "*Analyse de la situation des systèmes de sécurité sanitaire des aliments de la république de Madagascar*", FAO/WHO Regional Conference on Food Safety for Africa, Harare, Zimbabwe, 3-6 October 2005. Consulted at: ftp://ftp.fao.org/docrep/fao/meeting/009/af069f.pdf [10 September 2007].
[125] Basic Law of 1 August 1905 and its subsequent texts relating to the repression of fraud and the adulteration of food and non-food products; Law No. 88-021 of 24 November 1988 notifying Ordinance No. 88-015 of 1 September 1988 relating to export policy.
[126] Order No. 8671/2005 of 5 July 2005.

At the time of its first TPR, Madagascar did not have any contingency measure legislation and the situation has not changed since.

OTHER MEASURES

The authorities have notified the WTO of the Free Zone regime under the Agreement on Trade-Related Investment Measures (TRIMs) (section (3)(vi)).[127] No agreement has been signed with foreign governments or enterprises with a view to affecting the volume or value of goods and services exported to Madagascar. Likewise, the authorities are not aware of any such agreements between Malagasy and foreign companies. Madagascar complies with the international trade sanctions decided by the United Nations Security Council and the regional bodies to which it belongs.

MEASURES DIRECTLY AFFECTING EXPORTS

CUSTOMS PROCEDURES

The registration formalities applicable to the importation of goods for commercial purposes also apply to exports (section (2)(i)), and the corresponding customs procedures are the same (section (2)(ii)). Under Madagascar's foreign exchange regime, the State may "require the repatriation of foreign assets arising out of the export of goods"[128]; this requirement is implemented through the domiciliation of export transactions with approved intermediaries (for example, banks).[129] Four copies of the resulting document, namely, "the foreign currency repatriation commitment and declaration" (EDRD), must be lodged with the customs services for certification and attached to the customs documents. The currency must be repatriated within a period of 90 days.

Under the Mining Code and its implementing decree[130], only the approved collector is authorized to purchase mining products; to transport these products inside Madagascar it is necessary to have a pass, which must be attached to the customs export declaration. Hallmarking is compulsory for jewellery exported for commercial purposes. A similar regime applies to gold, except that the approved collector must sell to the *Comptoir de l'or* (Gold Agency), which carries out the export transactions.[131]

EXPORT DUTIES AND TAXES

According to the authorities, Madagascar does not impose any export taxes. However, it should be pointed out that some products are subject to a charge. Given that these products are almost entirely exported, these charges are *de facto* applicable almost exclusively to exports. Thus, a charge is applied to fishery products (Chapter IV(2)(iv)); a charge of 1.5 per cent of the f.o.b. value is applied to worked wood (Chapter IV(2)(v)); and a mining charge of 2 per cent is applied to mining products (Chapter IV(3)(i)). Furthermore, forestry charges are levied on the exportation of specimens of fauna and flora: at the rate of 4 per cent of the f.o.b. price for live specimens; 2

[127] WTO document G/TRIMS/N/2/Rev.8 of 19 July 2001.
[128] The information on the foreign exchange regime was obtained from the web site of the Central Bank of Madagascar: http://www.banque-centrale.mg/.
[129] Circular No. 005 of 30 June 1994.
[130] Law No. 99-022 of 19 August 2000 and Decree No. 2000-170 of 15 March 2000.
[131] Decree No. 95-325 of 3 May 1995.

per cent of the f.o.b. price for processed products (e.g., essential oils); and 1 per cent of the f.o.b. price for specimens that have been reproduced (e.g., by horticultural centres).[132]

PROHIBITIONS, QUANTITATIVE RESTRICTIONS, CONTROLS AND EXPORT LICENCES

Under the export regime notified to the WTO, numerous species of Madagascar's fauna and flora may not be exported, other than for scientific exchange and/or intergovernmental purposes. The authorities have noted that these measures were taken in conformity with the Washington Convention on International Trade in Endangered Species of Wild Fauna and Flora (CITES). Under CITES, Madagascar subjects the exportation of certain species of wild fauna and flora to prior authorization.[133] Madagascar has prohibited the exportation of any species of wood in rough or semi-finished form since July 2007[134], but authorizes exports in finished form (for example, works of art; craft articles or parts of musical instruments made of ebony, rosewood or palisander). The export of medicinal plants and archaeological or historical objects is prohibited.[135] An exit permit is required by anyone exporting more than 250 grams of jewellery for non-commercial purposes. At the same time, a tourist can export up to a kilogram of jewellery, but must declare the value and provide the mining administration with invoices and supporting foreign exchange documents.[136]

EXPORT SUBSIDIES, PROMOTION AND ASSISTANCE

Exports benefit from the zero rate VAT regime, which gives entitlement to the refund of the duties and taxes levied on the inputs used to produce them. Refunds are made, at the request of the economic operators concerned, within a period of 30 days. The temporary admission procedure is applicable to construction site plant and equipment, spare parts, construction materials, and accessories intended exclusively for re-exportation after use. Inputs, raw materials, and semi-finished or finished products used in the manufacture, market preparation, treatment, packaging or preservation of other products intended for export are eligible for the industrial warehousing regime.

INDUSTRIAL FREE ZONE

Enterprises approved for the Industrial Free Zone (ZFI) regime enjoy various tax advantages (Chapter II(4)); the authorities note that the regime will be amended, starting in 2008. In principle, free zone enterprises must sell as much as 95 per cent of their output, in value terms, for export. Their sales on the national customs territory are subject to import duties and taxes. Since 1999, in order to give the enterprises approved for this regime a further incentive to respect the threshold of 95 per cent of production for export, VAT at 20 per cent has been applicable to inputs introduced into the ZFI. The inputs can remain in the ZFI for 12 months. The VAT is refunded to the free zone enterprises within 60 days of their providing proof that the finished goods have been exported.

The sales of free zone enterprises are monitored by the Ministry of Finance on the basis of an examination of the documents submitted by the enterprise concerned, more particularly, the "foreign exchange repatriation undertaking and declaration" (EDRD) (Chapter I(2)). A financial penalty may be imposed if the domestic market sales quota is exceeded.

[132] Order No. 6833/2001-MEF/SG/DGEF of 28 June 2001.
[133] The requirements are listed on the site of the Ministry of Agriculture, Livestock and Fisheries (http://www.maep.gov.mg/fr/formulaire.php?maeplink=form_animaux.htm) [14 September 2007].
[134] Interministerial Order No. 10885/2007 of 3 May 2007.
[135] Decree No. 92-424 of 3 April 1992.
[136] Order No. 15269/2003 of 18 September 2003.

Some 202 free zone enterprises were active in 2006, employing a total of nearly 116,000 people. Exports under this regime amounted to around 300 million special drawing rights (SDR) in 2006 (about 56 per cent of the total for that year), with the textiles and clothing item accounting for approximately 70 per cent and shrimps and crustaceans for 15 per cent. Europe was the destination for about 70 per cent of sales, followed by the United States with 25 per cent. Imports by free zone enterprises amounted to around 190 million SDR in 2006, which resulted in a surplus of about 110 million SDR.

MEASURES AFFECTING PRODUCTION AND TRADE

INCENTIVES

Madagascar's notifications to the WTO indicate that it grants no aid or subsidy that might be inconsistent with its obligations under the Agreement on Subsidies and Countervailing Measures or under the GATT 1994.[137] However, support measures are granted to enterprises approved under the Free Zone regime (Chapter II(4)), as well as to large-scale mining investments (Chapter IV(3)(i)). Public services, such as electricity (Chapter IV(3)(iii), water (Chapter IV(3)(iv)), air and rail transport (Chapter IV(5)(i)) and postal (Chapter IV(5)(iii)) services, also benefit from State aid, as does agriculture (Chapter IV(2)(ii)).

COMPETITION AND PRICE CONTROLS

Madagascar adopted a new regulatory framework for competition in 2005[138], but the provisions concerning good practice are not yet operational. Because of funding difficulties, the budget for setting up the *Conseil de la concurrence* (Competition Council), which would act as the administrative authority for this framework, had still not been approved at the end of 2007.[139] The legislation establishes free enterprise and free pricing as a general principle, but, where prices are concerned, recognizes that the State, by regulation, can impose limits on this freedom in the presence of a monopoly situation or continuing supply problems, as well as at times of crisis, for a period of not more than six months; these provisions are already in effect. The framework also prohibits certain anti-competitive practices.[140] In particular, any merger (the criteria for which are to be established by regulation) will be subject to prior examination by the Competition Council (once established); the Council could decide to forbid it or to accept it under certain conditions to be fulfilled by the parties.

Madagascar's current policy is mainly aimed at monitoring the prices of basic necessities (PPN), namely, edible oils, condensed milk, baby food, cement, flour, bread, sugar, household soap, school exercise books, candles, packaging products. These are defined within the historical context of the price control policy followed by the authorities up to 1987 when the regime was first liberalized. Moreover, the Ministry of Agriculture monitors the price of rice on Madagascar's main markets; the results of the surveys conducted by the monitoring body are published weekly.[141] Exceptional measures to exempt rice from import duties and taxes were taken in 2005 to deal

[137] WTO documents G/SCM/N/95/MDG of 16 July 2003 and G/SCM/N/95/MDG/Suppl.1 of 21 October 2004.
[138] Law No. 2005-020 of 17 October 2005.
[139] "Madagascar: *Création du conseil de la concurrence en 2008*", *L'Express de Madagascar*, 11 August 2007, http://www.lexpressmada.com/index.php?p=display&id=10205&search=concurrence.
[140] The usual collective anticompetitive practices prohibited are: understandings aimed at or having the effect of preventing, restricting or appreciably distorting the free play of competition within the domestic market or a substantial part thereof; and abuses of dominant position. Mergers are subject to prior review. Monopolies are defined but not prohibited.
[141] Consulted at: http://www.maep.gov.mg/fr/donnee.php?maeplink=donobsriz.htm.

with shortages (section (2)(iv)(e)).[142] The prices of petroleum products were liberalized in 2004, in connection with the opening up to competition of the activities of the downstream petroleum sector (Chapter IV(3)(ii)).

According to the authorities, state-owned enterprises and those that benefit from a *de jure* or de facto monopoly (section (iii)) are granted autonomy in determining their pricing policies.

STATE TRADING, STATE-OWNED ENTERPRISES AND PRIVATIZATION

Madagascar has not made any notification to the WTO concerning State trading enterprises within the meaning of Article XVII of the GATT. However, HASYMA holds a *de jure* monopoly for the production of cotton lint, and KRAOMA one for the extraction and marketing of chromium. Moreover, the State-owned enterprise JIRAMA holds a de facto monopoly on the transport of electricity (Chapter III(3)(iii)) and on the production, transport and distribution of water (Chapter IV(3)(iv)). TELMA, a private-law enterprise, holds, until June 2008, a monopoly on the supply of basic fixed telecommunications services. Along the South rail corridor commercial transport services are provided exclusively by the State-owned enterprise RNCFM (Chapter IV(5)(i)).

The ambitious programme of State withdrawal from economic activity[143], begun in 1997, is currently entrusted to the Regulation Directorate of the Ministry of Finance and the Budget (MFB). Altogether, this programme involves 53 State-owned enterprises, across all sectors. The State withdrawal mechanisms comprise sales of shares, asset transfers, new equity issues with renunciation of preferential rights, liquidation and lease-management contracts, with account for the rehabilitation and/or environmental protection dimension. The methods of open or selective tendering, after open pre-qualification, and sale by auction are generally used for privatization purposes. It should be noted that as State land can only be acquired by nationals, long leases are offered to foreigners where the purchase of assets is involved. The difficulties faced by foreigners in obtaining access to land explain the policy of seeking strategic partners pursued by the State. Once it is set up, the *Fonds de portage et de privatisation* – FPP (Transfer and Privatization Fund) will manage the State's minority holdings in privatized companies and eventually open the way for the establishment of a stock market. In general, State participation in the Malagasy economy remains substantial (Table III.5). According to the authorities, this participation allows the State to sit on the boards of the companies concerned and defend its interests, particularly social.

Table III.5 State holdings, October 2006

Company	Activity	Equity capital (in MGA)	State share (percentage)	Current situation
Agriculture-fisheries-livestock				
Société agricole de l'Ankaratra (AGRIKA)	Farming	36,000,000	100.00	Subsidiary COROI – in course of liquidation
Bureau central laitier (B.C.L.)	Dairy farming extension	5,878,000	74.79	In course of liquidation

[142] Law No. 2005-015 of 26 July 2005 exempting rice imports from customs duty. Since 2006 the zero regime has applied to rice.
[143] Law No. 96-011 of 13 August 1996 established the programme and its regulatory framework; it was amended by Law No. 2003-051 of 30 January 2004.

Company	Activity	Equity capital (in MGA)	State share (percentage)	Current situation
Compagnie Nosy-béenne de l'industrie agricole (C.N.I.A.)	Perfumery plants	79,593,250	100.00	Subsidiary COROI – leased to Biolandes
Fikambanana Fampandrosoana ny Lemak'i Betsiboka (FIFABE)	Development of the Betsiboka plain	12,400,000	33.06	Liquidation closure pending
Fikambanana Fampandrosoana an'i Toliara (FIFATO)	Agricultural development of the Toliara region	6,000,000	75.50	In course of liquidation

Table III.5 (cont'd)

Hasy Malagasy (HASYMA)	Cotton growing	3,016,800,000	10.00	
Société langouste du Sud (LANSU)	Fishing and crayfish gathering	10,000,000	40.00	In course of liquidation
Malts et orges de Madagascar (MALTO)	Barley growing	467,449,000	39.40	
Société pour le développement de Matitanana (MATITANANA)	Agricultural extension	5,000,000	100.00	In course of liquidation filiale COROI
Les pêcheries de Nossi-Be (PNB)	Deep-sea fishing and fish farming	2,161,600,000	23.01	
Société d'aménagement et du développement de la plaine de bas – Mangoky (SAMANGOKY)	Agricultural extension	59,000,000	79.00	In course of liquidation closure EGM pending
Société Andapa Mamokatra (SOAMA)	Agricultural extension	20,000,000	100.00	In course of liquidation
Société pour le développement du moyen-ouest (SODEMO)	Agricultural extension	54,000,000	96.42	In course of liquidation minutes of EGM pending
Société malgache du Lac Alaotra (SOMALAC)	Agricultural extension	34,200,000	85.50	In liquidation
Société malgache de pêcherie (SOMAPECHE)	Deep-sea fishing and fish farming	1,344,266,000	1.00	
Société de pêcherie de Boina (SOMAPEBO)		1,622,740,000		State shares transferred to Codal in October 2006
Société theicole de Madagascar (SOTHEMAD)	Tea plantation	87,800,000	100.00	Exploitation of plantation transferred to SIDEXAM, no longer active – asset management

Company	Activity	Equity capital (in MGA)	State share (percentage)	Current situation
Société Lamoulie Valentin	Manakara & Farafangana plantation	5,000,000	100.00	co. Management COROI – in course of liquidation plantation Valentin abandoned
Ronono Malagasy (ROMA)	Dairy products	600,000	25.00	Closed down
Trade, collection and distribution				
Comptoir de représentation pour l'océan Indien (COROI)	Wholesale trade in staples – import/export	900,000,000	100.00	In course of liquidation
Société anonyme Maxime Darrieux (S.A. M Darrieux)	Office equipment and supplies – hardware	100,000,000	100.00	In course of liquidation
Tranombarotra Roso	Wholesale trade in staples – import/export	400,000,000	100.00	In course of liquidation
Société industrielle et commerciale de l'Emyrne (SICE)	Wholesale trade in staples – import/export	200,000,000	100.00	In course of liquidation
Société d'intérêt national des products agricoles (SINPA)	Collection and distribution of staples	66,000,000	100.00	In course of liquidation
Société générale de distribution (SOGEDIS)	Distribution of goods and retail trade	27,800,000	100.00	In course of liquidation
Société malgache de collecte et de distribution (SOMACODIS)	Import, export, supermarket	280,000,000	100.00	In course of liquidation
Société pour l'exportation du café du Sud (SECA)	Export of coffee, pepper, cloves	30,000,000	100.00	Subsidiary COROI In course of liquidation
Société pour le conditionnement de l'exportation des products agricoles (SCEPAG)	Rice	27,000,000	100.00	Subsidiary COROI In course of liquidation
Société des products de Madagascar (SPM)	Coffee, pepper, cloves	60,000,000	100.00	Subsidiary COROI In course of liquidation
Omnium de maintenance de véhicules de transport (OMAVET)	Spare parts for Japanese industrial vehicles	1,750,000,000	69.00	State holding assigned to CUA; payment for the shares assigned by CUA pending

Table III.5 (cont'd)

Company	Activity	Equity capital (in MGA)	State share (percentage)	Current situation
Petroleum distribution				
Total Madagasikara S.A.	Petroleum distribution	14,956,152,000	20.00	Operation concluded
SHELL	Petroleum distribution	3,600,000,000	20.00	Operation concluded
JOVENNA	Petroleum distribution	7,888,760,000	10.00	Operation concluded
GALANA DISTRIBUTION	Petroleum distribution	5,103,200,000	30.00	Operation concluded
GALANA RAFFINERIE TERMINAL	Petroleum distribution	3,000,000,000	20.00	Operation concluded
Logistique pétrolière	Petroleum distribution	19,889,380,000	31.00	Operation concluded
Industry				
La Laiterie de soja D'Ambatolampy (Unité LALASOA)	Soya processing	92,400,000	100.00	In liquidation
Famokarana Mahabibo Malagasy (FA.MA.MA)	Cashew-nut plantation and processing	115,500,000	99.56	Plantation remains
Société d'exploitation commerciale et industrielle de l'abattoir de Morondava (SECIAM)	National abattoir	40,400,000	72.18	In course of liquidation
Société d'exploitation de viandes de Madagascar (SEVIMA)	Canning	14,400,000	100.00	In course of liquidation
Société malgache de conserverie (SOMADCO)	Tomato canning	12,000,000	93.75	In course of liquidation
Société STAR	Carbonated beverages and health drınks	4,290,000,000	11.21	
Société des jus de fruits d'Antsirabe (SOJUFA)	Fruit juice and mineral water	20,000,000	15.00	Serious difficulties with working capital
Société industrielle de stockage et de traitement des products agricoles (TRAPAG)	Storage and processing of agricultural products	40,000,000	100.00	Subsidiary COROI In course of liquidation
Société Siramamy Malaigasy (SIRAMA)	Sugar cane plantation and processing	1,874,800,000	74.40	
Société Siramamin'Analaiva (SIRANALA)	Sugar cane plantation and processing	100,000,000	65.00	Operation entrusted to SUCOMA
Société des palmiers à huile de Madagascar (SOMAPALM)	Oil palm plantation and refinery	23,600,000	65.85	In course of liquidation

Company	Activity	Equity capital (in MGA)	State share (percentage)	Current situation
Société Sambava Voanio (SOAVOANIO)	Coconut plantation and processing	300,000,000	78.50	
La cotonnière d'Antsirabe (COTONA)	Spinning and weaving	12,951,000,000	38.32	
Filature et tissage de Madagascar (FITIM)	Jute sacks	780,200,000	37.40	
Société Sud Madagascar textile (SUMATEX)	Spinning and weaving	280,000,000	58.33	In course of liquidation
Société industrielle du bois (SIB)	Plantation and woodworking	5,780,000,000	99.98	
Société industrielle du bois (SIB)	Woodworking	17,200,000	100.00	In course of liquidation
Société pour le développement du machinisme agricole (SIDEMA)	Agricultural mechanization	16,000,000	73.00	
Entreprise "TOLY"	Agricultural mechanization	132,000,000	100.00	In course of liquidation
Société d'étude, de construction, de réparation navale (SECREN)	Shipbuilding	400,000,000	37.50	
Torginol Madagascar	Paint	12,000,000	100.00	In course of privatization
Orin'Asa Fanaovana Fanafody (OFAFA)	Pharmaceuticals	118,000,000	50.00	
Energy				
Jiro sy Rano Malagasy (JIRAMA)	Production and distribution of electricity and water	87,665,421,521	100.00	
Solitany Malagasy (SOLIMA)	Refining and distribution of petroleum products	500,810,000	100.00	In course of liquidation

Table III.5 (cont'd)

Mines and drilling				
Kraomita Malagasy (KRAOMA)	Extraction of chromium	308,000,000	100.00	
Société marbre et granit de Madagascar (MAGRAMA)	Extraction of marble and granite	1,700,000,000	1.00	
Forages, essais, travaux spéciaux (FORESTRAS)	Drilling	4,000,000	25.00	In course of liquidation
Transport				
Société nationale des transports aériens "Air Madagascar"	Air transport	17,685,440,000	90.59	
Réseau national des	Rail transport	2,000,000,	100.00	Management of

Company	Activity	Equity capital (in MGA)	State share (percentage)	Current situation
chemins de fer Malgache (RNCFM)		000		remaining assets
MADARAIL	Rail transport	5,000,000,000	25.00	
Filaterana Malagasy (FIMA)	Passengers and freight - urban and national lines	80,000,000	70.92	In course of liquidation
Société nationale de transports et de services "Air Route Service/ATO" (ARS/ATO)	Road transport	110,000,000	90.90	In course of liquidation
Société malgache de transports maritimes (SMTM)	Long-haul maritime transport	1,049,750,000	75.33	In course of reorganization
Compagnie malgache de navigation (CMN)	Local and regional cabotage	196,000,000	97.51	In course of liquidation
Société d'exploitation du bac automoteur Katsepy (SEBAK S.A)	Passenger and freight transport Katsepy zone	250,000,000	49.00	
Port and airport services				
Aéroport de Madagascar (ADEMA)	Management of 12 air terminals	130,000,000	68.00	In course of privatization
Société d'exploitation du Port de Toamasina (SEPT)	Port infrastructure	2,311,414,000	100.00	
Communications				
Société anonyme Telecom Malagasy (TELMA SA)	Telephony	41,156,200,000	32.00	
CINEMEDIA	Film distribution	120,000,000	75.00	
Tourism				
Madagascar Airtours (MAT)	Travel agency	270,553,840	16.72	
Société malgache d'hôtellerie (SMH)	Management company for the Madagascar Hilton hotel	679,800,000	46.57	
Société touristique et hôtelière de Madagascar (SOTOHOMA)	Owner of Palm Beach Nosy Be and casinos	10,000,000	100.00	Closed down real estate problems (hotel built on others' land)
Casino Club de Madagascar (CCM)	Owner of Andilana Beach Nosy-Be	11,000,000	98.20	Leased to SMTH under management contract
Société d'études immobilières et d'exploitation hôtelière "ZAHA MOTEL" (SEIXEHO-	Owner of ZAHA hotels	71,730,000	50.89	Lease of ZAHA Mahajanga to SOFITRANS

Table III.5 (cont'd)

Company	Activity	Equity capital (in MGA)	State share (percentage)	Current situation
ZAHAMOTEL)				
Building and public works				
Société d'intérêt national des travaux publics (SINTP)	Public works	160,000,000	100.00	Closed down since 1992
Société sino–malgache des travaux publics (SMATP)	Public works	400,000,000	30.50	
Laboratoire national des travaux publics et des bâtiments (LNTPB)	Public works	2,000,000	100.00	Unable to convert to limited company
Antok'Asa Ambanivohitra (A.A.A.)	Rural engineering	160,000,000	100.00	Closed down since 1993 In course of privatization
Société d'équipement immobilier de Madagascar (SEIMAD)	Construction and management	271,760,000	98.00	
Société "Ny Antsiva"	Construction and civil engineering	50,000,000	30.00	In course of liquidation
Consultancy				
Cabinet "RINDRA"	Advice and assistance	10,000,000	100.00	
Société d'étude et de réalisation pour le développement industriel (SERDI)	Advice and assistance	33,000,000	85.00	In course of privatization
Financial services				
BNI – Madagascar	Bank	10,800,000,000	32.58	
BFV – SG	Bank	14,000,000,000	28.50	
BOA – Madagascar	Bank	18,000,000,000	10.00	
Fonds de garantie malgache (FDGM)	Bank	400,000,000	49.00	
Caisse d'épargne de Madagascar (CEM)	Bank	5,460,000,000	100.00	
SGR	Bank	1,200,136,500	100.00	
SOFIRE	Bank	439,000,000	100.00	
ARO	Insurance company	7,013,30	73.25	
NY HAVANA	Insurance company	5,435,60	47.61	
Autres				
Société d'exploitation de loterie (SEL)	National lottery	20,000,000	57.50	Closed down
Société nationale de participation	Equity participation	850,000,000	56.77	

Company	Activity	Equity capital (in MGA)	State share (percentage)	Current situation
(SONAPAR)				
Société mixte libyo – malgache "LIMA HOLDING"	Equity participation	326,400,000	19.00	
Fonds de portage et de privatisation (FPP)	Equity participation	20,000,000	100.00	
Société du port à gestion autonome de Toamasina (SPAT)	Equity participation	20,000,000	100.00	
Société du port à gestion autonome de Toliary (SPATO)	Equity participation	250,000,000	51.00	Being formed
Société du port à gestion autonome de Manajanga (SPAM)	Equity participation	300,000,000	47.00	Being formed
Société du port à gestion autonome d'Antsiranana et de Nosy-Be (SPAAN)	Equity participation	250,000,000	51.00	Being formed

Source: Malagasy authorities.

The first wave of privatizations, starting in 1998, involved the banks. It was followed by the liberalization of the importation, storage, processing, transport and distribution of fuels (Chapter IV(3)(ii)). The change of economic strategy in 2002 (Chapter II(2)) revitalized the process of State withdrawal and liberalization. Out of the ten major projects identified by the authorities, three were completed in 2004, with the privatization of TELMA[144], in the telecommunications sector (Chapter IV(5)(iii)) and HASYMA[145], in the cotton sector (Chapter IV(2)(iii)), and the granting to Madarail of a 25-year concession to operate the RNCFM Nord rail network (Chapter IV(5)(i)).[146] Altogether, the revenue derived from privatization between 2000 and 2006 amounted to US$69 million. The privatization of ADEMA (airport services), Air Madagascar, SOFITRANS (tourism services), SIRAMA (sugar mills), and SBM (banking services) has been suspended, while the transfer of the remaining assets and final involuntary liquidation of SOLIMA (former State-owned oil company) are in progress. The reorganization of JIRAMA is one of the authorities' current priorities because of the difficulties with the supply of electrical energy.[147]

GOVERNMENT PROCUREMENT

[144] Transfer by the State of 34 per cent of TELMA's shares to the Consortium Distacom for US$12.6 million. Distacom also acquires France Cable Radio's 34 per cent holding. The State retains 32 per cent of the shares.

[145] Transfer by the State of 52 per cent HASYMA's shares to DAGRIS for US$1.6 million. DAGRIS already held 38 per cent of the shares. The State retains 10 per cent of the shares.

[146] Madarail is the company set up to manage the concession and the State investment fund for renovation of the rail network. This company is owned by Madarail Holdings (51 per cent), Manohisoa financière (12.5 per cent), First immobilière (9 per cent), Financière Aro (2.5 per cent) and the State (25 per cent).

[147] IMF (2007b).

Madagascar's government procurement regime has been completely revised since its first TPR. The new regime adopted in 2004 was devised with the technical assistance of the World Bank.[148] It has been progressively introduced since 2005 through the adoption of the corresponding administrative and procedural regulations. The *Autorité de régulation des marchés publics* – ARMP (Government Purchasing Regulatory Authority) was set up in 2005[149], and has been busy promoting the adoption of the Code.[150] The ARMP is made up of two entities, namely, the *Comité de réglementation et des recours en matière d'attribution des marchés publics* – CRR (Committee for Regulation and Appeals concerning the Award of Public Contracts) and the *Commission nationale des marchés publics* – CNM (National Public Contracts Commission), established in 2006.

The ARMP is responsible for monitoring compliance with the provisions of the Code, applied within each entity covered by a *Commission d'appel d'offres* – CAO (Tender Commission) chaired by the person responsible for government procurement; for example, within a ministry, that person would be the Minister, while at regional level the person responsible would be the head of that region. The CAO is responsible for examining bidders and assessing their bids, while the person responsible signs the contract. Anyone involved in the award and execution of a public contract is subject to the code of good conduct drawn up in 2006[151] and must undertake in writing to fulfil all the ensuing obligations. Madagascar is neither a member nor an observer at the Plurilateral Agreement on Government Procurement concluded under the aegis of the WTO, but the authorities are interested in observer status.

The Code is intended to "ensure that government purchasing is efficient and that public monies are properly used".[152] In principle, it applies to purchases made by State and public institutions, local authorities and their public institutions; any public or private entity whose resources are derived from public funds; and any enterprise in which the State has a majority holding (Table III.5). In practice, the Code is being progressively introduced by the entities concerned. However, many State-owned enterprises have their own contract award procedures. Contracts financed from external resources are also subject to the Code, provided there is nothing to the contrary in the clauses of the finance agreements concerned.

The thresholds for the application of the Code are defined by regulation; certain large contracts may be reviewed *post facto* by the administrative authority (Table III.6).[153] Beyond these thresholds, contracts are, in principle, subject to the tender procedure; recourse to direct negotiation must be justified in a report to the ARMP by the person responsible. In principle, tender notices are published in advance in a specialized government journal and in at least one daily newspaper with a wide circulation.[154] Tendering may be open (with or without pre-qualification) or selective. In principle, the lowest bid is accepted, but national enterprises may be accorded a price advantage of 10 per cent at most. Selective tendering requires at least three suppliers or enterprises. Inviting at least three suppliers to bid is a principle that is also applied to contracts below these thresholds, which are awarded by issuing a purchase order as specified in the regulations.

[148] Law No. 2004-009 of 26 July 2004.
[149] Decree No. 2005-215 of 3 May 2005. Its officials were appointed in June 2006. The information on the ARMP was obtained from the web site: http://www.armp.mg/ [26 December 2007].
[150] See, for example, the *Guide de l'utilisateur*. Consulted at: http://www.armp.mg/files/GUIDE-UTILISATEUR-SUR-LA-PASSATION-DE-MARCHE.pdf [26 December 2007].
[151] Decree No. 2006-343 of 30 May 2006.
[152] Article 4, Law No. 2004-009 of 26 July 2004.
[153] Order No. 11179/2006/MEFB of 29 June 2006, as amended.
[154] Publication online is also offered by the ARMP at http://www.armp.mg/avis_g_n_raux.

The new regime is struggling to become established. Thus, no contracts were put out to tender in 2004, only three in 2005, and seven in 2006. According to the authorities, 22 per cent of contracts awarded in 2007 were awarded by direct negotiation; according to the International Monetary Fund (IMF)[155] recourse to tendering does not appear to be widespread, and a survey carried out for the *Conseil supérieur de lutte contre la corruption* – CSLCC (Anti-Corruption Council) showed that corruption is a phenomenon that often affects government procurement.[156]

Table III.6 Thresholds for the award of public contracts (in MGA)

Contracting authority	Threshold	Works: Highway: Construction rehabilitation	Works: Highway: Maintenance	Works: Other	Supplies	Provision of services/ intellectual services
State and ex-category[a] urban communes and their public institutions	Award	1 billion	200 million	140 million	80 million	25 million
	Prior review	4 billion	750 million	300 million	200 million	90 million
Regions, urban communes of categories 1 and 2[a] and their public institutions	Award	500 million	100 million	75 million	50 million	20 million
	Prior review	2 billions	350 million	150 million	120 million	80 million
Rural communes and their public institutions	Award	250 million	50 million	35 million	20 million	6 million
	Prior review	1 billion	200 million	80 million	50 million	25 million
State-owned companies and Industrial and Commercial Public Institutions (EPIC)	*Post facto* review	1 billion	200 million	140 million	80 million	25 million

a The urban communes of categories 1 and 2 are the six provincial capital urban communes and the urban communes of Antsirabe, Nosy-Be and Sainte Marie. The other urban communes are ex-category.

Source: Order No. 20 476/2007/MEFB of 20 November 2007.

PROTECTION OF INTELLECTUAL PROPERTY RIGHTS

OVERVIEW

There has been no substantial revision of Madagascar's intellectual property regime since its first TPR in 2001. It still consists of a regime specifically for the protection of industrial property[157],

155 IMF (2007b).
156 Casas & Associates (2006).
157 Ordinance No. 89-019 of 31 July 1989 and Decree No. 92-993 of 2 December 1992.

and another regime covering copyright and related rights.[158] The authorities point out that they are continuing their efforts, already mentioned in the first TPR, to bring the national legislation into conformity with the provisions of the TRIPS Agreement, as they apply to LDCs (including Madagascar), and expect the provisions relating to the protection of industrial property to be revised in the course of 2008.

Madagascar has been a member of the World Intellectual Property Organization (WIPO) since 22 December 1989. In 1963, Madagascar acceded to the Paris Convention for the Protection of Industrial Property and in 1972 to the Stockholm Act; in 1966 it acceded to the Brussels Act of the Berne Convention for the Protection of Literary and Artistic Works, and in 1978 to the Patent Cooperation Treaty (PCT). Madagascar has signed the Patent Law Treaty (2000), and in 2007 ratified the Protocol relating to the Madrid Arrangement for the International Registration of Marks. The authorities would like to build national capacity in order to speed up the process of ratification of the treaties administered by WIPO.

INDUSTRIAL PROPERTY

In Madagascar, industrial property is administered by the *Office malgache de la propriété industrielle* – OMAPI (Malagasy Industrial Property Office).[159] There is provision for four titles, namely, patents, trademark registrations, industrial design registrations, and trade name registrations, accompanied in each case by a term of protection and sanctions in the event of infringement of the protected rights. Software, plant or animal varieties, and essentially biological processes for the production of plants or animals, together with pharmaceutical, veterinary, cosmetic and food products, are excluded from patentability[160], contrary to the provisions of the TRIPS Agreement. However, software is protected under the copyright regime (see below). Moreover, the authorities point out that patent applications for pharmaceutical products mainly concern the manufacturing processes, which are patentable, rather than the products themselves.

The obtaining (or renewal) of an industrial property title is based on an application made out on a form available from OMAPI, in accordance with an established scale of fees.[161] After receiving the form, OMAPI proceeds to initiate the procedure and register and examine the application. The industrial property titles issued are published in the *Gazette officielle de la propriété industrielle* – GOPI (Official Industrial Property Gazette). Since 1994, OMAPI has received 502 patent applications (64 per cent from non-residents under the PCT, and the rest from residents) and has issued 336 patents (Table III.6). Patent protection is granted for a term of 15 years; this term of protection is less than the 20 years stipulated in the TRIPS Agreement, although the authorities point out that an "additional five-year term of protection may be granted on request, provided that the national interest so requires and local exploitation is serious and satisfactory". Moreover, protection of trademarks and trade names is granted for ten years and can be renewed for further ten-year periods, while industrial designs are protected for five years, twice renewable.

In the event of industrial property rights being infringed, the holder, by virtue of an order made by the president of the competent court, may proceed with the designation and detailed description, with or without seizure, of the allegedly counterfeit objects. The sanctions for violation of industrial property rights are six months to three years' imprisonment and/or a fine of

[158] Law No. 94-036 of 9 December 1994.
[159] Decree No. 92-994 of 2 December 1992.
[160] Article 8, Ordinance No. 89-019 of 31 July 1989.
[161] Information on the regime, the texts of the laws, and the procedures, forms and taxes was obtained from the OMAPI web site: http://www.omapi.mg/.

MGA 100,000 to 2 million, plus damages. In the event of a repeat offence, the penalty is doubled.

OMAPI also undertakes missions to raise the awareness of economic operators and keep them informed. In Madagascar, the products most likely to be counterfeited are clothing, perfumery articles, and film and music CDs and DVDs. Article 29 of the Customs Code (2007) describes products bearing a trademark identical to that registered as being those prohibited, and this provides the authorization for seizures at the customs cordon. So far, however, OMAPI has not intervened in the local market to seize counterfeit articles that have passed through customs.

Table III.7

Industrial property applications and titles issued, 1994-2006

	Number of applications filed		Number of titles issued	
	Residents	Non-residents	Residents	Non-residents
Patents	133	369	72	264
Trademarks for products and services	3,173	5,510	2,605	4,980
Industrial designs	2,363	112	1,851	91
Trade names	684	14	618	4

Source: Malagasy Industrial Property Office (OMAPI).

COPYRIGHT AND RELATED RIGHTS

In Madagascar literary and artistic property is administered by the *Office malgasy du droit d'auteur* – OMDA (Malagasy Copyright Office)[162], whose tasks include the protection, defence and management of copyright and related rights. The regulatory framework for copyright is harmonized with certain relevant provisions of the WTO's TRIPS Agreement. This applies, in particular, to the term of copyright protection which, under the Malagasy regime, covers the life of the author and 70 years after his death. Software is protected for 25 years after its creation (contrary to the provisions of the TRIPS Agreement which call for a 50-year term of protection), the *droit de suite* (resale royalties) lasts 70 years, the rights of performers are protected for 50 years after fixation, and the rights of radio and television broadcasting organizations for 20 years.

The OMDA collects royalties for the use or exploitation of literary and artistic works and, after deducting management costs, distributes them to those entitled (including foreigners). For radio stations, restaurants and hotels, the OMDA proposes lump-sum payments in the absence of systematic monitoring of the works broadcast. The OMDA has 4,877 members and by mid-2007 had registered 89,517 works.

The OMDA participates in the seizure of counterfeit products (25,000 CDs, VCDs, and DVDs between 2004 and 2006). Since 2006, it has been possible to carry out seizures without a prior complaint from the authors or their beneficiaries.[163]

[162] Decree No. 98-434 of 16 June 1998.
[163] Interministerial Order 12226/2006 of 17 July 2006.

STRATEGIC INFORMATION FOR BUSINESS AND INVESTMENTS

(TRADE POLICIES BY SECTOR AND INVESTMENT OPPORTUNITIES)

Madagascar has considerable agricultural potential, although it is little exploited. The farming population is estimated to be around 13.3 million (some three quarters of the total population), but is generally poor because of rudimentary cultivation techniques and low crop yields. Nevertheless, since the first review of Madagascar's trade policy (TPR), the authorities have redefined the country's economic and social development strategy in the hope of achieving a "sustainable green revolution". Rapid progress has been made with the policy to ensure more secure land tenure. Although the State no longer intervenes in the prices paid to farmers, it does subsidize the supply of seed and inputs. In order to facilitate public-private interaction, the authorities have set up forums for consultation by branch of agriculture (rice, litchis and vanilla). In the case of rice, a basic foodstuff, a monitoring centre keeps an eye on prices on local markets and gives out information in order to help these markets to function better. A number of projects financed by external funds support rural development. One of the objectives of agricultural policy is to improve food security and to generate surpluses that can be exported to subregional markets.

The fisheries and aquaculture subsector (together with the mining and tourism subsectors) are three of the major activities on which the authorities are relying to boost the country's medium-term economic development. Shrimps are one of Madagascar's most important export products and appear to be produced in accordance with the sanitary requirements in force on the European market, which is their main destination. Tuna resources are exploited under bilateral agreements with the European Union and Japan. Timber in the rough has not been exported since 2007 in order to encourage processing.

The mining sector has attracted large-scale investment since the introduction of an incentive framework and a sharp increase in the production of mineralized sands, cobalt and nickel is expected in the near future. In accordance with current provisions, such investment must meet environmental protection criteria. Investment is needed in the country's rail transport infrastructure and in building new mineral ore ports. Madagascar is still a large producer of chromium (under a State monopoly) and of gemstones.

Since the first TPR, the manufacturing sector has grown, particularly those companies manufacturing textiles and clothing under the free zone regime and enjoying preferential access to the United States market under the AGOA. Despite the tax and customs incentives they have been given, Madagascar's manufacturers complain, *inter alia*, of the recurrent electricity supply problems. Since 2004, Madagascar has opened up activities downstream of the petroleum subsector by eliminating the ceiling prices on petroleum products, although these are still monitored.

Since 2003, there has been a sharp rise in tourism, partly as a result of the open skies policy. The authorities are also hoping to develop ecotourism by creating *réserves foncières touristiques* (tourism land reserves), although the supply of the requisite water, internal transport and telecommunications services is not satisfactory. Financial services (banks, micro-finance institutions and insurance) are open to competition from foreign suppliers. Under the GATS, however, Madagascar only bound measures concerning the supply of certain tourism services.

AGRICULTURE AND RELATED ACTIVITIES

Madagascar's surface area is 595,790 km^2, and it has 4,500 km. of coastline. Its exclusive economic zone (EEZ) covers 1,225,259 km^2, giving Madagascar the fourteenth largest EEZ in the world. It has natural resources and a climate conducive to agriculture (including raising livestock, fishing and forestry), and its contribution to the GDP is substantial (Chapter I(1)). Some 60 per cent of the agricultural GDP comes from crops, 25 per cent from raising livestock and fishing and 15 per cent from forestry.[164] Agricultural products (shrimps, vanilla, litchis and cloves) are also among Madagascar's important exports (Chapter I(3)(i)).

The farming population is estimated to be around 13.3 million (around three quarters of the total population). Each farm covers an average area of 0.87 hectares. Cultivation techniques are rudimentary and there is little mechanization (the *angady*, a type of spade, is still the tool most commonly used on family farms) and there is little use of inputs (improved seeds, fertilizer, pesticides). The production zones are isolated, which makes it difficult to reach the crops and market them. The rural population mainly produces for its own consumption and is usually poor. Because of the relatively high demographic growth there is growing demand for food, which in turn has an effect on the means of production, particularly land tenure, water and financing. It should also be noted that 70 per cent of household spending is on food, so its price has a marked impact on purchasing power and the level of poverty.

Madagascar is an agricultural producing country with some 36 million hectares of arable land (out of 58 million hectares)[165], but only just over 2 million hectares are under crops. The three major crops are: rice, the basic foodstuff, roots and tubers; industrial crops (groundnuts, sugar cane, cotton, tobacco), which provide the raw material for local agro-industrial units producing edible oils, sugar, cotton lint and cigarettes (see section (4)); and cash crops mainly intended for export (vanilla, cloves, pepper, coffee, cocoa). Since the first TPR of Madagascar in 2001, rice production has increased, whereas the production of industrial crops has stagnated and cash crops have shown a downward trend with the exception of cocoa (Table IV.1). There has been an increase in the production of fruit and vegetables, particularly in outlying areas.[166]

Madagascar also has considerable potential for raising large and small ruminants. The majority of households in rural areas raise livestock and look on their herds as a source of food and the prime source of savings. Bovine cattle are the large animals most commonly raised and, together with pigs, are increasingly being reared. Madagascar has a herd composed of 9.7 million bovine cattle; 1.3 million pigs; 700,000 sheep; 1.3 million goats; and 29 million head of poultry. Milk production does not meet national needs so a large volume of powdered milk is imported.

Table IV.1 Production of food crops, 2001-2005 (Tonnes)

	2001	2002	2003	2004	2005
Coffee	64,530	61,520	70,315	67,780	55,474
Tea	441	516	570	365	351
Cocoa	4,410	4,413	4,410	4,410	6,470
Oilseeds	35,240	..	35,610	34,590	64,841

164 Over the period 1984-2005, the primary sector was made up of crop production (on average 47 per cent of the agricultural GDP), livestock breeding and fishing (42 per cent), and forestry (11 per cent). Since 1984, crop production has therefore increased its share of the agricultural GDP, notably as a result of the expansion of rice growing caused by growing demand from the population, to the detriment of forestry, livestock and fishing.

165 Embassy of France in Madagascar, Economic Mission (2006d).

166 Embassy of France in Madagascar, Economic Mission (2006a).

Fresh vegetables	..	..	..	..	263,659
Dried grains (leguminous vegetables)	82,450	77,550	77,660	77,300	166,064
Tropical fruit	..	..	..	..	1,041,424
Temperate fruit	..	..	..	..	33,722
Rice	2,662,465	2,603,965	2,800,000	3,030,000	3,392,460
Other cereals	..	..	..	..	397,171

Table IV.2 Trend in the food balance sheet for rice, 2000-2005 (Tonnes)

	2000	2001	2002	2003	2004	2005
Production of paddy rice	2,480,500	2,662,500	2,604,000	2,800,000	3,030,000	3,400,000
Equivalent in milled rice	1,637,130	1,757,250	1,718,640	1,848,000	1,999,800	2,244,000
Population	14,814,000	15,229,000	15,655,000	16,093,000	16,908,000	18,040,300
Requirements	2,074,000	2,132,100	2,191,700	2,253,000	2,367,100	2,525,600
Imports	207,700	330,300	170,500	283,800	151,400	278,000

Source: Malagasy authorities.

Fishing and aquaculture potential amounts to around 480,000 tonnes annually, of which 300,000 tonnes are of commercial interest. In 2005, Madagascar's total exports of fisheries products were some 34,515 tonnes (Table IV.3), not including deep-sea fishing by foreign ships under bilateral agreements. The overall value of these exports was MGA 358 billion, mostly shrimps (around 60 per cent) and different types of fish (32 per cent).

According to the FAO[167], forest covers some 22 per cent of Madagascar's land area. Around 80 per cent of this is classified as "primary" forest. Total forest cover is receding despite reforestation because demographic pressure continually raises the demand for land. Primary forest is inhabited by exceptional fauna and flora that are the basis for ecotourism (see section (5)(ii) below). The exploitation of forest resources provides wood and by-products that meet most of households' energy needs. There is also a flourishing trade in processed tropical wood (section (v) below).

Table IV.3 Trend in the export of fisheries products, 2003-2006 (Tonnes)

Product	2003	2004	2005	2006
Shrimps	15,255	13,650	11,716	12,218
Crabs	492	852	1,228	775
Spiny lobsters	383	555	565	222
Beches de mer	205	300	223	243
Cephalopods	999	1,668	1,606	1,237
Shark fins	18	43	58	26
Fish	2,796	891	1,900	19,773

[167] FAO (2006).

Product	2003	2004	2005	2006
Eels	12	8	7	5
Other	565	31	258	17
Total	**20,726**	**17,999**	**17,561**	**34,515**

Source: Malagasy authorities.

AGRICULTURAL POLICY[168]

The Ministry of Agriculture, Livestock and Fisheries (MAEP) is responsible for drafting, implementing and coordinating the Malagasy State's policy on agriculture, livestock and fishing, as well as that on State-owned and private land. This policy was redefined in the 2003 poverty reduction strategy (Chapter II(2)). The *Programme national pour le développement rural* – PNDR (National rural development programme), adopted in 2005, focuses on raising income in rural areas, in principle taking into account the environmental aspects. According to the "Madagascar Action Plan" (MAP)[169] concerning the country's economic and social development strategy for the period 2007-2011, rural development will consist of a "sustainable green revolution" and agri-business centres will be set up to assist in training and in meeting needs such as irrigation, seeds, fertilizer and storage facilities. The expansion in production needed to accomplish the green revolution will be achieved through more intensive cultivation, expansion of the area under crops, as well as the supply of seeds and fertilizer and assistance in using them. The authorities hope that this green revolution will lead to greater food security and to surpluses that can be exported to subregional markets. A transport policy aimed at ending the isolation of production zones and supporting entrepreneurship in agriculture complements this effort.

The MAP has defined six main challenges: to achieve secure land tenure; to improve access to rural financing; to launch a sustainable green revolution; to promote market-oriented activities, in both internal and external markets; to diversify rural activities; and to increase the agricultural value added and promote agri-business. In order to meet these challenges, the State intends to make the sector's institutional framework more effective and more efficient; to facilitate access to capital and production factors; to improve food security, expanding production and agricultural processing; to develop natural resources and protect natural production factors; and to develop markets and organize key branches. The latter have been identified for each of the 22 regions. In the case of agriculture, the most important branches are rice, maize and sorghum, and for fishing, shrimps, tuna, spiny lobsters and traditional fishing are priorities.

Since the end of 2005, the State has been pursuing its *Programme national foncier* (national land ownership programme) in order to make land tenure more secure.[170] The lack of an operational property market represents a handicap to securitization of financing for agricultural activities and, consequently, private investment in this activity. According to the authorities, only 10 per cent of national territory was the subject of land ownership deeds in 2005. The State's property services, under MAEP's responsibility, were unable to meet the demands from families seeking to obtain recognition of their land rights or requests to buy State-owned land so the Government rapidly decided to expand the network of property offices. A property office is a neighbourhood community service responsible for administering land that is not the subject of title deeds and for the community's land. It issues a property certificate, which has full legal effect and allows all property transactions to be conducted. The State also intends to reform land ownership legislation and update its application by computerizing topographical data and property deeds

[168] The exploitation of Madagascar's fisheries and forest resources is the subject of special subsectoral policies defined by regulatory frameworks (section (iii) below).
[169] IMF (2007a).
[170] For further details, see the State's relevant web site: http://www.foncier.gov.mg.

and certificates. It should be noted that State-owned land or land registered in the name of the Malagasy State may not be bought by foreigners but may be the subject of a long lease for a maximum period of 99 years.

There are three types of intervention in the agricultural sector in Madagascar through the following: the traditional activities of the MAEP (which has around 3,588 officials); projects; and parastatal structures. Research (into seeds and new growing techniques) is carried out by the *Centre national pour la recherche appliquée au développement rural* – FOFIFA (National Centre for Applied Research for Rural Development), set up in 1974, whose activities are financed by the State. The FOFIFA produces breeder seed, pre-foundation seed and foundation seed. The latter are then multiplied at *Centres multiplicateurs de semences* – CMS (seed multiplying centres), which have the status of a State-owned industrial or commercial enterprise, by *Groupements de producteurs de semences* – GPS (seed producers' groups) or by private operators. The cost of the seed produced by the FOFIFA is determined according to its quality and the market price. The MAEP also finances projects in support of modern agriculture by providing inputs and agricultural equipment (with a subsidy of 40 per cent). Overall, the MAEP's budget (for operations and investment) amounted to MGA 195 billion in 2007, almost twice that in 2006.

There are many projects in the field (creation of reservoirs, support for purchasing agricultural equipment, eradication of animal disease) financed by external funds; for example, the World Bank is financing a development support project (2001-2008), and the European Union and its member countries are also closely involved. Payment for services and goods supplied depends on the donors and complies with the provisions laid down in the financing agreements signed between Madagascar and the donors. The FIFAMANOR, a parastatal structure, produces foundation seed for potatoes, sweet potatoes and wheat, which is then sold to farmers at a fixed subsidized price. In addition, many NGOs are working in the field.

The State is planning to set up an agricultural development fund in the near future, partly financed from external sources. In order to promote activities oriented towards internal and external markets, the State intends to increase the number of structures (farmers' organizations, markets, price monitoring centres such as that for rice) able to relay market trends to producers. Value added is low because the majority of agricultural products are exported without processing. The State plans to set up agri-business centres to train and support farmers in relation to production, marketing and export. It is also a question of producing goods that meet consumers' expectations as far as sanitary and quality standards are concerned. Madagascar's Chamber of Agriculture was set up in 2002 to facilitate the exchange of information among producers and allow them better to defend their interests *vis-à-vis* the central authorities.

At present, the principal tax-related support measures for farmers, livestock breeders or fishermen are: exemption from the company profits tax (IBS) and the minimum tax on new companies engaged in agriculture for the first two financial years with a 50 per cent reduction for the third financial year[171]; the summary tax (applicable to individuals or companies whose turnover or annual gross income does not exceed MGA 6 million) at a reduced rate of 6 per cent[172]; as well as various tax benefits under the free zone regime for export-oriented companies (Chapter II(4)). The authorities point out that only those who are formally registered as farmers or

[171] Article 01.01.16, General Taxation Code (2006 edition).
[172] Article 01.06.02, General Taxation Code (2006 edition).

authorized as collectors[173] pay tax. Since 2002, the import of agricultural inputs such as seed, fertilizer and herbicide has been subject to a zero tariff; VAT must be paid.

Madagascar's tariff policy gives relatively higher nominal protection to agricultural products than to non-agricultural products. The simple average of tariffs applied on agricultural products in 2008, according to the ISIC definition (including livestock, fishing and forestry), is 14.4 per cent (Table AIV.1), higher than the overall average of 13 per cent. Agricultural products, including foodstuffs, may be subject to sanitary and phytosanitary measures (Chapter III(2)(vi)).

Subsectoral policies apply, *inter alia*, to rice, cotton, tobacco, litchis, and to fishing and aquaculture and forestry. The State is also pursuing its policy of withdrawing from agro-industrial units (section (i) above).

POLICY BY SUBSECTOR

RICE

According to the MAEP formula, "for Madagascar, rice is simultaneously an economic, social and political product"[174], which explains its importance. Rice is grown on 2,144,739 of the total 2,994,501 farms.[175] The area sown with rice is estimated to be 1,330,000 hectares (around three quarters of the area under crops). Village-level rice farms have low yields (around 2 tonnes/hectare annually). The production is mainly for private consumption and only 26 per cent of the national crop is marketed.[176] Annual rice consumption per capita is around 120-140 kg.; although production continues to increase (by 21 per cent since 2001), it does not cover national requirements. Imports are needed and mostly come from Asia. Despite population growth of 2.8 million between 2001 and 2005, rice imports have remained stable (Table IV.2).

In order to reach the PRSP objectives and because of the sustained growth of Madagascar's population and the key role played by rice in the rural economy, development of the rice market is one of the authorities' main concerns. According to the plan adopted, the first stage in development is to increase rice production and then to improve its management and remove the constraints (particularly road transport) on its marketing in Madagascar from the farm to the table. Since 2005, the consultation and guidance forum for the rice subsector has organized regular consultations among the various actors in the subsector and the State.

In order to increase the yield per hectare, the authorities plan to make the seed improved by the FOFIFA available. Training is proposed in order to develop producers' professional skills and make it easier for them to adopt new rice-growing techniques. The State invests in improving the operation of irrigation channels. It also assists storage by establishing village-level community stores. In order to lessen the isolation of the regions producing rice, as well as to reduce the time taken to bring rice to local markets and lower transport costs, the State is also investing in rehabilitating rural roads.

The authorities are seeking to facilitate the operation of local markets in order to prevent shortages of rice that upset price trends, as happened during the rice crisis of 2004-2005. Collectors are the only persons authorized to collect agricultural products such as rice from

[173] Decree No. 65-046 of 10 February 1965 provides that agricultural products or livestock or fisheries products may only be collected by authorized collectors. The purpose of this requirement is to encourage efficient collection and transfer to wholesalers.
[174] Directorate-General of the Economy, Ministry of the Economy, Finance and Budget (2004).
[175] Embassy of France in Madagascar, Economic Mission (2006b).
[176] Directorate-General of the Economy, Ministry of the Economy, Finance and Budget (2004).

farmers and sell them to wholesalers; their role is intended to avoid large numbers of intermediaries and to place such activities on a formal basis. Since 2005, prices on local markets have been monitored by the rice monitoring centre, whose findings are available online and in other media in order to inform the various actors in the subsector (Chapter III(4)(ii)).

Rice imports help to make good the deficit in national production and avoid shortages when there is a seasonal shortfall (between September and March). Although only small quantities of rice are imported in comparison with domestic production, they in fact supply one third of the market on average and only 26 per cent of domestic production is sold. Tariff policy on rice varies according to the needs of the domestic market; since 2005, the import of any type of rice (seed, paddy, husked, etc.) has been subject to a zero tariff. Other taxes are usually levied. In the medium term, Madagascar hopes to become a net exporter of rice.

VANILLA

Since May 1995, the vanilla subsector has been liberalized and the Vanilla Fund abolished. The vanilla-producing zones are concentrated in the east of Madagascar and are estimated to cover 29,500 hectares. Since 2001, when the producer price rose sharply, there has been a marked expansion in the growing of vanilla although prices have tended to drop since 2004. Madagascar nevertheless remains the leading exporter of vanilla (around 67 per cent of the world total). Vanilla is all exported in a raw state and vanillin is extracted in the importing countries; artificial vanillin competes with the natural form. Vanilla exports are subject to a quality standard (Chapter III(3)(iv)), which is controlled by the Ministry of Trade's analytical laboratory.

In order to place them on a more professional basis, since 2001 the activities of vanilla planters and preparers have been regulated.[177] The SAVA Enterprises Group (GES) is responsible for the professional licences given to planters and preparers and also plays a key role in organizing markets and the subsector (dates of the harvest and opening of the season, monitoring the market for green vanilla, reinforcing control systems). The *Groupement national des exportateurs de la vanille* – GNEP (National Group of Vanilla Exporters) is composed of some 240 small groups comprising over 15,000 planters. Since 2007 there has been a forum for consultation in the vanilla subsector in order to encourage regular consultations among the various actors in the subsector and the State.

In Madagascar, vanillin is highly protected. It may not be imported into Madagascar without prior authorization (Chapter III(2)(v)). The maximum tariff of 20 per cent applies, together with VAT of 20 per cent and excise duty of 180 per cent. Nevertheless, vanillin is still not produced on an industrial scale in Madagascar.

COTTON

Despite the privatization of the former State-owned company HASYMA in 2004[178], the cotton subsector has not been radically reorganized. HASYMA has a monopoly of the production of cotton lint in Madagascar and is still the only buyer of the seed cotton produced. It directly

[177] Decree No. 2001/234 of 24 March 2001.

[178] HASYMA is 90 per cent owned by Dagris, while the State still has 10 per cent of the shares. According to the terms and conditions of sale, Dagris must sell some of its shares to cotton growers in order to incorporate them into the new company; this stage has not yet been completed. The Malagasy company, a subsidiary founded in 1973 by the *Compagnie française pour le développement des fibres textiles*, the former name of Dagris, was nationalized in 1978 when the capital was increased. "*Dagris s'offre HASYMA pour 1.6 millions de dollars*" (Dagris takes over HASYMA for US$1.6 million), 20 September 2004. Consulted at: http://www.sobika.com/fich_news/v2/news_436.htm [29 October 2007].

employs 500 workers and supports growers, some of whom are organized into groups. The objective of HASYMA is to achieve production of 50,000 tonnes of seed cotton in the medium term, i.e., twice the 2006 level. The State does not intervene directly in HASYMA's support policy, but is represented on the company's governing board.

The company determines a set price for buying seed cotton from growers; in 2005, this price (in lint equivalent) was effectively two thirds of the global price. HASYMA provides seed, fertilizer and phytosanitary products (the latter mostly imported) on credit, as well as equipment. It issues an international tender for the supply of fertilizer and phytosanitary products to cotton growers at cost price without any margin. Since 2003, however, it would appear that the increased price of inputs greatly exceeds the price of seed cotton, which makes cotton growing less profitable. Cotton growers also finance their purchase of equipment through micro-finance, but this source appears to be inadequate.

The seed cotton produced is stored and then collected by HASYMA. Its transporters are private persons selected through a bidding procedure, with the cotton being delivered to the factory on trucks leased by HASYMA. After being ginned (the average rate is 40 per cent), HASYMA exports the cotton lint or delivers it to the only spinning company, COTONA, a free enterprise. HASYMA sells cotton seed separately. The cotton spun in Madagascar has become of increasing economic importance since the country started to participate in the textile initiative under the United States AGOA (Chapter II(3)(ii)(f)); Madagascar has been given a special waiver for the incorporation of fabrics from third countries, renewed until 30 September 2012. In addition, it supports several initiatives in favour of African cotton.

Cotton yarn and fabrics are given the maximum tariff protection of 20 per cent (Table AIII.1). VAT of 20 per cent applies both to imported cotton lint and to that domestically produced.

LITCHIS

Litchis, a tropical fruit, are one of Madagascar's major exports. The domestic crop is estimated to be some 100,000 tonnes, a quarter of which is exported. Litchis are a highly seasonal fruit and are harvested after a short growing period. The harvest is then sold on export markets between November and January. The fresh fruit is exported as Madagascar does not have any processing capacity, with export mostly being transported by sea, although some go by air. The main export market for Malagasy litchis is France[179], where it competes with litchis produced by neighbours (South Africa and Mauritius). Litchis are subject to an optional export standard (Chapter III(2)(vi)). The total export earnings are around €14 million. A consultation forum for the litchi subsector was set up in 2006 in order to encourage regular consultations among the various actors in the subsector (producers, collectors, transporters and exporters) and the State.

Litchi imports are subject to the maximum tariff of 20 per cent and VAT of 20 per cent also applies.

TOBACCO

Tobacco is the subject of a special regime in Madagascar because its cultivation plays an important role in the rural economy. Some 29,000 tobacco planters are listed. The *Office malgache des tabacs* – OFMATA (Malagasy Tobacco Board) has had a monopoly of tobacco production in Madagascar since 1969. It gives producers support, determines a floor price for purchases of tobacco and supplies inputs on credit. The OFMATA supplies tobacco in stable and

[179] COLEACP EXPRESS, No. 25, June 2006. Consulted at: http://www.coleacp.org/fo_internet/doc/Fîle/Coleacp_Express/FR_COLEACP_EXPRESS_025.pdf [29 October 2007].

fermented leaves to the two factories manufacturing cigarettes and chewing tobacco. Domestic production was estimated to be around 3,000 tonnes in 2006. The OFMATA also has a monopoly of tobacco imports, and may import those varieties that are not produced locally in order to make cigarettes. In addition, imported cigarettes are subject to the maximum tariff protection of 20 per cent and VAT of 20 per cent is also levied, together with excise duty of 230 per cent (the local product is subject to 20 per cent VAT, but the excise duty is lowered to 135 per cent).

FISHERIES AND AQUACULTURE

The fisheries and aquaculture subsector (together with the mining and tourism subsectors) is one of the three major activities on which the authorities are relying to boost the medium-term economic development of Madagascar. The master plan for fisheries and aquaculture for 2004-2007 aims to increase freshwater fish production in order to help to meet the population's food needs and increase foreign currency earnings by exporting fisheries products. Madagascar has around 42,500 fishermen.

The regulatory framework for fisheries dates from 1993[180], and the separate regulatory framework for aquaculture from 2001.[181] Fishermen must obtain a fishing licence and pay a royalty which varies according to the type of ship and the catch (tuna, shrimps, crustaceans, fish or other).[182] The *Agence malgache de la pêche et de l'aquaculture* – AMPA (Malagasy Fisheries and Aquaculture Agency) issues fishing licences. The authorities do not have any policy on quotas for catches by species but aim to manage fisheries resources by managing the fleets. Nevertheless, it may be decided to stop fishing for certain periods in order to protect stocks.

The *Groupement des armateurs de pêche crevettière de Madagascar* – GAPCM (association of owners of shrimp fishing vessels of Madagascar), set up in 1994, is involved in managing the shrimp fishing subsector.[183] With backing from Madagascar's development partners, support structures have been set up, such as the research programme, the fisheries monitoring centre and the economic observatory. Since 2000, the system for granting licences and monitoring the environmental aspects has been totally revised. The GAPCM is involved in identifying the periods for closure and reviewing production methods in order to optimize the catches, lower fuel consumption and reduce the incidental capture of other fish and turtles. Since 2004, fishing gear on shrimp fishing vessels has been equipped with turtle exclusion devices (Chapter III(3)(iv)). The GAPCM considers that shrimp fishing meets the criteria for responsible fishing within the meaning of the FAO Code of Conduct. In 2004, it signed an agreement with the WWF in order to obtain eco-certification for exports by shrimp farms.

Shrimp farming (part of marine aquaculture) on average accounted for 36 per cent of the total annual production of shrimps during the period 2000-2005[184]; part of this production is exported. Shrimp farming experienced a crisis in 2004, but since then has continued to grow and accounted for 40 per cent in 2005. In 2007, some 7,000 tonnes were exported. As relatively large investment is needed for this activity because the ponds have to be installed, shrimp farms are often to be found under the free zone regime (Chapter II(4)), which explains why shrimp farming is geared towards exports. Malagasy exports consist of whole shrimps, shrimp tails and shelled shrimps and the principal export market is the European Union. Exports of fisheries products to

[180] Ordinance No. 93-022 of 4 May 1993.
[181] Law No. 2001 of 12 December 2001.
[182] Interministerial Order No. 5558/97 of 18 June 1997.
[183] Rojat, D. and Andriantosa, M. (2004).
[184] Embassy of France in Madagascar, Economic Mission (2005a).

the EU are subject to Malagasy sanitary standards drawn up to meet the requirements of this market and to strict regulations applicable to fisheries establishments (Chapter III(3)(iv)).

The fisheries subsector enjoys relatively high tariff protection of 18.8 per cent, way above the global average of 13 per cent (Table AIV.1). This tariff structure does not encourage the quest for competitiveness in the subsector and consequently production is oriented towards exports in the absence of various benefits. This explains why operators in the subsector are mostly to be found under the free zone regime.

Foreign vessels may fish in Madagascar's EEZ under bilateral agreements. Deep-sea fishing for tuna takes place in the EEZ under bilateral agreements with the European Union (EU) and Japan. The EU and Madagascar have signed a new six-year fisheries partnership agreement, which took effect on 1 January 2007.[185] This allows 43 tuna freezer seiners and 76 long-liners belonging to EU member countries to fish in Malagasy waters subject to a fishing licence to be issued by the Malagasy authorities, with compensation amounting to €1,197,000 for a total catch of 13,300 tonnes of tuna annually. Japan and Madagascar signed a protocol of agreement on fishing on 24 October 2005 for a period of three years allowing access to 44 Japanese long-liners. The financial counterpart is set at US$2,000 and US$5,000 per ship per month, in addition to an entry fee for the EEZ amounting to US$1,000 per entry. Japan finances investment in the fisheries sector (for example, building a market).

FORESTRY

Madagascar's regulatory framework for forestry has not changed since the first review of its trade policy in 2001.[186] The objective of forestry policy is the sustainable management of forest resources and their beneficiation in order to contribute towards economic development. This policy mainly concerns the management of State-owned forests, 24 per cent of whose total surface area is composed of zones (preservation forests, national parks and special reserves) to which the timber industry in principle has no access, while the remainder may be used for commercial forestry. Since 2003, the State has gradually put in place protected areas (1 million hectares annually with a view to reaching 12 million hectares by 2015).

Commercial forestry policy is implemented by the Ministry of the Environment, Water Resources and Forests (MAEF)[187], through forestry commissions on which forestry companies and NGOs involved in environmental protection are represented. The main forestry authorization is an agreement on forest exploitation, which is accompanied by terms and conditions, setting out the company's rights and obligations together with those of the State. The terms and conditions include a management plan based on a model drawn up to ensure the sustainable management of the forests concerned and operating permits are issued annually in accordance with this plan. Signatories to such agreements undertake to pay forest royalties, including a levy on export of the products.[188] For wood forest products, since 1994 the tax has been 1.5 per cent of the f.o.b. price for processed wood and 4 per cent of the f.o.b. price for logs and wood in the rough[189]; in principle, however, Madagascar does not allow the export of unprocessed forest products, since

---

[185] European Union press release IP/06/847, "EU and Madagascar initial new fisheries partnership agreement", 26 June 2006. Consulted at: http://europa.eu/rapid/pressReleasesAction.do?reference=IP/06/847&format=HTML&aged=0&language=EN&guiLanguage=en [14 October 2007].

[186] Law No. 97/017 of 8 August 1997 and Decree No. 98/781 of 16 September 1998 determining the general conditions for application of this Law.

[187] Decree No. 98/782 of 16 September 1998.

[188] The other levies are: the operating permit tax (wood forest products); the tax on collection (non-wood forest products); the logging permit tax; the tax on entry into forest stations; and the tax on transactions.

[189] Order No. 5139/94 of 15 November 1994.

2006 for processed woods (rosewood and ebony)[190], and since 2007 for all products coming from natural forest.[191] Before it is allowed to leave the forest, any resource exploited must bear the regulatory marks laid down in the terms and conditions.

Because of these bans, it would appear that no wood in the rough of any species is any longer exported and only pinewood (grown on plantations) is exported in a processed state (Table IV.4). In 2006, earnings from the export of all forest products amounted to MGA 24 billion (of which 1.5 per cent came from export levies). The exports consisted of various processed woods (55 per cent), handcrafted products and other finished products (12 per cent), essential oils and medicinal plants (32 per cent). France is the main destination, but other markets are being developed, for example, Belgium, Switzerland, Germany, Italy and Singapore.

Using the ISIC definition, the simple average of the tariff on imported products in the timber subsector is 6.8 per cent (Table AIV.1), below the overall average of 13 per cent. Internal taxes are also levied on timber (Chapter III(2)(iv)(b)).

Table IV.4 Exports of forest products, 2006

Type of product exported	Volume	Value (MGA)	Taxes levied (MGA)
Main products			
Anakaraka wood	340 m²; 25.683 m³	61,895,611	1,130,348
Rosewood	457m; 3,565 m²,and 338.42m³	831,653,168	12,481,754
Pinewood	202 m²; 43,563.697 m³	13,221,466,437	243,310,444
Sohihy wood	445.24 m²; 4.7 m³	41,550,547	655,642
Sohy wood	68 m²	2,144,405	32,166
Teak wood	5.580 m³	8,667,972	130,020
Eucalyptus wood	10.524 m³	12,055,296	180,829
Ordinary wood	70 m²; 55.383 m³	113,550,164	2,172,301
Katrafay	135.740 m²	8,275,164	124,127
Varongy		6,002,100	90,032
By-products and other products			
Charcoal	33,000 kg.	5,605,120	84,078
Copal	1,043 kg.	3,573,745	105,858
Raffia	4,842 kg.	12,939,519	194,093
Finished products			
Miniature model boats		187,985,787	2,819,788
Furniture and/or furnishings		788,404,749	11,826,073
Display units		98,296,447	1,474,446
Handcrafted products		1,921,976,045	28,759,490
Essential oils and medicinal plants			
Essential and plant oils		6,277,101,275	24,494,766
Medicinal plants	412,254	1,577,881,441	31,828,910
Medicinal seeds	72	3,858,305	39,796
Total		**24,904,883,399**	**361,934,968**

Table IV.4 (cont'd)

[190] Interministerial Order No. 16030/2006 of 14 September 2006.
[191] Interministerial Order No. 10885/2007 of 3 May 2007.

Source: Malagasy authorities.

MINING, ENERGY AND WATER

MINING PRODUCTS

Madagascar has considerable mining potential. Mining is one of the three major growth sectors (together with fisheries and aquaculture and tourism) on which the authorities are counting to form the basis for the country's medium-term economic development, but currently, its contribution to Madagascar's GDP is marginal (Table I.1). Although Madagascar produces chromite, graphite and gemstones, these are almost all exported in the rough state without any value added; in 2006, the value of exports was MGA 86 billion, approximately twice the value in 2000. These exports could increase in the near future when large new mines (ilmenite and nickel) start to operate under the Mining Code and in accordance with the environmental provisions (section (b)). These projects may be eligible for the special regime on large-scale mining investment (section (b)). Mining is the activity that has attracted the largest amount of foreign direct investment since the first review of Madagascar's trade policy in 2001.

Currently, Madagascar produces chromite ore with a content of 48 to 49 per cent in the mines at Ankazotaolana and Bemanevika, operated exclusively by the State-owned company Kraomita Malagasy (KRAOMA), which also has a monopoly of the marketing of Madagascar's chromium.[192] In 2006, output was around 132,330 tonnes, of which 116,290 were exported, the main destinations being China, Japan and Sweden, for a turnover of MGA 28 billion. The ore is transported by rail to the port at Tamatave. Chromite is used for chemical and metallurgical purposes and the KRAOMA has a project for vertical diversification of production by means of value added. Its price is fixed quarterly on the international market and is rising (from US$51/tonne in 2001 to US$161/tonne in 2007). The Bemanevika mine has reserves amounting to 3 million tonnes, but resources at the mine at Ankazotaolana will soon be depleted. Madagascar also produces graphite.

Madagascar produces and exports precious, semi-precious and ornamental gemstones. Production is almost entirely on a small scale and is virtually all exported in the rough state to markets in Asia for cutting and making jewellery. The subsector is dominated by illegal exports, which makes it difficult to evaluate its contribution to the economy and, consequently, that of the mining sector as a whole to the GDP, to employment and to exports.

MINING POLICY

Since Madagascar's first TPR, the Mining Code has changed[193], notably with a view to improving the collection and the shares of the earnings from the 2 per cent mining royalties accruing to the autonomous provinces, regions and local authorities (70 per cent in all) and the State (30 per cent).[194] With the support of development partners, the mining policy adopted in 2003 has enabled the geophysical information to be updated, thereby making prospecting easier. Since 2006, this information has been available to interested persons through the *Base de données sur la promotion et la gouvernance des ressources minérales* – BPGRM (database on the promotion and management of mineral resources); there is a charge for access to the site (MGA 700 to

[192] United States Geological Survey (2005).
[193] Law No. 99-022 of 19 August 1999 and its Implementing Decree No. 2000-170 of 15 March 2000.
[194] Law No. 2005-021 of 27 July 2005.

100,000).[195] Madagascar intends to observe the requirements of the Extractive Industries Transparency Initiative, and all its large mining companies have belonged to the Initiative since 2007.[196]

The Code governs prospecting, exploration, operations, possession, holding, transport, processing and marketing of useful mineral substances found in the soil or subsoil (with the exception of liquid or gaseous hydrocarbons or underground water, which are the subject of separate regulatory frameworks), which are owned by the State. Mining prospection may be freely undertaken within Madagascar, except in protected zones, temporarily reserved classified zones and areas covered by mining permits or by an "exclusive area reservation authorization (AERP)".[197] The three types of mining permit are: an R permit (for prospecting and exploration), valid for five years and renewable twice for three years; an E permit (for exploitation), valid for 40 years and renewable for several further 20-year periods; and a PRE permit, exclusively for small-scale operators for prospecting, exploration and operations, valid for eight years, renewable for one or more four-year periods. Gold panning is a separate activity.

Since 2001, Madagascar has had a special framework to encourage large-scale mining investment[198]; since 2005, this framework has been amended to lower the threshold for eligibility from MGA 200 to 50 billion[199] because the results obtained were disappointing. This special regime gives the right to a series of tax and customs incentives applicable throughout the term of the original mining permit, including: a tax of 25 per cent on the company's profits and those of subcontractors (instead of the standard rate of 35 per cent), which falls to 10 per cent for processing companies and their subcontractors[200]; and in the case of companies whose entire output is exported, the right to import the machinery and equipment covered by the investment project free of VAT. Investors may also freely convert into foreign currency and transfer the sums needed for their day-to-day operations and, subject to authorization, may transfer capital. They may opt for the regime giving taxation and customs stability while at the same time being eligible for more favourable measures if the State so agrees.[201]

Mining projects under E permits are subject to environmental impact requirements, under the responsibility of the Ministry of the Environment.[202] For example, QIT Madagascar Minerals S.A. (QMM)[203] exploits Madagascar's mineralized sands with a view to producing ilmenite; the commencement of operations at the Tolognaro mine by QMM was the subject of studies on the environmental impact on the coastal area in order to minimize the negative impact. The first stage of this project, affecting Mandena, was given an environmental permit in 2001.[204] The project includes the building of a new mineral ore port at Ehoala. The other large mining site, at Ambatovy, exploiting nickel deposits, has not yet gone through all the stages needed to obtain its

---

[195] La Gazette, "*Le centre unique de données ouvre ses portes*" (The single data centre opens), 30 September 2006. Consulted at: http://www2.gaf.de/bpgrm/pdf/Dossier-Press_BPGRM-300906.pdf [2 November 2007].

[196] Madonline, "*Secteur minier: pour plus de transparence*" (Mining sector: greater transparency), 29 August 2007. Consulted at: http://www.madonline.com/article.php?article_id=2340&lang=fr [2 November 2007].

[197] An AERP is granted for a non-renewable period of three months and gives the exclusive right to prospect and then, where applicable, to request a mining permit with a view to exploration and/or operations within the area covered.

[198] Law No. 20-2001 of 8 October 2001 and its Implementing Decree No. 2003-784.

[199] Law No. 2005-022 of 27 July 2005.

[200] The IBS rises to 35 per cent in the case of an internal rate of return (IRR) after tax of 20 per cent, and to 40 per cent when the IRR exceeds 25 per cent.

[201] Article 159 of the Mining Code.

[202] Decree No. 99-954 of 15 December 1999 covers the environmental impact of all types of investment, including that in mining.

[203] The company is 80 per cent owned by Rio Tinto and the rest by the State.

[204] Consulted at: http://www.pnae.mg/mecie/QMM/index.html [2 November 2007].

environmental permit. In order to protect Madagascar's natural assets, some NGOs are highly active in the area of the environment.

Possession and transport of mining products requires registration and a special pass; the mining authorities ensure that exports conform to the declaration made by the exporter. The conformity certificate issued by the mining authorities is required for the export of precious stones and metals and also semi-precious stones. It would appear, however, that trade in these products is also through informal channels. The authorities hope to orient production to the formal outlets that are gradually being introduced; the KRAOMA has set up a pilot gold agency in Brieville, which buys gold from authorized collectors at a price that is some 60 to 70 per cent of the international price.

The average tariff on mining products is 7.1 per cent. The import of cut precious stones is subject to the maximum rate of 20 per cent and VAT of 20 per cent. This tariff structure does not encourage investment in local jewellery-making activities.

PETROLEUM PRODUCTS AND NATURAL GAS

Although Madagascar does not at the moment produce oil, following the boom in global prices since 2003, investment by oil companies in exploring and exploiting oilwells has risen sharply. It is expected that Madagascar will produce its first crude oil in March 2008. Since the first TPR of Madagascar, the regulatory framework for petroleum activities has not changed.[205] By means of three types of mining title (exploration, operations and transport)[206], it governs prospecting, exploration and exploitation of liquid or gaseous hydrocarbons found in the soil or subsoil, including those within the EEZ, which belong to the State; as well as activities (and facilities) for storage, transport and processing of hydrocarbons within Madagascar.

The *Office des mines nationales et des industries stratégiques* (OMNIS) (National Mines and Strategic Industries Board), a State-owned enterprise, is in charge of the national hydrocarbons mining subsector.[207] It centralizes geological information (which is available for purchase) describing the potential onshore and offshore; 21 mining titles for exploration had been granted by the end of 2007. In addition, OMNIS may propose two types of operating contract to oil companies: joint ventures; and production sharing. In the former case, the mining titles may be held by the partners, while OMNIS holds the titles in the case of production sharing contracts. Oil companies holding mining titles for exploitation must pay a royalty per barrel produced, depending on the volume, and also a direct tax on hydrocarbons (IDH) amounting to 30 per cent, based on the profits (the IDH gives exemption from profits tax).[208] A temporary admission regime is available for machinery and equipment used for prospecting, exploration and surveying of hydrocarbons. Investment is subject to environmental impact requirements[209] under the responsibility of the Ministry of the Environment.

Madagascar imports oil to meet its population's fuel needs. In 1999, activities downstream of the petroleum subsector (import of hydrocarbons and gas, their processing, transport, storage and distribution) were liberalized.[210] In 2000, the components of the formerly State-owned company SOLIMA, which had a monopoly of these activities, were privatized. The *Office malgache des*

[205] Law No. 96-018 of 4 September 1996.
[206] Decree No. 97-740 of 23 June 1997.
[207] Decree No. 96-113 of 7 November 1996.
[208] Law No. 96-010 of 12 August 1996.
[209] Decree No. 99-954 of 15 December 1999 covers the environmental impact of all types of investment, including that in mining.
[210] Law No. 99-010 of 17 April 1999.

hydrocarbures (OMH) (Malagasy Hydrocarbons Board) is the regulatory authority for the downstream sector and issues authorizations to operators for the import, processing, transport, storage and sale of hydrocarbons; these activities are open to natural or legal persons (both Malagasy nationals and foreigners). The exercise of such activities, however, requires an operating licence and the payment of certain costs.[211] Currently, licences to import hydrocarbons are held by JOVENNA, TOTAL, GALANA (and its refinery), Shell, JIRAMA, Madagascar Petroleum International Gas Station (MPIGS) and Madagascar Energy International Gas Station (MEIGS). The only refinery at Toamasina, privatized in 2000 and taken over by GALANA, is winding up its activities. Several operators also hold licences for the storage and transport of hydrocarbons and for the sale of fuel.

The OMH ensures that the products imported or sold and the petroleum facilities comply with the standards in force. It monitors fuel supplies in Madagascar. Until 2004, it was also responsible for drawing up price lists. Since then, however, pricing policy has changed from one of fixed ceilings to free pricing by operators.[212] The OMH still monitors prices and margins in order to exert pressure on operators in the sector if their margins are excessive. The OMH is awaiting the effective introduction of the new framework so that there can be proper competition. Import of petroleum products is subject to special tariffs which vary from MGA 12/kg. net to MGA 390/litre depending on the product and also to special taxes (the tax on petroleum products (TPP)), VAT of 20 per cent, and a number of special levies (a tax on shipments to finance the OMH, another for the environment and one for road maintenance).

ELECTRICITY AND WATER

Madagascar's national electricity scheme is composed of the Antananarivo and Fianarantsoa interconnected networks and independent centres. A large proportion of the electricity generated (70 per cent) comes from hydroelectric power stations and the remainder from thermal stations. The total installed capacity is currently 233 MW. Furthermore, the Antananarivo interconnected network, with a peak of 111 MW in 2000, has reached the limit of its capacity.

In 1998, the State started to liberalize production, transport and distribution of electricity[213], but these activities have attracted few investors. The *Office de régulation de l'électricité* – ORE (Electricity Regulation Board) is responsible for granting permits and concessions to suppliers (both from Madagascar and abroad), which should be granted following an invitation to tender although in practice they are granted as a result of a spontaneous candidature. Permit holders must pay a levy of 1.2 per cent on their turnover and the sums collected are used to fund the ORE.[214] The State-owned company JIRAMA holds ten-year concessions for three activities, the generation, transport and distribution of electricity. Following liberalization, other producers have come on the scene and supply JIRAMA, which is still the only company engaged in transport and distribution. Electricity producers are free to fix the selling price; currently, the State sets ceiling prices for transport and distribution. The latest price-list dates from November 2007, with a price increase of 30 per cent in order to bridge the gap between the price and JIRAMA's operating costs.

[211] Decree No. 2004-669 of 29 June 2004 covers the types of licence. The procedure generally takes about 120 days. A licence to import hydrocarbons is issued against the equivalent of US$40,000 in MGA; it is valid for seven years and its renewal or transfer costs the equivalent of US$20,000 in MGA. Overall, the OMH offers 18 types of licence.
[212] Law No. 2004-003 of 24 June 2004.
[213] Law No. 98-032 of 20 January 1999 and its Implementing Decree No. 2001-173 of 28 February 2001.
[214] Interministerial Order No. 1055/2005 of 14 March 2005. For information on the ORE, consulted at: http://www.ore.mg/ [29 December 2007].

Production as a whole is unable to satisfy demand so the rate of electrification is low, particularly in rural areas where less than 2 per cent of the population has access to electricity. The infrastructure is insufficient and a large number of the generation and distribution facilities are obsolescent. Load shedding is common in the capital. In the short term, reorganizing the JIRAMA is one of the State's priorities because of electricity supply problems.[215]

Forestry, mining, tourism or industrial companies produce their own electricity, with authorization[216], and are free to supply rural communities. Rural electrification is financed through the *Fonds national d'électricité* – FNE (National Electricity Fund).[217] In addition to grants from donors, the FNE is financed, *inter alia*, through a special contribution levied on each kilowatt-hour consumed in all exploitation centres (with the exception of electricity consumption billed at the social rate). In 2007, 21 villages were being connected to the electricity supply and US$110 million had been allocated for the electrification of 100 villages a year up to 2010.

The JIRAMA also holds a ten-year concession for the production, transport and distribution of water.[218] In 2004, 27 per cent of the population had access to drinking water and less than 20 per cent to a basic sanitation infrastructure, although in rural areas the rate of access to water was 12 per cent. In 2006, JIRAMA's total production amounted to 110 million m^3, of which 60 per cent came from the city of Antananarivo and 40 per cent from the six other large cities in Madagascar. JIRAMA determines the price of water. Following a constant increase in production, sales and consumption between 1996 and 2000, production is now stagnating because use of the infrastructure is reaching saturation point while the number of subscribers continues to increase. JIRAMA's disastrous financial situation and its low investment capacity hamper development of the subsector in urban areas. The company LAHMEYER was given a management contract to modernize the JIRAMA in 2005.

With the support of donors, the Government has decided to open up the water subsector to private companies[219] which will be able to carry out their activities alongside the JIRAMA. The *Autorité nationale de l'eau et de l'assainissement* – ANDEA (National Water and Sanitation Authority) was established[220] and in 2003 regulatory texts for implementing the Water Code were adopted. Nevertheless, the regulatory body has still not been set up and the reorganization of JIRAMA remains a challenge with external financing still to be mobilized. Outside the area covered by the JIRAMA, water sources are managed collectively.

MANUFACTURING

Manufacturing only plays a minor role in GDP formation in Madagascar and there have been no important changes since 2001 (Table I.1). In 2006, the manufacturing sector was essentially composed of companies set up under the free zone regime (43 per cent), a substantial increase compared with 2001 when these enterprises' share was only around 24 per cent (Table IV.5). The companies concerned manufacture textile articles, process fisheries or timber products or are involved in shrimp farming. In the manufacturing sector outside the free zone (Table IV.5), which is mainly oriented towards the domestic market, agro-industry (beverages, foodstuffs and tobacco) plays the leading role (accounting for some 49 per cent of the sub-total), followed by the manufacture of building materials and metal articles (amounting together to 19 per cent). The manufacturing sector also includes workshops making clothing or engaged in other small-scale activities, bakeries and some other small industries.

[215] IMF (2007b).
[216] Order No. 6678/2001 of 19 June 2001.
[217] Law No. 2002-001 of 7 October 2002.
[218] Embassy of France in Madagascar, Economic Mission (2005b).
[219] Implementing Decrees for Law No. 98-029 (Water Code) of 20 January 1999.
[220] Decree No. 2003/192.

Companies in the free zone are export-oriented and are generally more competitive than those outside this regime (Chapter III(3)(vi)). The concerns of Malagasy firms, particularly manufacturers, include the high cost of access to financing, problems of electricity and water supplies, transport services and telecommunications, and macroeconomic instability, without forgetting poor governance.[221] In addition, the multilateral liberalization of textiles and clothing from 2005 onwards made Malagasy exports of these products more open to competition on foreign markets to which they had preferential access.[222] Nonetheless, exports of these goods manufactured in the free zone amounted to US$195 million in 2006.

Table IV.5 Breakdown of activities in the manufacturing sector outside the free zone, 1999-2006

	1999	2000	2001	2002	2003	2004	2005	2006
Agro-industry	7	6	5	6	5	5	5	4
Foodstuffs	21	20	20	21	22	21	21	22
Beverages	28	27	26	25	24	24	22	21
Tobacco	7	7	7	7	8	7	7	6
Oils and fats	3	3	3	2	3	3	3	3
Pharmaceuticals	8	7	7	7	7	7	8	7
Textiles	2	2	2	1	1	1	1	1
Leather	0	0	0	0	0	0	0	0
Wood	3	3	3	3	3	3	3	2
Building materials	5	5	6	5	5	5	6	7
Metal industry	6	7	8	9	9	10	12	12
Transport equipment	2	2	2	2	2	2	2	2
Electrical appliances	7	8	9	8	8	8	9	9
Paper	1	2	1	1	2	2	1	1
Other industries	0	0	0	0	0	0	0	0
Total	100	100	100	100	100	100	100	100

Source: WTO Secretariat calculations based on statistics provided by the Malagasy authorities.

Sugar[223] is produced by two State-owned companies (outside the free zone), namely, SIRAMA[224] and SUCOMA.[225] Protocol No. 8 on sugar (under the Cotonou Agreement) gives Malagasy sugar guaranteed access to the European Union market for around 10,760 tonnes of sugar a year. This volume is purchased at the guaranteed community price, which should fall by some 36 per cent

[221] World Bank Group, Africa Region, Private Sector Unit, "Madagascar: Investment Climate Statement", Note 3, September 2005. Consulted at: http://siteresources.worldbank.org/EXTAFRSUMAFTPS/Resources/note_3_screen.pdf [2 September 2007].
[222] Ernst C., Ferrer, A.H. and Zult, D. (2005).
[223] Le Quotidien, "Dossier Sucre", No. 766, 14 April 2006. Consulted at: http://www.cite.mg/malagasie/article.php?IdArticle=162 [9 September 2007].
[224] The SIRAMA is composed of four sugar refineries (Ambilobe, Namakia, Nosy-Be and Brickaville) with nominal annual production capacity of 119,000 tonnes of sugar and 100,000 hl of pure alcohol, but it only produces some 20,000 tonnes/year. The Ambilobe and Namakia refineries are subcontracted out to the SUCOMA.
[225] The Chinese company SUCOMA took over the SIRANALA under a management leasing contract in 1997. This company has a sugar refinery in the Morondava plain; its annual production capacity is 20,000 tonnes of sugar.

between 2006 and 2009.[226] Madagascar also has preferential quotas of 2,500 tonnes/year under the Special Preferential Sugar (SPS) scheme and 4,200 tonnes/year under the Everything But Arms (EBA) initiative. In addition, Malagasy sugar is given a preferential quota of 7,258 tonnes/year of raw sugar to the United States of America. These preferential quotas are not utilized. Domestic production, however, cannot meet internal demand and large imports of sugar are needed (over 100,000 tonnes in 2005). Imported sugar is in principle subject to customs duty of 20 per cent, plus VAT of 20 per cent and excise duty; the latter's rate is lower on domestically-produced sugar (Chapter III(2)(iv)(c)).

Milk is collected from farmers and processed into dairy products by the private firms SOCOLAIT and TIKO; domestic production is complemented by imports of powdered milk for the manufacture of dairy products.[227] Madagascar also produces beer under licence, rum, mineral water, sweetened beverages and local wine and alcohol. These local products compete with similar imported products despite customs duty of 20 per cent. In the case of beer, wine and alcoholic beverages, the excise duty on local products is lower than that on imported products (Chapter III(2)(iv)(c)); the same applies to cigarettes. In general, the manufacture of beverages, foodstuffs and cigarettes is given MFN tariff protection of 16.7 per cent (Table AIV.1), with a large number of products subject to the maximum rate of 20 per cent and also to other import duties and taxes (Chapter III(2)(iv)(b)).

The tariff structure does not encourage investment, particularly in agri-food industries, because of the relatively high cost of agricultural raw materials, together with their relatively strong tariff protection so exporting firms tend to utilize the free zone regime. In addition, the high effective protection in the majority of industries, with a few exceptions (Chart III.2) does not encourage competitiveness and consequently export because of the lack of incentives.

SERVICES SECTOR - POLICIES AND OPPORTUNITIES

TRANSPORT

WATER TRANSPORT AND PORT SERVICES

Madagascar is served by large shipping lines (Maersk, Mediterranean Shipping Company) as part of their Indian Ocean routes. The *Société malagasy des transports maritimes* – SMTM (Malagasy Maritime Transport Company), a State-owned company, only operates one ship; it is included in the privatization programme.

Maritime transport is through the two main commercial ports:[228] Toamasina, Madagascar's principal port on the east coast, 380 km. from the capital, and Mahajanga on the west coast, 570 km. from the capital. Toliara and Diego are other two major ports in Madagascar. The building of a mineral ore port started at Ehoala in 2007 as part of the QMM project for extracting ilmenite and it is also planned to build a mineral ore port at Soalara in connection with the exploitation of the cobalt and nickel mine at Ambatovy (section (3)(i)).

The regulatory framework for maritime transport has not changed since Madagascar's first TPR in 2001.[229] The State's policy has, however, been modified to hand management over to private

[226] WTO document WT/TPR/S/177/Rev.1 of 15 May 2007.
[227] Embassy of France in Madagascar, Economic Mission (2007a).
[228] Consulted at: http://portfocus.com/madagascar/index.html.
[229] Law No. 99-028 of 3 February 2000. The framework is being revised to reflect the State's new approach to transport policy, both as regards maritime, river and land transport (section (b)) and air transport (section (c)).

operators. The *Agence portuaire, maritime et fluviale* – APMF (Port, Maritime and River Agency), set up in 2004[230], is responsible for controlling and monitoring independently managed ports and acts as the port authority in non-autonomous ports until 2008. It is responsible for maintaining maritime signalling and river and maritime navigation routes.

The four independently managed ports, i.e., those in the hands of private companies in the context of public-private partnerships, are Toamasina, Mahajanga, Toliary and Diego. The *Société du port autonome de Toamasina* – SPAT (Toamasina Autonomous Port Company) has been modernizing the port facilities since 2005 in order, *inter alia*, to develop its role as a regional centre in Madagascar.[231] The GasyNet (Chapter III(2)(ii)) is operating in the port. Each year, 1.5 million tonnes of goods go through the port, of which almost 60 per cent are in containers. In June 2005, the SPAT gave a 20-year concession for the new container terminal to Madagascar International Container Terminal Services Limited (MICTSL).[232] The International Ship and Port Facility Security (ISPS) Code applies in the independently managed ports.

Madagascar's specific commitments under the GATS only relate to a small number of business services but not to any transport services.[233]

LAND TRANSPORT

There have been changes in the regulatory framework governing land transport (by rail or road) since Madagascar's first TPR in 2001.[234] The new policy for the sector aims to confine the State's activity to strategy and the design of infrastructure, particularly for government investment in this area; to define the public land transport service; and to introduce a system for regulating operators and users in the subsector. Responsibility for regulation, granting concessions and management has been handed over to the *Agence des transports terrestres* – ATT (Land Transport Agency).[235] The Agency issues driving licences, car registration documents and permits for operating transport vehicles, as well as giving approval to road carriers; the fees paid go towards the ATT's operating budget.

The road network covers 50,000 km., of which only 8,000 km. are in fair condition.[236] The poor state of this infrastructure is an important obstacle to Madagascar's economic development, particularly its agriculture, its mining sector and tourism. The rural transport policy, adopted in 2001, is aimed at expanding the network of sealed roads and rehabilitating rural roads and at resolving problems relating to their financing by decentralizing responsibility for their maintenance.[237] Since 2004, the land transport policy has been incorporated into the Integrated Growth Poles (IGP) project in order to make the best use of the investment. Large-scale road infrastructure rehabilitation projects are financed by development partners with a contribution from the *Fonds d'entretien routier* – FER (Road Maintenance Fund), whose resources come from a special tax on the import of petroleum products (section (3)(ii)). Some 16 per cent of budgetary expenditure in 2007 was allocated for government investment in the transport subsector.

---

[230] Decree No. 2003-659 of 4 June 2003.
[231] http://www.port-toamasina.com/.
[232] http://www.ictsi.com/operations.aspx?p_id=3&category_id=72&operation_id=136&id=193.
[233] WTO document GATS/SC/51 of 15 April 1994.
[234] Law No. 2004-053 of 28 January 2005.
[235] Decree No. 2006-279 of 25 April 2006.
[236] http://www.worldbank.org/transport/rural_tr/gp_docs/madagascar.htm.
[237] Government of Madagascar, "*Déclaration de politique et stratégies de transport en milieu rural*" (Statement on rural transport policy and strategies), May 2001. Consulted at: http://www.worldbank.org/transport/rural_tr/gp_docs/mad_rt_pol&strat.pdf [3 November 2007].

In large cities, authorized taxis and minibuses provide the majority of urban public transport services. Fares can be determined freely, but any increase must be communicated 15 days before it comes into effect for information purposes.

Because of the poor state of the highway infrastructure, rehabilitation and extension of the railway network should be priorities. There are two railways in Madagascar: the northern route has been operating since 2004 under a concession given to Madarail for 25 years; while the *Réseau national des chemins de fer* – RNCFM (Malagasy National Railway Network) for the south is included in the privatization programme. The Madarail (north) route is 750 km. long and is divided into three sections: the TCE line (from the port of Toamasina to the capital Antananarivo), the TA line (from the capital to Antsirabe), and the MLA line (between Moramanga and Lake Alaotra). The company has promised substantial investment (€37.5 million over five years) to modernize the railway and meet demand for rail transport by mining companies. The RNCFM is a major transporter of passengers and goods in the south of Madagascar. The cost of rail transport may be determined freely. For companies under Malagasy law, an operating authorization may be required.

AIR TRANSPORT

The regulatory framework governing civil aviation in Madagascar is being revised in order to prepare the ground for liberalization of this activity. According to the new Code adopted in 2004[238], regulation, granting operating licences and any other documents to air carriers (including suppliers of services at airports and airfields), and administering safety standards will be delegated to the *Agence de l'aviation civile* – AAC (Civil Aviation Agency). For the time being, *Aviation civile de Madagascar* – ACM (Madagascar Civil Aviation) remains the authority responsible for the subsector.[239] The AAC negotiates Madagascar's bilateral agreements on air transport and these have changed radically since Madagascar's first TPR in 2001. For a long time Madagascar protected its air space because it was determined to guarantee the continuity of the national company Air Madagascar (still in the privatization programme), but is now in favour of increasing the number of routes and their frequency by all airlines and lowering prices in order to develop its tourism (section (ii)).

In 2004, Madagascar signed an open skies agreement with the United States of America. The Franco-Malagasy Bilateral Air Agreement of 1962 was renegotiated in 2005[240], and the agreement with Italy came into effect on a provisional basis in 2004. In 2006, the 1992 agreement with Mauritius was renegotiated. The new agreements signed with Egypt (2006), Ethiopia (2007) and Senegal (2007) allow each of the parties to nominate an African multinational company as the national airline in conformity with the "Decision on the implementation of the Yamassoukro Declaration concerning the liberalization of air transport and market access in Africa, signed on 14 November 1999 and approved by the Heads of State of the African Union in July 2000". Madagascar is seeking to sign more reciprocal bilateral agreements covering destinations in Asia such as India and China in order to promote tourism, both for business and leisure purposes.

Air carriers are free to determine their fares, but these must be set at "reasonable" levels taking into account the relevant factors; they are submitted to the other party 30 days before they come into effect. A dispute settlement procedure is provided if there is any disagreement. Flight frequency is negotiated but may be increased on demand. Commercial activities are allowed, as is the transfer of the net earnings derived therefrom. All the recent agreements provide for the

[238] Law No. 2004-027 of 9 September 2004.
[239] Decree No. 99-821 of 20 October 1999.
[240] Since 2007 the "Chirac tax" has applied to routes between France and Madagascar.

first four freedoms, although the agreement with Italy also includes the fifth freedom. None of the bilateral agreements authorizes domestic traffic.

Madagascar's open policy has allowed it to be linked by international flights offered by airlines such as Air France, Corsair, Air Madagascar and Air Austral (via the island of Réunion). In addition, Air Madagascar has 20 weekly regional flights (Kenya, South Africa, Mauritius, Réunion, Comoros, Mayotte) and flights to Paris, Milan, Kuala Lumpur, Bangkok (via Réunion) and Singapore.[241] Air Madagascar also serves 40 domestic destinations; under its agreement with the State, the company is obliged to service some unprofitable lines. Since 2007, Air Madagascar has no longer been the only airline providing a domestic service. Some dozen small national private companies provide domestic passenger transport on demand.

Madagascar has 12 airports and 43 airfields; the international airports are at Antananarivo, Nosy-Be and Fort-Dauphin. The company ADEMA (Aéroports de Madagascar), a State-owned company included in the privatization programme, has a monopoly for managing these airports. It sets the rates for its services subject to approval by the Ministry in charge of transport. Madagascar decided to leave the ASECNA which provides aviation assistance in the form of meteorological services to all its member countries (except France), because the budget allocated to the airports managed by the agency is deemed insufficient.[242]

TOURISM[243]

Madagascar is well known for its biodiversity and the large variety of its fauna and flora and since 2003 (with 2001 and 2002 being less fruitful years) the number of tourists has continued to increase. Between 2003 and 2004, this increase was around two thirds and then between 2004 and 2005 the number of tourists (between January and September) rose to 202,485 (non-residents), a 21 per cent increase, with turnover of US$150 million. This increase mainly consists of European tourists seeking discovery tourism, adventure sports and eco-tourists, although business tourism (for the purposes of investment, humanitarian action or development aid) has also been important in the capital.

In general, tourism in Madagascar is less developed than in other destinations such as Mauritius.[244] Its tourism infrastructure, particularly transport, accommodation and related services, is confined to certain regions only, including Antananarivo, Nosy-Be and Fort-Dauphin. Having identified them as having considerable development potential, the World Bank's IGP project has identified three priority zones for development, including two devoted to tourism: Nosy-Be and Fort-Dauphin. In 2003, a master plan for tourism in Madagascar, incorporating sustainable management, was adopted. In order to encourage the development of eco-tourism, tourism land reserves have been set up (Isalo is the first, eight others are set up and more are being established).[245] In order to facilitate access to land by foreign investors (Chapter II(4)), the land is bought by the Ministry in charge of tourism and becomes the subject of an international

---

[241] Air Madagascar, flight schedule, 28 October 2007 to 29 March 2008. Consulted at: http://www.airmadagascar.com/jcms/index.php?option=com_content&task=view&id=36&Itemid=100 [3 November 2007].

[242] *L'Express*, "*Madagascar: L'Asecna dans une mauvaise passe*" (Asecna in bad straits), 2 November 2007. Consulted at: http://fr.allafrica.com/stories/200711020586.html [3 November 2007].

[243] Embassy of France in Madagascar, Economic Mission (2006c).

[244] World Bank (2005).

[245] Ministry of the Economy, Trade and Industry, "*Madagascar, une île paradisiaque, offre à tous les investisseurs qui veulent entrer dans le tourisme, une grande opportunité*" (Madagascar, a paradise island, offers all investors in tourism a great opportunity) http://www.meci.gov.mg/ index.php?option=com_content&task= blogcategory&id=106&Itemid=282 [3 January 2008].

invitation to tender[246]; investment in this subsector is subject to the ordinary law regime, but foreign promoters may utilize the services of the GUIDE when setting up their businesses (Chapter II(4)). Tourism facilities must respect the eco-tourism standards. Tourism reserves are poorly served by domestic transport and lack water, electricity and telecommunications. Another obstacle to the development of tourism in Madagascar is the high cost of air transport, despite the policy of opening up to competition pursued by Madagascar since 2004 (section (ii)(c)), as well as the limited availability of trained managers.

There has been no change in the regulatory framework for tourism since Madagascar's first TPR in 2001.[247] In principle, tourism facilities require authorization and must observe the prescribed standards. In practice, only the facilities in Antananarivo appear to comply with these obligations and these were last surveyed in 2006. The price of hotel services depends on their classification. In Nosy-Be and Fort-Dauphin, the authorities are surveying facilities (many of which lack authorization) and are encouraging them to meet the standards.

Madagascar's specific commitments under the GATS relate to a small number of business services, including "maintenance and repair of equipment (CPC 886); preparation and control of basic equipment in the following sectors: tourism and hotels, with the exception of transport activities relating to tourism".[248] Madagascar has expressed reservations on the supply of these services through a commercial presence, although in practice such investment is eligible for the same ordinary law regime as that applicable to other sectors.

Madagascar has been a member of the World Tourism Organization (UNWTO) since 1975.

TELECOMMUNICATIONS AND POSTAL SERVICES

The Malagasy authorities attach great importance to the development of the telecommunications subsector, pursuant to their commitment in the MAP to make Madagascar a "linked nation". Currently, the telecommunications subsector comprises TELMA[249], which has the exclusive right to the commercial supply of basic fixed telecommunications services (telephone lines, national and international fixed calls) until June 2008 (i.e., four years after its privatization); GULFSAT Telephony, which has provided telephone services since 2005 through the VSAT network to 11 isolated localities; three mobile telephone companies, Orange, Madacom (a subsidiary of Celtel) and TELMA Mobile (a subsidiary of TELMA, launched in 2006)[250]; as well as many Internet service providers (ISPs), a large number of distributors of telephone cards and mobile telephone booths. Voice-over-the-Internet (VoIP) services are not allowed. As a result of the growth in mobile telephony (Table IV.6), teledensity has progressed sharply in Madagascar since 2001 and in 2006 was 6.4 lines per 100 inhabitants. Access to the Internet, however, which depends on fixed lines (only 105,538 in 2006) or a satellite link, is still low.

TELMA is currently investing in the installation of a backbone infrastructure so as to develop its high speed and telephony fixed services. This scheme will eventually be linked to the outside because Madagascar is participating in two major regional projects for links using submarine fibre optics, which should in principle come about in 2008: the Indian Ocean Islands network project, launched by the Indian Ocean Commission (COI) and COMESA; and the EASSy project

[246] Consulted at: http://www.tourisme.gov.mg/.
[247] Law No. 95-017 containing the Tourism Code. Decree No. 96-773 laying down standards applicable to companies, tourism companies, facilities and operators.
[248] WTO document GATS/SC/51 of 15 April 1994.
[249] TELMA is 60 per cent owned by Distacom and the remainder by the State. Distacom's share is the result of the sale (in June 2004) by the State and France Cable & Radio of 34 per cent of TELMA (each) for a total amount of US$25.2 million.
[250] Embassy of France in Madagascar, Economic Mission (2007b).

(Eastern Africa Submarine Cable System)[251], to link Madagascar to the global submarine fibre optics network. At the end of 2007 only the latter project was under way with Alcatel as the supplier.

Table IV.6 Telecommunications service indicators, 2001-2006

	2001	2002	2003	2004	2005	2006
Subscribers, fixed lines	48,166	45,921	47,003	46,527	54,159	105,538
Subscribers, mobile telephones	147,500	163,010	279,357	333,001	510,269	1,045,888
Total subscribers	195,666	208,931	326,360	379,528	564,428	1,151,426
Teledensity (lines per 100 inh.)	1.32	1.32	1.96	2.3	3.2	6.39

Source: Malagasy authorities.

The *Office malagache d'études et de régulation des télécommunications* – OMERT (Malagasy Telecommunications Studies and Regulation Board), set up in 1997, is the regulatory authority for the subsector. The obligation to provide universal basic services in principle lies with TELMA and their supply is financed through a special fund, the Telecoms Development Fund, administered by the OMERT, whose resources come from a fixed levy of 2 per cent on the annual turnover of all fixed or mobile telephony companies. Mobile telephony licences are awarded through a bidding procedure. Tariffs for those areas open to competition may be fixed freely, whereas the cost of services that are a TELMA monopoly are regulated; the rates freely fixed by operators are transmitted to the OMERT for information. Interconnection rates are negotiated among operators. Telephone equipment must comply with the international standards recommended by the ITU and be approved by the OMERT.

Madagascar did not take part in the negotiations on telecommunications services at the WTO after the Uruguay Round, which ended in 1997. The regulatory framework was revised in 2005[252], following TELMA's privatization in 2004. Sweeping changes in the competition regime and in opportunities for investment in the subsector will, however, not occur until TELMA's monopoly ends (after June 2008). In principle, the OMERT should be replaced by the *Autorité de régulation des télécommunications et des communications* – ARTC (Telecommunications and Communications Regulatory Authority). The latter will be responsible for issuing licences to operators of telecommunications networks; the declaration regime will apply to ISPs; and the free regime to call centres, *inter alia*. Implementing decrees will be adopted to regulate the opening up to competition.

The government enterprise, La Poste, is responsible for administering postal services. It has a monopoly of reserved postal services (universal mail service, postal financial services), and proposes a number of financial services through the postal savings bank. A number of private operators have been given licences to offer express mail services (for example, DHL), in addition to those proposed by La Poste.

[251] The member countries of this consortium are: Botswana, Djibouti, Ethiopia, Kenya, Madagascar, Malawi, Mozambique, Rwanda, Somalia, South Africa, Sudan, Uganda and the United Republic of Tanzania. "EASSy (Eastern Africa Submarine Cable System)", April 2005. Consulted at: http://www.uneca.org/disd/events/accra/ AccessAndinfrastructure/EASSy.ppt [4 November 2007].

[252] Law No. 2005-023 of 17 October 2006.

FINANCIAL SERVICES

BANKING AND MICRO-FINANCE SERVICES

In Madagascar, commercial banking activities (except those provided by La Poste) are subject to the national banking regulations, which have not changed since the first TPR in 2001[253]; the principal new feature is special regulations on micro-finance institutions (MFIs), in force since 2005.[254] Pursuant to the banking law, activities by any credit establishment require approval by the *Commission de supervision bancaire et financière* – CSBF (Banking and Financial Supervisory Commission).[255] The minimum capital required to set up any of these establishments is as follows: MGA 3 billion for Malagasy banks, non-Malagasy banks and specialized financial institutions; MGA 1 billion for financial establishments; and MGA 15 to 700 million for MFIs in levels 2 and 3 of their classification[256], if individual or collective approval (for a network) is required and if the MFI takes savings from the public.[257] Conditions for engaging in banking are the same for all loan establishments whether owned by Malagasy nationals or foreigners. The CSBF supervises the requirements for operating loan establishments, monitors their financial situation and ensures respect for the profession's ethics, as well as exercising such control over MFIs in levels 2 and 3.

Since 2001, the banking and micro-finance services subsector has expanded from 12 to 25 loan establishments. Madagascar has eight commercial deposit banks, two of which are new; eight financial establishments, six of which were set up recently, notably for the purpose of proposing micro-credit services; and nine MFIs (mutualist or not authorized to engage in micro-credit operations), seven of which are new. The privatization that occurred in the subsector reduced the State's holding in several commercial banks in favour of French banking partners, even though the State's retains a sizeable share (Table III.5). Among the commercial banks, the State Bank of Mauritius specializes in large accounts and banking operations between Madagascar and Mauritius, and the BICM covers Malagasy imports of Chinese products. Other banks mainly offer finance to individuals and small- and medium-sized enterprises (SMEs).

The borrowing and lending rates proposed by the banks appear to be determined freely. The lending rate does not seem to follow the trend laid down by the Central Bank of Madagascar (BCM) through its management of a reference rate.[258] For example, the latter fell from 16 to 12 per cent during 2006, but the maximum borrowing rate remained fairly stable at around 14 per cent for fixed deposits for less than one year. The lending rate applied ranges from 14 to 26 per cent for short-term loans, 12 to 17 per cent for medium-term loans and 11 to 17 per cent for long-term loans.

INSURANCE SERVICES

Since Madagascar's first TPR in 2001, the regulatory framework governing insurance services has not changed.[259] Companies wishing to offer insurance services must be set up as public limited companies and comply with the law governing businesses. They must obtain approval for

[253] Law No. 95-030 of 22 February 1995.
[254] Law No. 2005-016 of 27 July 2005.
[255] Instruction No. 002/97/CSBF of 2 June 1997 (banks and financial establishments) and Instructions No. 002/2007, No. 003/2007, No. 004/2007, No. 005/2007 of 11 May 2007 (micro-finance institutions).
[256] Articles 14 to 17 of Law No. 2005-016 of 27 July 2005 define three levels of MFI (1 to 3). All MFIs in level 3 may offer long-term loans, but only non-mutualist MFIs in this level may receive savings. MFIs in levels 1 and 2 only offer short- and medium-term loans within the limits laid down in the regulations.
[257] Decree No. 2007-013 of 9 January 2007.
[258] Central Bank of Madagascar (2007).
[259] Law No. 99-013 of 2 August 1999.

each branch of activity – injury, life and capitalization – but may offer services in all branches. The minimum capital required to set up an insurance company offering personal insurance is MGA 100 million; MGA 600 million for an insurance company offering insurance against injury; and MGA 1 billion for life insurance and capitalization services. The requirements for setting up a company are the same for foreign and Malagasy insurers. Approval for each branch is given by the Minister in charge of finance after the request has been reviewed.

Madagascar's insurance market comprises five approved suppliers: the *Compagnie d'assurances et de réassurances omnibranches* – ARO (Insurance and Reinsurance Company for All Branches); the *Compagnie malgache d'assurances et de réassurances* – NY HAVANA (Malagasy Insurance and Reinsurance Company); the *Mutuelle d'assurances Malagasy* – MAMA (Malagasy Mutual Insurance Fund); and the *Société d'assurances et de réassurances* – AGF-Madagascar (Insurance and Reinsurance Company); the *Société d'assurances et de reassurances* – COLINA-Madagascar (Insurance and Reinsurance Company). The State has holdings in two of these companies, ARO and NY HAVANA.[260]

A company established in Madagascar may not cover risks outside the country. Likewise, risks in Madagascar may not be covered by non-resident companies; residents may not take out direct insurance abroad in order to cover a risk situated in Madagascar. The only compulsory insurance is that for civil liability of owners of motor vehicles. The policy on premiums is free but is monitored by the Ministry in charge of finance in order to ensure that the premiums are reasonable and take into account relevant factors, including the company's solvency and prudential standards.

[260] The State owns 73.35 per cent of ARO and 47.61 per cent of NY HAVANA.

TRADE AND CUSTOMS REGULATIONS: IMPORTANT INFORMATION

TRADE REGULATIONS, CUSTOMS AND STANDARDS

IMPORT TARIFFS

Custom duties range from 5% to 20%. Based on the 2011 budget law, inputs and capital goods for agriculture are exempt from customs duties as well as inputs for EPZ companies in the textile sector. Products for health security (medicine, vaccine, mosquito nets, glasses), equipment related to renewable energy and sports equipment are also exempt from custom duties.

VAT is fixed at 20% for all goods except rice, agricultural equipment, agricultural inputs (seeds, fertilizers, animal food and vitamins), newspapers, magazines, and sports equipment which are all exempt.

TRADE BARRIERS

Like many developing countries, Madagascar collects a significant share of government revenue through customs duties, import taxes and value added taxes (VAT) on imports.

Although they have been lowered recently, tax and customs duty rates are still relatively high. Madagascar does not have significant formal non-tariff barriers to trade.

IMPORT REQUIREMENTS AND DOCUMENTATION

Import documentation

The following documents are required for imports:

BSC (Bordereau de Suivi des Cargaisons - cargo follow-up form)

Commercial invoice

Bill of lading or Air Way Bill

Packing list

Import declaration

Certificate of origin

Export requirements and documentation

Most exports have been liberalized. However, export authorization is required for some protected animal and plant species, as requested by the Convention on International Trade in Endangered Species (CITES), of which Madagascar is a member. These include crocodiles and crocodile skin products, live animals, and orchids. Since September 2010, exports of rosewood have been included in Annex III of CITES, requiring importers to obtain an import permit signed by CITES authorities.

Exporters are obliged to repatriate their foreign exchange earnings within 180 days following shipment.

The following documents are required for exports:

Commercial invoice

Bill of lading or Air Way Bill

Certificate of origin (under GSP regime, JADE Act)

Phyto sanitary certificate, if required

Packing list

Export declaration

Customs declaration

Quality certificate, if required

U.S. EXPORT CONTROLS

There are no U.S. export controls specifically related to Madagascar which companies must respect when exporting. However, companies should ensure that imports of flora or fauna from Madagascar to the U.S. adhere to the provisions of the Lacey Act, which does not allow the import, export, transport, sale, receipt or purchase of plant materials taken, possessed, transported, or sold in violation of U.S. or foreign laws. American law enforcement officials took action in 2010 against companies that imported rosewood that had been illegally felled in Madagascar.

TEMPORARY ENTRY

Personal effects of diplomatic corps and international organizations are not subject to import taxes upon entry, but if personnel sell their effects before leaving the country, they must pay the import duties. Madagascar has a temporary admission regime under which certain items may enter duty free for up to 12 months. These items include imported goods that are expected to be re-exported (as is or after transformation), goods subject to experiment, repairs, and testing, goods exhibited during an international trade fair, and equipment used in public works.

LABELING AND MARKING REQUIREMENTS

For each certified product, labeling and marking are required on the packaging of the product before sale or export. All perishable foods must bear a label, in French or English, indicating the origin, the sell-by or use-by date, the ingredients, the method of storage, the name of the manufacturer together with his registration number, where appropriate, and the intended use. The utilization of the metric system is compulsory in Madagascar.

For further information, point of contact is:
Bureau National des Normes (BNM)
P.O. Box 1316
Antananarivo 101 – Madagascar
Tel: (261 20) 22 279 70
E-mail: bnm@moov.mg

PROHIBITED AND RESTRICTED IMPORTS

Imports into Madagascar are liberalized and no longer require any import license except for a few categories of items which are considered by the GOM as strategic and which are specially regulated. The importations of radioactive waste from nuclear power stations; pornographic materials; counterfeit branded products, pirated goods and goods bearing false indications of origin are prohibited: The importation of such products as arms, explosives and narcotic drugs is subject to prior authorization. The same applies to imports of diamonds, gemstones, gold and platinum jewelry, and vanillin. Madagascar also maintains a special regime for imports of leaf tobacco. An import license is required for lubricants. In addition, Madagascar applies prohibitions and licenses under multilateral environmental agreements to which it is party.

CUSTOMS REGULATIONS AND CONTACT INFORMATION RETURN TO TOP

Customs are valued at C.I.F. Madagascar is a member of the World Customs organization (WCO). Since November 2000, the Malagasy customs authorities have implemented the "transactional value" definition of the WCO.

Customs contact information
Mr. Vola Razafindramiandra Ramiandrasoa
Director General of Customs
Ministry of Finance, Budget and Economy
Antaninarenina, Antananarivo 101
Madagascar
Tel: (261 20) 22 229 16
Fax: (261 20) 22 646 80

STANDARDS

The Bureau de Normes de Madagascar (BNM) (Madagascar's Standards Office), is the official body in charge of standards and conformity assessment in Madagascar. BNM's objective is to draft and publish national standards, manage the national trademark conformity, promote and apply standards, certifications, and quality, represent Madagascar at regional and international standards organizations such as ISO, CEI, OIML, and Codex Alimentarius. When developing standards, BNM follows international standards, mainly ISO.

PRONABIO, a local organization, has developed its own standards called NATIORA to certify its natural goods such as vegetables, spices, and essential oils.

STANDARDS ORGANIZATIONS

The main national testing laboratories are:

- Laboratoire de Chimie et de Microbiologie d'Antananarivo (LCMA): quality control of food and agricultural goods, classification and conformity assessment. Standards used are AFNOR, ISO, and Codex Alimentarius.

- Laboratoire de Chimie de Tamatave (LCT): quality control of agricultural goods such as coffee, vanilla, cloves, litchi, pepper, and essential oils; classification and conformity assessment. Standards used are AFNOR and ISO.

- Laboratoire de Métrologie Légale (LML): control and standardization of measuring equipment in the commercial and industrial sector. LML belongs to the ministry of trade.

- Laboratoire du Centre National de Recherche pour l'Environnement (LCNRE): analysis of environmental samples; monitoring of impacts of industrial activities of environment; scientific support to the industrial sector; control and analysis in the nutritional and food sector; scientific support to the private sector in product quality (shrimp, lobster, agricultural goods, etc).

- Laboratoire de Biochimie Nutrition du Département de Recherche Zootechniques et Vétérinaires (LBN): chemical and microbiological analysis of raw materials for animal food.

- Laboratoire du Centre National de Recherches Industrielles et Technologiques (CNRIT): conformity assessment in the following sectors: water, various chemical products, construction material, civil engineering, electronics. Technical support to enterprises.

- Laboratoire de Chimie et de Recherches des Fraudes Alimentaires (LCFRA): quality control of all physic-chemical food (whether local or imported) for consumption certification.

- Laboratoire de Contrôle des Pesticides (LCP): control of agro-pharmaceutical products and pesticides (local or imported).

- Laboratoire de Microbiologie, des Eaux et des Denrées Alimentaires de l'Institut Pasteur de Madagascar: bacteriological analysis of food, water, and medicines.

- Laboratoire National des Mines du Ministère de l'Energie et des Mines (LNM): certification of jewelry and precious stones for exports; LNM belongs to the ministry of energy.

- Laboratoire National de Recherches en Télécommunications (LNRT): verification, inspection and certification of telecommunication equipment.

- Laboratoire de l'Institut National des Sciences et Techniques Nucléaires (LINSTN): standardization of ionizing radiation detection apparatus; radioactivity control of food and metallic waste; analysis of geological samples; detection of heavy metal; control of heavy metal in seafood and meat; quantitative/qualitative analysis of atomic elements in powder, solid, and liquid samples.

- Laboratoire National des Travaux Publics et du Bâtiment (LNTPB): certification of construction materials (cement, iron, etc); study of road materials; study of soil in view of construction stability assessment; control of construction; description of maintenance works; development of standards; training of engineers.

NIST Notify U.S. Service

Member countries of the World Trade Organization (WTO) are required under the Agreement on Technical Barriers to Trade (TBT Agreement) to report to the WTO all proposed technical regulations that could affect trade with other Member countries. **Notify U.S.** is a free, web-based e-mail subscription service that offers an opportunity to review and comment on proposed foreign technical regulations that can affect your access to international markets. Register online at Internet URL: http://www.nist.gov/notifyus/

CONFORMITY ASSESSMENT

The BNM and the testing laboratories stated above are the organizations in charge of conformity assessment in Madagascar.

PRODUCT CERTIFICATION

Vanilla, coffee, meat, seafood, and mining products should be certified before export.

A few forestry products (under CITES regulations) should be certified before export.

No mutual recognition agreement (MRAs) with U.S. organizations.

ACCREDITATION

Accreditation body and contact information:

BNM
P.O. Box 1316
Antananarivo 101 – Madagascar
Tel: (261 20) 22 279 70
E-mail: bnm@moov.mg
Accreditation is mainly required in the construction sector.

PUBLICATION OF TECHNICAL REGULATIONS

Technical regulations and standards developed by the different laboratories are published in the national gazette of the Republic of Madagascar if required by law. U.S. or foreign entities can approach the different laboratories or related departments to comment on final regulations.

LABELING AND MARKING

For each certified product, labeling and marking are required on the packaging of the product before sale or export. All perishable foods must bear a label, in French or

English, indicating the origin, the sell-by or use-by date, the ingredients, the method of storage, the name of the manufacturer together with his registration number, where appropriate, and the intended use. The utilization of the metric system is compulsory in Madagascar.

CONTACTS

For any information about standards or certification, BNM is the key contact (see address above)

TRADE AGREEMENTS

Madagascar is a signatory to the following regional and international agreements:

- 1964: United Nations Convention on Trade and Development (UNCTAD)

- 1992: Indian Ocean Commission. Since 1998, elimination of tariffs on goods originating from the COI countries.

- 1993: Common Market for East and Southern Africa (COMESA): Free Trade Area since 2000 and customs union expected in 2010

- 1995: World Trade Organization (WTO)

- 2000: Cotonou Agreement

- 2005: SADC. Free Trade Area since 2008

- 2009: Interim Economic Partnership Agreement with the European Union.

FOREIGN TRADE

Madagascar historically has remained outside the mainstream of African affairs, although it is an active member of theOrganization of African Unity and the Non-Aligned Movement.In contrast to former President Ratsiraka's "all points" policystressing ties with socialist and radical regimes, includingNorth Korea, Cuba, Libya, and Iran, President Albert Zafy hasexpressed his desire for diplomatic relations with all countries.Early in his tenure, he established formal ties with South Korea and sent emissaries to Morocco. Active relationships have been maintained with Europe, especially France, Germany, and Switzerland, as well as with Russia, Japan, India, and China.

FOREIGN EXCHANGE

Foreign currency may be imported into Madagascar without restriction (provided that a written declaration is made to customs).
Local currency may not leave Madagascar with non-residents except FMG 25000.
Exchange Control is administered by the External Finance Office of the General Directorate of the Treasury.
The Floating System is in operation.
Some approval authority for exchange control has been delegated to authorised intermediaries, and all exchange transactions relating to foreign countries must be effected through such intermediaries.
No restrictions apply to the opening of credit or the means of financing imports; importers may use their own resources, borrow from the banking system, or avail themselves of external loans including suppliers' credits, to finance imports.

DOUBLE TARIFFS

Non-residents are quoted prices generally in French francs with an exchange rate that works out to an FMG figure about twice the price paid by residents. It may be worthwhile to note at this point that the average income of residents is $250 a year.

EXPORTS

(1992)--$328 million: vanilla, sugar, cloves,shrimp, chromite, graphite. Major export markets--France, U.S.,Germany, Japan, Singapore, Italy. Imports (1992)--$547 million:consumer goods, foodstuffs, crude oil, machinery and vehicles,iron and steel. Major suppliers--France, Iran, Japan, Germany, Saudi Arabia, Hong Kong..

IMPORTS

Labradorite is a type of feldspar displaying a unique labradoresence. The presence of feldspar lamellae gives rise to the Schiller effect, an iridescence due to light refraction.

Schiller is best developed in labradorites creating a lovely color play in shades of green, blue, gold and yellow. The color play is iridescent like the feathers of a peacock or the Northern Lights.

Each Labradorite item that we offer is unique in its coloration. In addition, they are hand carved, so the sizes listed are approximate. The quality of the carving and polish is especially fine.

These objects are all made from Petrified Wood found in Madagascar.

No, we haven't identified the kinds of trees these came from - scientists haven't even succeeded in doing that with all the existing trees in Madagascar!

These beautiful Star Rose Quartz spheres from Madagascar have naturally occurring 6 ray stars.

The stars are best seen in direct sunlight or through the use of a single ray of light.

The Ammonites from Madagascar are members of an extinct order of mollusks. These creatures died out about 65 million years ago.

They are related to the modern day squid, octopus and chambered nautilus.

The ammonites found in Madagascar are unique because of their well-defined chambers.

We also offer beautiful Madagascar Quartz Crystals. They are in matrix as shown, and are available in two different sizes.

WORLD BANK ROLE

There are 18 active International Development Association (IDA) projects in Madagascar and current commitments are US$629 million. About 33 percent of projects are in the social sectors, 18 percent in infrastructure, 8 percent in energy, 7 percent in agriculture sector, 7 percent in the private sector, 5 percent in environment, and 22 percent are multi-sector.

The International Finance Corporation (IFC) has committed $11.3 million to seven operations in Madagascar, and some new operations are under consideration. In the 1998-1999 financial year,

IFC focused on projects in hotel and tourism, energy, agribusiness, telecommunications, air cargo transport, and export-oriented activities. IFC's advisory program is likely to focus on privatization in the telecommunications, tourism and banking sectors.

The Multilateral Investment Guarantee Agency (MIGA) has three guarantees in the tourism sector for a gross exposure of US$1.4 million. Once the project is constructed, the total amount of foreign direct investment facilitated is expected to reach US$117.6 million. It also has two active applications for Madagascar for a total investment potential of US$41 million in the oil and gas sector.

The World Bank Institute (WBI) organized two regional workshops in which a Malagasy delegation took part. The themes that were the most popular with the Malagasy were utility regulation and competition in telecom sector.

TRADE GENERAL

Import licences are not required, except for a short list of goods which are subject to administrative control for security or health reasons.
Before importing, importers are required to submit their "Fiche Statistique d'Importation" (Import Data File) with the proforma invoice to their bank. A copy must be submitted to the Ministry of Commerce.
Madagascar is a contracting party of the Harmonised Commodity Description and Coding System.
Customs duties and import taxes are assessed on an ad valorem basis; the basis for valuation is C.I.F..
Samples having no commercial value are entered free of duty.
Valuable samples may be admitted temporarily free under deposit or bond or bank guarantee.
South African businessmen are encouraged to visit the island personally to re-initiate contact.
According to the financial law of 1999, there are four types of duties
- Import tax (TI): 0 - 25%

- Custom fees (DD): 0 - 25%
- Consumption tax (DA): 0 - 10%
- Value Added Tax (VAT): 20%The government has eliminated most quantitative restrictions on imports.

Director General of Customs - Tel: (0926120) 2222916, Fax: (09261 20) 2264680

DEVELOPMENT

Multilateral and bilateral donors, including the World Bank and the IMF, are active in Madagascar. Under Bank and IMF-sponsored economic reforms, stabilization has been satisfactory, and donor coordination is strong. The transport sector, education financing, rural development, locust control, and post-cyclone reconstruction projects are instances where there is multiple donor participation. Progress in structural reforms and debt relief during the year will be key to ensure that Madagascar can adopt a high growth path conducive to poverty reduction.

MADAGASCAR INTERNATIONAL TRADE

TOURISM

The tourism sector is quite well structured because of several existing associations, which are organized by function and national scope. Tourism in Madagascar specializes more and more on niche markets based on its natural resources. Madagascar is a key destination, thanks to the endemic fauna and flora (respectively 80 and 90%), 70% of the lemurs species in the world, 1.000 of orchids species, 46 classified sites, its other tourist attractions are resort sites (thanks to its 5 000 km of coast with many beaches and bays) and the diverse culture of its population.

Tourism indicators show a constant growth over the years and Madagascar will benefit for being remote from international political and health burdens (terrorism and SARS)
For the high season for this year 2003, 9 flights are scheduled weekly to Europe, 3 on the national airline company AIR MAD, 4 with AIR FRANCE and 2 with CORSAIR.

Madagascar has:

- 5 national parks: Montagne d'ambre, Isalo, Mantadia, Ranomafana, Mananara nord
- Special reserves of which the main ones are: Andasibe, Bezaha mahafaly, Ankarana, Sainte Marie, Nosy Mangabe
- 11 integral natural reserves
- 70% of the world's lemur species
- 1000 species of orchids
- 146 classified monuments and sites, 27 restored
- 125 unclassified sites and monuments
- 23 special reserves for the protection of animal and plant species
- 6 hunting reserves and 2 private reserves
- A high endemic rate for batrachians, reptiles and butterfly species
- An extra ordinary wealth of crafts
- A botanical treasure of dry spiny deserts

Sector potentialities and opportunities

Without any doubts, Madagascar possesses the most exceptional fauna and flora of this part of the world when one considers the incredible number of endemic species - 80% for the fauna and 90% for the flora. This fact, combined with a unique climatic diversity, gives country an exceptional tourism potential. The number of visitors is estimated at 150,000 per year, but this only represents one tenth of the total number of visitors of the south western part of the Indian Ocean.

Madagascar has around 5,000 kilometres of coastlines, a part of which is protected by coral reefs with rich aquatic fauna, to the delight of divers and ordinary swimmers. Inland, the diversity in climates, cultures and landscapes, combined with an exceptional bio-diversity, make Madagascar a unique destination: island-continent, it provides the eager traveller with wide open spaces with great opportunities for adventure and discovery. Referred to as nature sanctuary, Madagascar is a paradise for botanists, paleontologists and primatologists.

The seaside tourist resorts will also soon be launched on the market. At this day, Madagascar's capacity to receive tourists is still not enough; the coming of new investors will give the possibility to increase the attraction to the destination.

FOODSTUFF

Madagascar is a country with great agricultural potential. The food sector is the heart of the Malagasy economy. Large areas of usable land are still unexploited (there is 9.5 million hectares of usable land).

80% of the population is involved in the agricultural sector and in 2000, contributed to 31.8% of Gross Domestic Product (Source: Madagascar Central Bank). The country has an important agri-business potential taking into account the enormous agricultural potential. 26% of all formal Malagasy industrial businesses accounted for in the agricultural sector.

Agri-business is the most important branch since it represents more than 37% of the total industrial production. For "canned and vegetable" products, Madagascar is the main exporter in the Indian Ocean region. Other products also represent a potential for export, such as green beans, green pepper, pickled mushrooms, frozen vegetables... Ddry vegetables are also part of the main exporting products in this sector.

Below are some statistics on export trends.

(Quantities are expressed in thousands of metric tone)

products	2003	2004	2005
Sugar	1.70	8.24	6.56
Vanilla	1.04	0.47	1.7
Cloves	15.75	12.40	9.60
Pepper	1.05	1.20	1.32
Prawns	8.09	6.13	3.68
Cocoa	0.56	4.25	1.64
Coffee	7.14	7.07	5.95

(Source: The Central Bank of Madagascar)

Sector potentials and opportunities

Madagascar's diversified climates and relief offer a range of agricultural possibilities. Indeed, each area of the Great Island is characterized by a climate favorable for any kind of cultivation which do not require a cold climate below O°C.

The Malagasy soils represent significant arable surfaces: 5 000.000 ha constituting 8,4% of the total of the national territory.

FISHERIES SECTOR

Madagascar, as an island, possesses a large fishing zone and various "deposits" seawater and freshwater, with 5,000 kilometres of coastline, 2 miles of continental marine plateau, 2,000 km2 of lakes, rivers and several aquaculture centres.

The Government of Madagascar is very keen on developing the fishing sector because of its economic (source of foreign currency), social role (employment creation), and a development factor (through the increase revenues to local communities and balanced nutrition of the population).

The fishing sector can be divided into three fields:

1- "Inland fishing", consists of freshwater (streams and lakes) fishing which is mainly traditional,
2- "Coastal fishing", consists of seawater fishing, which is divided into three fishing categories based on the technique used: Industrial fishing, on a Large scale, by specialized Businesses with professional material; Fishing as family businesses and fishermen's associations with small motored boats not exceeding 50 horsepower. The most common fishing technique used is the trawl,
Traditional fishing (by foot or by paddling boat).

3- "Aquaculture", which is further divided into two types of cultures depending on the environment, seawater and freshwater: The marine aquaculture today the main culture is the shrimp. The branch also includes the culture of sea cucumber and sealgae.

The freshwater fish farming

Production

Items	1997	1998	1999	2012
Inland fishing	30 000	30 000	30 000	30 000
Coastal fishing	85 841	84 904	87 970	87 435
Aquaculture	5 127	4 503	5 087	7 241
Total Production	120 968	119 407	123 057	124 676

Source: Ministry of Fishing and Seafood resources

Fishing production

1996	2012
118 877	142 193 t

Sector opportunities and potentialities:

The fishing sector presents many potential and opportunities according to the following points:

- Many waters still not enough exploited
- Possibility to triple the aquaculture production in the next 10 years
- Large water ways in the country, favourable to the culture of other species like trout
- The production of tuna still needs to be improved (10 000 Tons per year only)
- The emergence of the culture of marine algas

Madagascar has quickly adopted a textile culture with the increasing arrival of foreign investors, attracted by investment incentives. In 2001, the manufacturing export oriented firms under the EPZ regime, were 220, all sectors included, but the garment industry is dominant. The search for an increasing vertical integrated textile industry remains a challenge for Madagascar. Production of cotton seeds, yarn and fabric are declining though many areas are available for such activities.

The development of raw material production is necessary for the success of the manufacturing sector and textiles in particular. Indeed, regarding the spinning and textiles manufacturing, the units equipped themselves with efficient tools and techniques to ensure a quality of competitive products on the international market.

The EPZ regime boosted the development of textile industry in Madagascar, production capacity was increased to supply the American market. Moreover the AGOA reinforcedthe competitiveness of the products coming from Madagascar. AGOA provides duty-free, and quota free access to the US market. Important US brand names are now transferring their orders to the country to get more benefit from its competitiveness. Among others GLORIA VANDERBILT, VICTORIA□S SECRET, GAP, LIZ CLAIRBORNE, THE LIMITED are some brands produced here. Textiles have become the engine for development in Madagascar.

Sector potentialities and opportunities:

Existing of local or proximity supplier

In the region of the Indian Ocean, one of the main fabric producers (COTONA of the Group

SOCOTA) is established in Madagascar, and possesses one international branch in Mauritius. This one has benefited of 8.5 million USD as a loan in 2001, to modernize and replace its equipments. This company plays an important role in supplying the Malagasy EPZ companies. The other supplying countries in terms of fabrics and accessories are: Mauritius, France, east Europe, Taiwan, Hong Kong, Pakistan.

AGOA Opportunity

In the framework of the AGOA, Madagascar benefits of a special regulation for garments items, at the intention of the Less Advanced Countries. This regulation offers access to the US market with exemption of duties on textile items, wherever the origin of fabrics and yards may be until September 30, 2004, and then from countries benefiting AGOA.

A skilled labour at a competitive cost

Thanks to structured development policy, the Malagasy textile sector benefits of a skilled labour, especially by the establishment of a specialized training centre, and as wage cost still competitive in the world.

A tax-free regime

The free tax regime offers many advantages:
- a fiscal regime with low rate including total exoneration on profit taxes during a period of 2 to 15 years, then a fixed rate of 10% for the following years.
- a custom regime insuring tax exemption when importing, free access to currencies, and transfer
- relaxing regulations on employment, visa and exchange matters.

ESSENTIAL OILS

In this sector, Madagascar has been known for its traditional essential oils such as Ylang ylang, clove and Palmarosa essence. It is only more recently that Malagasy producers have begun producing and exporting new types of essential oils, for example geranium, niaouli and helichryse. This new interest for non-traditional essential oils has led to the development of the sector for the past three years, especially with the support of USAID and UNIDO.

The essential oils field is emergent. It constitutes even one of the economy's country pillars from the entry of currencies it generates and the number of created jobs "80 to 90% of the products are exported. The remaining 20% are intended for the domestic market".

Because of the insufficiency of the transformation units (perfume industry, aromatherapy, the foodstuffs one...), most of the exported products are raw products.

To show the quality and the origin of the natural and organic products of Madagascar (cloves, ginger, pepper, cinnamon...), the professional traders association in agri-business (PRONABIO) is in a phase of launching the label "natiora" (test period of 6 months) during which the analyses in laboratories will be carried out in parallel from the local laboratories partners and those of the Rutgers University of New Jersey.

More than 3 tons of essential oils of cloves per month, 1 ton of ravintsara per month, 2-3 tons of niaouli, these are in one hand the needs for the firms and foreign companies.

Biological exports of products

Products	1999 (kg)	2012 (kg)
Essential oil Ylang Ylang	23 190	3 500

Essential oil Niaouli	1 600	825
Essential oil Ravitsara	980	725
Essential oil stems of clove	645	-
Other Huilles essential	1 205	2 006

Sector potentials and opportunities
Madagascar, from its climate, presents an enormous potentiality in terms of essential oils. One can count a score of plants from which can be extracted oils or oleoresins. More than 35 varieties of aromatic and medicinal plants are exploited and transformed by the traders.

In addition, with an useful surface area corresponding to 11,8% of the country's surface, the potential of the agricultural sector (export culture) is still important. Moreover with the participation of a population whose labour is among the less expensive, the products are competitive on the international market.

MINING

The global objective of the project is to assist the Malagasy government in implementing strategy to accelerate the sustainable development of the mining sector and contribute to reducing poverty in Madagascar by improving management and transparency of mineral resources, particularly pertaining to traditional and small-scale mining activities.

Specific objectives of the Project :

- Reinforcing transparency and governance in the mining sector.
- Promoting institutional reforms essential for the community based management of mineral resources.
- Promoting private investments and added value in the mining sector.
- Fast and sustainable development of the mining sector and increase of economic spin-offs for populations within the framework of fighting against poverty.
- Improving natural resources management to prevent deterioration in the environment.

The different main actions to be considered by PGRM in order to fulfill the aforementioned objectives regroup :

- Improvement and application of the legal and regulatory framework
- Implementation of the community based management of crisis and rush situation of precious substances
- Establishment of a national capacity to certify and control gems quality and improve their marketing through the creation of the "Institut de Gemmologie de Madagascar" (IGM)
- Establishment of a trade center (purchase/sale) of precious stones and a one-stop-shop to facilitate export formalities.
- Promotion of a vocational focus to lapidary artisans to improve added value of gems production
- Reinforcement of the private sector entities
- Pursue of institutional reforms to improve the sector administration and the community based management of mineral resources
- Reinforcement of the decentralised management of the environment
- Creation of the Agency for the Promotion of the Mining Sector to improve the ability of the Government to attract private investments
- Support to traditional mining sector through the extension of services and a small donation program
- Reinforcement and update of the geological infrastructure through the realisation of the airborne

geophysical surveys, geological and geochemical surveys, synthesis and valuation researches of mineral resources
- Establishment of a Base for the Promotion of the Governance of Mineral Resources, an unit specialised in geological infrastructure operation for promotion activities

HANDICRAFT

The Malagasy craft industry is characterized by its diversity, as well as in its form, production as its geographical situation. It is more than ever present in the everyday life of the Malagasy and knows even a regular expansion.

One distinguishes generally, three categories of craft industry production in various forms:

- The craft industry which produces utility goods representing basketries, weaving, leather, wood and metal work, foodstuff transformation, the paper work, the manufacture of charcoal, the brickyard, tile-works, the pottery, mirror manufacture, the manufacture of articles from greasy substance, bakery, confectionery etc.);
- The service craft industry which is constituted of mechanical reparation, electric domestic appliances, watches reparation and audio-visual appliances, hairdresser, etc.);
- The art craft industry gathers the sculpture, marquetry, standard lamp, jewelry, the work of horn, ceramic pottery, painting, gold silver plated, etc.).

The craft industry contributes in the export increase and diversity. It takes part in the satisfaction of the essential need adapted to the purchasing power for the rural and urban population, and brings complementary incomes to the peasants and underprivileged population.

For a certain time, with the support of the national and international assistance structures, the sector tries to be organized while gathering in professional associations.
- UAMA (union des artisans Malagasy)
- FEDNAM (federation nationale de l'artisanat Malagasy)
-GROUPROAMA (groupement des professionnels des artisans de Madagascar)
- FIMPITAMA (groupement descommerçcants de produits artisanaux Malagasy)
- UNAPM (union des artisans d'arts plasticiens de Madagascar)
- GAAA (groupement des artisans d'arts d'Antsirabe)
- ATA (Chambres des métiers d'Antananarivo)
- Madagascar Magic Fingers

It should be noted that other associations with limited scale also exist

Sector potentialities and opportunities

Handicraft is integrated into the Malagasy culture. Indeed, it is an activity of master key time and passion that has assumed for the last 10 years an economic and professional dimension. The structuring of the trade of craftsman, the development of training programs and growing position on the international markets reinforce the image of this diversified craft industry. The availability of the various raw materials (available locally, silk, "landy be", raffia, sisal, cotton, banana leaves, horns...) widens the variety of item possible such as baskets, bags, shoes, woodwork, jewelry

Handicraft clusters will contribute to improving the production system. Malagasy craft products are eligible for AGOA benefits.

Madagascar has many natural resources as well of mineral origin, vegetable as animal which show the importance and the diversity of the craft productions.

The majority of craft technologies can be implemented easily.
The craft industry can create a high number of jobs.

INFRASTRUCTURE

Air transport

The 12 main airports of the island are managed by ADEMA (Airports of Madagascar) whose ADP Management (Airport of Paris) is shareholder to a total value of 33%. The attribution of deputy management of the international airport of Antananarivo is currently on study.
In addition to the national company Air Madagascar, two companies ensure the connection Madagascar-Europe, Air France and Corsair. The domestic flights are ensured by Air Madagascar only. For the peak season this year 2003, 9 flights are scheduled weekly (4 flights on Air France, 3 on Air Madagascar and 2 on Corsair).

Rail transport

The Malagasy rail network possesses 870km road, but the obsolescence of the fixed infrastructures and the material is an obstacle for the development of the traffic. The evolution of the traffic has been falling for ten years. The number of travellers passed from nearly 2 million in 1990 to less than 100 000 in 2000 and the tonnage of the transported goods decreased by 90%, passing over the same period from 597.000 to 54.000 tons.

The northern network was allotted in concession to COMAZAR Group in 1997. The created local company, MADARAIL is supposed to exploit the Northern network for 25 years with an investment program (road and material) estimated at 35 M USD, to which the European Investment Bank will take a significant share. The concession contract will be finalized in second half-year period 2003.

The southern network will be subjected to a significant rehabilitation (in particular Manakara-Fianarantsoa) through the World Bank finance. The USAID recently intervened for reparation of cyclonic damages.

Road transport

Madagascar's road system is 25,500 kilometres long and consists of 5,500 kilometres of asphalted roads and 20,000 kilometres of secondary roads. One of the present government's main priorities is the road construction.

Road transport is very fluid on the main axes. There exists an important fleet of private merchandise haulers and passengers transporters.

Sector potentialities and opportunities

Madagascar's economic future will essentially depend on the transport sector. The current President of Madagascar has emphasized on several occasions that a better transport system will contribute to the development of the country. To this effect, the government has established the following objectives:

- The decentralization of construction and maintenance work;
- The maintenance of a 15,000 kilometres priority network linking the major economic regions.

It is obvious that rapid development cannot be achieved if certain regions of the island remain isolated.

NET & TECHNOLOGY

The development of data processing firms was included in the EPZ success from the beginning of the nineties: firms specialized in data-processing or subcontracting data-processing work. This sector, between 1998 and 2000, experienced a growth rate in export of about 30% (US $ 4 million turnover in 1999). In 2001, 65 firms were operational all over Madagascar among which 16 were operating under the EPZ regime. They crated 3 000 jobs in Antananarivo alone.

Telecommunication

The telecommunication system has been Significantly modernized. All the major cities are served by automatic exchanges and all international communications are automatic. The national telecommunication company TELMA going through a process of privatisation Competition in this sector has become Increasingly important since the establishment of many mobile phone networks. Regarding the phone subscription in 2001, one counted approximately 50.000 subscribers. 3 private mobile companies share the market of the mobile telephony (Intercel, Madacom, Orange) which one counted approximately 150.000 subscribers in 2001. Several companies ensure the Internet service supply. One counts more than 10.000 subscribers to Internet. The cyberspaces grow in Antananarivo and open gradually in provinces, all that generates a sales turnover of 100 million US dollars

Currently, there are 11 companies working in networks, 11 service providers and approximately 70 suppliers of terminal equipments.

Sector opportunities and potentialities:

- The necessary investments are not heavy financially
- the local labor profits from a good training given by the existing of a University specialized in Computer Sciences.
- the small training centres in software are numerous.
- the activity lends itself to the Export Processing Zone Company in Technology (EFI) and profiting from incentive measurements.
- the labour cost makes Madagascar a competitive contractor.

OPERATING PROCEDURES, STANDARDS OF ACCOMMODATION FACILITIES SUBJECT TO CLASSIFICATION AND QUALIFICATION OF MANAGERS.

Article One: Under Article 65 of Decree No. 2001-027 of 10 January 2001, this regulation sets out the modalities of operation, standards of accommodation facilities subject to classification and qualification of responsible.

Are considered accommodations subject to filing hotels, motels, ecolodge relay and defined by the provisions of Articles 41, 42, 43 and 48 of the Decree.
Section 2: Pursuant to Article 7 of Decree No. 2001-027 of 10 January 2001 cited above, obtaining a prior opinion of the Minister of Tourism or authority to whom he delegates his power is mandatory.

The implementation of ecolodge should respect the provisions in the specifications which may be established for this purpose, the specifics of each area.
Rule 3: Before the operation of any establishment, an application for authorization to open shall be filed with the Tourism Authority having jurisdiction over the location of the institution which issues a certificate of posting.

Article 4: Provisions common to all these institutions appear in Annex I to this Order.

Article 5: hotels, motels, ecolodge and relays, are classified in categories ranging from one (01) to three (03) "RAVINALA" and one (01) to five (05) "STARS".
Hotels, motels, ecolodge relay and ordered "RAVINALA" are those whose equipment and the maintenance condition correspond to the standards set out in Annex II of this Order.
Hotels, motels, ecolodge and relay classified as "STARS" are those facilities, the maintenance condition and level of staff qualifications match the standards set out in Annex III of this Order.

Article 6: The application of classification of the establishment must be filed simultaneously with the initial request from the Tourism Authority having jurisdiction over the location of the institution which issues a certificate of posting.
Article 7: The standard models of demand for notice, authorization for the opening and grading as well as the list of files accompanying those applications are appended to the Decree No. 4889/2001. / MINTOUR of 19 April 2001 establishing the composition of application files for review prior to project construction, improvement and expansion of accommodation facilities and / or catering as well as records request permission opening and grading.
Article 8: are and remain abrogated all previous provisions contrary to those of this Order.
Article 9: This Order shall be registered, published in the Official Gazette of the Republic and communicated wherever necessary.
Done at Antananarivo, 19 April 2001

THE MINISTER OF TOURISM Razafimanjato Blandin

ANNEX I THE ADOPTED No. 4902/2001 / THE MINTOUR April 19, 2001

PROVISIONS COMMON Atousa ESTABLISHMENTS ACCOMMODATION SUBJECT TO CLASSIFICATION

The accommodations subject classification must comply with regulations defined by:
- Law No. 90-033 of 21 December 1990 the Malagasy Environment Charter;
- Ordinance No. 60-167 of 03 October 1960 on the Town Planning;
- Ordinance No. 62-072 of 29 September 1962 Consolidation of Legislative Texts on Public

Health;
- Decree No. 89-017 of 18 January 1989 establishing the work of water and sanitation;
- Decree No. 99-954 of 15 December 1999 on the conformity with the investment environment;
- Interministerial Circular No. 98/001 MINATV / HBD / MI of 12 June 1998 on the management of urban space.

These institutions must:
- Be implemented according to safety standards ensuring adequate protection of customers;
- Be designed to the specifics of each region;
- Be organized according to a plan for internal circulation, if necessary, evacuation of people living easy;
- Designed and organized to ensure safety, including connection to a collective system of sewerage, sewage and storm or have clean equipment performing the same function, and be served by a system collective disposal of garbage and solid waste or dispose of specific

equipment, safe and away from the institution, which perform this function.

ANNEX II
THE ADOPTED No. 4902/2001 / THE MINTOUR April 19, 2001

STANDARDS OF ACCOMMODATION ESTABLISHMENTS FOR THE CATEGORY RAVINALA

The accommodations are listed RAVINALA coherent sets of physical facilities and services provided to customers.

I - THE COMMON OPEN FOR GUESTS
They include:
1 - Entrance
2 - Reception
3 - The waiting room
4 - The corridors and aisles serving different rooms and areas open to customers
5 - The breakfast room
6 - The sanitary and other equipment.
Establishments classified Ravinala must have an effective protection against insects and pests
Designation 1

· I - THE COMMON OPEN TO GUESTS
ENTER · It must be clearly identifiable, specific to the hotel and drive directly to the reception · It must be well lit.

RECEPTION · It includes a counter and equipment (lockers or other), not accessible to customers, where the keys and messages are deposited.
A room in which the customers arriving at or departing may deposit his luggage
WAITING ROOM · a health facility in a perfect state of maintenance and cleanliness at any time of day should be installed near the waiting room. · The waiting room must be equipped with seats

Minimum Area:

8m2 8m2 10m2

· A telephone available to the client must be installed in the room. · The waiting room should have a small lounge equipped with armchairs.

AREAS OF OUTSTANDING CUSTOMER · The corridors must have a width according to safety standards (minimum 1.20 m) and sufficient light leaving no areas remain obscure. · Corridors must be properly ventilated and clean permanent. · The ladder must be equipped with a handrail. Its width must conform to safety standards (minimum 1.20 m). It must have adequate lighting.
BREAKFAST ROOM A small room to serve breakfast is mandatory.

HEALTH AND OTHER EQUIPMENT near bedrooms are not equipped with private toilet and shower must be installed: - A toilet with toilet paper and a shower in perfect condition and cleanliness permanent for every five rooms .- The shower must be installed in a cabin that can be completely closed from the inside and having a separate division for undress.

II - THE LOCAL PRIVATE USE
ROOMS AND FACILITIES Minimum Number of rooms:
6 July 8

Minimum area (excluding health) of the unit available to each customer:
Single room: 8m2

Room for 2 people:
10 m2 10 m2 12 m2

All rooms must be equipped with: - a sink - a mirror - a lamp - a tablet effects of personal grooming - 1 outlet.

All rooms must be linked to the receipt by a ringing call
A telephone is required per floor

A window opening onto the outside is required for proper ventilation.
Lighting should be sufficient and allow playback at any point of the room.

The minimum installation around each bungalow is to:
20 m2 20 m2 25 m2

BATHROOM and WC, the proportion of rooms to be equipped with private bathroom and WC is:
10% 20% 30%

DETAILS OF BATHROOM AND WC suite or shared · a window opening to the outside or a ventilation system should permit the escape of water vapor or odor. · Lighting should be sufficient.

· The area of the bathroom should allow convenient use of facilities: - private bathroom: 2 m - shared bathroom, cabin included: 3 sqm · The area of private or shared toilet is 2 sqm · The walls and floors must be designed so as not to be damaged by moisture or by the regular use of disinfectant or detergent.

THE ELEMENTS OF STORAGE Each room must have a closet or a wardrobe with hangers and shelves in sufficient numbers. The volume and surface storage must be sufficient to allow the storage of items of clothing.

THE FURNITURE Each room must be furnished: - a bed of a size less than 90 x 200 cm for individual clients and 140 x 200 cm for double beds - allowing a table of write and a chair - bed linen regularly maintained.
The presence of a wastebasket in every room is required.
The bedside lamps are mandatory

RESERVED TO THE COMMON SERVICE institution must have: - one (1) local to store the products and maintenance equipment - one (1) premises for storing sheets, blankets and other linen.

SERVICES DIRECTLY RELATED TO THE SERVICE OF THE ESTABLISHMENT OF ACCOMMODATION - The home must be provided by competent staff speak at least one foreign language .- The display near the reception area, specific operating characteristics of the institution must be in Malagasy and French .- The written information in the rooms on the property (rates, institutional rules for clients, meal times) must be written in Malagasy and French .- The First aid services are required including the existence of a medicine box containing emergency instruments, objects, dressing and essential drugs .- The daily room and bathroom is required .- The supply sheets, pillowcases, blankets, soap, towels (size less than 70 x 50 cm) and toilet paper is required .- The change of sheets and towels should be made to each guest's departure and all three nights when it is several nights in the same room.

SAFETY - The equipment against fire are required at each level. They should be kept in excellent operating condition at all times .- outings and / or fire escapes should be provided and their locations must be clearly identified .- The security establishment must be permanently maintained.

STAFF - to be serviced by a competent staff, good looking and dressed in outfits appropriate .- The institution must be managed by a skilled executive.

APPENDIX III THE ADOPTED No. 4902/2001 / THE MINTOUR April 19, 2001
GRADING STANDARDS OF ACCOMMODATION ESTABLISHMENTS SUBJECT TO THE CLASSIFICATION OF CLASS STAR

The accommodation establishments classified as "STAR" are coherent sets of physical facilities and services provided to customers.

I - THE COMMON OPEN FOR GUESTS
They include:
1. The entrance
2. The reception
3. The local host and shows,
4. Traffic areas (corridors, lifts, walkways, ...) serving various rooms and areas open to customers,
5. The breakfast room,
6. The garages or parking.

The accommodation establishments classified as "Star" should have an effective protection against insects and parasites.

For residential homes for categories 4 and 5 stars, architectural design should allow people with physical disabilities to access the hotel entrance, reception and all public areas at the same level as thereof. This requirement is desired for other categories.

Designation 1 STAR 2 STARS 3 STARS 4 STARS 5 STARS

COMMON They must possess: - heating equipment or air conditioning to ensure in closed rooms, regardless of the season and time, a temperature between 18 and 25 ° C - a device to to ensure, in case of breakdown or failure of electricity distribution networks or water: § minimum electrical service for lighting move, § elevator service, § equipment to alleviate the temporary impairment of utilities water and wastewater disposal, stormwater and solid waste and garbage

ENTRY The entry whose size and interior are related to the category of the establishment must be clearly identifiable, specific to the institution and lead directly to the reception. It should benefit the whole hour of a exterior and interior lighting for reading at any point of the room.
RECEIVING It must be visible from the entry and include: - A counter on which it is possible to write and behind which stands permanently at least one person - Equipment (lockers or other), not accessible to customers, where the keys and messages must be left on deposit - A confined space in which customers arriving at or departing luggage may file .- A safe where guests may deposit their valuables in the except the category "1 Star"

THE PREMISES AND HOME SHOW institutions must have local or host salons, enabling customers to meet and to receive visitors other than in the rooms.
The minimum area due depends on the number of rooms and varies between the limits indicated below:
10m ² 20m ² 35m2 35m2 35m2
Beyond 10 rooms increase of 1m ² per additional bedroom Beyond 10 rooms increase 2m ² per additional room

Over 25 rooms minimum area required 25 sq.m. 30 rooms minimum area required 40 sq.m. 55 rooms minimum area required 80 sq.m. 95 rooms minimum area required: 120 sq.m. 135 rooms area required: 160 sq.m.

The local host or lounges should be provided with seating of a quality commensurate with the classification

The local host or shows must have a television.

TRAFFIC AREA OF THE CUSTOMER - The corridors must be a width according to safety standards (1.20 m minimum) included in the same block - Aisles should be designed to ensure the absence of sludge and puddles for detached housing units - The staircase must follow the safety standards (minimum width of 1.20 m, installation of handrails, non-skid system) - The circulation area should be sufficiently illuminated 24 hours 24 from mannered to leave only the dark areas - The area of movement must be properly ventilated, free of moisture and odors even transient.

The elevator, whose capacity must be commensurate with that of the institution. is required, once the property is built on more than:

Three floors (R 3) Two storey (R 2)

The corridors must be covered with carpet or other soundproofing materials
BREAKFAST ROOM Seats must be equal to half the number of persons to be accommodated in the rooms of the hotel.

COMMON HEALTH AND OTHER FACILITIES FOR COMFORT Implanted near the reception and accommodation: - Sanitary facilities should be in perfect condition and cleanliness at any time .- The importance of these health facilities varies depending on the number of rooms : separate toilet (men, women) with toilet paper, wash basins topped by a mirror with hot water from the 3-star, soap and equipment for dry hands .- A telephone communication system must be the provision of clientèle.A near bedrooms: - If the hotel has rooms not equipped with private toilet (1 and 2 Stars), a toilet in perfect condition and cleanliness at all hours for every 4 bedrooms with toilet paper is required .- If the hotel has rooms not equipped with phone (1 and 2

Stars), a telephone for every six rooms is required. These positions are located in areas of outstanding rooms with a minimum of one post per floor

PARKING GARAGES OR The ratio between the number of rooms and number of parking spaces or parking is presented as follows: 30% 50%

II - THE LOCAL PRIVATE USE

Designation 1 STAR 2 STARS 3 STARS 4 STARS 5 STARS
Each element of housing available to the customer includes the room itself, with a private bathroom and a private bathroom and fitted storage and an adequate furniture.
The rooms and their equipment

General Provisions The minimum number of bedrooms is:
October 20 suites including 10%

Windows opening to the outside, allowing good ventilation and equipped with a system to be dark in the room at any time of day are required.

An adequate light for reading at any point of the room, with control at the entrance of the room and head of the bed (back and forth) is required.

The layout of the room must provide sound insulation.

The installation of bells connecting rooms at the front desk phone if necessary.
The rooms and their equipment

GENERAL PROVISIONS A heating and / or air conditioning must maintain an indoor temperature between 18 and 25 ° C in all seasons and at any time. The operation of the air conditioner must not be a source of noise.

A telephone for communicating with the outside of the establishment in each chamber is required.
A safe must be installed in each room.
A TV set must be installed in each room.
The presence of a minibar in each room is required.

PART THE PRIVATE PROVISION OF EACH CLIENT minimum area of the unit is set as follows:
Single room
10 m^2 12 m^2 20 m^2 25 m^2 30 m^2
Room for two
12 m^2 14 m^2 25 m^2 30 m^2 35 m^2
Triple room
14 m^2 16 m^2 28 m^2 35 m^2 40 m^2

HOTELS IN THE CASE OF FORMS OF UNITS The minimum area of each room should conform to the surface presented to the line "unit available to each customer" above.
The installation surface surrounding each bungalow is set as follows
30 m^2 50 m^2 80 m^2 90 m^2 100m^2
The provision of bungalows and openings must preserve the privacy of customers

EQUIPMENT IN PRIVATE BATHROOM AND PRIVATE WC The proportion of rooms to be equipped with private bathroom and private WC in% is determined as follows:
Bathroom suite
50% 100%
Private WC
50% 75% 100%
The rooms without private shower room must have a sink fitted in the same way as the private shower room (see "Minimum Equipment for private bathrooms" below.)
THE ELEMENTS OF STORAGE The storage volumes and surfaces in the form of cabinet or wardrobe or closet or dressing room should be sufficient for storing luggage and effects.
The hangers and shelves in sufficient numbers must be available at least 3 per person.
THE FURNITURE The room must contain: - A bed of a size less than 90cm x 200cm for beds and 140cm x 200cm for the double beds. The bedding should be in good condition and in relation to the type of the school .- A table with chairs for writing and wastebasket bedside lamps-A-Rack Dressing table with mirror must be installed.

The bathrooms and toilets
DESIGN The window opening on the outside or the ventilation system must allow the evacuation of water vapor and odors.

Adequate lighting and power supplies comply with safety requirements are mandatory and no electrical outlet must be at hand when you're in the tub or shower.
The size of the bathroom must allow convenient use of facilities, including the smallest dimension is at least 1 meter.

Walls and floors must be designed so as not to be damaged by splashing water (tile or other materials made of materials specific to the regular use of disinfectant or detergent).

MINIMUM EQUIPMENT ROOM DEPRIVATION WATER Installing a sink dimensions at least equal to 55 cm x 35 cm, equipped with an overflow and a removable strainer is mandatory.
Beside the sink must be installed a mirror, a lamp, a shelf which can be deposited on the effects of personal toiletries, a socket with an indication of voltage and trash.
A shower tray with specific dimensions at least equal to 70 cm x 60 cm flexible tip apple or apple sets, curtains, skid-powered hot water and cold water must be installed.
The lavatory must be equipped with a mixing valve.
Installing a tub of hot water supplied is required in the bathrooms.
The sink and shower must be equipped with a faucet of hot and cold.
A hair dryer is required.

PRIVATE toilet installation with a toilet seat, flush toilets and septic system is required

III RESERVED TO DIFFERENT PARTS OF HOTEL SERVICES

These parts are made: premises for the storage, circulation areas and facilities reserved for staff.

Designation 1 STAR 2 STARS 3 STARS 4 STARS 5 STARS

STORAGE Must be provided: - A place to store the products and maintenance materials .- A room for storing linens necessary for the operation of the facility.

TRAFFIC ZONES For hotels built on several levels:

A staircase should be provided

A service elevator must be installed where there is a lift for customers.
RESERVES THE LOCAL PERSONNEL Must be isolated from operating areas
A man and a cloakroom cloakroom woman must be installed.
The complete bathroom (shower, toilet, washbasin).
IV - SERVICES RELATED TO THE FUNCTION OF ACCOMMODATION
Services directly related to the function of accommodation are made either in public areas or in rooms.

Designation 1 STAR 2 STARS 3 STARS 4 STARS 5 STARS
SERVICES IN THE COMMON The home must be provided 24 hours / 24 by staff speaking Malagasy and foreign language. The home must be insured by 24hours/24 staff speak at least two foreign languages in addition to the Malagasy.
Porters should be provided.

The hotel must provide a breakfast service.
The display of the operating characteristics of the specific property, near the reception, is required.

The service, first aid, such as emergency medical service must be provided.
Written information about the hotel (price, instructions in case of fire, information on telephone usage, numbers of all facilities) must be displayed.
The sign "do not disturb" should be provided.
Service Parking must be provided.
IN HOUSE SERVICES daily cleaning and sanitation must be done.
The towels should be changed daily. (Supplies of toilet soap).
Sheets, blankets must be changed after each departure and at least every three (03) night when the client is still several nights in the same bedroom.
The change of sheets, blankets should be every two nights.

ROOM SERVICE The provision of two towels not smaller than 80 cm x 50 cm plus one towel per person housed in the chamber is required.
Possibility to have breakfast in the rooms.
The daily change of sheets, towels supply two sizes of at least 80cm x 50cm and towel size at least equal to 120 cm x 80 cm per person accommodated in the room as well as soaps and other Home products are mandatory.

Writing paper with envelopes should be available in the rooms.
Wake-up calls at all hours must be ensured.
A fast food service from 5:00 until midnight must be ensured.
Room cleaning on request until midnight must be ensured.
The bathrobe, shower cap, bath foam, shaving cream, shampoo, deodorant waxing products must be available in the rooms.

V - SERVICES FOR FACILITATING THE STAY AND MAKE MORE PLEASANT
Designation 1 STAR 2 STARS 3 STARS 4 STARS 5 STARS

The service of washing and ironing it must be insured
SERVICES TO FACILITATE THE STAY AND MAKE A MORE PLEASANT express service washing, ironing and a postal service must be ensured:
- A tourist information service to be provided at the reception .- The transfer service to airport,

train station or the port must be provided .- Possibility to use in building or near a sports facility or fitness (swimming, sauna) - Allowing the establishment or near the services of a hairdresser or beauty salon .- A taxi must exist near the hotel.

VI - ADDITIONAL SERVICES FOR HOTELS, MOTELS AND RELAY
Designation 1 STAR 2 STARS 3 STARS 4 STARS 5 STARS

ADDITIONAL SERVICES Possibility of booking show

Possibility to find a newsstand

Ability to use in establishing or near: - meeting room - a business center
The institution must have: - a business center, a meeting room
Enable customers to access the facility or in close proximity to services: - a travel agency - a car rental with or without chauffeur.Sinon, the institution must provide customers necessary information and services related thereto.

VII - SECURITY
Designation 1 STAR 2 STARS 3 STARS 4 STARS 5 STARS

SAFETY equipment against fire are required at each level. They must be kept in excellent operating condition at all times.

Exits and fire escapes must be provided and their locations must be clearly indicated.
The security establishment must be permanently maintained.

VIII - PERSONNEL

Designation 1 STAR 2 STARS 3 STARS 4 STARS 5 STARS
QUALIFICATIONS The service must be provided by competent staff, good presentation, and having held the appropriate function.
The facility must be supervised by a qualified person, assisted by: - 1 head room - a responsible host - one responsible for lingerietous, with knowledge of the trade (2 years experience minimum)
The establishment must be managed by a highly qualified person having under his direction - an accommodation manager - responsible for a receipt - a floor manager - a manager's lingerie - a charge all qualified animation (holders diplomas or certificates in this area) and having at least 5 years experience, able to pass on their knowledge personnel.La presence of at least one employee who can speak fluent English or another language is required.
The establishment must be managed by a highly qualified person having under his direction: - hosting a director - responsible for a receipt - a chief seamstress - a housekeeper room - a charge animation - one count of entretien.tous highly skilled, able to provide training to staff and to recycle

IMPORTANT INFORMATION FOR TRADE AND BUSINESS ACTIVITY

PRODUCTS FOR EXPORT DEVELOPMENT

With its membership in a large number of regional (SADC, Indian Ocean Commission, COMESA) and global trade agreements (AGOA, Cotonou), Madagascar has the capability of becoming a viable investment and export location. Compared to other countries of similar revenue, Madagascar is relatively integrated into the global economy. Economic Priority Zones, referred to as Zones Franches, have raised the productivity levels of industries and facilitated the establishment of businesses especially with foreign capital.

FDI into Madagascar has steadily increased since the early nineties, with net inflows totaling USD 45 million in 2004 compared with USD 13 million in 2003 (see Figure 19). Estimates for 2005 suggest that inflows will amount to over USD 80 million. Most FDI originates from France, followed by Mauritius, China, luxembourg, Switzerland, Bermuda, Canada, the US, India and Sri lanka. In 2004, the total assets of foreign companies represented approximately USD 3 billion. The primary sectors receiving investment include textile and apparel, where Madagascar has seen an increase of Asian investment, seafood (shrimp), agro-industries and wood products. The Government of Madagascar is continuing to improve the country's investment climate as evidenced by current efforts to revise the Investment Code and to create an investment promotion agency, in order to develop its full FDI potential. Full ownership of land is permitted in Madagascar and most sectors are open to 100 percent foreign ownership. There are no restrictions on payments or transfers, though profits must be repatriated within 30 days.

FOCUS PRODUCTS

Below is a list of focus products, represented by the most current market assessment from EthnoPharm, and from our understanding of what Madgascar has to offer. One of the major purposes of this investigatory trip to Madgascar is to understand the various products and selling points of these products that might differentiate Malagasy products in the market, and therefore open up more opportunities. I expect there will be several other promising products that will emerge as our understanding of these products evolves, and we are able to communicate this effectively to potential buyers.

CINNAMON (CINNAMOMUM VERUM OR C. ZEYLANICUM)

There has been a tremendous amount of interest recently in cinnamon extracts due to recent studies that demonstrate cinnamon has promise as a potential treatment for type II diabetes. Cinnamon may lower blood sugar levels in hyperglycemic patients according to a few recent studies. Many new supplement products now contain cinnamon either as a stand-alone or in combination with other nutrients.

Cinnamon also seems to be enjoying a rediscovery in functional food markets in a wide variety of applications. Tea and coffee consumption is on the rise, and cinnamon is being used as a favorite flavor, spice and functional ingredient in many tea and coffee products. Other beverage applications, nutritional bars, cereals and confectionery products are all now potential functional food delivery systems and cinnamon is becoming more popular as a flavor as well as a potential functional nutrient or nutraceutical. In addition to its potential benefits in lowering blood sugar, flavonoids and essential oils found in cinnamon are considered to have anti-bacterial and preserving qualities, as well as to enhance immune system function.

Essential oil products from cinnamon are being used in perfumery, candle and potpourri applications, in essential oil blends for topical use or in vaporizers. In food, cinnamon is still a commonly used spice. Traditional markets for cinnamon, which include spice, flavor, potpourri, candle and other related industries seem to offer sustained growth opportunity for cinnamon. These markets will not be the direct focus of this report.

The problem with cinnamon is that it suffers from a problem many natural products suffer from; cinnamon is subject to commodity-like pressures where price is the driving force in the marketplace. Cinnamon can be sourced in many places; there are many different species and varieties used as cinnamon and consumers are unlikely going to be able to distinguish the many differences available in the market.

The challenge, and consequently, the opportunity, for Malagasy cinnamon producers is to distinguish themselves by offering a superior quality cinnamon, and/or a sustainable story (like a Fair-trade or community-supporting story). This might be accomplished by understanding then disseminating what species and varieties there are in Madagascar as well as how they differ from other places; the differences in aroma, flavor and chemical profiles. If there are small independent communities in Madagascar that produce cinnamon, then a community-supporting story and strategy may be created.

Sustainable cultivation and harvesting practices along with organic certification should help further differentiate cinnamon from that produced in other areas. There may be the possibility for growing or harvesting partnerships if we can package a quality and/or varietal difference along with organic, sustainable and fair-traded products. Should Madagascar not have the necessary means to manufacture (hot water extraction, filtration, concentration) and dry (spray, vacuum or belt dry) a cinnamon extract, a manufacturing partnership or supply relationship can be investigated with manufacturers, including ones that have the capacity to produce organically.

GREEN TEA (AND OTHER BUSH TEAS--ESP. ORGANIC OR COMMUNITY PRODUCED)

The market for green tea in the U.S. is in some respects mature, but still offers significant growth potential as new applications arise and consumer awareness to the benefits of green tea continue to increase. Most of the green tea consumed in the U.S. comes from China, South East Asia and India. There are many products derived from green tea, but most are presented as either extracts (for supplement and functional food applications) or in beverages, many of which have functional claims.

There may be a niche market to supply green tea (cut and sift) for use in beverage applications (mostly tea products). However, there would have to be a distinguishing quality to green tea, like a unique and desirable flavor or aroma profile or if it is certified organic and produced in a sustainable manner (or socially responsible manner).

There may be further opportunities to develop brewed extracts of green tea in Madagascar, and either ship concentrates (which would require preserving) or soluble dry extracts (which would require drying capabilities). This of course, is contingent on available processing capabilities within country. Again, partnership or supply programs may be considered if there are distinguishing properties (aroma, flavor, organic certification) to the green tea produced in Madagascar.

Green tea is also a commodity, coming from fairly low value producing nations like China, which means that it is even more important to develop and promote the distinguishing qualities and properties of Malagasy green tea.

Another area of opportunity is in other tea products. There may be a market for tea and beverage herbs, other than tea (Camellia sinensis), should there be a convincing history of local or traditional use, an interesting flavor and aroma, as well as any distinguishing or health properties. An example of this might be Voafotsy (*Aphloia theaformis*), a tea that has an apparently rich tradition of use in Madagascar. Though little is known in the

U.S. about Voafotsy or other types of teas, an educational project might be considered, to tell the story and tradition of other tea consumption in Madagascar. This kind of effort is likely to take some time to develop and may be beyond the scope of the work in this series of reports. However, there are many companies that have expressed interest in such teas, as they could be one of the first on the market to offer them, and they are suitable for both dietary supplement and functional food industries.

SPECIALTY ESSENTIAL OILS

One significant problem with developing business for Malagasy essential oils (EO) is that many EO products from Madagascar lack scalability. This is especially true for some of the endemic species and for less traded products. There are also consumer concerns regarding the quality and sustainability of many essential oil products. More education will be needed to inform the public about the benefits of trade in EO, especially from Madagascar, and that trade in EO actually promotes sustainability and helps community programs. The endemic, or primarily Malagasy essential oils that have the most promise for trade development are:

KATRAFAY EO (*CEDRELOPSIS GREVEI*)

Malagasy Ravintsara EO(*Cinnamomum camphora or Ravensara aromatica*)

Niaouli EO (*Melaleuca quinquenervia or M. viridifolia*)

Foraha or Tamanu oil (*Calophyllum inophyllum*)

Ginger EO (*Zingiber officinale*)

This is based on conversations with EO companies and traders. All the essential oils listed above have interesting properties. None of the essential oils though, with the possible exception of Ginger EO, are traded in large enough volumes to generate much money.

There is an opportunity for developing niche markets, especially with EO distributors and blenders, cosmetic companies and large retailing outlets (like Whole Foods, Williams Sonoma and so on). This is true if a story can be developed that differentiates EO products from Madagascar as being unique, exclusive, sustainable, organic and with a direct benefit to small and rural producers. A possible scenario would have a couple or a few Malagasy producers and exporters (like Phael Flor and HomeoPharma) link directly with clients in the U.S. and Europe, and have them establish the community programs on behalf of and with their clients.

Price and quality programs will need to be worked on and established. In the case of price, it will be important to demonstrate that prices and wages to small or rural growers, harvesters and producers are fair. At the same time, quality programs will need to be instituted that will offer clients standards of quality in traded products and assist in developing means for differentiating Malagasy EO products from those in other places.

CLOVE (SYZYGIUM AROMATICUM OR EUGENIA CARYOPHYLLATA) – WHOLE DRIED ORGANIC

Cloves have a long and established place in the spice and flavors markets. It has long been used in a variety of different culinary applications, and no one in the U.S. could imagine a Thanksgiving treat of pumpkin pie without its most important spice.

Clove also has many nutritional applications. Clove is used as an anti-bacterial, anti-fungal and anti-vital, as well as to treat worms. However, it is most commonly used externally to treat toothache and mouth and throat inflammation. Similarly to cinnamon, clove may help regulate how the body uses insulin and thus blood sugar balance. It is also thought that clove is an antioxidant. Cloves are also prepared whole, ground, as extracts or tinctures and as an essential oil.

There may be an opportunity to supply whole cloves and clove EO if there is some means of differentiating the clove products through quality, EO quantity or quality, flavor, organic certification or sustainability program. As there is a lack of organic cloves on the market (according to a couple sources), this was assessed as an immediate opportunity. One program might be to develop a Malagasy Spice Rack, that can contain many favorite Malagasy spices, like cinnamon, cloves, basil, pepper, and so on. The spice rack might be packaged for a large-scale retailer and marketed using a story of supporting products, labor and trade for Madagascar. The spice rack idea can even be developed with a similar program for essential oils. Another possible outlet for these kinds of rack products might be a handicraft retailer, since these products can be easily and attractively packaged and are also mostly non-perishable. Yet another thought is to produce sachets and potpourri based on Malagasy spices and EO products and distribute as well through a handicraft or other retail outlet.

VIRGIN COCONUT OIL (*COCOS NUCIFERA*)

Coconut and palm oils are produced in large-scale all over the world, and would not normally be considered a niche or high-value endeavor. Yet, there is a niche market developing for virgin coconut oil (see below for description of the difference between virgin and other oils). Virgin coconut oil is said to be nutritionally rich (including high content of lauric acid, a component of human mother's milk), and to have a positive effect on the immune system and on supporting energy levels. It is also touted as excellent for cooking and other food use, with an excellent flavor profile. A company based in the Philippines called Tropical Traditions (www.tropicaltraditions.com) is selling a certified organic virgin coconut oil and seems to be doing quite well. The demand is growing and sellers command a premium for this product (see Section 3.6 for pricing pointers).

Opportunities may exist to work via culinary academies, specialty retailers (like whole foods) and restaurants to promote such a product. Selling virgin coconut oil also with a functional or dietary supplement application is also possible.

Virgin coconut oil is minimally processed oil from the ground (usually fresh but can be dried under low temperature) and crushed coconut meat. The milk is then separated (decanted) or fermented to separate the oil from water. The ensuing oil is clear and stable. The product is not exposed to high heat, chemical, hydrogenation nor any other harsh processes.

It is possible to develop an extraction program with a fairly small investment in Madagascar, making it a possible candidate for investment and further development. Again, this must be certified organic, sustainable, and/or fair trade based.

HANDICRAFTS

This group has already begun developing commercial links and opportunities for Malagasy handicraft producers to U.S. based traders. One such organization is World of Good, in California. They are very interested in continuing to develop the relationships with Madagascar. Other possible links may be with companies like Ten Thousand Villages. The response thus far has been very interesting. Companies and organizations seem to be very impressed with the quality of handicraft products from Madagascar, though there is some concern with pricing on certain lines.

There is a need to continue developing these opportunities and an even stronger need to be responsive to client interests, requests and requirements.

PACKAGING RECOMMENDATIONS

General Recommendations

The natural and nutritional products industry in the United States is undergoing a new phase of development and growth. One of the principal movements in the changing natural products industry is a movement toward defining quality in products. This is due to many factors, including commercial, regulatory and business cycle variations. The new laws regarding Bio-Terrorism and state laws like Proposition 65 in California have placed quality and safety issues ahead of most matters in the industry. One of the areas for quality concerns has to do with packaging and labeling. Yet, this is also an opportunity, as compliance with laws and regulations will be rewarded with more business. A cinnamon extract manufacture recently reported that they lost business to other companies because their cinnamon extract, manufactured in China, had failed Proposition 65 requirements for heavy metals. An opportunity exists if Malagasy producers can demonstrate their products to be clean, safe and handled in appropriate conditions. This section will review some of the more important general, rather than product specific, packaging issues in the market currently.

Raw Materials Handling – The manner in which raw materials are handled is of vital importance. This is the first area of product quality, where serious issues like contamination and spoilage can be avoided. Raw materials should be handled, packaged and transported appropriately.

Manufacturing – Manufacturers and traders are typically the last to handle and package materials for export. As a result, their attention to packaging is of significant importance.

Quality Control – The responsibility for the packaging and quality of a product is usually with the manufacturer and/or a trading company. Defining and determining the quality of products is also important, as the shipper must usually attest to the fitness of the product for shipment.

Packaging – Some of the products covered in this report are powders, powdered extracts, or some other solid dosage form. These products are typically packaged in poly bags and placed into either food grade (cardboard) boxes, or fiber drums. The essential oils and liquids are typically packaged in food grade plastic (polyethylene or polypropylene) or glass; though glass is heavier and more fragile for transportation. Meanwhile the virgin coconut oil and bulk oils can be packaged in plastic drums or metal drums with plastic liners. In either case, the quality of packaging also affects short and long-term quality of the product. Due to the potential contamination of wood products, wood products should not be used anymore for shipment into the U.S., unless the wood products have been treated in advance. To read more about the quarantine requirements of wood products, go to: http://www.aphis.usda.gov/ppq/wpm/import.html.

Labeling Bulk – All products being imported into the U.S. must be accurately and completely labeled. All ingredients or components of the shipment must be declared and labels must be presented visibly. Documentation – Export documents need to be compliant with all regulations, and exporters are required to register with and notify agencies like the FDA (Food and Drug Administration) of any shipment coming into the U.S.

Labeling consumer products – All products must conform with nutritional labeling, structure function claims, DSHEA and other regulations. This will be discussed in greater length under section 4.0 Labeling Primer.

Cinnamon (*Cinnamomum verum* or *C. zeylanicum*) – Cinnamon is either shipped as a whole, cut and sift, powdered extract, or essential oil. As a whole, cut and sift or powdered extract, cinnamon is likely best packaged in double, poly bags and inside a food grade box or fiber drum. Cinnamon, whole bark or pieces can also be shipped in sacks or totes, but special attention should be paid to potential contaminants. Cinnamon tincture and essential oil, however, must be shipped in bottles or drums that are protected from heat, moisture and light. Bottles made from polyethylene or polypropylene can be used for essential oils and plastic drums or metal drums with plastic liners can be used for larger scale EOs and Foraha oil. Glass is discouraged from use as it is expensive, heavy, and creates more fragility.

Green Tea (and other teas) – Green tea can be packaged in a manner similar to cinnamon, as its solid dose/serving forms are similar to cinnamon's.

Specialty Essential Oils – The essential oils should be packaged in bottles or drums that are protected from heat, moisture and light. Bottles made from polyethylene or polypropylene can be used for essential oils and plastic drums or metal drums with plastic liners can be used for larger scale EOs and Foraha oil. Glass is discouraged from use as it is expensive and creates more fragility. Focus products that this applies to are the following:

KATRAFAY EO (*CEDRELOPSIS GREVEI*)

2.4.2 Malagasy Ravintsara EO(*Cinnamomum camphora or Ravensara aromatica*)

2.4.3 Niaouli EO (*Melaleuca quinquenervia or M. viridifolia*)

1. Foraha or Tamanu oil (*Calophyllum inophyllum*)
2. Ginger EO (*Zingiber officinale*)

2.5 Cloves (*Syzygium aromaticum or Eugenia caryophyllata*) – Whole Dried Organic – Cloves can be packaged in a manner similar to cinnamon, as its solid dose forms are similar to cinnamon's.

2.6 Virgin Coconut Oil (*Cocos nucifera*) – The coconut virgin oil should be packaged in tins or drums with liners. The tins can be offered in a variety of sizes (1 or 5 gallons for instance). It is important to protect the coconut oil from exposure to heat, light and moisture.

1. **Handicrafts (various)** -There are no major guidelines for packaging handicraft products as they vary so much in types, styles, materials and so on. However, it makes sense to

package products in such a way as to protect the products from breakage, contamination or other exposures. Again, please no wooden crates.

2. **Pricing Pointers**

GENERAL RECOMMENDATIONS

As the family of natural, health and wellness products continues to develop and grow, there is a movement toward commoditization of products. Products are too easily substituted and buyers shop for products based on price almost exclusively. This is partly due to the difficulty the industry has in establishing proprietary and added value products, as well as accepted standards in the dietary supplement and functional food industries. The major opportunities for differentiation and adding value may come through the development of partnerships, vertical integration, organic and science based products. Further differentiation with clean products that are solvent, residue and heavy metals free will also help sellers distinguish themselves and add value.

Pricing and value work like an inverse pyramid with most of the value captured at the top of the pyramid and little with the producer. One of the aims of projects like these is to reshape the pyramid slightly so that it is not so wide on the top and so narrow on the bottom.

Most of the recommendations for products have to do with increasing value (and consequently, price) through differentiation techniques like improved raw materials, improved handling or processing techniques, organic certification, sustainability, better quality control, pure and clean products and so on.

Cinnamon (*Cinnamomum verum* or *C. zeylanicum*) – The cinnamon extracts used for diabetes products (usually standardized to 8% polyphenols) have an estimated import price into the U.S. of $25.00 to $30.00 per kg and a wholesale price of around $65.00 per kg. Extraction ratios are said to be between 10 and 15:1. The extracts mostly come from China. The retail value of cinnamon extracts is described below:

- x New Chapter Cinnamon Force – 60 X 140 mg softgel capsules of a combination Cinnamomum aromaticum and C. verum. It is a blend of 94 mg water/ethanol extract at 8% polyphenols and 46 mg of supercritical CO2 extract at 35% cinnameldehyde. Price is $17.97 per bottle
- x Gaia Herbs Liquid Phyto-Caps Cinnamon Bark. 1 bottle of 60 capsules (per 2 capsules: Cinnamon bark, supercritical CO2 extract (Cinnamomum burmanii) 50 mg; cinnamon Bark, ETOH Extract (Cinnamomum burmanii) 200 mg—standardized to 33.75 mg total cinnamaldehydes and 16mg total phenol). Retail $ 21.99 1 bottle.
- x Gaia Herbs Cinnamon Bark Liquid extract. Same extraction procedures as above with 65% pure grain alcohol USP and spring water; standardized to 7.5 mg total total cinnamaldehydes and 2 mg mg total phenol. Retail $ 10.99 1 bottle.
- x Diabeticine – 60 X 300 mg. Includes, Banaba, Guggle, Bitter Melon, Licorice extract, Cinnamon herb powder, Gymnema sylvestre, Yarrow, Cayenne, Juniper berries, Huckleberry, and Vanadyl sulfate. Price for1 bottle - $74.95, 10 bottles - $374.95
- x Cinnamomum zeylanicum – 625 mg capsules powdered cinnamon. 30 count - $6.38, 60 count - $10.18, 350 count - $39.32
- x Wonder Labs – 350 X 600 mg Cinnamon powder - $24.95
- x Planetary Formulas Cinnamon extract – 120 X 200 mg tablets of Cinnamomum

aromaticum 10:1 at 8% flavonoids for $13.50 per bottle

- x FutureBiotics Cinnecare – 125 mg of CinnulinPF® (Cinnamomum aromaticum) extract 20:1, plus Chromax®, Activin®, Fenugreek, Vanadium and Bioperine (Black Pepper). Price is $21.25 per bottle
- x CinnaBetic II – 60 X 125 mg capsules of Cinnamomum extract. Retail price is between $19.99 to $24.99 per bottle
- x HerbPharm – Cinnamon tincture – Cinnamomum zyelanicum (verum) – 1:5 ratio
- x Cinnamon Essential Oil - $2.00 for 1 oz. – Indonesia
- x Nature's Sunshine Cinnamon Leaf EO – 1/6 fl oz (5 ml) - $7.95

Green Tea (and other bush teas)

Since there is an immediate opportunity for the possible sale of certified organic green tea (cut and sift, for use in tea), we will attempt to determine those values per client negotiation, depending on quality. Green tea pricing is highly variable, and can be anything from wholesale $ 20-120/k. Green tea that is packaged as individual tea bags is also highly variable, and can range from $2.49/box of 20 tea bags (retail) to close to $8/box. Traditional Medicinals offers one of the highest quality lines of tea on the market, and they consistently charge about $ 5/box of 16 teabags (see samples).

Specialty Essential Oils

Below are some broad retail and wholesale values for the focus product essential oils:

Katrafay EO (*Cedrelopsis grevei*) – Retail - $ 18.00 per oz – Wholesale - $185.00 per kg

Malagasy Ravintsara (*Cinnamomum camphora or Ravensara aromatica*)

EO – Retail - $ 8.00 per oz – Wholesale - $122.00 per kg

Niaouli EO (*Melaleuca quinquenervia or M. viridifolia*) – Retail - $ 4.0012 per oz – Wholesale - $48.00 per kg; in perfume roller (jojoba oil) application, retail $11.59 for 5 ml.

3.4.4 Foraha or Tamanu oil (*Calophyllum inophyllum*) – Retail - $ 6.00 per oz

– Wholesale - $85.00 per kg

Ginger EO (*Zingiber officinale*) – Retail - $ 20-35.00 per oz – Wholesale - $300.00 per kg

3.5 Clove (*Syzygium aromaticum or Eugenia caryophyllata*) – Whole Dried Organic There is not much information on the wholesale or retail prices for clove based products. x Morton & Basset, Whole cloves (not organic, I think) 1.3 oz bottle-$ 8.79 x Wholesale prices for clove EO are around $70.00 - $75.00 per kg.

Virgin Coconut Oil (*Cocos nucifera*)

There is not much information on the wholesale or retail prices for virgin coconut oil.

- x Jungle Products Extra Virgin Organic Coconut Oil 16 OZ -$ 13.99

- x Organic coconut oil unrefined (for medium heat) 14 FL OZ- $ 6.99
- x Organic coconut oil refined (for medium heat) 14 FL OZ- $4.99
- x Tropical Traditions retails a gallon of virgin coconut oil for about $65.00

Handicrafts (various)

Handicrafts can vary considerably in price depending on the item, quality, quantity, and sale channel. One of the potential clients, World of Good, focuses only on Fair Trade products, and is very interested in creating a relationship with Madagascar. However, they say that for their customer base rarely will pay more than $30 per item. With a mark up of about 6 X the FOB price, this means that the items from Madagascar need to be in the $5-6 range. We are currently exploring these possibilities. There may be higher end vendors that can pay higher prices but lower volumes, but this clientele has not yet been developed.

LABELING PRIMER

Labeling Primer Key

The first step in labeling finished products for the US market is to decide which into market the product will be sold and what regulations apply to the specific product, it will be labeled as either: a dietary supplement (see Section 4.2), a food or functional food (they are both labeled as foods; see Section 4.3); a cosmetic care/personal care product (see Section 4.4); or a handicraft (see Section 4.5).

To decide which market your product fits, use these questions as your guide:

x Is your product "a product, other than tobacco, intended to supplement the diet that bears or contains one or more of the following ingredients: a vitamin, a mineral, an herb or other botanical; an amino acid; a dietary substance for use by man to supplement the diet by increasing the total dietary intake; or a concentrate, metabolite, constituent, extract or combination of any of the aforementioned dietary ingredients; and is intended for ingestion in the form of a capsule, powder, softgel or gelcap, is not represented as a conventional food or as a sole item of a meal or the diet (Section 201 (ff), FD&CAact)?" If the answer is "Yes," see Section 4.2. If you are not sure, for clarification, what is commonly referred to as a "herbal medicine" is regulated as a dietary supplement in the U.S. If your product is an herbal tea that has a structure/function claim associated with it, then it is considered a dietary supplement (go to Section 4.2). If it is a beverage tea with no claims, then it is a food (go to Section 4.3). See Examples. If you answered "No" to the above questions, then go onto the next question.

x Is your product "articles used for food or drink for man or other animals, chewing gum, and articles used for components of any other such article (21 CFR 102.5(a))?" If the answer is "Yes," see Section 4.3. If you answered "No" to the above question, then go onto the next question.

x Is your product an "article intended to be applied to the human body for cleansing, beautifying, promoting attractiveness, or altering the appearance without affecting the body's structure or functions? Included in this definition are products such as skin creams, lotions, perfumes, lipsticks, fingernail polishes, eye and facial make-up preparations, shampoos, permanent waves, hair colors, toothpastes, deodorants, and any material intended for use as a component of a cosmetic product. Soap products consisting primarily of an alkali salt of fatty acid and making no label claim other than cleansing of the human body are not considered cosmetics under the law." If the answer is "Yes," see Section 4.4. If your product is a pure essential oil or a fragrance,

fragrance blend or perfume, see Section 4.4. If you answered "No" to the above question, then go onto the next question.

x Is your product a craft or other item that is not intended for consumption or topical use on the skin? If the answer is "Yes," see Section 4.5. If you answered "No" to the above question, then return to the top of Section 4.1 and review the questions again.

Dietary Supplement Labeling

The FDA (Food and Drug Administration; http://www.fda.gov/) is broadly responsible for ensuring compliance with the law for dietary supplement, including the law known as DSHEA (Dietary Supplement Health and Education Act of 1994; http://www.fda.gov/opacom/laws/dshea.html). This law governs, among many other things, labeling and permissible claims for dietary supplements. The FTC (Federal Trade Commission; http://www.ftc.gov/) also regulates dietary supplements from a consumer protection point of view. Therefore, when companies make outrageous claims on how their herbal or dietary supplements can cure disease, it is not only the FDA that can prosecute, but also the FTC that may prosecute companies. Often times, the heaviest punishments that are given to manufacturers regarding false claims come from the FTC.

Among the focus products that may be subject to dietary supplement labeling regulations are cinnamon extracts (for use as a dietary supplement) and herbal teas, possibly such as green tea and voafotsy.

General Dietary Supplement Labeling Guidelines

The finalization of dietary supplement labeling had been a controversial topic in the US, with much concern as to the types of claims that can be made for a product. The labeling regulations are very specific about font sizes and placement of certain items on the label, and these topics will not be covered by these guidelines. Instead, refer to the CD-ROM called "Dietary Supplement Labeling Compliance Review" for technical aspects of specific labels.

Dietary supplement labels must contain the following:

x An Identity Statement This statement is essentially the wording "Dietary Supplement," or other similar term that is placed on the front panel of the label, and must be the second most prominent (meaning the font is as large or the next size smaller to the name of the product or other larger font) type on the label.

x An Ingredient Statement & Nutrition Labeling Dietary supplements are required to list all the ingredients on the labels, and this is usually done in a Supplement Facts Box. Small label exemptions to apply, but not if there is a structure/function statement made. The common name of all herbs is used, as specified by the Herbs of Commerce, 2nd Ed. For more specific information on the Supplement Facts Box, see Section 4.2.2. In the case of excipients (or ingredients present at less that 2%), these are referred to as "Other ingredients," and listed directly below the Supplement Facts Box.

x Name and Address of the Place of Business The name and place of business of the manufacturer, packer or distributor is required on dietary supplement labels in a conspicuous manner. If it is not manufactured by the business, then qualifying words, such as "Manufactured for…." or "Distributed by…." may be placed on the label. The street address, city, state, and ZIP code is required. If the business is listed in a current city or telephone directory, the street address may be omitted.

x Net Quantity of Contents Statement The net quantity of the contents shall be stated on the front display panel of the label, and shall be expressed as either weight (if solid or semi-solid), fluid measure (for fluids), or numerical count (or maybe a combination of weight and numerical count).

x Nutrient Content Claims & Health Claims There are certain claims that can be made on labels of dietary supplements for dietary substances that have an established Daily Value, but only if they conform to the regulation for the meaning of that term. Example for a nutrient content claim is "healthy," a food product that has the word *healthy* on it has to conform to the specific implied nutrition content claims for as specified by law, the same is true for the words "high" or "low".

Specific health claims are also allowed, and there are less than 20 that have been approved. These health claims only refer to food substances.

x Other Claims as may Be Provided for by the FD&CA and 21 CFR Part 101 Other claims that are allowed on dietary supplements are referred to as "structure/function" claims because they are statements that are not disease claims (otherwise they would be regulated as pharmaceuticals), but rather statements that do not explicitly or implicitly claim an effect on a specific disease or health condition, but may alter a structure or function of the body. For more information see Section

Supplement Facts Box

See example Supplement Facts Boxes for the format, font sizes and example boxes for different products. In general, the supplement facts box may contain one or two sections of ingredients. If the product has nutritional contents (i.e. calories, fat, carbohydrates) or ingredients with daily values (the major vitamins and minerals), then those will be listed first in the order as specified by the FDA. If there are ingredients that do not have daily values, such as herbs or other dietary supplement products (like glucosamine sulfate), then those would be listed in the next section in descending order. If there are no products with daily values or nutritional content, then that section may be omitted.

Structure/Function Claims

Whenever a structure/function statement is made, there should be a premarket notification that is filed with the FDA. Also, there needs to be an asterisk next to the statement and then a bolded and boxed disclaimer (at the bottom of the same page or panel where the statement appears) that reads: "* This statement has not been evaluated by the Food and Drug Administration. This product is not intended to diagnose, treat, cure, or prevent any disease." See examples of Structure/Function Statements.

Functional Food/Food Labeling

The FDA (Food and Drug Administration) is broadly responsible for ensuring compliance with the law, as well as labeling. Foods and drugs are covered under CFR (Code of Federal Regulations) Title 21. Most functional food and traditional food manufacturers only use ingredients that are considered GRAS (Generally Regarded As Safe) or are on an "Approved Food Additives" list. The FTC (Federal Trade Commission) also regulates functional foods from a consumer protection point of view.

The labeling regulations are very specific about font sizes and placement of certain items on the label, and these topics will not be covered by these guidelines. Instead, refer to the CD-ROM called "Food Labeling Compliance Review" for technical aspects of specific labels. Also see example Nutrition Facts Boxes.

One of the focus products that is labeled as a food, and may also be considered a functional food is Virgin Coconut Oil. See sample product for labeling. Other focus products that may be subject to food labeling are green tea (and other beverage teas), whole or processed cloves and cinnamon.

4.3.1 General Food Labeling Guidelines Like dietary supplement labeling regulations, the food regulations are complex, more due to the wide variety of foods and package forms on the market. Functional foods are a marketing term, and as such do not have a specialized regulatory body that governs them. All "functional foods" are considered foods by the US regulations, and are governed as such (see more on this in Section 4.3.3). In general, the food or functional food label should contain the following items:

x Identity Statement

The common name or usual name of the food shall be placed on the most prominent panel of the label, along with any appropriate descriptive term. In the case of "imitation" products, this must also be stated.

x Designation of Ingredients & Nutrition Labeling Ingredients shall be listed in an ingredient statement if there are two or more ingredients present in the product. Ingredients should be listed in descending order of predominance by weight. Spices, flavorings, colorings and chemical preservatives may be declared as specified by 21 CFR 101.22. In this regulation, the word "spice" can be used as a blanket identity statement for the usual spices, including cinnamon and cloves. For more on Nutritional Facts Boxes, see Section 4.3.2.

x Name and Place of Business

The same regulations for listing the name and place of business for dietary supplements apply to foods (see Section 4.2).

x Net Quantity of Contents

Similar regulations on stating the net quantity of contents for dietary supplements apply to foods (see Section 4.2).

x Nutrient Content Claims & Health Claims

Similar regulations on nutrient content claims & health claims that were stated for dietary supplements also apply to foods (see Section 4.2).

x Statements about the Structure or Function of the Body

The label of a conventional food may bear a structure/function statement, similar to those discussed for dietary supplements. The difference, however, is that for a food, it must be able to produce this effect through the nutritive value of the food, otherwise it

is regulated as a drug. See more about this in Section 4.3.3.

Nutrition Facts Box See example Nutrition Facts Boxes. Generally, the Nutrition Facts Boxes only contain nutritive information about the food in the package and daily value information for the major vitamins and minerals.

Functional Foods As stated previously, functional foods are not regulated as such by the FDA. The term "functional food" is a marketing term that does not have any relevance or meaning to the FDA. However, what is commonly referred to as a functional food is a "food or food ingredient that has been shown to affect specific functions or systems in the body." Functional foods may take the form of conventional foods, such as yogurts that enhance digestive function, or still conventional but more innovative forms such as beverages with herbs (that are Generally Recognized as Safe) added. One of the characteristic differences with what are commonly referred to as functional foods may be the use of structure/function statements on the label. These are the same as those used by dietary supplements, except that disclaimers are not generally required.

4 Cosmetics/Personal Care Labeling

The definition of cosmetic under the law varies slightly between countries, but in general terms "cosmetic" means any article intended to be used by means of rubbing, sprinkling or by similar application to the human body for cleaning, beautifying, and for maintaining health of the skin and hair, provided that the action of the article on the human body is mild. The regulatory agency for cosmetics in the US is the Food and Drug Administration (FDA). The FDA does not require pre-market approval for cosmetics. The cosmetic product name and details of its ingredients are voluntarily reported to the FDA within 60 days of marketing. With the exception of color ingredients that require authorization for use, the FDA does not approve the use of any cosmetic ingredient, unless a safety problem arises after it has been put on the market, in which case the FDA can take action. The FDA's budget for cosmetic safety surveillance is less than 1%.

Essential oils (EOs) are the volatile, odorous oils that occur in certain plants. EOs are widely known for their scents and flavors, making the food flavor and fragrance (F&F), aromatherapy (including body care and cosmetics) industries among the largest users.

In addition to the federal regulations set by the FDA and FTC (see http://www.cfsan.fda.gov/~dms/cos-206.html; and http://www.cfsan.fda.gov/~dms/coshdb1.html) , the body care and cosmetics manufacturers also work with industry associations to provide additional guidelines and standards. The CTFA (Cosmetic, Toiletry and Fragrance Association) for example, works with manufacturers on developing safety and quality control standards that exceed those of the federal government. Industry associations like these have independent researching, testing and reporting capacity. Industry members are likely to abide by and uphold these standards, as they are the commonly accepted way to do business

Among the focus products that may be subject to these labeling guidelines are: Katrafay EO (*Cedrelopsis grevei*), Ravensara Aromatica EO (*Agathophyllum aromaticum*); Niaouli EO (*Melaleuca quinquenervia*); Foraha or Tamanu oil (*Calophyllum inophyllum*); and Ginger EO (*Zingiber officinale*).

General Cosmetic Labeling Guidelines [The following text is excerpted from an FDA Guidance Document at http://www.cfsan.fda.gov/~dms/cos-labl.html:]

Under the Food, Drug, and Cosmetic Act (FD&C Act) and the Fair Packaging and Labeling Act (FPLA), certain information must appear on the labels of cosmetic products.

All cosmetics, whether they are sold on a retail basis to consumers or marketed exclusively for salon or workplace use, are subject to the FD&C Act. This law and regulations enacted under its authority require the cosmetic label to state the name and place of business of the manufacturer, packer or distributor; an accurate statement of the quantity of contents; and any appropriate directions for safe use and/or warning statements. This information must comply with additional regulatory requirements. It must be prominent and appear in the proper location on the label.

Regulations enacted under the FPLA require ingredients to be listed on the labels of cosmetics sold on a retail basis to consumers -- even if the label states "For professional use only." Consumers can use the ingredient declaration to identify ingredients they wish to avoid. Ingredients are listed in descending order of predominance, that is, with the ingredient present in the greatest amount listed at the beginning and those present in the smallest amounts listed at the end.

Special rules apply to the ingredient declaration on products that are both cosmetics and over-the-counter drugs. An example of such a product is an anti-dandruff shampoo: A shampoo is a cosmetic, while an anti-dandruff treatment is a drug. Regulations enacted in 1999 require such combination products to have the drug ingredients listed separately as "Active Ingredients," in alphabetical order, followed by the cosmetic ingredients, which are listed as "Inactive Ingredients" in descending order of predominance.

In addition to the immediate label, FDA regulates all cosmetic product "label*ing*." The definition of labeling includes all written, printed, or graphic matter that appears on the product, its containers, or its wrappers, as well as any such matter that accompanies the product. Typically, materials such as promotional literature, product catalogs, and flyers fit this definition of labeling. FDA also has considered promotional statements appearing on Internet sites to constitute labeling, especially on those sites where the promoted product can be purchased. However, unfair or deceptive advertising that appears in magazines, in newspapers, or on television generally falls under the authority of the Federal Trade Commission.

Cosmetic firms should refer to FDA's Cosmetic Labeling Manual (http://www.cfsan.fda.gov/~dms/cos-lab1.html) and the regulations related to cosmetics (http://www.cfsan.fda.gov/~dms/cos-cfr.html) for more detailed labeling information.

General Essential Oil Labeling Guidelines

Essential oils may be regulated, and thus labeled, as cosmetics if they are included in lotions or other product delivery forms that fit within the cosmetic regulations (see Section 4.1). If essential oils are sold as fragrances or fragrance blends, however, the regulations are much less specific. In order to be perceived as a supplier of good quality essential oil, certain information should be included on the label, as follows:

x *The Latin Binomial*

As there are many common names for essential oils and the plants from which they are derived, to avoid confusion and to show the consumer that this is a quality product, the label should contain the Latin binomial (a two word scientific botanical name) for the plant that the oil was derived from. According to Christoph Streicher, aromatherapy expert (http://www.spiritualminds.com/articles.asp?articleid=6305), "All Eucalyptus oils are not alike. Eucalyptus Globulus is a great decongestant and antibacterial oil, but it is too strong to use in a baby's room. Eucalyptus Radiata is wonderful and safe for keeping your baby's nasal passages clear, so you both can have a good night's sleep. Eucalyptus Citriodora is a good insect repellant. Thyme, Pine, and Chamomile are several commonly used oils that have different subspecies."

x *How it was grown*

Whether a plant source for an oil was organically grown, wildcrafted or fair-trade/community supporting should be listed on the label. The source location and even region may be excellent ways of distinguishing your essential oil, and can be included on the label.

Toxic Oils

As a few oils are considered toxic, there should be cautionary statements listed on the label, and should listed for use only by trained aromatherapists. A few of the oils that are considered toxic are White Birch, Sassafras, Thymus zygis, Hyssop, and Camphor.

Handicrafts

Handicrafts and craft products do not have a consolidated agency for regulation of labeling (unless it is a child's toy). Standards and criteria for handicrafts may arise as a result of an interest in trading under sustainable practices and the desire to carry a seal or certification of some kind. As in the case of the Sustainability Markets, certifiers establish standards based on social, environmental and economic principals and benefits.

One area for attention regarding crafts and arts is that any product that may be used or seen as a child's toy, must conform to regulations set up by the FTC (Federal Trade Commission) and the CPSC (Consumer Product Safety Commission). Mostly, these agencies are concerned with protecting children from toys and crafts that may cause safety problems. Some toys require age appropriate labels for example, to inform adults of the possible risk of exposing toys to younger children these toys need to be labeled with recommended minimum ages and safety information. It is important for exporters to work with their American clients to ensure the products comply with these important safety measures.

MARKETING PLAN STRATEGY

Our market plan is still best summarized as a "three pronged" approach. First we will be looking for general distributors that can handle Madagascar essential oils, spices, possibly other botanicals, and handicrafts. We are specifically looking for the distributors that will make an effort or take a larger interest in Madagascar, and not just selling its products as commodity items. We may need as little as two distributors, and as many as four to cover the range of market channels we are interested in entering. The distributors that have the highest potential for covering the markets are Frontier Natural Products Co-Op, The Lebermuth Company Inc., RFI Ingredients, Pharmline, PharamChem, Lemur International, Tri-K Industries, Ecotrend, Trout Lake Farm, BDS Natural Products, and World of Good. These distributors are well positioned in the functional food, dietary supplement, cosmetic and skin care, as well as craft markets. Further negotiations are needed to narrow down this list or carve out areas of sales territories (or products) for effective promotion of the Malagasy products.

The "second pronged" approach is to develop direct relationships with either a) large or established and innovative companies that might be interested in developing a "Madagascar-themed" product line in the medium to long-term, or b) other companies that are interested in carrying one or more product from Madagascar as a stand-alone product in the short-term. An example of (a) might be a line of Aveda body care and cosmetics that features Malagasy essential oils and tells the story of Madagascar and the sustainable promotion of its products; or (b) any size company that sees an immediate need for a stand alone product from Madagascar, such as the "focus products" that are recommended with this report. Examples of companies that fit this approach are Aveda or Estée Lauder, Access Business Group (Nutrilite and Amway), Frontier Natural Products Co-Op (through Simply Organics or Aura Cacia), Aubrey Organics, GNC, Whole Foods (introduce a branded line of functional spices and essential oils), Williams Sonoma, Exalted Extracts, and Threshold Enterprises. Negotiations with these companies are in very early stages, and will need more time to develop. Shorter-term relationships and sales may be formed once samples and introductions are made, or perhaps after meetings at the Natural Products West conference.

The "third pronged" approach is what I have been referring to as developing "fair deal" or direct-to-community relationships. The idea is to find smaller companies or product innovators in the natural products and handicrafts industry and help them to make direct relationships with a community (or more than one) from Madagascar that is similar to Fair-trade (provides higher prices or living wages to farmers or suppliers), and/or may provide other socioeconomic benefits to the community (such as building roads, schools, etc). This is becoming a popular marketing strategy in the U.S. that can also help to alleviate poverty and possibly create longer-term (rather than those based on price) relationships than the usual supplier relationship. An added benefit is that the larger consuming public may become educated and the awareness of Madagascar may increase, helping other sectors of business. An example of a company that has done this successfully is HonesTea, who support a South African community with their ready to

uring this investigatory trip to Madagascar, I hope to accomplish certain goals that will be crucial in my ability to establish business relationships with US companies and Malagasy producers.

Visits with Key Producers

One of the key purposes for this first trip to Madagascar is to meet with a few of the key producers with which we hope to work. Hopefully, I will be able to meet various producers that represent the variety of products that are available in Madagascar, along with specific producers with whom we are already working, such as the handicraft producers, Homeopharma, and Phaelflor. During these visits I hope to personally meet the people with whom we will be communicating, and who will be responsible for sending sample, answering emails, etc. for each producer. I also hope to see their current products, and gather samples and/or take pictures (that I can post on our website), as appropriate. I also would like to gain an understanding of the production capacity of each producer. In this regard, I would like to know the following types of questions: -What is the volume they can produce of each product, and at what times of year do they produce? -What is their understanding of potential applications for their products? -What other production capacities do they have—do they have manufacturing machinery to add value to a product like in the bulk handling (drying and handling of herbs), drying capabilities (spray drying, vacuum drying, etc.), and any other scalable capabilities that they have? -Do they have quality control procedures in place, and if so, what kind? -What is the optimal type of relationship they would like to form with a US company?

Of course, as I am looking for the producers to help me understand the answers to these questions, I will also be happy to meet with each producer and answer questions about the marketplace from my understanding and the potential I see for their products. I am also happy to give feedback on labeling and other specific technical questions when I can.

Visits to Regions where Products are Produced

I am hoping to also get an opportunity to visit the various producing regions for the key products or other potential products we are working with, as well as meeting with growers and grower cooperatives. As part of the strategy for creating successful long-term value added products out of Madagascar includes telling the story, or creating a perceived higher value through "community-supporting" products, it is essential for me to know these regions. In a visit to a region I hope to understand what about that region of Madagascar is special for producing a higher quality (or ethnic) product, and to get to know the peoples with whom such relationships might be possible. One example might be the Malagasy Magic Fingers cooperative. I will also hope to bring home pictures of the peoples and lands with which we might find business linkages in the US, for posting on the www.madagascarnatural.com website.

Learning about the Selling Points and Story Associated with Products

I am constantly asked from potential clients, "What from Madagascar is interesting? Can they compete on price with products from India or China, or are there products that are unique to Madagascar in quality or identity?" I need to gain a thorough understanding of what Madagascar has to offer, and why businesses should pay a premium (value added or even just the extra shipping costs) that are associated with doing business with Madagascar.

Visiting with Research Institutions

A few of the businesses that I have been talking with would like to explore the possibility of working in tandem with research institutions in Madagascar to help develop the science and/or quality of products out of Madagascar. Additionally, I believe often times these type of research institutions have already performed certain scientific studies, application work or have prospected plants (along with creating relationships with traditional healers) that could be very useful for our work in developing the markets in the US. Therefore, if it would be possible to arrange a meeting with key researchers or institutions in Madagascar so that I can help to promote relationships with them, and also learn from them what products are promising, I believe it would be very useful. An example of such an institution is the IMRA (Institut Malgache de Recherches Appliquées).

THE MOST PROMISING SECTORS FOR BUSINESS AND INVESTMENT

Aside from management, which is typically staffed by expatriates, investors can expect consistently below average wage levels for all employment categories. Investors also reported low real estate and construction costs in many sectors, which create lower initial startup costs. Among the benefits, investors specified low lease prices for industrial and hotel land, low cost office space rental and relatively low farmland prices. The country's low corporate and property tax rates were also cited. Firms found a higher level of economic freedom, as recorded by the Transparency International Index, in Madagascar than in almost any other sub-Saharan African country, and rated corruption levels to be lower than in any other surveyed country. Investors also reported quick customs clearance times and competitive transportation costs for a number of destinations.

Each sector included in this chapter (textile, apparel, food and beverage processing, horticulture, shared services and tourism) begins with a global sector brief, followed by country specific sector briefs and a SWOT analysis. In order to study the viability of the sectors studied in this report, each sector's market trends and future prospects within the global context was analyzed. The country-specific sector briefs highlight information and factors relevant to the sector in that country.

The SWOT analysis at the end of every sector brief provides a general overview of strengths, weaknesses, opportunities and threats that investors in each country experience while investing in the relevant sector. The strengths and weaknesses for each sector present whether the country is among the three countries that performed worst in the six most important surveyed site selection factors as reported by investors presently operating in Africa. Three of the six factors pertain to quality factors and three to operating cost factors (see Table). The opportunities and threats have been summarized for all countries. It is worth noting that not all countries were benchmarked in all sectors. lesotho is benchmarked in only the textile and apparel sector, while Mozambique and Uganda were not benchmarked for the textile sector and the tourism (hotels) sector respectively.

TOP SIX SITE SELECTION FACTORS ACCORDING TO SURVEYED INVESTORS

Textile Apparel Horticulture Food and Beverage

Quality factors (In order of importance)

1	Access to markets and supplies	Access to markets and supplies	Access to markets and supplies	Access to markets and supplies
2	General business environment	General business environment	General business environment	General business environment
3	local potential to recruit staff	local potential to recruit staff	Availability of real estate/Arable land	local potential to recruit staff

Cost factors (In order of importance)

1 Wage levels Wage levels Wage levels Wages levels

2 Cost of real estate Cost of real estate Cost of real estate Cost of real estate

3 Cost of water and Cost of water and Cost of transport Cost of construction power power

Tariffs

Though tariff levels are an important factor for sectors such as textile, apparel, horticulture and food and beverage processing, most sub-Saharan African countries have tariff-free access to a number of major markets within a wide range of export products. It is, for this reason, that tariffs are not a general worry for investors in Africa. Among the more popular trade agreements are the African Growth Opportunity Act (USA), the Cotonou Agreement (EU), the Everything But Arms (EBA) amendment to the EU's Generalized System of Preferences (EU), the Common Market for Eastern and Southern Africa (COMESA), the East African Community (EAC), the Economic Community of West African States (ECOWAS) and the Southern African Development Community (SADC).

Tourism

Access to markets Access to markets and supplies and supplies

General business General business nvironment environment

local potential local potential to to recruit staff/ recruit staff/ Real Infrastructure estate

Wages levels Cost of real estate

Telecommu-Wage levels nications Cost of real estate Cost of construction

SNAPSHOT AFRICA -**MADAGASCAR**

↑

TEXTILE SECTOR

Between 2000 and 2004, the value of world exports of textile products grew at an average annual rate of 4.4 percent. With exports from emerging economies growing at a slightly higher rate, their share of world exports increased by 1.5 percentage points to 46.7 percent in 2004. Currently, the major players in the global textile market are China, the US, the EU, India, Pakistan, Japan, Republic of Korea and Turkey. low cotton prices provide cheap inputs to textile operations worldwide. According to the EIU, estimated global consumption of cotton in 2004/05, at 23.4m tons, is slightly higher than expected and represents an increase of almost 10 percent over the last year. Overall, world cotton consumption in 2005/06 is forecast to reach 24.35m tons, an increase of 4 percent.

The elimination at the end of 2004 of quantitative import restrictions under the World Trade Organization (WTO) Agreement on Textiles and Clothing (ATC) has greatly affected the textile industry (see Table). A recent study predicts the following trends as a result of the elimination of quotas on textiles: an increase in the share of world exports for textiles emanating from emerging economies; a considerable gain in the export shares of countries with low labor costs, such as China, India and Pakistan; heightened competition among suppliers in low-cost countries; and increased specialization of products among source countries.

The textile industry is usually characterized as capital intensive and highly automated, with a reliance on unskilled labor. Although labor costs in Africa are generally competitive with those in China or India, the main factor decreasing the competitiveness of Africa in the global textile trade is high utility costs, particularly for electricity and water, coupled with supply unreliability. A number of successful textile producing countries, such as China and India, rely on strong backward linkages for production inputs, and textile industries in Africa have yet to create such linkages to the local economy.

A number of countries benefit from AGOA's third-country fabric sourcing allowance, which permits African countries, exporting under the AGOA agreement, to source raw material inputs from non-AGOA countries. This arrangement is slated to expire in 2007, which will increase the need for AGOA countries to source inputs from local suppliers. African textile exports under AGOA totaled USD 1.4 billion in 2005, which represents a 12 percent decline from the previous year, due to increased global competition, brought about by the elimination of the multi-fiber agreement (MFA). Africa has had little success thus far in attracting FDI into the textile sector. According to loco Monitor, an online FDI tool, Africa receives just 2 percent of global FDI, while Asia Pacific and Europe together account for almost 80 percent. The largest share of FDI in Africa in the textile sector is from the EU, followed by North America and Asia Pacific, while Africa and the Middle East account for many small-scale projects.

Sub-Saharan Africa does possess a number of advantages that increase its attractiveness as an investment location, particularly its low labor costs and abundance of unskilled labor. Investors in Africa can also benefit from preferential access to a number of global markets, including AGOA, and large and still developing regional trade zones. A number of sub-Saharan African governments are putting increased emphasis on developing EPZs that provide improved access to global markets and infrastructure. Successful EPZ investments are evident in African countries such as Mauritius and lesotho.

APPAREL SECTOR

During the last two decades, trade in apparel has grown significantly and developing countries have made a considerable contribution to this growth. In this period, apparel exports from developing countries increased sevenfold. According to UNCTAD, developing countries accounted for 76 percent of total world clothing exports in 2003, compared with a 1985 figure of only 8 percent. Total global apparel trade was USD 462 billion in 2003 and has grown at a compounded annual rate of

6.6 percent since 1990. Market leaders in apparel exports include China, EU, Turkey, Mexico, India, the US and Indonesia. The expiration of the MFA in December 2004 has greatly affected global trade and investment in the apparel sector.

The clothing industry is labor-intensive and offers entry-level jobs for unskilled labor in developed as well as developing countries. The majority of clothing is produced from textiles and fabrics across a very wide range of products, materials, styles and usage. There are many stages in the production of apparel such as pattern making, cutting and sewing, trimming, garment dyeing, ticketing, folding and packaging. The variations are unlimited and as fashions change and materials develop, new garments are being developed all the time as well as being re-invented. Moreover, it is a sector where relatively modern technology can be adopted even in poor countries at low investment costs. This feature of the industry has made it attractive as the first step towards industrialization for many poor countries such as Bangladesh, Sri lanka, Viet Nam and Mauritius. Some of these countries have experienced a very high output growth rate in the sector.

With the disappearance of the global quota system, which is expected to further consolidate production in a few super competitive countries, increased competition for FDI is expected. Elimination of quotas has benefited China, though increased fear of dumping of cheap Chinese apparel products has raised caution in markets such as the EU and the US. From this perspective, Africa could still benefit from a number of preferential trade agreements such as AGOA and the EU's lomé Accord. As pointed out by a Value Chain Study conducted by UNIDO, sub-Saharan Africa currently lags behind other developing regions mainly due to poor transportation and communications infrastructure. These factors are very important to the functioning of apparel firms. Apparel exporters require ready access to inputs and global markets, streamlined customs procedures and reliable transport infrastructure. A number of countries are making an effort to both improve their communications infrastructure and to develop EPZs, and firms have benefited by establishing in these zones in countries such as Mauritius and Madagascar. Apparel production in sub-Saharan African countries also suffers from a weak cotton-textile-apparel value chain.

Good current export performance Increase in trade competitiveness Good rating on corruption perception Good availability of skilled workers low wage rates for professionals low wage rates for technical workers low wage rates for skilled workers low wage rates for unskilled workers low water costs

Opportunities in the sector exist and despite the end of MFA, the Ministry of Industry declared that 10 new foreign companies registered in 2005 within the apparel sector to benefit from tax incentives and the inexpensive but well-trained labor force available in the country. Madagascar offers opportunities for investors developing export oriented apparel companies in the EPZ, called the Zone Franche, which gives lucrative incentives to export companies, including tax-breaks. Unlike other countries, Madagascar's EPZ expands across the whole island. EPZ status can be granted to companies anywhere in Madagascar and is not restricted to specific geographic zones.

Difficulty of sourcing local component inputs Weak country credit rating High country risk rating Business start-up procedures are numerous Unfavorable labor relations Poor availability of managers Poor availability of professionals Poor availability of technical workers Poor availability of unskilled workers High wage rates for managers International competition is the biggest direct threat to Madagascar's apparel industry.

HORTICULTURE SECTOR

The horticulture sector is defined as the production and marketing of highly perishable products destined for fresh consumption, with relatively high-value per unit. Average annual worldwide production and trade in horticultural goods (fresh fruits, leguminous vegetables, cut flowers, nuts, and spices) have grown steadily. From 1993-2002, world trade in fruits and vegetables increased by 37 percent to an estimated USD 75 billion. While production has risen steadily in most regions of the world, an increasing share of this production growth has occurred in developing countries. Today, according to FAOSTAT, Asia is the leading exporter of fresh fruit and vegetables (USD 607 million), followed by latin America (USD 408 million). Sub-Saharan Africa's export value is USD 89.6 million, behind the US (USD 205 million) and the EU (USD 96 million).

Among developing regions, Africa has shown relatively higher growth not only in the export growth of fruits and vegetables, but also in terms of the share of fruits and vegetables in the region's total agricultural exports. In many African countries, horticulture exports have become a bright spot with vegetable and fruit exports now ranking first in total sub-Saharan Africa agricultural exports. More than 60 percent of this volume comes from the Southern African Customs Union (SACU), with Kenya's in particular, a successful example. A number of other countries across Africa have moved aggressively in recent years in efforts to duplicate Kenya's success story and several have achieved some notable success in diversifying their production and accessing export markets.

In export markets, supermarkets are increasingly playing an important role in the horticulture industry, particularly in the retail of fruits and vegetables. This trend, combined with the increased concern for food safety issues, is the force shaping the new supply chain structure in the horticulture sector. There is heavier reliance on fewer but trusted suppliers whose relationship is based on stringent and detailed contracts. In some cases, this relationship may also involve technical and other assistance. However, there has not yet been a trend for these supermarkets and hypermarkets to become direct investors. In fact, the majority of horticulture commodities in Africa today are produced by smallholders, who, in turn, depend on medium-to large-scale agri-businesses to organize their produce for exports.

While the amount of FDI in the horticulture sector is not substantial compared to other sectors, such as light manufacturing, it is a factor. In fact, FDI is behind almost all the successful horticulture development stories in Africa, and continues to play an important role. Opportunities are sought by entrepreneurs, particularly in the final-market country, who see climate and other production advantages in Africa. In the horticulture sector there appear to be export opportunities in the growth in demand for high quality pre-packed vegetables. An advantage for Africa is that these industries require a combination of labor-intensive activities such as pre-packaging work, and lower labor costs. Africa's position with regard to fresh cut flowers, starting material for cut flowers (seeds, young plants, cuttings, etc.) and pot plants, is currently strong. In particular, starting material presents good opportunities because of its relatively high levels of labor intensity, which now makes it impossible to produce it in Europe.

For potential investors, in addition to the climatic requirements, good logistics in order to comply with just-in-time-and-shape delivery required by buyers is critical. Equally important is the availability of inputs such as pesticides, fertilizers, and packaging materials. Market access questions will be determined by the ability to comply with trade standards rather than tariff levels.

Average Investment Characteristics

Ownership	51 % local owned
	21 % joint ventures 28 % completely foreign owned
Investment size	USD 4.9 million
Size of site	195 ha
Number of employees	462
Sales	USD 18.7 million
Company exports	Roses beans vanilla gum arabic mangoes tomatoes cashews live plants pineapples citrus fruit banana baby corn peppers

Madagascar's climate is its biggest attribute for horticulture operations. It is conducive to year-round growing of fruits, vegetables, nuts, and ornamental plants, making it an attractive location from which to serve markets in temperate and cold climates such as the USA and Europe. Horticulture products traditionally grown in Madagascar include: citrus fruit, bananas, mangos, coconuts, litchi, pineapple, avocados, peach, nectarines, apples and pears. Opportunities also exist for establishing large farms or consolidating small ones, as there is high demand in the local food and beverage processing market for the stability and predictability in crop supply that large farms provide.

FOOD AND BEVERAGE PROCESSING SECTOR

The food and beverage processing sector refers to the manufacturing, processing and preservation of meat, fish, fruit, vegetables, oils and fats; manufacture of dairy products;

manufacture of grain mill products, starches and starch products and prepared animals feeds; manufacture of other food products (e.g. bread, sugar, chocolate, pasta, coffee, nuts and spices); and the manufacture of bottled and canned soft drinks, fruit juices, beer, wines, etc.

Global market growth for processed food and beverages has been strong in recent years, with sales totaling an estimated USD 3.2 trillion, or about three-fourths of total world food sales. Africa is no exception. Agro-processing is one of the most significant manufacturing activities in Africa. In fact, agribusiness activity, of which food processing represents a large share, accounts for approximately one-fifth (or USD 70 billion) of the region's GDP and just under half of the region's value-added in manufacturing and services.

Despite strong production and sales growth of processed foods and beverage in recent years, growth in trade has been slow, at about 6 percent of sales. The presence of tariff escalation and growing use of trade remedy measures (such as antidumping and countervailing duties and safeguard measures) are partly to blame. Such mechanisms favor trade in raw commodities at the expense of processed products, reflecting countries' efforts to encourage domestic processing. As a result, firms looking for access to foreign markets often opt to make foreign direct investment. Market saturation at home and the search for higher profit margins in new underserved markets is pushing food manufacturers to seek overseas markets. These companies are looking to capitalize on increased local demand for higher value foods, a trend driven by rising incomes and increased urbanization. At the same time, consumer-driven changes are increasingly pushing food suppliers to meet consumer demand and preferences at a local level. This requires food suppliers to be capable of tailoring their products to the unique characteristics of consumer demands in each market that they serve, for which FDI offers a better tool than exports.

The largest food companies such as Nestlé, Kraft, Unilever, Coca-Cola and Pepsi already have a strong presence across the developing world. In Africa alone, the Coca-Cola Co. has more than 100 bottling and canning plants; Nestlé has 27 factories supplying African consumers with a wide range of products including powdered milk, soluble coffees, bottled water, breakfast cereals, chilled dairy and ice cream and infant nutrition. Unilever is currently operating in 13 countries with more than USD 2 billion sales annually. In recent years, South African firms in particular have expanded into the region with new retail food formats, fast food outlets, and pan-African processed food brands. Given the importance of the size of the local or regional market, formulating regional trade blocs is one way to enhance attractiveness to investors. According to the UN's Food and Agriculture Organization (FAO), the East African milk market alone is due to double by 2030 to 475 million metric tons. Fisheries is a constantly expanding sub-sector, especially in East Africa, as the region is endowed with some of the largest freshwater lakes and abundant fishery resources, including the Nile perch, the most widely processed fish for export in the region. From 1995-2001, exports of fish and fish products from the EAC nearly tripled in value. In West Africa, Ghana successfully tapped into the endowment of fish supply and attracted FDI: Starkist's investment in canned tuna manufacturing tripled Ghana's export capacity of processed tuna.

Ownership	37 % local owned 25 % joint ventures 38 % completely foreign owned
Investment size	USD 38.1 million
Factory floor space	35,795 m²
Number of employees	518

Sales	USD 52.9 million
Company exports	Dried fruits and vegetables bottle beverages and fruit juices palm oil peanut oil sugars jellies and jams powdered milks biscuits cookies candy canned fruits and vegetables

SHARED SERVICES (CALL CENTERS) SECTOR

Call center operation is a segment within the outsourcing trend. Outsourcing occurs when one company delegates responsibility for performing a function or series of tasks to another company. Outsourcing services span a wide range – from call center functions (outbound tele-marketing campaigns, data-cleaning, surveys, help desks, inbound services) to business process functions such as fulfilling financial, insurance, healthcare, human resource, tax compliance functions, data conversion, and IT services. In sub-Saharan Africa, where the sector is still nascent, outsourcing is almost exclusively in call center operation, with the exception of South Africa. Offshore outsourcing now represents a USD 100 billion market that is growing at more than 30 percent per annum. The majority of current demand for offshore outsourcing services comes from developed countries: the United States and Canada (15.9 percent) and Western Europe (44.8 percent). The primary countries exporting services to satisfy this demand include Ireland, India, and Canada. In sub-Saharan Africa, South Africa and Mauritius are the only countries that have begun to emerge on the radar screen of investors, but their estimated market size is still miniscule compared to competitors around the world.

Behind the rapid growth in offshore outsourcing are the improved quality and lower costs of telecommunications and Internet infrastructure. The development of the industry has led to an increased general knowledge and experience in offshore outsourcing. This means there is now less risk associated with including offshore outsourcing in the evaluation and implementation process of a company's business plan. As a consequence, there is international competitive pressure to include offshore outsourcing as a component of overall business strategy to reduce cost and/or to increase productivity.

The factors making a foreign country an attractive base for offshore outsourcing services, according to an index developed by A.T. Kearney, are the following: financial structure, people skills and availability, and business environment. The market growth of offshore outsourcing does not necessarily lead to higher levels of FDI in the industry, as the relationship between offshore outsourcing service providers and their clients is generally contractual. Nevertheless, there is plenty of opportunity for FDI growth.

Trends in offshore outsourcing indicate a promising future. As with any maturing market, offshore outsourcing moves up the value chain, reflecting increased levels of provider competence and confidence among their customers. Customers will multi-source from more than one provider (and country), depending upon type of services required, costs and risks. Due to increased competition and risk management, providers extend their services offerings (e.g., call-center services extend to back-office services) and offer new value-added services. Mature offshore markets then outsource to new, lower cost countries or locations within the same country. Higher value outsourcing services (IT and financial) migrate to those countries with greater protection of intellectual property and privacy. Increased demand and competition for offshore outsourcing services is likely to lead to rising labor costs, resulting in decreased service levels and the tendency to move offshore to lower cost countries.

TOURISM (HOTELS) SECTOR

After a drop in tourism caused by the events of September 11, 2001, and other natural disasters, global tourism has seen a rebound since 2004. According to the UN World Tourism Organization (UNWTO), the number of international tourist arrivals in 2005 is estimated at 808 million, up from 766 million in 2004. The UNWTO is expecting tourism arrivals to double by 2010 and reach 1.56 billion by 2020. Globally, tourism accounts for roughly 35 percent of exports of services and over 8 percent of exports of goods, and is the world's largest employer.

According to the UNWTO, sub-Saharan Africa saw the strongest growth in tourism in 2005 estimated at 13 percent, with particularly remarkable results for Kenya (26 percent between January and October compared with the same period of the previous year), and Mozambique (37 percent Jan.-Sept.). South Africa (11 percent Jan.-Aug.) as well as Seychelles (7 percent) and Mauritius (6 percent), all improved on their 2004 results. Tourism is often a leading generator of foreign exchange in African countries. Total tourist expenditure in Africa was estimated at about USD 33 million in 2004, and is anticipated to increase to USD 47 million by 2010 and to USD 77 million by 2020.

Sub-Saharan Africa is heavily endowed with exceptional attractions for the local and international tourism markets. These include natural resources, biodiversity and a number of historical heritage sites. The greatest numbers of tourist arrivals to sub-Saharan African countries were visitors from other countries within the region. Nonetheless, arrivals from Europe, Asia and North America are also growing. Europeans tend to visit single countries, while North American travelers usually visit several countries as part of a circuit tour. While North Americans number fewer than Europeans, their expenditure tends to be higher. Asians form a smaller part of African tourism, but are growing in importance.

African countries offer unique opportunities for investment in safari, beach, adventure, cultural and ecotourism holidays as well as opportunities for business travel. At the early stages of investment, anchor or magnet projects create the base for future investment. Some cities have become hubs for tourism investment with a full complement of hotels catering to local and foreign tourists. These investments are typically made by foreign investors, but often with local partners who are skilled at negotiating with government. These anchor – or greenfield -investments require financial engineering suited to the hotel sector. Ownership and operations are often separated, with one company owning the building and an operating company managing or leasing the property. Ownership companies are suited to local and foreign investment with substantial equity (20-50 percent of investment) and long-term loans consistent with real estate financing. In this context, investors look for the additional comfort that guarantees can offer on the equity and associated long-term lending.

Most international chains, on the other hand, are management companies providing skilled management services. A limited number will also take equity positions as a demonstration of goodwill and a few are exploring long-term investment as a new strategy. Anchor projects of course also attract the smaller investments characteristic of tourism investment – small guest houses, new restaurants and vastly improved travel agency and tour operator services. Financing of tourism SMEs conforms to schemes for SMEs in general and typically does not lend itself as well to guarantees – although technical support is often a feature of such operations and some countries are experimenting with credit and guarantee schemes.

IMPORTANT LAWS AND REGULATIONS

CUSTOMS CODE

TITLE 1 - GENERAL PRINCIPLES OF THE CUSTOMS REGIME

Chapter 1 - Definition of the laws and customs regulations

S.1 .- The term "customs laws and regulations" means both the laws and regulations relating to arrangements for assessment and collection of customs duties and obligations to the Customs Administration as the subject, as applicable to taxes or tax collected by customs.

Art.2 .- The term "customs duties" means the rights whose purpose is to protect the trade, industry and agriculture of the Republic of Madagascar and the rates of which may vary the minimum rate (conventional law) or general rate by origin or destination of goods imported or exported.

They can be "ad valorem", calculated from a percentage of the value of the goods, or "specific", when the plate is the quantity of goods, weight, volume or number.

Art.3 .- The term "tax duties and taxes" means taxes and duties which aims to provide revenue to the budget of the Republic of Madagascar. They can be "ad valorem" or "specific".

TITLE 2 - GENERAL

Art.4 1 .- The customs area includes the national territory, internal waters, territorial waters and contiguous zone.

2 ° zones exempt from all or part of the legislation and regulations may be established in the customs territory.

Art.5 .- In all parts of the customs territory, we must follow the same laws and customs regulations.

Art.6 .- 1 ° customs laws and regulations should be applied, regardless of the quality of the natural or legal persons, private or public, that are subject to.

2 ° The only immunities or exemptions that may be granted are those set out in this Code.

Art.7 .- The Customs Administration is responsible for implementing the provisions of this Code.

TITLE 3 - TARIFF ACT

Section 1 - Rates of duties

Art.8 .- The goods entering the customs territory or leaving, are liable, as the case of import duties or export duties included in the tariff of customs duties. The rate of duty is fixed by law.

Section 2 - Rates of duties and taxes tax

Art.9 .- Goods entering the customs territory, or leaving, are liable, as appropriate, duties or import taxes tax or output tax rates listed.

The rates of duties and taxes are set by tax law.

These duties and taxes are subject to the provisions of this Code and, in particular by the special rules laid down in Title IX below.

Section 3 - Common provisions

Art.10.-The provisions of this Code relating to goods that are "heavily taxed" refer to goods that are subject to duties and taxes that in total exceed 20% in the case of ad valorem tax or more than 20% of the value of goods in the case of specific taxation.

Art.11.-payment instruments (bank notes, checks, bills, etc..) Are considered goods under customs regulations.

Chapter 4 - General powers of the government

Section 1 - Restrictions on entry, exit, tonnage and packaging

Art.12.-Orders of the Minister of Customs may:

° 1 ° limit the jurisdiction of certain customs and identify those which should be made mandatory for certain customs;

° 2 ° decide that certain goods can not be imported or exported only by vessels of that tonnage determined and set;

° 3 ° set, after consultation with the Ministers concerned if necessary, and for certain commodities, specific rules of conditioning.

Section 2 - Grant of the transitional clause

Art.13.-Goods that can justify being shipped directly to the customs territory prior to insertion of an instrument establishing or changing of customs and tax in the Official Gazette, are admitted to the previous regime more favorable when they are declared for home use without being placed in storage or incorporated deposit.

The justifications must result of the last tickets set to direct destination from the customs territory, prior to insertion in the Official Journal of the act aforesaid

Chapter 5 - Applicability of the Tariff Act

Section 1 - Background and refund of duties and taxes

Section 1 - General

Art.14.-1 products imported or exported are subject to the Tariff Act in the state where they are when they it becomes applicable.

2 ° However, the Customs may allow the separation of goods in the same load would have been damaged as a result of events occurring before registration of the declaration in detail the goods to be damaged or destroyed immediately be re-imported or shipped back within as appropriate, be taxed according to their new state.

3 ° The duties, taxes and surcharges are levied specific regardless of the relative value or degree of conservation of the goods.

Paragraph 2 - Reimbursement of duties and taxes

Art.15.-1 Reimbursement of duties and taxes levied on imports or exports shall be provided is found to have been improperly collected.

2 ° The refund of duties and taxes levied on imports is granted when it is established that at the time of importation the goods were defective or not in accordance with the terms of contract under which they were imported.

The refund of duties and taxes shall be subject to re-export of goods to or on behalf of the foreign supplier or to their destruction under the supervision of the Customs Administration, with payment of taxes relating to residues of the destruction.

3 ° The order of the Minister of Customs shall determine the conditions of application of this section, including the period within which the claim must be filed after the importation of goods.

Section 2 - Species of goods

Section 1 - Definition, classification and assimilation

Art.16.-1 The species of goods is the name given them by the tariff only so-called "Harmonized Commodity Description and Coding System" which is the basis for customs tariffs and tax.

2 The goods are not included in price shall be treated as objects most similar in general interpretative rules and explanatory notes of the Harmonized Commodity Description and Coding System.

Section 2 - Complaints against the decisions of assimilation and classification

Art.17.-In case of any discrepancy in the decisions referred to in Article 16 above, the claim is subject to an administrative commission called "Commission for Conciliation and Customs Expertise," which gives its opinion on this claim . The composition and functioning of this commission are defined in Articles 112-115 of this Code

Art.18.-The costs of the operation of the Commission of Conciliation and Customs Expertise are the responsibility of the state.

Art.19.-destruction or deterioration of goods or documents submitted to the Commission for Conciliation and Customs Expertise can result in the awarding of compensation.

Section 3 - Origin of goods

Art.20. A-1 imports, tariffs are levied according to the origin of goods, except under special provisions provided for in international agreements in force for the granting of preferential rates.

2 ° The country of origin of a product is when the product was harvested, extracted or manufactured soil.

3 ° The rules for determining the origin of products harvested, extracted from the soil or manufactured in one country and then worked in another country are determined by order of the Minister of Customs.

4 Imported products are entitled to the preferential treatment given to their origin if it is regularly justified this origin. Orders of the Minister of Customs shall determine the conditions under which the original justifications must be produced and where they are not required.

All violations of the corresponding rules of origin customs offenses are punishable under Articles 360 and following of this Code.

A Art.21.-export, the Customs Administration authenticates the certificates and documents certifying the origin of Malagasy exports.

Section 4 - Origin of goods

Art.22.-The country of origin is the country from which the merchandise is shipped direct to destination customs territory.

Transit, stop, stop or transshipment of goods through a country does not confer the qualification of origin

Section 5 - Value of goods

Paragraph 1 - A import

Art.23.-1, the customs value of imported goods is the transaction value, that is to say the price actually paid or payable for the goods when sold for export to Madagascar, where appropriate, adjusted in accordance with paragraph 4 of this section, provided that:

• a) that there is no restriction on the sale or use of goods by the buyer other than restrictions which:

- I) are imposed or required by law or by public authorities of Madagascar,

- Ii) limit the geographical area in which the goods may be sold, or

- Iii) do not substantially affect the value of the goods;

· B) the sale or price is not subject to some condition or consideration for which the value is not determinable with respect to the goods being valued;

· C) no portion of the proceeds of any subsequent resale, disposal or use of the goods by the buyer will accrue directly or indirectly to the seller, unless an appropriate adjustment can be made in accordance with paragraph 4 of this section , and

• d) the buyer and seller are not related or, if they are, the transaction value is acceptable for customs purposes under the provisions of paragraph 2 of this article.

· A) In determining whether the transaction value is acceptable for the purposes of paragraph 1, that the buyer and seller are related shall not in itself sufficient grounds for regarding the transaction value as unacceptable. In this case, the circumstances of the sale shall be examined and the transaction value shall be accepted provided that the relationship did not influence the price. If, based on information provided by the importer or other sources, the Customs has reason to believe that the relationship influenced the price, it shall communicate its grounds to the importer and gives him a reasonable opportunity to answer. If the importer so requests, the reasons are communicated in writing.

· B) In a sale between related persons, the transaction value is accepted and the goods valued in accordance with the provisions of paragraph 1 whenever the importer demonstrates that such value is very close to one of the following values, ranging at the same time or at about the same time:

- I) the transaction value in sales to unrelated buyers of identical or similar goods for export to Madagascar;

- Ii) customs value of identical or similar goods, as de-terminated under the provisions of Article 24-2 ° C);

- Iii) the customs value of identical or similar goods, as determined under the provisions of Article 24-2 ° d)

In applying the above criteria, it is due account of the demonstrated differences in levels of trade, quantities, items listed in paragraph 4 of this article and costs incurred by the seller in sales in which the seller and I buyer are not related and that does not support them during the sales in which the seller and buyer are related.

° C) the criteria set out in paragraph 2 b) are used at the initiative of the importer and for comparison purposes only. Substitute values can not be made under paragraph 2 b).

· A) The price actually paid or payable is the total payment made or to be made by the buyer to the seller, or for the benefit of celuici for imported goods and includes all payments made or to be made as a condition of sale of imported goods by the buyer to the seller or the buyer to a third party to satisfy an obligation of the seller. The payment need not be made in cash. It can be done by letters of credit or negotiable instrument and may be made directly or indirectly;

· B) activities, including those related to marketing companies or by the buyer on his own account other than those for which an adjustment is provided in paragraph 4 of this Article shall not be regarded as an indirect payment the seller, even if we can consider that the seller has or have been undertaken with his consent, and their cost is not added to the price actually paid or payable in determining the value of the value for duty of imported goods.

° 4 ° To determine the customs value under the provisions of this section is added to the price actually paid or payable for the imported goods:

· A) the following to the extent they are incurred by the buyer, but were not included in the price actually paid or payable for the goods:

- I) commissions and brokerage, except buying commissions,

- Ii) the cost of containers which are treated for customs purposes, as being one with the goods, packing costs, including both labor and materials;

· B) the value, apportioned as appropriate, products and services below where supplied directly or indirectly by the purchaser and used in the production and sale for export of imported goods in the Since this value was not included in the price actually paid or payable:

· - I) materials, components, parts and similar items incorporated in the imported goods;

· - Ii) tools, dies, molds and similar items used in the production of imported goods;

· - Iii) materials consumed in the production of imported goods;

· - Iv) engineering, development, art and design, plans and sketches undertaken elsewhere than in Madagascar and necessary for the production of imported goods;

· C) royalties and license fees related to the goods being valued that the buyer must pay, either directly or indirectly, as a condition of sale of the goods being valued to the extent that such royalties and license fees were not included in the price actually paid or payable;

• d) the value of any portion of the proceeds of any subsequent resale, disposal or use of imported goods that accrues directly or indirectly to the seller,

° E) expenses relating to services and benefits following occurred to the port or place of introduction to Madagascar:

- I) transport and insurance of imported goods and

- Ii) loading and handling associated with the transport of imported goods.

5 ° Anything that is added by subsection 4 of this section to the price actually paid or payable is based exclusively on objective and quantifiable data.

6 In determining the customs value, nothing is added to the price actually paid or payable, except those provided for in paragraph 4 of this article.

7 The Customs may conduct research and surveys to see if the criteria for assessing the value declared or presented to customs for the purpose of determining the customs value are complete and correct. In this regard, importers must cooperate with the Customs Administration, under threat of prosecution under section 286 of this Code.

Art.24.-1 When the customs value can not be determined under section 23 of this Code, it is necessary to pass successively in a), b), c), d) and e) paragraph 2 of this Article, until the first of these paragraphs can be determined, unless the order made under paragraph c) and d) must be reversed at the request of the declarant, it is only when this customs value can not be determined under subparagraph a given that it is permissible to apply the paragraph that immediately follows it, in the order established under this paragraph.

Customs values determined under this section are:

· A) the transaction value of identical goods sold for export to Madagascar and exported at the same time or at about the same time as the goods being valued;

· B) the transaction value of similar goods sold for export to Madagascar and exported at the same time or at about the same time as the goods being valued;

· C) value based on the unit price at which sales of Madagascar imported goods or identical or similar goods imported, accounting for the highest amount and made to persons not related to the sellers;

• d) computed value, the sum of:

- The cost or value of materials and fabrication or other processing employed in producing the imported goods;

- An amount for profit and general expenses equal to that usually reflected in sales of goods of the same species as the goods being valued which are made by producers in the exporting country for export to for Madagascar,

- The cost or value of the items referred to in paragraph 4 e) of section 23;

• e) value determined on the basis of data available in Madagascar, using reasonable means consistent with the principles and general provisions:

of the Agreement on Implementation of Article VII of the General Agreement on Tariffs and Trade 1994, of Article VII of the General Agreement on Tariffs and Trade 1994,

- The provisions of this Section.

3 ° The customs value determined under the provisions of paragraph 2 e) of this section will not be based:

· A) the sale price, Madagascar, goods produced in Madagascar;

· B) a system which provides for the acceptance for customs purposes of the higher of two possible values,

° C) on the price of goods on the domestic market of the exporting country,

• d) the cost of production other than! Are computed values which have been determined for identical or similar goods in accordance with article 24-2 ° d)

° E) on the price of goods for export to countries other than Madagascar,

° F) minimum customs values, or

· G) on arbitrary or fictitious values.

Notwithstanding the provisions of paragraph f) above, the officially established minimum values may be retained on a limited and transitional basis.

4 ° Where the evidence used to determine the customs value is expressed in a foreign currency, the conversion must be made on the basis of the official exchange rate published by the Malagasy authorities and in force at the date of registration of the declaration .

5 ° The value determined under the conditions above should, where appropriate, be rounded al'unité below.

Art.25.-1 Unless otherwise by decision of the Minister of Customs, a declaration of particulars relating to customs value must be filed with the accounting.

2 ° The declaration of particulars relating to customs value shall be signed by the importer and by the registrant.

3 The form and the particulars of the elements related to the customs value shall be determined by decision of the Director General of Customs.

Paragraph 2 - Export

Art.26. A-1 export, the value is to declare goods at the exit point plus, where applicable, transport costs to the border but not including the amount:

· A) the rights of exit,

· B) domestic taxes and similar charges that have been granted discharge to the exporter.

2 papers due. the original invoice included., together with the declaration does not bind the sovereign appreciation of the Customs Department nor the Commission of Conciliation and Customs Expertise.

Section 6 - Weight of goods

Art.27.-Orders of the Minister of Customs shall determine the conditions under which verification must be made of goods charged by weight and diet of packings imported filled. The dutiable weight of goods charged to the net weight can be determined by applying a flat tax.

Chapter 6 - Prohibitions

Section 1 - General

Art.28.-1 For the purposes of this Code, are considered prohibited any goods the import or export is prohibited in any capacity whatsoever, or subject to restrictions, rules or quality fitness, health, or to particular formalities.

2 ° Where the import or export is permitted only on presentation of an authorization, license, certificate, etc.. The goods is prohibited unless it is accompanied by a regular or if presented under the guise of a non-applicable.

All 3 titles authorizing import or export (licenses or other similar securities) can not, under any circumstances, be a loan, sale, assignment and, In general, any transaction by the holders to whom they were nominally granted.

Section 2 - Prohibitions relating to counterfeit trademark goods and pirated goods

Art.23.-1, the customs value of imported goods is the transaction value, that is to say the price actually paid or payable for the goods when sold for export to Madagascar, where appropriate, adjusted in accordance with paragraph 4 of this section, provided that:

• a) that there is no restriction on the sale or use of goods by the buyer other than restrictions which:

- I) are imposed or required by law or by public authorities of Madagascar,

- Ii) limit the geographical area in which the goods may be sold, or

- Iii) do not substantially affect the value of the goods;

· B) the sale or price is not subject to some condition or consideration for which the value is not determinable with respect to the goods being valued;

· C) no portion of the proceeds of any subsequent resale, disposal or use of the goods by the buyer will accrue directly or indirectly to the seller, unless an appropriate adjustment can be made in accordance with paragraph 4 of this section , and

• d) the buyer and seller are not related or, if they are, the transaction value is acceptable for customs purposes under the provisions of paragraph 2 of this article.

· A) In determining whether the transaction value is acceptable for the purposes of paragraph 1, that the buyer and seller are related shall not in itself sufficient grounds for regarding the transaction value as unacceptable. In this case, the circumstances of the sale shall be examined and the transaction value shall be accepted provided that the relationship did not influence the price. If, based on information provided by the importer or other sources, the Customs has reason to believe that the relationship influenced the price, it shall communicate its grounds to the importer and gives him a reasonable opportunity to answer. If the importer so requests, the reasons are communicated in writing.

· B) In a sale between related persons, the transaction value is accepted and the goods valued in accordance with the provisions of paragraph 1 whenever the importer demonstrates that such value is very close to one of the following values, ranging at the same time or at about the same time:

- I) the transaction value in sales to unrelated buyers of identical or similar goods for export to Madagascar;

- Ii) customs value of identical or similar goods, as de-terminated under the provisions of Article 24-2 ° C);

- Iii) the customs value of identical or similar goods, as determined under the provisions of Article 24-2 ° d)

In applying the above criteria, it is due account of the demonstrated differences in levels of trade, quantities, items listed in paragraph 4 of this article and costs incurred by the seller in sales in which the seller and I buyer are not related and that does not support them during the sales in which the seller and buyer are related.

° C) the criteria set out in paragraph 2 b) are used at the initiative of the importer and for comparison purposes only. Substitute values can not be made under paragraph 2 b).

· A) The price actually paid or payable is the total payment made or to be made by the buyer to the seller, or for the benefit of celuici for imported goods and includes all payments made or to be made as a condition of sale of imported goods by the buyer to the seller or the buyer to a third party to satisfy an obligation of the seller. The payment need not be made in cash. It can be done by letters of credit or negotiable instrument and may be made directly or indirectly;

· B) activities, including those related to marketing companies or by the buyer on his own account other than those for which an adjustment is provided in paragraph 4 of this Article shall not be regarded as an indirect payment the seller, even if we can consider that the seller has or have been undertaken with his consent, and their cost is not added to the price actually paid or payable in determining the value of the value for duty of imported goods.

° 4 ° To determine the customs value under the provisions of this section is added to the price actually paid or payable for the imported goods:

· A) the following to the extent they are incurred by the buyer, but were not included in the price actually paid or payable for the goods:

- I) commissions and brokerage, except buying commissions,

- Ii) the cost of containers which are treated for customs purposes, as being one with the goods, packing costs, including both labor and materials;

· B) the value, apportioned as appropriate, products and services below where supplied directly or indirectly by the purchaser and used in the production and sale for export of imported goods in the Since this value was not included in the price actually paid or payable:

· - I) materials, components, parts and similar items incorporated in the imported goods;

· - Ii) tools, dies, molds and similar items used in the production of imported goods;

· - Iii) materials consumed in the production of imported goods;

· - Iv) engineering, development, art and design, plans and sketches undertaken elsewhere than in Madagascar and necessary for the production of imported goods;

· C) royalties and license fees related to the goods being valued that the buyer must pay, either directly or indirectly, as a condition of sale of the goods being valued to the extent that such royalties and license fees were not included in the price actually paid or payable;

• d) the value of any portion of the proceeds of any subsequent resale, disposal or use of imported goods that accrues directly or indirectly to the seller,

° E) expenses relating to services and benefits following occurred to the port or place of introduction to Madagascar:

- I) transport and insurance of imported goods and

- Ii) loading and handling associated with the transport of imported goods.

5 ° Anything that is added by subsection 4 of this section to the price actually paid or payable is based exclusively on objective and quantifiable data.

6 In determining the customs value, nothing is added to the price actually paid or payable, except those provided for in paragraph 4 of this article.

7 The Customs may conduct research and surveys to see if the criteria for assessing the value declared or presented to customs for the purpose of determining the customs value are complete and correct. In this regard, importers must cooperate with the Customs Administration, under threat of prosecution under section 286 of this Code.

Art.24.-1 When the customs value can not be determined under section 23 of this Code, it is necessary to pass successively in a), b), c), d) and e) paragraph 2 of this Article, until the first of these paragraphs can be determined, unless the order made under paragraph c) and d) must be reversed at the request of the declarant, it is only when this customs value can not be determined under subparagraph a given that it is permissible to apply the paragraph that immediately follows it, in the order established under this paragraph.

2 Customs values determined under this section are:

· A) the transaction value of identical goods sold for export to Madagascar and exported at the same time or at about the same time as the goods being valued;

· B) the transaction value of similar goods sold for export to Madagascar and exported at the same time or at about the same time as the goods being valued;

· C) value based on the unit price at which sales of Madagascar imported goods or identical or similar goods imported, accounting for the highest amount and made to persons not related to the sellers;

• d) computed value, the sum of:

- The cost or value of materials and fabrication or other processing employed in producing the imported goods;

- An amount for profit and general expenses equal to that usually reflected in sales of goods of the same species as the goods being valued which are made by producers in the exporting country for export to for Madagascar,

- The cost or value of the items referred to in paragraph 4 e) of section 23;

• e) value determined on the basis of data available in Madagascar, using reasonable means consistent with the principles and general provisions:

of the Agreement on Implementation of Article VII of the General Agreement on Tariffs and Trade 1994,of Article VII of the General Agreement on Tariffs and Trade 1994,

- The provisions of this Section.

3 ° The customs value determined under the provisions of paragraph 2 e) of this section will not be based:

· A) the sale price, Madagascar, goods produced in Madagascar;

· B) a system which provides for the acceptance for customs purposes of the higher of two possible values,

° C) on the price of goods on the domestic market of the exporting country,

• d) the cost of production other than! Are computed values which have been determined for identical or similar goods in accordance with article 24-2 ° d)

° E) on the price of goods for export to countries other than Madagascar,

° F) minimum customs values, or

· G) on arbitrary or fictitious values.

Notwithstanding the provisions of paragraph f) above, the officially established minimum values may be retained on a limited and transitional basis.

4 ° Where the evidence used to determine the customs value is expressed in a foreign currency, the conversion must be made on the basis of the official exchange rate published by the Malagasy authorities and in force at the date of registration of the declaration .

5 ° The value determined under the conditions above should, where appropriate, be rounded al'unité below.

Art.25.-1 Unless otherwise by decision of the Minister of Customs, a declaration of particulars relating to customs value must be filed with the accounting.

2 ° The declaration of particulars relating to customs value shall be signed by the importer and by the registrant.

3 The form and the particulars of the elements related to the customs value shall be determined by decision of the Director General of Customs.

Paragraph 2 - Export

Art.26. A-1 export, the value is to declare goods at the exit point plus, where applicable, transport costs to the border but not including the amount:

· A) the rights of exit,

· B) domestic taxes and similar charges that have been granted discharge to the exporter.

2 papers due. the original invoice included., together with the declaration does not bind the sovereign appreciation of the Customs Department nor the Commission of Conciliation and Customs Expertise.

Section 6 - Weight of goods

Art.27.-Orders of the Minister of Customs shall determine the conditions under which verification must be made of goods charged by weight and diet of packings imported filled. The dutiable weight of goods charged to the net weight can be determined by applying a flat tax.

Chapter 6 - Prohibitions

Section 1 - General

Art.28.-1 For the purposes of this Code, are considered prohibited any goods the import or export is prohibited in any capacity whatsoever, or subject to restrictions, rules or quality fitness, health, or to particular formalities.

2 ° Where the import or export is permitted only on presentation of an authorization, license, certificate, etc.. The goods is prohibited unless it is accompanied by a regular or if presented under the guise of a non-applicable.

All 3 titles authorizing import or export (licenses or other similar securities) can not, under any circumstances, be a loan, sale, assignment and, In general, any transaction by the holders to whom they were nominally granted.

Section 2 - Prohibitions relating to counterfeit trademark goods and pirated goods

Art.29.-are prohibited at the entrance and exit:

· A) goods, including packaging, bearing a trademark or trade name that is identical to the trademark validly registered or trade in such goods;

· B) any trademark or trade without authorization designed to be attached to the goods, presented separately or even in the same situation that the goods referred to under a);

· C) any sign or any combination of signs, particularly words, including personal names, letters, numerals, figurative elements and combinations of color;

• d) any particular brand of piracy on the phonograms (sound recordings) for the circulation without the authorization of the producer, performer, foreign or domestic.

In accordance with the provisions on customs procedures in law enforcement for fraud, counterfeit trademark goods or pirated goods seized are forfeited after court decision or settlement transaction.

The Customs has the power to destroy them without compensation of any kind or to give them any other destination specified in the framework of its powers, provided they are not introduced into commercial channels and it is not prejudice the holder of the registered trademark or copyright holder.

Re-exportation of counterfeit trademark goods or pirated goods is prohibited. The same prohibitions imposed on imports non-commercial nature.

Section 3 - Prohibitions relating to the protection of trademarks and indications of origin

Art.30.-1 are prohibited at the entrance, excluded from the warehouse, transit and traffic, all foreign products, natural or manufactured, labeled either on themselves or on packaging, boxes, bales , envelopes, labels or tapes, etc.., a trademark or trade name, sign or any indication likely to believe they were manufactured in Madagascar they are from Madagascar.

2 This also applies to foreign products manufactured or natural, obtained in a town of same name as a town of Madagascar, which do not, along with the name of this locality, the name of the country of origin and the word "Imported" in letters clearly visible.

Art.31.-are prohibited at the entrance to all foreign products that do not meet in the indication of origin, the conditions imposed by law.

Chapter 7 - Control of external trade and foreign exchange

Art.32.-Regardless of obligations under this Code, importers and exporters must comply with the regulation of control of foreign trade and foreign exchange.

Division 2 - Organization and functioning of the customs administration

Chapter 1 - Scope of the customs administration

Art.33.-1 The action of the Customs Administration is carried across the customs territory under the conditions laid down in this Code.

2 An area of special monitoring is organized along the maritime border. It is the customs radius.

Art.34.-1 ° The customs radius includes a marine area and land area.

2 ° The sea area is between the coast and the boundary of the maritime exclusive zone of Madagascar.

3 ° The land area extends:

· Between the coast and a line sixty kilometers below the sea shore;

Œ at a radius of sixty kilometers from the international airports

4 ° To help prevent fraud, the depth of the land area can be increased, in varying degrees not exceeding 100 km, by order of the Minister of Customs after consulting the Minister of the Interior.

5 Distances are calculated in a straight line regardless of windings of the roads.

Chapter 2 - Immunity, backup and obligations of customs officers

Art.35.-1 Customs officers are under the special protection of the law. It is prohibited to all persons

· A) of the abuse, mistreat them or disturbing them in the performance of their duties;

· B) to object to this exercise.

2 ° The civil and military authorities are required to first request to lend a hand to customs officials for carrying out their mission.

Art.36.-1 Subject age requirements established by the laws, customs officials of all ranks must take an oath before the civil tribunal of first instance in whose jurisdiction the residence where they are appointed.

2 The oath is recorded free in the court. The act of the oath is exempt from stamp and registration. It is transcribed free employment commissions referred to in the following article.

Art.37.-In carrying out their duties, customs officers must have their employment commission mentioning their swearing and they are required to show it to the first request.

Art.38.-are bound by professional secrecy, in accordance with the provisions of the Criminal Code, the customs officers and all persons to the course of their duties or their duties to perform in any capacity whatsoever functions at headquarters or in the external services of customs or to intervene in the application of customs legislation.

Art.39.-1 Customs officials have, for the performance of their duties, the right to bear arms. 2 ° In addition to self-defense, they can use:

· A) when violence or assault are brought against them or when they are threatened by armed individuals;

· B) when they can not stop other vehicles, boats and other means of transport drivers fail to comply with the stop;

° C) when can not otherwise oppose the passage of a meeting of people who do not respect warnings addressed to them.

• d) when they can capture live dogs, horses and other animals used for fraud, or that one attempts to import or export fraudulently or illegally circulating in the customs radius.

Art.40.-1 Customs officers are also authorized to use all appropriate means and equipment such as harrows, hedgehog, cables, to secure the means of transport when drivers do not stop at their summons.

2 The first paragraph of this section and those of Article 39 above shall be applicable throughout the customs territory and in all cases where customs officials may legally exercise their function.

Art.41.-Customs officers have, for the performance of their duties, the right to wear the uniform. The composition of the uniform and the conditions of the port are set by decision of the Director General of Customs.

Art. 42 .- A customs officer who was dismissed from his job or leaves must immediately return his commission in the administration of employment, records, seals, weapons and items of equipment which is responsible for its service and to make its accounts.

Art.43.-1 Customs officers to leave for two years the customs radius, in case they will be fired unless they return home they had in the department, before into the Customs Administration.

2 officers dismissed who fail in the month, with the demand to leave the department are pursued by the prosecutor about the criminal court, arrested and sentenced to the same penalties as those determined by Articles 271 and 272 Penal Code.

Art.44.-1 are prohibited customs officers, under the penalties under the Penal Code against public officials who are bribed to receive directly or indirectly any gratuity, reward or present.

2 ° The culprit denouncing corruption is absolved of penalties, fines and forfeitures.

Art.45.-1 The Customs Administration is authorized to disclose information it holds in foreign trade and financial relations with foreign services under other ministries and the Central Bank of Madagascar by their activity involved in public service missions which contributes the Customs Administration. The information provided must be necessary for the fulfillment of these missions or better use of public spending on the development of foreign trade.

2 ° The provision of such information may be made to officers completing at least the position of Director.

3 People who know and use the information provided is, in the manner and subject to the penalties s under the provisions of the Penal Code, held to professional secrecy regarding such information.

Chapter 3 - Powers of customs officers

Section 1 - Rights of access to goods, means of transport and people

Art.46.-For the purposes of the provisions of this Code and to the pursuit of fraud, customs officers may enter and inspect the goods, conveyances and people whether in the office radius or anywhere in the country. To this end, Customs officers may require production of documents proving the origin of goods held or transported.

In addition to the regulations applicable in the area of the radius of Customs and the goods referred to in section 254 of the Customs Code, failing to produce these documents to the first request, the customs officers can, to avoid diversion of the goods, the transfer, the owner's expense at the customs office nearest you or if necessary, put them under customs supervision by affixing weights or on the container or on the openings of the places where they are deposited.

Art.47.-1 driver of a conveyance shall be subject to the orders of customs officials.

2 ° They can use all appropriate devices to secure the means of transport when drivers do not stop on their signal.

Art.48.-Customs officers can visit all vessels below 100 GRT that are in the maritime zone of customs.

Art.49.-1 Customs officers can go on all buildings, located in ports or harbors or up or down the rivers. They can remain there until their discharge or departure.

2 Captains and Commanders must receive customs officers, to accompany the visiting ships. They must also submit to such agents the overall condition of the ship loading.

Customs officers can request the opening of the hatches, rooms and closets of these buildings and the parcels designated for the visit.

In case of refusal, customs officials require the assistance of a police officer who is required to open the hatches, rooms, cabinets and packages.

Minutes shall be prepared for offenses punishable under Articles 35-1 ° and 361 of this Code, without prejudice to infringements after the opening of the hatches, rooms, cabinets of their building or parcel.

If the police officer so required refuses assistance, customs officers fail to observe this refusal, inform the prosecutor and mention of the incident is made in the minutes.

However, the rooms the crew being treated as homes, a search warrant must be obtained from the Public Prosecutor, in accordance with Article 13 of the Constitution.

3 ° The officers of the testing of vessels and cargoes can, at sunset, close the hatches, which can be opened in their presence.

4 Of the warships, visits can only be made after sunset.

Art. 50 .- For the exercise of visitation rights, audits, inspections and surveillance provided for in this Code and the enactments for its enforcement, customs officials can use seals which forms and characteristics are defined by decision of the Director General of Customs.

Only establishments approved under the conditions set by the Customs seals can provide

Such establishments may be inspected Administration of Customs.

Art.51.-As part of the exercise of rights of access to people, and when there are serious indications can be assumed that a person crossing the border carrying narcotics hidden in his body, customs officials can submit it to of medical screening after having obtained the consent. In case of refusal, customs officers are the President of the Court with territorial jurisdiction an application for authorization.

The magistrate seized may authorize Customs officers to carry out medical examinations, it means the doctor immediately responsible for the practice.

The test results reported by the physician, the observations of the person and the conduct of the proceedings must be recorded in a report submitted to the magistrate.

In addition, Customs officers may carry out, in the rooms provided for that purpose, to visit the bodies of those believed to have on the body of the fraudulent merchandise.

Section 2 - Home visits

Art.52.-1 for the search for goods held unlawfully in the customs radius, and for research in all places of the goods subject to the provisions of section 254 below, customs officials may conduct home visits. Except in the case of flagrante delicto, each visit must be authorized by an order of the judicial authority which means the Judicial Police Officer responsible for assisting in the operation.

2 ° The visits are conducted in the presence of the occupier or his representative. If this is impossible, the judicial police officer requires two witnesses chosen outside of those within his authority or that of the Customs Administration.

3 Customs officers can intervene without the assistance of a police officer, to search for goods, continued to view without interruption as provided by Article 275 below, are introduced into a same house or other building located outside the radius.

However, after finding they must immediately notify the Prosecutor

4 visits can not be started before six o'clock in the morning or after six pm at night.

The visits started can be continued until the close of trading.

Section 3 - Post-clearance

Art.53.-The Customs Administration may, after issuance of the authorization of the release of the goods, to revise the statements, the control of documents relating to the goods in question or verification of such goods when they can still be made.

When the result of the revision of the declaration or subsequent verification that the provisions governing the customs procedure concerned have been applied on the basis of incorrect or incomplete, the Customs Administration shall, in accordance with the laws and regulations, measures to restore the situation in the light of new evidence in its possession.

Section 4 - Right of communication especially in the Customs

Art.54.-1 Customs officers with the rank of inspector or customs officer, or responsible for the Receiver or police chief of Customs may require the submission of papers and documents any kind relating to transactions affecting their service, including data on computer media:

· A) in the railway station (bills, invoices, load sheets, books, records, etc.).

· B) the premises of the shipping companies and river and among owners, agents and ship brokers (cargo manifests, bills of lading, bills of board, shipping notices, delivery orders, etc.).

° C) in the premises of the airlines operating (dispatch, notes and

delivery notes, records, stores, etc.).

• d) the premises of the business of road transport (records management, record book packages, permit books, waybills, bills of lading, packing slips, etc.).

° E) in the local agencies, including the so-called "rapid transit" that char-gent of the receipt, consolidation, shipping by all modes of transportation (rail, road, water, air) and delivery of all packages (detailed schedules of collective shipments, receipts, delivery permits, etc.).

· F) in or freight forwarders;

· G) dealers warehouse docks and general stores (books and records of deposit, warrants and pledges books, records of entry and exit of goods, status goods, records, etc.).

• h) in actual recipients or senders of goods declared to customs;

· I) and, in general, in all persons or entities directly or indirectly interested in regular or irregular transactions within the jurisdiction of the Customs Administration;

2 ° Customs officers not below the rank of controller also have the right of communication under the 1st paragraph above, when acting on written order of an officer not below the rank of Inspector and under which they serve directly. This order must be presented to the subject must indicate the name of the latter.

Officers entitled to exercise the right of communication under paragraph 1 above may be assisted by officials of a lower grade, as they obliged and under the same sanctions to secrecy.

3 ° The various documents mentioned above must be retained by the parties for a period of five years from the date of the customs declaration of export goods for shippers. and as of the date of customs declaration of import. for recipients.

4 In the examinations and investigations made for people or companies referred to in paragraph I of this Article, the designated customs officers in that paragraph may proceed with the seizure of documents of any kind (accounts, invoices, copies of letters , checkbooks, bills, bank accounts, storage media for computer data such as CPU, disk etc.). to facilitate the accomplishment of their mission.

5 ° As part of International Mutual Administrative Assistance, the Customs Administration is authorized, subject to reciprocity, to provide qualified authorities of foreign countries any information, certificates, minutes and other documents that may establish violation of applicable laws and regulations at the entrance or exit from their territory.

Section 5 - Customs control of mailings

Art.55.-1 Customs officials have access to post offices, including the sorting rooms, in direct correspondence with the outside world, to seek, in the presence of authority staff, the items enclosed or not , original interior or exterior, except for transit shipments, containing or appearing to contain objects of the kind referred to in this article.

2 The Post Office is authorized to submit to customs control, as provided by the conventions and agreements of the Universal Postal Union, the items which are prohibited to import, subject to duties or taxes levied by the Customs Administration or subject to restrictions or formalities at the entrance.

3 The Post Office is also authorized to submit to customs control items which are prohibited for export, subject to duties and taxes collected by the Customs and subject to restrictions or formalities at the exit.

4 It can not, under any circumstances, be deprived of the secrecy of correspondence. Section VI of passports

Art.56.-Customs officers may check the identity of persons entering the customs territory or leaving, or circulating in the customs radius.

Division 3 - Conduct of goods to customs

Chapter 1 - Import

Section 1 - Transport by sea

Section 1 - General

Art.57.-1 Goods arriving by sea must be registered on the manifest or loading condition of the ship;

2 This document must be signed by the master, he must state the species and number of packages, their marks and numbers, nature, the gross weight and net weight of goods, place and date of shipment;

3 It is forbidden to present as a unit in the manifest, more packages sealed together in any manner whatsoever;

4 Prohibited goods must be brought to manifest in their true name, by nature and species.

Art.58.-captain of a ship arrived in the maritime zone of Customs shall, at the first request:

· A) submit the original manifest to the visa varietur customs officers who go on board;

· B) give them a copy of the manifest.

Art.59.-1 ships can dock in the ports provided with a customs office except in cases of force majeure duly justified. In this case, the master shall, upon landing, to appear before the Head of Department of Merchant Marine, or failing that, the Chief of the Brigade of the National Gendarmerie, the Police Commissioner or the Mayor of the City of place, and submit for approval, where the log should be recorded in advance the causes of docking.

The customs office nearest must be immediately notified of the event by the master and the administrative authority which granted the endorsement of the log.

2 ° The Director General of Customs may permit operations outside of these places and it then sets the conditions under which these operations are subject.

Art.60.-A entered the port, the captain must submit his logbook to the approval of the customs officers.

Except Art.61.-1 deadline set by a statutory instrument on the vessel's agent, representing the captain ashore, must submit to the customs office, starting ten days before the arrival of the ship until the date of ship's arrival

· A) as a summary declaration:

· The manifest of the cargo and, where appropriate, their authentic translation, providing at least the information on the bill of lading, the identification of the container, the number of packages, the trade description of the goods, indicating the shipper, the responsible for receiving (Bank, actual recipient). The manifest of the cargo will be filed in five copies and written on magnetic media or electronic processes, they are not payable for non-computerized offices.

· The obvious special stores and shoddy goods belonging to members of the crew;

· B) The charter parties and bills of lading, certificate of citizenship and other documents as may be required by the Customs for the customs enforcement;

° 2 °

· A) If a ship is chartered by two or more charterers, they or their duly authorized representative shall, within the time limit, submit to the customs office a summary declaration of goods to land which they are responsible

· B) The summary declaration must be filed even when ships are in ballast.

° C) when the ship should land any goods or is in ballast, the summary declaration shall contain only a reference to land goods "nil" or "ballast".

3 ° The period prescribed in subsection I above does not run on Sundays and public holidays. Only the cargo manifest do varietur referred under the provisions of Article 58 paragraph a) above is admissible, to the exclusion of any obvious correction or supplemental, filed during or outside of this period.

4 The summary declaration, submitted in advance, shall take effect until the arrival of the vessel. It can be canceled by the Customs if the ship did not arrive within the time fixed by decision of the Director General of Customs.

Art.62. 1-unloading vessels can take place within the walls of the ports where customs offices are located.

2 ° No goods can be unloaded or transferred without the written permission of customs officials and that their presence. The unloading and transshipment to take place during school hours and under the conditions laid down by the decisions of the Director General of Customs.

Art.63.-Commanders of ships of the Navy are required to complete the entry, all procedures that govern the captains of merchant vessels with the exception of the deposit in advance of the manifesto.

Paragraph 2 - Breaks forced

Art.64.-captains who are forced to release by perils of the sea, pursuit of enemies or other acts of God, shall:

· A) upon entry into the maritime zone of Customs to comply with its obligations under section 58 above;

· B) within twenty four hours of their arrival, to justify a report, the causes of the break and to comply with what is prescribed by section 61 above.

Art.65.-Goods on board the ships forced the release is fully justified are not subject to any duty or tax, except where the captain is obliged to sell them. Otherwise, the goods may be unloaded and placed at the expense of owners or captains in a closed room with two different keys one of which is held by the Customs Administration, until they are re-exported.

The captains and owners can even transfer them from edge to edge on other vessels, after having declared in the statutory requirements.

Paragraph 3 - Goods rescued from shipwrecks, wrecks

Art. 66.-are deemed foreign, unless otherwise justified, the goods saved from the wrecks and wrecks of any kind re-collected or recovered on land or at sea

Art.67.-Goods or wrecks are placed under the joint supervision of the Customs Administration and the Department of Merchant Navy until their final destination is given in accordance with laws and regulations.

Art.68.-Goods rescued from shipwrecks and shipwrecks can be paid on the domestic market after payment of duties and taxes on imports.

When they were not declared for a by the beneficiaries, they can be sold by the Customs at the request of the Administration in charge of the Merchant Marine for all destinations permitted by law.

In this case, the proceeds are used to pay duties and taxes that may be due after deduction of expenses related to the rescue, the filing and sale. If, after deduction of fees and charges and taxes, there is a surplus, it is paid to the Treasury Deposit where it is made available to the owners or tenants within the period of one year. After this time, it is definitely acquired the Treasury.

Section 2 - Transport by air

Art.69.-1 Aircraft must carry out an international career, to cross the border, take the air route imposed on them;

2 Except in cases of force majeure or operation assistance or rescue, aircraft conducting an international shipping can not land on the airport customs.

Art.70.-Goods transported by aircraft must be given in a manifesto signed by the commander of the unit, this document should be prepared under the same conditions as those for ships, in Article 57 above.

Art.71.-1 The aircraft commander shall present to customs officers at the first request, the cargo manifest and any other documentation that may be required for the customs enforcement.

2 It must provide this document as a summary declaration, the customs office at the airport, and, where appropriate, the authentic translation, on arrival of the aircraft, or, if the unit arrives before the opening of the office, at the opening.

3 ° The manifest can also be transmitted to the Customs by Internet or e-mail prior to the arrival of the aircraft for the purposes of international trade and to regulate mandatory under the provisions set forth above in this article.

4 When the aircraft is chartered by two or more charterers, they or their duly authorized representative shall, upon arrival of the aircraft, remove the customs office a summary declaration of goods under their charge.

5 ° where the aircraft must unload any goods, the summary declaration shall contain only a reference to unload merchandise "nil"

6 ° However, the filing of the summary declaration may be made before the arrival of the aircraft. In this case, the summary declaration shall not take effect until the arrival of the aircraft concerned.

7 If at the expiry of a deadline set by Decree of the Minister of Customs, the aircraft concerned has not arrived, the summary statement filed in advance, is canceled by the Administration.

8 The summary declaration may be made by the party's manifesto for the only goods to be unloaded.

Art.72.-1 are prohibited, and all jets unloading of goods in transit.

2 ° However, the aircraft commander has the right to take along the way the ballast, the mail in places officially designated for this, and the goods loaded with jet is essential to the salvation of the aircraft .

Art.73.-The provisions of paragraph 2 of Article 62 concerning the unloading and transshipment are applicable to carriage by air.

Section 3 - Duty of goods which have been subject to summary conviction.

Art.74.-Goods have been the subject of a summary declaration, under the provisions of Articles 61-1 ° and 71-1 ° of this Code, must be presented at the first request of customs officials, by the captain of the ship or his representative on the ground, except to justify that they were regularly removed or transferred or placed in a store or area clearance with express commitment of the operator of that store or area clearance to assume the full responsibility in respect of the Authority, in accordance with the provisions of this Code.

Section 4 - Correction of summary statements

Art.75.-Without prejudice to any contentious suites, the registrant or the agent may be authorized to correct clerical errors can not affect the name of the goods.

Chapter 2 - Export

Art.76.-goods intended for export must be taken to a customs office or in places designated by the Customs to be accounted for.

Chapter 3 - stores and clearance areas

Art.77.-Where goods upon arrival at the customs office, are not subject to regulatory accounting information, they can be discharged in areas designated for that purpose to stay under customs control until the filing of the customs declaration. These places are called stores and clearance areas.

Stores and clearance areas may also receive, pending their dispatch the goods to be exported or re-exported which were accounted for and verified.

Art.78.-area stores and clearance can be created by natural or legal persons.

Their creation, their location, their construction and design are subject to prior approval of the Customs Administration.

The obligations and responsibilities of the operator vis-à-vis the Customs Administration, are subject to an annual commitment endorsed.

The terms of store management and areas of clearance and expenses of the operator in the provision, maintenance and repair of facilities necessary to perform the service and the conditions under which customs control is exercised established by decision of the Director General of Customs.

Art.79.-stores and clearance areas can also be opened for the exclusive use of persons.

Goods that are dangerous or are likely to spoil other goods or require special facilities may be allowed only in stores or clearance areas specially equipped to receive them.

Art.80.-The maximum length of time goods in stores and clearance area is fifteen clear days.

The operations required to maintain unchanged the goods placed in stores and clearance areas such as cleaning, dusting, sorting, refurbishment or replacement of defective packaging can be made after approval by the Customs Administration.

May also be authorized transactions such as usual, subdivision, weighing, marking, meeting of parcels to form one sent to facilitate their removal and subsequent delivery. These various operations are performed in the presence of customs officers.

Art.81.-Goods damaged or damaged by accident or duly established cases of force majeure before leaving stores and areas of customs clearance, customs clearance are allowed in the state where they are at the date of recording of accounting.

However, these provisions apply only to goods that have remained continuously under customs control.

Art.82.-goods placed in stores and clearance areas that are destroyed by accident or duly established cases of force majeure, are not subject to the application of duties and taxes.

Debris and waste resulting, if this destruction shall be liable in case of home use, rights and taxes on waste or scrap imported in that state

-A Art.83. the expiration of the stay in the stores and clearance areas as provided in Article 80 above, the operator is required to drive the goods to a place designated by the Administration Customs when they consist of office under the Queen's warehouse in accordance with Articles 236, 237, 238 and 239 of this Code.

TITLE 4 - CUSTOMS CLEARANCE

Chapter 1 - Accounting

Section 1 - Mandatory nature of the accounting

Art.84.-1 All goods imported or exported must be an accounting;

2 ° The Accounting is the act in the manner prescribed by the provisions of this Code, in which the registrant shall indicate the customs procedure to be communicated to the goods and items required for the application of duties and taxes and for requirements for customs clearance.

3 ° The exemption of duties and taxes is at the entrance or exit, does not exempt from the requirement under this section.

Art.85.-A import, home use is the customs procedure under which all imports, except for privileged operations provided for in this Code shall be subject to payment of taxes and duties, in order to have freely of the goods into the customs territory.

For exports, the export output is simply the outright exportation of a good grip on the market.

Art.86.-1 The goods shall be deposited in a customs office open for customs operation considered.

2 ° For imports, it can be made before the goods arrive in stores and clearance areas provided that the manifest entry of the vessel or aircraft that brought it has reached and must be filed within a maximum period of fifteen clear days after the goods arrive at the office (not including Sundays and holidays) and during office hours unless authorized by the Collector of Customs.

In the case of a rate change after such filing and before the arrival of the ship, duties and taxes are collected under the provisions of Articles 13 and 14 above.

3 ° export, it must be lodged once the goods arrive in stores and clearance areas, or if the goods have arrived before the opening of the office, at the opening.

In-Art.87. customs offices equipped with computer systems for the clearance of goods, the filing of accounting documents, statements and summary of the receipts to deposit provided for in Articles 61, 71-1 °, 84-1 °, 86, 88, 101, 129, 131, 132, 136-1 ° of this code is made by electronic or computer processes, except where exempted by order of the Minister of Customs.

Deposit of the documents annexed to the summary declaration, with acknowledgments to question in detail and statements referred to above may, upon approval of the Customs Administration, carried out by electronic or computer.

The signature of the declarant may be replaced by an electronic signature. Rules for the implementation of these provisions are laid down by regulation.

Art.88.-1 The declarations filed in advance for the benefit of the exemptions provided for in Article 86-2 ° above, shall take effect, with all the consequences attached to the registration on the day of the arrival of the goods and provided that such statements meet the requirements of section 98 below;

2 These statements can be rectified under the conditions laid down in Article 103-2 and 4 of this Code.

Section 2 - Persons entitled to declare for the goods: customs brokers

Art.89.-1 Goods imported or exported must be accounted for by their owners, shippers or consignees by the real or natural or legal persons having obtained the approval of the customs agent or the authority to release under the conditions under Articles 90-97 of this Code.

2 are deemed owners, holders and travelers regarding the objects that accompany them, provided they meet their social situation.

Art.90.-1 No one can do for others the customs formalities for the declaration for the goods if it has been approved as a customs broker, otherwise fall under the provisions of Article 361 of this Code.

2 This approval is given by the Minister of Customs on the proposal of the Director General of Customs. The decision sets the customs offices or for which approval is valid;

The use of the approval is conditional on the provision of a bond to cover claims in respect of the Customs Administration

3 ° The Minister of Customs may, following the same procedure as in 2 above, withdraw approval of a temporary or permanent.

Art.91.-1 ° Any recipient or sender's real goods, not practice as a customs agent, intends, on the occasion of his industry or his business, to the customs declarations in detail for its own account must obtain permission to clear issued by the Minister of Customs.

2 This permission is granted on a temporary and revocable, and for operations on specific goods under the conditions set by paragraph 2 of Article 90 above.

Art.92.-1 Approval of customs agents is given in a personal capacity. In the case of a corporation, it must be obtained for the company and any person authorized to represent the company.

2 ° In any case, the refusal or temporary or permanent withdrawal of the approval or authorization can not be opened to clear right to compensation or damages.

The Art.93.-approved customs agents may form trade associations whose statutes are subject to the approval of the Minister of Customs.

Art.94.-Applications for approval of the customs agent must also be accompanied by a bond to cover possible with regard to the Customs Department of the Treasury claims against the approved customs agents and their deposit.

Art.95.-1 Every natural or legal person who does for others or for his own account of customs operations must record on annual directories under the conditions established by the Director General of Customs.

2 ° It is required to keep those directories as well as correspondence and documents relating to its customs operations five years from the date of registration of customs declarations related.

Art.96.-rates of remuneration that customs brokers are authorized to receive are determined in accordance with the laws and regulations on prices.

Art.97.-1 ° The conditions of application of Articles 89 to 96 are fixed by decree of the Minister of Customs;

2 ° These orders determine the conditions under which the companies operated in direct control by the state can do for others customs clearance and their obligations in this regard.

Section 3 - Form, statements, registration statements and cancellation details

Art.98.-1 statements in detail must be made on paper or electronically.

They must contain all information required for customs enforcement and the establishment of customs statistics.

They must be signed by the registrant.

2 ° The Director General of Customs shall determine, by making:

- the form of the declaration, the particulars it should contain and the documents that must be attached;

- conditions and procedures for clearance of goods by the Customs computer system.

It may authorize the replacement of the written statement by an oral declaration or simplified.

Art.99.-When several items are listed on the same declaration form, each item is considered to have been an independent statement.

Art.100 .- It is forbidden to make statements as a unit in the closed meeting more packages in any way whatsoever.

Article 101 .- 1 ° Persons entitled to submit statements in detail, when not in possession of the necessary elements for establishing, may be allowed to examine the goods before declaration and to take samples. They must then make an interim customs which can not, in any case, waive the requirement of accounting.

2 ° Any manipulation likely to alter the presentation of the goods having been interim statements is prohibited.

3 The shape of the provisional returns and the conditions may occur prior review of goods are determined by decisions of the Director General of Customs.

Art.102.-1 statements admissible in detail recognized by the customs officers are immediately registered by them

2 are considered inadmissible statements irregular in form or not accompanied by the documents whose production is required.

Art.103.-1 After registration, the statements can not be changed, they become authentic linking declaring the Authority;

2 ° However, the day of filing the accounting, and prior to the commencement of the audit, tax filers may correct clerical errors such as the discrepancy between the handwritten and the encrypted part. This correction concerns only the weight, number, measurement, the value of the statements in detail on the condition that represent the same number of packages bearing the same marks and numbers as previously stated and the same types of goods.

3 ° Where, for reasons valid estimated by the Customs, the declarant can not immediately produce the required documents in support of the statement is allowed in the terms and conditions set by the

Customs Administration, to file a statement with a commitment to produce the missing documents later in the timeframe set by the Customs Administration.

4 In addition, the declarations filed in advance can be rectified later than when it is appropriate to the goods arrive.

Art.104.-1 The registrant may request cancellation of the declaration:

· A) the importation,

· - If he proves that the goods have been accounted for in error or that the statement is no longer justified because of special circumstances;

· B) for export:

- If he has the goods have not left the customs territory

- If the statement is redundant with other statements previously recorded.

2 ° Where the Customs Administration has informed the registrant of its intent to conduct an audit of the goods, the cancellation request can be accepted only after the audit took place and no offense has been found.

3 A decision of the Director General of Customs shall, as appropriate, the modalities for implementing this article.

Art.105.-Decisions of the Director General of Customs may determine simplified customs clearance procedures including requirements that certain statements in detail information will be provided later in the form of additional global statements, periodic summary.

S.106 .- The provisions of Article 105ci above can be applied in investment and output of petroleum products from bonded warehouses.

Chapter 2 - Verification of freight

Section 1 - Conditions under which the audit takes place of goods

Art.107.-1 After recording the accounting, the Customs Administration shall, at its discretion, verification of all or part of the goods declared;

2 ° In case of dispute, the registrant has the right to challenge the results of the partial audit and request verification of full particulars of the declaration to which the dispute.

Art.108.-1 verification of the goods declared to customs offices can be made in stores and clearance areas or in places designated for that purpose by the Customs Administration.

2 ° The transportation of goods to the places of the audit, unpacking, repacking and any other handling required by the audit is undertaken at the expense and under the responsibility of the declarant.

3 The goods were carried in stores and clearance areas or on the premises of the audit can not be moved without the permission of the Customs Administration.

4 Persons employed by the registrant for the handling of goods in customs must be approved by the Customs Administration, in the absence of the approval, access to the stores of the customs and places designated for testing are prohibited.

Art.109 .- 1 The audit conducted in the presence of the declarant.

2 ° Where the declarant does not appear to attend the examination, the Customs shall notify by registered its intention to begin operations visit, or to continue them if he had stayed, if at the end a period of eight days after this notification, it has had no effect, the judge in whose jurisdiction is located the customs office, ex officio, at the request of the customs collector, a person to represent registrant fails to attend and verification.

Art.110.-For purposes of analysis or examination by experts, customs officials can take in the presence of the declarant, samples of the goods declared, if the kind, value or origin can not be made satisfactorily by other means.

Analysis or examination, the samples are not destroyed are returned to the declarant.

Section 2 - Settlement of disputes relating to the species, origin or value of goods

Art. 111 1 .- In the event that challenges the Customs at the time of examination of goods, the particulars of the statement concerning the nature, origin or value and where the declarant n not accept the appreciation of the service, the dispute is brought before the "Board of Conciliation and Customs Expertise" sitting in Antananarivo.

2 ° In the case provided for in paragraph 1 above shall be drawn up at the end of an act of expertise and there shall be a sampling necessary expertise.

3 ° Upon service of the appeal, the Receiver shall release the goods in dispute, subject to:

• that the release does not preclude the examination of samples of the goods by the Commission;

• that the goods are not affected measures prohibitions opposing their release;

• that the amount of the difference in duties and taxes recognized and declared them to be recorded or guaranteed by a guarantor.

Art.112.-1 The composition of the Commission of Conciliation and Customs Expertise is determined by a decree made by the Minister of Customs.

The President of the Commission may appeal, if necessary, assistance of any person whose technical input is considered useful.

2 The magistrate and the members are appointed by decree presented by the Minister of Customs. Alternates are appointed in the same way.

3 ° The members are bound by professional secrecy.

Art.113.-The Commission for Conciliation and Customs Expertise can be entered by the Director General of Customs in case the economic operator or the registrant does not accept the opinion of the Administration.

Art.114.-1 Unless decides not to proceed with the dispute, the Director General of Customs shall, within two months from the date of the act-end expertise, the declarant to notify the grounds on which the

Administration bases its assessment and invite or acquiesce is to provide a response within two months from the date of notification.

2 ° If the disagreement persists, the Director General of Customs within two months of the response or expiry of the period provided above to answer, seized the Commission of Conciliation and Customs Expertise by transmitting its Secretary the record of the case.

Art.115.-1 The parties to the dispute must provide to the Commission for Conciliation and Customs Expertise samples necessary expertise and their documents and information relating to the dispute.

2 ° The President of the Commission may prescribe any person hearings, research or analysis that it considers relevant to the investigation of the case.

3 ° Where the dispute is not about the species, origin or value of the goods, he noted, by a decision not subject to appeal, the jurisdiction of the Commission.

4 After consideration of the submissions may be produced and after having summoned the parties or their representatives to be heard together and contradictory in their comments, the Commission, unless agreed between the parties set a deadline after which, after deliberating, it must communicate its conclusions, which are taken by majority vote of its members.

5 ° When the parties have agreed before the expiry of the deadline to 4 of this section, the Commission gives note of that agreement specifying its content.

6 In its conclusions, the Commission shall indicate the names of those who deliberate, the subject of the dispute, the name and address of the registrant, a summary of the arguments, disputes and technical reasons for the solution adopted. When the dispute relates to this case, the tariff of the infringing goods must be also specified.

7 The conclusions of the Commission shall be notified to the parties.

8 If the parties disagree on the opinion of the Commission, the case is brought before the competent court in accordance with the provisions of Title X of this Code.

Art.116.-material and technical findings made by the Commission of Conciliation and Customs Expertise, on the species or origin of the infringing goods or for determining the value of a commodity, are the only ones that can be retained by the Tribunal.

Art.117 .- 1 ° When disputes relating to this case, the source or value is made after the clearance of goods during inspections and investigations carried out in accordance with this Code;

· A) one or the other party may, within two months of notification of the administrative act of finding of infringement, see the Commission for an opinion of Conciliation and Customs Expertise, which provides for this purpose , the powers specified in section 115 above;

· B) the party that initiated the consultation simultaneously inform the other party or his use of the consultation;

° C) the opinion of the Commission must be notified to the parties within a maximum period of twelve months during which the course requirements under the provisions of this Code is suspended;

• d) in case of subsequent proceedings in the courts, the finding by the Commission as part of the consultation referred to in paragraphs a) and b) of this section shall be paid by the chairman of this commission to the court record.

2 ° In all cases where proceedings are brought before the courts, whether or not prior consultation of the Commission of Conciliation and Customs Expertise, forensics, if prescribed by the competent court to decide on customs disputes, is entrusted to this Commission.

Section 3 - Implementation of audit results

Art.118.-1 fees, taxes and other customs measures are applied according to the results of the audit and, where appropriate, in accordance with the undisputed findings of the Commission of Conciliation and Customs Expertise or in accordance with decisions justice with the authority of res judicata.

2 ° If the Administration does not conduct verification of the declared goods, rights, duties and other customs measures are applied according to the particulars of the declaration.

Chapter 3 - Liquidation and payment of duties and taxes

Section 1 - Payment of duties and taxes

Except Art.119.-transitional provisions under Article 13 above, duties and taxes to be collected are those in effect at the date of registration of the accounting.

Art.120.-When lowering the duty rates of customs, the declarant may request application of the new price more favorable than that which was in effect at the date of registration of the declaration for consumption if authorization under s. 125 of the Code has not yet been given.

Art.121.-The duties and taxes for each item of the same statement are rounded to the lower Ariary.

Section 2 - Cash payment

Art.122.-1 fees and taxes assessed by the Customs are payable in cash;

2 officers charged with the collection of duties and taxes are required to give a discharge;

3 Records of payment of duties and taxes may consist of sheets prepared by electronic or mechanical procedure and then connected.

Art.123.-1 fees and taxes are not due on goods that the Customs accepts the abandonment to his advantage;

2 The goods whose abandonment is accepted by the Customs Administration are sold by public auction by the latter under the same conditions as the goods left behind by transaction.

Section 3 - taxation and off PIP PIP

Art.124.-products in the form of donations and aid in kind, or acquired externally funded of all types of external (loan funds, grants, funding competitions, etc..) Falling within the national territory, to pay to the State taxes and duties under the regulations in force.

The public, semi-public or private beneficiaries pay to the Customs Administration, their budget, duties and taxes due for the clearance of these products.

If any agency would replace the recipient for payment of fees due, the agency pays the fees of substitution due before removal of the goods in question under the same conditions as above.

If the state would replace the recipient to pay the fees due, it is established on presentation of the commitment of the State with indications of budget lines to support the payment, a statement of the rights of blue state . Regulation of the state and established blue takes place during the year of settlement in order to appropriation under the budget to provide a provisional basis and outside the evaluative framework for establishing the economic state budget .

Regularization of any overruns on the budget line and takes scheduled at the next Finance Bill or at the latest by the law of regulation.

Instructions are determined by circular of the Minister for the Budget.

Chapter 4 - Removal of goods

Section 1 - General

Art.125.-1 No goods can be removed from the offices of Customs duties and taxes if not previously paid, recorded or guaranteed.

2 The goods can not be removed without the permission of the Customs Administration.

3 ° Upon receipt of this authorization, the goods must be removed.

Section 2 - Credit collection

Art.126.-1 ° The customs collector can leave off the goods as and when checks and before liquidation and payment of duties and taxes, with penny-mission duly sanctioned for taxpayers:

· A) to pay duties and taxes and all other amounts owed to the Authority within a week at the latest

· B) to pay extra taxes and duties, a discount calculated on the amount of such duties and taxes.

2 Rules for the purposes of this section shall be fixed by order of the Minister of Customs.

Section 3 - Boarding and conduct foreign goods for export

Art.127.-After customs formalities, the goods to be exported by sea or air shall be immediately put on board ships or aircraft.

Art.128.-loading and transhipment of goods for export are subject to the same provisions as provided:

· A) paragraphs 1 and 2 of Article 62 above if it is an export by sea

· B) in paragraph 2 of that article, in the case of export by air.

· Art.129.-1 No vessel, laden or in ballast, may leave the port before the completion of customs formalities and without being provided with:

· On shipments customs on the ship itself and its cargo;

• or a clearly covered by the Customs;

File Number Identification of marine vessel

2 ° The manifest, bills of lading and shipping of the building should be represented whenever required by customs officers.

Art.130.-commanders of the navy leaving ports must complete all formalities that govern the captains of merchant ships.

Art.131.-1 ° The civil and military aircraft that are outside the customs territory may not take their flight as customs airports;

2 ° The same provisions as provided for in Articles 69-1 °, 70, 71-1 ° and 72 of this Code shall apply to such aircraft and their cargo.

TITLE 5 - TRANSIT AND ECONOMIC SYSTEMS

Chapter 1 - General scheme of the receipts to deposit

Art.132.-1 The goods must be placed under cover of acknowledgments to bail when transported by land, sea or air from one point to another within the customs territory of the rights suspended and taxes, or prohibitions.

2 ° The Director General of Customs may require the establishment of acknowledgments to ensure security for the arrival of certain goods or completion of certain formalities.

Art.133.-The receipt has to guarantee, in addition to the summary declaration or details of goods, joint and several liability of the principal and his surety to satisfy, on time and under the penalties of law, the obligations under the laws and regulations.

Art.134.-If the goods are not prohibited, the guarantee of the security may be replaced by the deposit of duties and taxes.

Art. 135 .- 1 After finding that the commitments were met, the Customs shall refund the duties and taxes may be recorded, cancel the engagement and give a discharge to the bidder.

2 ° The Customs Administration may condition the discharge of the receipts to bond or regulatory documents in lieu thereof, by producing a certificate issued by the authorities that, as evidence that the goods have actually purchased the system customs which it was previously intended.

3 The Director General of Customs may, to prevent fraud, making the discharge of the receipts to deposit underwritten to ensure the export of certain goods by producing a certificate issued either by the consular authorities or by the Customs of the destination country.

Art.136 .- 1 ° The discharge shall be granted only for quantities represented at the destination.

2 The quantities represented are liable to duties and taxes in effect at the date of registration of the receipts and penalties are determined, if necessary, according to the same duties and taxes. If the goods are prohibited, the principal and his surety are liable for payment of their value.

3 ° When the loss is due to force majeure duly noted, the Customs may exempt the principal and his surety for payment of duties and taxes or, if the goods are prohibited, to the payment of value.

Art.137.-Rules for the application of sections 132 to 136 above shall be determined by decisions of the Director General of Customs.

Art. 138 .- The provisions of this chapter shall apply to all the receipts to deposit to which this Code does not provide other rules.

Chapter 2 - Transit

Section 1 - General

Art.139 .- 1 Transit is the customs procedure under which are placed the goods transported under customs control from one office to another suspension of duties and taxes and measures of prohibition.

2 To qualify for the transit, the bidder must sign a declaration in detail with a commitment backed by which it undertakes, under the penalties of law, to send the goods declared at a particular office, the seals intact within limit and follow the prescribed itinerary.

Article 140 .- Excluded from transit as absolute goods bearing false trademarks of Malagasy origin and those falling under articles 29 and 30 above.

Art.141 .- Goods shipped in transit that are entered for consumption at the customs office of destination are subject to duties and taxes in effect at the date of registration of the accounting for consumption.

Art.142.-Decisions of the Director General of Customs shall determine the conditions for implementing the provisions of this chapter.

Section 2 - Regular Transit

Art.143 .- The goods subject to duties, taxes or import prohibition were shipped in transit on receipt to deposit.

Art.144 .- 1 ° At the entrance, the goods shipped under the common transit are accounted for and verified under the same conditions that the goods declared for home use.

2 In respect of goods declared for export, transit guarantees, in addition, the performance conditions which are subject to effects associated with exporting.

3 Goods presented initially to the Customs Administration should be represented along with the receipts or documents for deposit in lieu thereof:

· A) along the way whenever required by the Customs;

· B) to, at the customs office or in places designated by the Customs Administration.

Art. 145 1 .- Upon arrival, the goods and the declaration must be submitted to the customs declaration must be made and the customs procedure to be the goods. Pending the filing of the latter, the goods may be unloaded in the shops and areas of clearance for the discharge of transit.

2 ° The bidder and his surety are jointly and severally liable vis-à-vis the Customs Administration on the implementation of the obligations of the transit.

3 ° The release for consumption of goods that benefited from the transit system is under the same conditions as those imported directly from abroad.

Section 3 - The national road transit (TNR)

Art.146 .- The Customs Administration may dispense with the accounting in the first customs office that goods must be shipped on a second office to be subjected to this step.

Art.147.-In the case provided for in Article 146 above, carriers of goods are the first port of entry:

· A) produce the tickets for the goods;

· B) sign a receipt to deposit on which they must report the number and kind of packages, their marks and numbers, and the weight of each of them and the nature of the goods they contain.

Art.148.-Customs officers of the first port of entry may proceed with the verification of the particulars of the receipt to deposit. The tickets must be attached to the receipt.

Art.149.-The summary declaration can be corrected by the accounting filed in the office of destination.

The National Transit Art.150.-road is free to companies, container terminal operators established in Madagascar as well as businesses and corporations that have concluded a Memorandum of Understanding with the Customs Administration, for the delivery of their containerized cargo:

· A) import, a customs office of arrival to the office of Attachment for container terminal operators in order to make customs clearance regulations, or until firm to the EPZ , free enterprises or enterprises and companies have concluded a Memorandum of Understanding with the Customs pending the completion of customs clearance regulations;

· B) export from the office of attachment, after having fulfilled the formalities prescribed for export to a customs office for final boarding.

· The beneficiaries of the national road transit must:

· A) an undertaking to pay any annual endorsed the penalties

regarding acquired to bail for violations;

• b) have means of road approved by the Customs identified by a plaque TNR.

The modalities for implementing this Article shall be by decision of the Director General of Customs.

Section 4 - Transit international

Art.151.-1 The arrangements provided for in Section III of this chapter may be allowed as general transport companies designated by order of the Minister of Customs. He took the name of international transit.

2 Companies benefiting from the International Transit must make available to the Customs Department stores where goods will be received until a final customs system and be assigned their facilities and equipment necessary for their release. This obligation may by agreement or contract, be transferred to other bodies approved by the State.

Chapter 3 - Overview of economic systems

Art.152.-1 plans allow economic storage, processing, use of goods suspension of customs duties and all other fees and charges and measures of prohibition of an economic nature which they are liable

2 ° the customs regimes include:

· The bonded warehouse;

· The industrial warehouse;

· The temporary admission;

· The temporary admission for inward processing;

· The temporary export;

· The temporary export for outward processing;

• the processing under customs control;

· The temporary import and export of personal items belonging to travelers;

• Factory applied.

Art.153.-Without prejudice to the exclusions specific to each economic customs regimes listed above are excluded from these schemes the goods subject to restrictions or prohibitions based on considerations of safety, or public order, public safety, health or public health or veterinary phytopathological considerations, or relating to the protection of patents, trademarks, copyrights and reproduction regardless of quantity, country of origin of origin or destination.

Art.154.-To monitor the operations carried out under commercial economic regimes, the Administration and the bidder are, respectively, which trace entries:

· Firstly, species, quantities and values of goods placed under economic

· To the other, species, quantities and values of the compensating products and goods admitted clearance and, where appropriate, species, quantities and values of waste.

The writings of Bidders must identify by species, quantities and values, the goods in stock on their premises and those that are eventually delivered under contract to the conditions laid down in Article 197 below.

A decree of the Minister of Customs will determine the form and procedures for keeping records.

Art.155.-The bidder and the surety are finally released or, if appropriate, the court are fully reimbursed, given the clearance certificate duly authenticated given by agents of the Customs Administration.

However, if clearance successive partial account of the economic system under which the goods are placed, the bidder and the deposit is partially released from the guarantee or refund of duties and taxes recorded, in view of the clearance certificate, duly authenticated, given by officers of the Administration, at the end of each clearance operation part and up to amounts discharged.

Art.156.-competent Customs offices open to the import and export of the goods declared under an economic customs regimes are appointed by decree of the Minister of Customs.

Chapter 4 - Bonded Warehouse

Section 1 - General

Art.157.-1 ° The bonded warehouse is a customs procedure which allows the storage of goods under customs control in accommodation approved by the Customs Administration suspended from duties and taxes and economic measures.

2 There are four types of bonded warehouses:

· The public warehouse;

· The special warehouse;

· The private warehouse;

· The industrial warehouse.

Art.158.-The public warehouse is open to all users for the storage of goods of any kind except those excluded under the provisions of section 153 of this Code.

The public warehouse is said to be special when it is used to store goods:

° whose presence in the warehouse is dangerous or is likely to affect the quality of other goods;

· Whose preservation requires special facilities.

Section 2 - Public Warehouse

Art.159.-Can be admitted into public warehouse, the goods:

· Imported, they leave the store or area clearance;

· Placed under a customs procedure;

· For export for the purpose of obtaining reimbursement of fees and charges and, where applicable, the benefits of this export.

Art. 160 .- Apart from the exclusions provided for in section 153 referred to above, certain goods may also be excluded from the warehouse by order of the Minister of Customs, after consultation with the Ministers concerned.

Paragraph 1 - Grant of the public warehouse

Art.161.-1 ° The public warehouse is granted by decree in order of priority to the municipality or the Chamber of Commerce;

2 ° The public warehouse is granted if it meets the general needs duly recorded, in which case the costs of exercise are the responsibility of the state. It can also be granted on condition that the concessionaire to bear all or part of the costs of exercise, given the degree of public interest it presents;

3 ° The concession decrees determine the conditions to impose on the dealer and shall, where appropriate, the initial share of the costs of exercise to be borne by it;

4 ° The dealer collects taxes for shopping with fee must be approved by order of the Minister after consultation with the Customs authorities and bodies referred to in paragraph 1 above;

5 ° The public warehouse may be surrendered by tender, with competition and advertising;

6 Decisions of the Director General of Customs may also be in public customs warehouse, temporary, facilities for receiving goods for competitions, exhibitions, fairs and other events of samples of the same type.

Paragraph 2 - Construction and installation of public warehouse

Art.162.-1 The location, construction and management of local public warehouse must be approved by the Minister of Customs.

2 ° The warehouse at the facility, free of charge, to guard, offices and housing, reserved for customs officers.

3 ° For construction, repair and maintenance are charged to the dealer.

Paragraph 3 - Monitoring the public warehouse

Article 163 .- 1 ° The public warehouse is under the supervision of the Customs Administration, but under the physical custody of the dealer shops.

2 ° All exits from the warehouse are closed on two different keys, one of which is held by customs officials.

Paragraph 4 - Stay of the goods in storage and handling authorized public.

Art. 164 .- Goods guests in a public warehouse for a year.

Art.165.-1 Orders of Minister of Customs operations which determine the products placed in a public warehouse can be and the conditions under which these operations are subject.

2 ° These are stopped in the interest of export trade or re-export, derogate from the prohibitions of the laws or special regulations.

Art.166.-1 ° The warehouse must pay duties and taxes on goods they can not represent to the Customs in the same quantities. If the goods are prohibited, they are required to pay their value.

2 ° However, the deficits from either the extraction of dust, stones and dirt, from natural causes, are admitted free.

3 ° When the loss of goods in public warehouse due to a case of force majeure duly noted, the warehouse are exempt from payment of duties and taxes, or, if the goods are prohibited from paying value.

4 When there was theft of goods placed in a public warehouse, the warehouse are also exempted from payment of duties and taxes or value, as appropriate, if the evidence of flight is properly established.

5 If the goods are insured, it must be justified as insurance covers only the value in the store, in the absence of this justification, the provisions of paragraphs 3 and 4 of this Article shall not apply.

Paragraph 5 - goods remaining in public warehouse at the end of time

Art.167 .- 1 ° the deadline set by Article 164, goods placed in a public warehouse must be re-exported or if they are not prohibited, subject to duties and taxes on imports;

2 Otherwise, summation is the warehouse at his home if present, or the office of mayor or district if absent, having to meet one or other of these obligations. If the summons has no effect within one month, the goods are sold by public auction by the Customs Administration.

The proceeds, net of fees and charges in the case of home use, and storage costs and any other nature, is paid on deposit in the Treasury to be given to the owner if claimed within two years from the date of sale or, failing that, a claim within that period, finally acquired the state budget. Goods whose importation is prohibited can not be sold for re-export.

Section 3 - Special Warehouse

Paragraph 1 - Opening of the special warehouse

Art.168 .- 1 ° The special warehouse may be allowed:

· A) for goods whose presence in the public warehouse is dangerous, or is likely to affect the quality of products;

· B) for goods whose preservation requires special facilities. Orders of the Minister of Customs means products eligible special warehouse.

2 The permission to open a special warehouse is granted by the Director General of Customs.

3 The premises of the special warehouse are provided by the dealer and must be approved by the Customs Administration and are closed under the same conditions as the public warehouse.

4 ° The cost of the exercise of special warehouse are the responsibility of the concessionaire. The provisions for public warehouse under Article 162-2 ° above apply to the special warehouse.

Art.169.-The warehouse must make a commitment to re-export sanctioned goods or, if they are not prohibited, to pay duties and taxes in force at the time it will benefit the consumer, and this, in the deadline set by Article 170.

Paragraph 2 - Stay of the goods in the warehouse special

Art.170.-Goods guests in a special warehouse for a year.

Art.171 .- The rules set for real warehouse in articles 165 and 166-1 °, 2, 3 and 5 are applicable to the special warehouse.

Section 4 - Private Warehouse

Art.172 .- 1 ° The private warehouse may be granted to any person or entity for its exclusive use in order to store goods in connection with its business until their assigned a different customs procedure allowed.

2 ° The private warehouse is called trivial when it is granted to natural or legal persons by occupation, principal or accessory storage of goods on behalf of third parties.

The concession is granted by decree of the Minister of Customs on the advice of the ministers concerned.

3 ° The private warehouse is said especially when given to business enterprises for their exclusive use. The authorization to open a particular private warehouse is granted by the Director General of Customs. This authorization fixed expenses of the beneficiary under the supervision of that warehouse.

4 ° The natural or legal person in receipt of an order for grant of a bonded warehouse is called "dealer warehouse."

Art.173.-The procedure of concession or grant and the conditions of installation, control, supervision and operation of the warehouse shall be fixed by order of the Minister of Customs.

Section 1 - Establishment of a private warehouse

Art.174 .- 1 Orders of the Ministry of Customs means products eligible private warehouse and localities where s private warehouses may be established.

2 ° The private warehouse is made in the stores trade under the guarantee of a surety commitment to re-export the goods, or, if they are not prohibited from paying duties and taxes in force at the time will benefit the consumer, and this within the deadline set by Article 175 below.

Paragraph 2 - Stay of the goods in storage and handling authorized private

Art.175.-Goods guests in a private warehouse for six months, extendable once for the same period.

Art.176.-set rules for public warehouse by paragraph 1 of section 166 above shall apply to the private warehouse, even in case of theft or disaster.

Art.177.-Orders of the Minister of Customs may, under certain conditions, allow manipulations in private warehouse, and if necessary, allocate free of duties and taxes deficits resulting from these operations.

Section 5 - Industrial Warehouse

Art.178.-The industrial warehouse is the customs regime applicable to companies which, for export or for both export and domestic market, may be authorized to proceed with the implementation of goods suspension of customs duties and taxes which they are liable by reason of importation.

To this end, these companies are under the control of the Customs Administration.

Art.179 .- The benefit of the industrial warehouse may be granted by decision of the Minister of Customs.

The decision sets the period for which the plan is paid, where appropriate, the quantity of goods likely to benefit, the period of stay in the warehouse, the respective percentages of processed products for export and those that must be paid to consumption.

At the expiration of the time in industrial and warehouse unless extended, the duties and taxes on goods that are still under this regime become due immediately.

Art.180.-Except as authorized by the Customs, goods imported under the warehouse and industrial products resulting from their implementation may be subject to assignment during their stay under this regime.

If Art.181.-home use of compensating products, fees and charges to be collected are those of imported goods used for obtaining the compensating products, according to the species and condition of the goods recorded at entry into industrial warehouse.

The duties and taxes are current on the date of registration of the declaration of release for consumption.

Art.182 .- The rules for implementing the provisions of this chapter shall be fixed by order of the Minister of Customs.

Section 6 - Miscellaneous Provisions applicable to all warehouses

Art.183 .- During their stay in the warehouse, the goods must be produced whenever required by customs officers who can carry out all inspections and surveys that they consider necessary.

Art.184.-exceptional and provided the goods are in good condition, the deadline set by sections 164, 170 and 175 above may be extended by the Customs, at the request of the warehouse.

Art. 185 .- shipments from a warehouse to another warehouse or a customs office shall be under the transit procedure.

S.186 .- 1 ° In the event of consumption in response to warehouse duties and taxes applicable are those in effect at the date of registration of the accounting for consumption.

2 ° When they are to be liquidated on deficits, the applicable duties and taxes are current on the date of the last exit of the warehouse.

3 ° When they are to be assessed on goods removed from the warehouse, duties and taxes are current on the date of the determination of the subtraction.

4 ° If goods are taxed "ad valorem" or prohibited, the value is to consider, as appropriate, that the said goods to one of the dates referred to in paragraphs 1, 2 and 3 of this Article is determined under the conditions laid down in Articles 23 and 24 above.

Art.187 .- 1 ° Where goods which have undergone manipulation or processing in the warehouse are declared for home use, the collection of duties and taxes may be authorized by product category according to the species of these goods and the Basic amounts recognized or accepted by the Customs at the time of their entry into a warehouse.

2 ° When goods placed in storage at the landfill for temporary accounts are entered for consumption, the collection of duties and taxes may be authorized by product categories and according to the kind of goods and on the basis amounts recognized or accepted by the Customs at the time of their temporary admission.

3 ° If the provisions of paragraphs 1 and 2 of this Article, the applicable duties and taxes are those in effect at the date of registration of the accounting for the consumption, the value to be considered for application of such duties and taxes, if the goods taxed "ad valorem" or prohibited in the state where they are taxable, being determined on the same date, under the conditions laid down in Articles 23 and 24 above .

4 ° authorizations required for admission to the provisions of this Article are granted by the Director General of Customs.

Art.188.-dealers warehouse remain obligated with respect to the Directors until the actual removal of goods on regulatory approval issued by the Customs Administration

Art.189.-Orders of the Minister of Customs shall determine the conditions for implementing the provisions of this chapter.

Chapter 5 - Temporary

Art. 190 1 .- The term "temporary", the customs procedure which allows the admission into the customs territory, suspended from duties and taxes, without application of economic prohibitions of imported goods for a purpose and intended for re-export within a specified period:

· A) is in the state without having undergone any change except normal depreciation of goods following the use made in the conditions fixed by decree of the Minister of Customs on the proposal of the Ministers concerned;

· B) after having suffered under the inward processing, a working, additional labor or repair.

• 2 ° However, the Director General of Customs may grant under conditions agreed with the Ministers concerned for temporary entry in the following cases:

• Introduction of objects for repairs, tests or experiments;

• Introduction of equipment and wheeled vehicles in the framework of an agreement or an agreement made between foreign and Madagascar;

• Introduction to materials, equipment and / or input as part of an international fair;

• Introduction to have individual character and special which can not be generalized;

• Introduction of full containers to re-empty;

• Introduction of equipment for the execution of public works.

In these cases, decisions and orders granting temporary admission may not suspend a fraction of the amount of duties and taxes.

3 The orders or decisions of this article indicates:

• a) the conditions under which goods are to be used as is;

· B) the nature of the additional labor, the working or processing which must be the goods and, in the latter case, the products admitted to compensation for temporary accounts and the conditions in which take place this compensation.

· Art.191 .- To be eligible for temporary importation, importers must sign a receipt to deposit in which they undertake:

· A) to establish or re-export the products in storage temporarily admitted, within twelve months, this period may be extended by the Administration at the duly justified request of the principal;

· B) to fulfill the obligations prescribed by the regulations on temporary and bear the penalties for violations or non-discharge of the receipts.

The findings Art.192.-official laboratories of the State concerning the composition of goods presented to the dump of the receipts for temporary are final.

Art.193.-1 Unless otherwise authorized by the Customs, goods imported under the temporary entry and where appropriate, products resulting from processing or workmanship, must be d in any assignment during their stay under this regime.

2 ° The diversion of goods benefiting from a temporary to their destination falls within the provisions of Articles 358-5 ° and 370-4 ° of this Code.

Chapter 6 - Temporary admission for inward

Art.194.-1 Temporary admission for inward processing is a system that allows people with or may have the equipment needed for manufacturing, the working or in addition to labor considered, of suspension of import duties and taxes applicable to them to receive goods for processing, working or additional labor and goods which are listed by order of the Minister of Customs on the advice of the ministers concerned which are not found in the processed products but allow the production of those products, even if they are entirely or partially in use.

However, sensitive and strategic goods whose importation is subject to special authorization and on a list established by regulation can not benefit from this plan only with the authorization given under the conditions laid down by regulation;

2 Unless otherwise approved by the Minister of Customs, the maximum length of time goods under temporary admission for inward processing is twelve months from the date of registration of the import declaration.

3 unless exceptions are granted by the Director General of Customs, the declaration for temporary admission date should be in the name of the person who will implement or use imported goods.

4 ° The goods, after receiving processing, the working or the complement of labor, must be, unless waived by the Director General of Customs, or re-exported or incorporated in a bonded warehouse before expiry of the period in 2 ° above.

5 ° When the expiry of the period allowed, the goods are not exported or released for consumption after authorization or incorporated warehouse, duties and taxes which the goods are normally liable to import immediate payment.

6 Notwithstanding the provisions of this section 4, part of the compensating products may be released for consumption under the conditions and the proportions laid down by regulation.

7 Permits may be canceled by decision of the Director General of Customs if they have been issued on the basis of incorrect or incomplete or revoked when the conditions for regime are no longer fulfilled or if the holder does not comply obligations.

Art.195.-1 accounts for temporary admission for inward processing can be cleared on the basis of items reported by the bidder.

However, for the goods on a list established by regulation, the clearance of these accounts can be made at the option of the Bidder:

· A) in accordance with the first paragraph of this article

· B) according to the conditions laid down by regulation.

2 ° The elements relating to conditions of discharge reported by the bidder are controlled by the Administration in a period not exceeding two months from the date of registration of the re-export declaration filed in response to temporary for inward considered.

3 ° Where the checks provided above indicate clearance conditions different from those reported by the bidder, the results of these checks automatically replace the elements declared for both the quantity remaining to implement than those already used for what that is the customs procedure already booked to compensating products.

Art.196.-1 To enable the accomplishment of manufacturing split, the sale of processed products, regardless of the degree of development achieved by these products can occur in the following conditions:

· A) authority to the Customs Administration;

· B) filing with the Administration of a receipt to deposit with the agreement of the transferor and the joint and several liability of the transferee and a bond to meet the requirements of laws, regulations and decisions relating to the customs procedure suspension for whose benefit the goods are declared.

The deposit where required, may be replaced by a deposit in an amount not exceed the amount of duties and taxes or by any other guarantee approved by the Minister of Customs. Where the security takes the form of a blanket position bond, a statement upon receipt of deposit to the approval number of the guarantee is in lieu of the undertaking of the guarantor.

2 ° The transferee must meet the conditions laid down in Article 194 .- 1 ° above or be allowed as stated in that article.

3 ° The transfer of fully finished compensating products to be marketed abroad by a third person can also occur under the conditions referred to in 1 a) and 1 b) above.

Art.197.-declared goods under temporary admission for inward remittances may be under the responsibility of the bidder, under contract to a person with the necessary tools, provided that the person accused receives a delivery to be retained by the bidder. The latter shall record in its pleadings, in accordance with section 145 above, the delivery made.

Art.198.-When the quantitative and qualitative composition of exported products must be determined by a laboratory, it must be by the laboratory designated by the Minister of Customs.

Art.199.-1 Notwithstanding the provisions of Article 194 above, the Director General of Customs may authorize, without prejudice to the provisions relating to breaches of legislation on the matter, the regularization temporary accounts for inward:

· A) through the consumption of goods is in the condition they were imported, or the processed products from the processing of goods previously imported subject, in particular, the formalities of control of foreign trade and exchange rate applicable to such goods;

· B) by re-export or warehousing, as they are or they were imported, goods that could not receive processing, the working or the complement of labor indicated in the declaration of temporary admission for inward processing.

2 ° When it is applied 1 a) of this section and subject to the provisions of 4, 5 and 6 below, duties and taxes are payable according to the species and quantities of goods admitted temporarily and depending on the amount of duties and taxes applicable on the date of registration of the declaration for temporary admission for inward processing increased, if the said duties and taxes have not been recorded, including the default interest the rate is fixed by order of the Minister of Customs.

This delay is due to interest from the date of the registration of the declaration for temporary admission for inward until the collection included.

3 ° The value to be considered is that of those goods on the date of registration of the declaration.

4 Notwithstanding the provisions of 2 and 3 of this section, when the compensating products referred to in Article 5 of 194 above are released for consumption, taxes and duties are payable according to the species and the quantities accepted temporarily and according to the amount of duties and taxes applicable on the date of registration of the accounting for home use.

The value to be considered is that of goods previously imported, the date of registration of the accounting for home use.

5 ° When circumstances warrant, the bidder can not proceed with the re-export or home use of compensating products or goods previously imported, these products can be abandoned to the Customs or destroyed in the presence agents of the latter.

The destruction is done at the expense of petitioner.

6 The Authority may, under the conditions laid down by regulation, authorize the release for consumption, duty-and tax purposes and scrap production lots offered to the State, local governments, public institutions and registered charitable associations of public utility by decree.

Chapter 7 - Temporary export

Art.200 .- 1 A "temporary export", the customs procedure that allows the temporary export without applying measures of economic and prohibitions for a purpose, of goods to be re-imported within a specified period :

· A) is in the state without having undergone any change except normal depreciation of their male as a result of the use made of it;

· B) is in the outward, after undergoing a transformation, a working, additional labor or repair.

2 ° The benefit of the temporary export is subject to a prior request to the Customs Administration stating the nature of the use of the working, repair or processing the goods are to undergo abroad.

Art.201.-A decree of the Minister of Customs establishes rules under section 200 of this Code and the conditions under which the added value of goods resulting from the working, repair or alteration is subject to the payment of taxes and duties on reimportation.

Art.202.-Goods sent abroad for use as is or outward show at a fair or other similar events can be exported permanently from abroad within the laws and regulations force.

Art.203.-timeout which goods temporarily exported must be re definitely under section 200 above, is set according to the time required for the performance of the proposed transactions.

Chapter 8 - Temporary export for outward processing

Art.204.-1 Temporary exportation for outward processing is a plan for temporary export of goods and commodities, or Malagasy origin released for consumption or imported under temporary admission for inward processing, which are sent out territory subject to receive a working or processing.

2 A re-importation, the products and goods that have been temporarily exported for outward processing are either reinstated temporarily for outward initially purchased or released for consumption as provided in 3 above below and in Article 199 above.

3 ° When they are released for consumption upon re-importation, the products or goods are subject to the payment of customs duties and other duties and taxes according to the kind of products and imported goods.

Customs duties and other taxes are current on the date of registration of the declaration of reimportation.

The value to be considered is that of the products and goods in the state they are imported, less the value of the products previously exported goods.

However, the release for consumption takes place with total relief from duties and import taxes if it is established that the working or processing carried consisted of a repair for free, either because of a contractual obligation or statutory warranty or by reason of the existence of a manufacturing defect.

4 ° When economic necessity or justified by trade, the provisions of 3 above may apply, under the same conditions, products and goods of similar technical characteristics to those products and goods previously exported.

5 Without prejudice to the suites litigation, failure to re-import within the time fixed by regulation, products and goods temporarily exported for outward processing is considered a permanent export and resulting in the deposition by the tenderer of a new customs declaration, in discharge of that originally recorded, with all the consequences arising from the export procedure.

6 ° The conditions for implementing this Article shall be fixed by regulation.

Chapter 9 - Processing under customs

Art.205 .- 1 Processing under customs control is a plan to import, suspended from duties and taxes, of goods for them to undergo operations that modify the species or the state in order to make consumer products resulting from these operations, under the conditions set out below:

• a) the duties and taxes are those in effect at the date of registration of the accounting

· B) based on the tariff and quantity of processed product to the consumer;

° C) the value to be considered is that of goods on the date of registration of the declaration of such goods under processing under customs control.

2 ° the resulting products are termed processed products.

Art.206 .- may not benefit from the scheme that people have or could have the equipment needed for the proposed alteration and the following conditions:

· The processed products must be given, under specific regulations, the total or partial exemption from taxes and duties on imports or a reduced fee compared to goods to be implemented;

• the use of the procedure for processing under customs should not have the effect of diverting the effects of rules on quantitative restrictions on imported goods;

· The goods to be implemented must be identified in the processed products.

Art.207 .- 1 ° The procedure for processing under customs control shall be granted by decision of the Director General of Customs, after consultation with the Minister concerned, where the processed products are exempt all or part of duties and taxes on imports under the legislation;

2 The regime transformation is granted by joint decision of the Minister of Customs and the Minister concerned where the processed products have a reduced fee compared to goods to be implemented.

Art.208.-1 unless otherwise approved by the Minister of Customs on the advice of the Minister concerned, the maximum length of time goods under processing under customs control is twelve months from the date of the registration of the declaration of goods under this regime.

2 ° The conditions for granting such extension shall be determined by regulation.

3 ° When the expiry of the period allowed, processed products or, where appropriate, to put the goods under the scheme are not released to the market, duties and taxes which they are liable to become due immediately.

Art.209.-1 rates of clearance of accounts for processing under customs are established in the decisions to grant the regime, under Article 207 above.

2 These rates are determined based on the actual conditions under which is or will be made the transformation.

Art.210.-In the event of consumer goods in the condition they were imported or products that are at an intermediate stage of processing compared to that provided in grant decisions referred to in Article 207, the duties and taxes are payable according to the species and quantities of goods placed under the processing and function of amount of duties and taxes applicable on the date of registration of the declaration for processing under customs increased If such fees and charges have not been recorded, of which the default interest rate is fixed by order of the Minister of Customs. This delay is due to interest from the date of registration of the declaration of processing under customs control until the collection included. The value to be considered is that of those goods on the date of registration of the declaration.

Art.211 .- When the composition and other elements characteristic of the processed products must be controlled and determined by a laboratory, they must be by the laboratory designated by the Minister of Customs.

Art.212.-The conditions of application of this Chapter shall be fixed by regulation.

Chapter 10 - Temporary Import and export of personal items belonging to travelers

Section 1 - Temporary Importation

Art.213. 1-Travelers who come to stay temporarily in the customs territory may import suspension of duties and import taxes articles for personal use they bring with them, except for prohibited items import.

Items must be re-exported to the same end of the stay, except for home use under the conditions of the regulations.

2 Passengers are allowed to make a verbal declaration for goods with them.

However, when the goods presented him consider to be commercial in nature, the Customs may require a written statement.

3 ° The conditions for implementing this Article shall be fixed by order of the Minister of Customs.

Art.214.-The holder of a temporary importation papers may be exceptionally allowed to keep in Madagascar for personal use goods imported temporarily for the payment of duties and taxes in effect at the date of passing of the document, plus, if duties and taxes were not recorded, the default interest provided for in section 210 above, calculated from that date.

Section 2 - Temporary export

Art.215. 1-Travelers who have their principal residence or principal place in the customs territory and will stay temporarily outside the territory, can only export the objects for their own use they take with them to excluding the goods prohibited for export.

2 The export of such objects results in the issuance of a transit permit description.

3 ° the condition of being re-imported within one year by the person himself who exported the objects referred to in paragraph one of this article are not subject on reimportation into the customs territory rights , taxes and prohibitions of entry.

4 ° The conditions for implementing this Article shall be fixed by order of the Minister of Customs.

Chapter 11 - Plants exercised

Art.216 .- The Customs Treatment plants exercised is reserved for institutions and companies that perform:

· A) the extraction, collection and transportation of crude petroleum oils obtained from bituminous minerals, petroleum gas and liquid or gaseous hydrocarbons;

· B) processing and refining of crude petroleum oils obtained from bituminous minerals, petroleum gas and other gaseous hydrocarbons for petroleum products and related dutiable domestic consumption and other taxes or charges;

· C) to the liquefaction of gaseous hydrocarbons;

• d) the production of petroleum products and related dutiable domestic consumption and other taxes or charges;

° E) in the production and manufacture of chemicals and allied products, petroleum derivatives;

° F) to the manufacture of other related petroleum products;

· G) to the implementation or use of goods that benefit from a customs procedure or special tax.

Art.217 .- The goods placed under the plant exercised shall be allowed entry into the suspension of duties and taxes and restrictions on economic and other paperwork.

Art.218.-Goods from plants are released exercised the following conditions:

· Those for export, free of duty and taxes;

· Those for the domestic market on payment of duties and taxes, the value plate is fixed by regulation.

S.219 .- Where the goods referred to in section 216 of this Code are used for purposes other than those for which the suspension of duties and taxes or the application of the preferred pricing were given, duties and taxes formalities and whose products are normally liable to be immediately due according to the rules in case of release for consumption.

Art.220 .- Decisions of the Minister of Customs as the rules regulating the plants performed and determine the conditions to be met by institutions and companies under this regime and the obligations and burdens that result for operators.

Art.221 .- are placed under the plant exerted facilities and institutions that carry out the following:

· A) processing or refining of crude petroleum oils or bituminous minerals, petroleum gases and other gaseous hydrocarbons and their liquefaction;

· B) production and manufacturing of pétroléochimie and chemicals and allied products derived from petroleum.

· Art.222.-A entry in the plants carried the suspension of duties and taxes and economic prohibitions which they are liable is limited to the following goods:

· A) for crude oil, reduced to raw oil, mineral sands and other gaseous hydrocarbons to be processed or refined;

· B) products specified in Article 216 f).

· Articles 223 .- Entering the factory exercised imports other than those mentioned in the preceding article, are placed:

· Or under the home use;

· Or under temporary admission.

Art.224.-Orders of the Minister of Customs may be placed under the plant exercised, institutions other than those referred to in Articles 220 and 221 of this Code which is made in the implementation or use of goods receiving a customs procedure or special tax.

Chapter 12 - Industrial Free Zone

Art.225 .- means Export Processing Zone (EPZ) any territorial enclave established in order to consider the goods in it as not being in the customs territory for the application of customs duties and taxes which they are liable because of the imports and quantitative restrictions.

Art.226.-The creation of categories of companies constituting the EPZ enterprises defined in Article 3 of Law Institut that are in the defined area or outside of the area, in which case the company's industrial transformation is called Honest Company (EF), is authorized by decree on the proposal of Minister of Industry.

Art.227 .- 1 ° Subject to the provisions of paragraphs 2 and 3 below, as well as those provided for in Article 40 of the Law Institute are allowed in EPZ goods of all kinds, regardless of their quantity and whatever their country of origin, consignment or destination.

2 ° The above provisions do not preclude the application of prohibitions or restrictions justified on grounds of public morality, public order, public security, protection of health and life of people and animals or plant health, protection of national treasures possessing artistic, historic or archaeological value or the protection of industrial and commercial property.

3 Access to the EPZ may be limited by decree, to certain goods on grounds of technical or administrative.

Art.228 .- The goods placed in the EPZ or in EF may be subject to:

· A) of loading, unloading, transhipment or storage;

· B) manipulation;

° C) processing, working or supplements to labor conditions and in the manner provided in factories or industrial warehouses exercised.

Art.229.-1 Goods placed in EPZ or EF can not be re-exported or placed in use, or mutated in other suspensive in the state.

However, can be

· Returned to the sender or to the principal materials, raw materials and / or imported inputs do not comply with the order or not used and the remaining hardware and installation of imported building materials, not installed and / or not used,

· Re-exported to the sender equipment leased or imported on loan,

• re-exported to another company installed on the open country, as part of a national subcontracting, industrial or business located outside the national territory, as part of an external partnership . or transferred temporarily to a local law, raw materials and / or inputs for manufacturing, processing or additional labor.

2 The goods that have been in accordance with the EPZ c. of Article 228 above, transformations, working or supplements of labor must be re-exported.

However, provided that the goods have been an assumption by the Customs when they were introduced in EPZs, they are released for consumption may be exceptionally allowed by regulation.

Duties and taxes to be collected are those relating to the finished or semi-finished compensating in this case and the status of these products carried at EPZ output.

The rates applicable are those in effect at the date of registration of the declaration of release for consumption. The value to be reported is that of finished or semi-finished goods determined under the conditions laid down in Articles 23 and 24 above.

3 ° The length of time goods in EPZs and EF:

· Is not limited to equipment and plant equipment;

· But it is twelve months for inputs and raw materials.

Art.230 .- The provisions of this chapter does not violate the rules established by international treaties.

TITLE 6 - FILING OF CUSTOMS

Art.231.-A "'s warehouse" regime whereby the goods are stored on the premises designated by Customs for a specified period, after which the goods are disposed of under the conditions laid down in this code.

Art.232.-The Queen's warehouse is made, or in stores belonging to the Customs or in the premises approved by it, the buildings can be made especially in public warehouses or in stores or clearance areas

Chapter 1 - Constitution of goods deposited

Art.233.-1 consist of office in trust by the Customs:

· A) goods, import, have not been accounted for within the legal deadline;

· B) goods remain in customs for some other reason.

2 ° Where the goods are not market value, Customs may initiate their destruction.

Art.234.-Goods incorporated's warehouse are placed on a special register.

Art.235.-1 °'s warehouse goods remain at owner's risk, deterioration, alteration or loss while in deposit may give rise to damages, whatever the cause.

2 ° The costs of any kind resulting from the constitution and stay on deposit are paid in goods.

Art.236.-Customs officers can proceed to open the packages made by Queen's warehouse and verification of their contents in the presence of the owner or consignee or, failing that, a person designated by judge held as provided by section 109 above.

Chapter 2 - Sale of goods deposited

Art.237.-1 goods that have not been removed within the period of two months from the date of their registration deposit is sold at public auction.

2 ° perishable goods or in poor condition, and those whose stay in custody may be hazardous to health or safety of the neighborhood or may damage the quality of other goods deposited, can be sold to OTC by the Customs immediately after approval of the President of the Court of First Instance or the President of Section.

3 ° goods worth less than

10,000 Ar that are not removed at the expiration of two months referred to in paragraph I above are considered abandoned. The Customs may sell by public auction or donate them to hospitals, hospices and other charitable institutions.

Art.238 1 .- The sale of goods is done through the efforts of the Customs at the bidder.

2 The goods are sold free of all duties and taxes collected by Customs with the option for the contractor, to dispose of all destinations permitted by the laws and regulations.

Art.239.-1 Proceeds from the sale shall be applied in order of priority and pro rata:

· A) the settlement of fees and other incidental expenses of any nature incurred by the customs for the constitution and stay on deposit and for the sale of goods;

· B) the collection of duties and taxes to be imposed on goods by reason of the destination given to them.

2 ° When the proceeds are sufficient, there shall be a settlement of all other charges that may encumber the goods. Any remaining balance is paid on deposit in the Treasury where he stayed for a year available to the owner of the goods or assigns. After this time it is acquired in the state budget. However, if Ar is less than 400, the remainder is taken immediately as revenue in the final state budget.

3 ° Where the proceeds of the sale are insufficient to pay the debts listed in paragraph 2 above, the amounts are paid on deposit in the Treasury and allocated, if necessary, following the procedure of distribution of contribution at the behest of Administration. The judge of the place of deposit is competent.

TITLE 7 - PRIVILEGED OPERATIONS

Chapter 1 - Admission free

Art.240.-1 Notwithstanding sections 7, 8 and 9 above, the Minister of Customs may allow the duty-free import duties and taxes:

· A) of donations to the Head of State

· B) donations from organizations of foreign states to Ministers and Parliamentarians in office, on the occasion of official visits abroad,

° C) for sending ambassadors, consular and foreign members

some international officials residing in Madagascar

• d) of items intended for the Red Cross and other works of solidarity funded from external sources,

° E) of consignments intended for charities legally constituted and recognized as public utilities by decree

· F) donations of materials and equipment for the regions and municipalities,

· G) materials and specific products within the scope of prospecting, research and exploration of hydrocarbons,

• h) in small packages with no outstanding commercial nature;

2 ° The conditions for implementing this Article and the list of official international solidarity and works referred to in paragraph 1 above shall be determined by the orders signed by the Minister of Economy, Finance and Budget , the Foreign Minister and Minister of Population.

Chapter 2 - ship and aircraft

Section 1 - Special provisions for vessels

Art.241.-are exempt from duties and taxes due to the entrance, petroleum products, coal, spare parts, products and equipment for the refueling of vessels engaged in international shipping and boats in the armed great fishing, offshore fishing and inshore fishing zone 2.

Art.242.-1 ° The provisions and stores not exceeding the required brought by ships from overseas are not subject to duties and taxes when they remain on board.

2 These provisions and stores may be paid in the customs territory after accounting and payment of duties and taxes.

Art.243.-1 ° The provisions and stores not exceeding the required aboard vessels bound from abroad are not subject to duties and taxes at the exit.

2 ° The number of crew, and passengers, the amount and kind of food are brought on board the shipping permit which must be endorsed by the customs officers.

Art.244.-The food and stores that are embedded in a port other than port of departure for the outside are listed on the shipping permit except in case of difficulties in determining quantities, to comply with the provisions of the preceding article.

Art.245.-Ships and vessels not covered by Article 241 above can refuel in petroleum, coal, food and other stores with products that made for local consumption, and these operations are not subject to duties and taxes on output or the output prohibitions.

Section 2 - Special provisions for aircraft

Art.246.-are exempt from duties and taxes due to the input oil for refueling aircraft, military or civilian, who make a navigation across borders.

Art.247.-Any transfer or sale of equipment, materials and goods placed under economic or having benefited from a privileged treatment and whose duties and taxes have not been paid after expiry of the deadline, is prohibited without prior authorization from the Customs Administration.

Chapter 3 - Plan Returns

Art.248 .- To benefit from the returns and exemption from duties and import taxes, the goods originally exported from the territory must:

· Either be returned by the recipient for non-compliance with the order or defective,

· Or refused for reasons relating to the applicable regulations in the country of destination.

· Art.249 .- The regime defined above is granted subject to exporters:

· To justify pre-export goods,

· To meet the specific obligations laid down in Article 248 above.

Art.250 .- The benefit of the back is reserved for the original exporting. The request for re-importation shall be filed within two years from the date of export.

TITLE 8 - TRAFFIC AND DETENTION OF GOODS WITHIN THE CUSTOMS TERRITORY

Chapter 1 - Traffic and detention of goods in the land area of customs radius

Section 1 - Movement of goods

Art.251.-1 Some goods can move within the radius of Earth customs without being accompanied by a transit or other customs shipment taking place.

2 ° The list of such goods shall be fixed by order of the Minister of Customs. These orders shall also lay down conditions for applying the first paragraph of this article.

Art.252.-1 carriers are required not to deviate from the route shown on the catwalk, except in cases of force majeure duly justified;

2 ° They must represent the goods and the catwalks and other securities in lieu thereof:

· A) For the different customs offices which are on their way;

· B) Outside the office, whenever required by customs officers and tax or any other representatives of the police.

Section 2 - Detention of goods

Art.253 .- It is prohibited in the customs radius:

• a) the detention of goods prohibited or heavily taxed at the entrance where we can produce, at the first request of customs officials, or receipts showing that the goods have been properly imported, or purchase invoices, manufacturing slips or other proof of origin from individuals or companies lawfully established within the customs territory;

• b) the holding of stocks of goods other than the thought of the country, prohibited or heavily taxed at the exit, not justified by the needs of normal operation, or the importance of which clearly exceeds the supply needs of the family appreciated according to local custom.

Chapter 2 - Special rules apply throughout the customs territory to certain categories of goods

Art.254.-1 Those who hold or transport the goods specially designated by the Minister of Customs must first request to customs officials, or produce receipts showing that the goods have been properly imported, or purchase invoices , manufacturing slips or other proof of origin from individuals or companies lawfully established within the customs territory.

2 ° Those detained, transported, sold, transferred or exchanged these goods and those who established the original justifications are also required to submit the documents referred to in paragraph I above whenever required by customs officers made in a Within four years, from the time the goods were no longer in their hands, either from the date of issue of the original justifications. However, if the holders or carriers say they have another place of proof required, customs officials may accompany them to enable them to present such evidence or give them the opportunity to submit these documents within forty eight hours.

Chapter 3 - Boat Repairs and air

Art.255 .- Any goods incorporated into a vessel or aircraft of Malagasy nationality outside the customs territory, shall, within fifteen days after his arrival from a customs office, subject to a detailed declaration repairs or adjustments made abroad.

Art.256.-Goods imported to be used as is or after processing, construction, armament, rigging, repair or alteration of marine vessels of the merchant marine or fishing shall be allowed as suspension from duties and taxes.

After inspection by the Customs Administration, the allocation of goods to marine vessels, the procedure is discharged permanently, depending on the case, for a re-export to the buildings listed in section 241 above and by making consumption to regulatory conditions, for others.

TITLE 9 - MISCELLANEOUS TAXES COLLECTED BY THE CUSTOMS

Chapter 1 - Excise duties

Art.257 .- Some products consumed in the customs territory, that they have been imported, manufactured or harvested, are subject to a tax called "excise tax".

This tax is established under the conditions laid down in Articles 3, 9 and 16 above.

For imported goods, excise duty shall be charged and collected by customs officers, under the conditions and according to the rules laid down in this Code.

In addition, Art.258. imports referred to in Article 240 of this Code, may be exempt from excise duty (AD) when importing:

° 1 ° products that are in the manufacture of products subject themselves to an excise duty;

° 2 ° the products covered by the Tax Administration under the acquired to bail, which subsequently provides the perception of excise duty by the rules of its own;

° 3 ° the objects of the plant raw or semi-wrought, imported to undergo further processing and then allowing the assembly or manufacture of finished in the care of a national workforce;

° 4 ° certain air navigation equipment and parts, petroleum products and chemicals for the refueling of aircraft, equipment for fixed equipment Aerodrome and marking the lines of air navigation;

° 5 ° for complete engines for tractors, tractor parts and special tires for tractors, subject to employment in agriculture or forestry;

° 6 ° of materials and products for companies in research and exploitation of oil and gas, bitumen, asphalt, sandstone and shale;

° 7 ° of equipment for carrying out the work of installation and operation carried out by companies for extraction, separation and processing of useful minerals of beach sands (monazite, ilmenite, zircon);

° 8 ° materials from all sources for the creation of old firms when these firms have been the subject of an approval as contributing to the implementation of plans of economic and social development;

° 9 ° raw materials, finished or semi-finished products need to import both the manufacturing and packaging, and packaging for transport, the goods produced by firms approved under the 8 above;

° 10 ° alcohol type for the preparation of drugs or used by health facilities or scientific as well as denatured ethyl alcohol in accordance with regulations.

The conditions for implementing this Article shall be fixed by order of the Minister of Customs. These orders determine, as appropriate, the categories of beneficiaries of the exemption.

The charge-Art.259. the benefit of the general counter purchase and sale of tobacco, due on manufactured tobacco imported by individuals, is wound and collected by customs officers under the same conditions and following the same rules as excise duty and is taken cumulatively recipe with it.

Chapter 2 - Redemption

Art.260 .- Some products originating in the customs territory declared for export are subject regardless of their destination, a tax law says "exit fee".

This right is established in the requirements of Articles 3, 9 and 16 above.

It is calculated and levied by customs officers in the manner and according to the rules laid down in this Code.

Companies that have been the subject of an approval as contributing to the implementation of plans of economic and social development, will be eligible for full or partial exemption from export duties on products from their farms or their manufacture. Accreditation decisions will determine the percentage of deduction of exit rights granted to each company.

Chapter 3 - Tax on Value Added

Art.261 .- It is a perceived value added tax (VAT) on imports regardless of their origin and provenance, and this, according to the tariff of customs duties and taxes.

This tax is paid, levied, collected and recorded by customs officials under the conditions and according to the rules laid down in this Code.

Chapter 4 - Right Navigation

Art.262 .- is charged for any vessel from the outside right global navigation established in the requirements of Articles 3 and 9 above.

This duty is charged and collected by customs officers in the manner and according to the rules laid down in this Code.

The rate of duty is 18 Ariary per net ton per trip.

This rate is halved for ships entering and leaving in ballast with a cargo, or incoming and outgoing with a load of ballast. Is considered to ballast the ship whose cargo volume does not exceed one-twentieth of its usable capacity. Captain wishing to benefit from the reduced rate should apply to the customs collector, to produce any necessary evidence and submit any visit to his ship deemed necessary.

Is considered for the application of the above as being a journey, all hit a ship in port or the customs territory of Comoros during a journey "back and forth." During this trip, the route may include one or more stopovers in the ports of the island of Réunion, Mauritius and its dependencies, the Union of South - Africa, Mozambique, Tanzania , Kenya, interposed between the affected Madagascar.

Vessels used solely for navigation between ports or the customs territory of the Comoros must pay an annual fee of 36 Ariary per ton net. This right, liquidated on the basis of the statement of the captain, is payable by him at the beginning of the year, from a customs office. No other right of navigation is payable if the coastal vessel performs during the calendar year, up to ten trips to a port on the island of Réunion, Mauritius and its dependencies, the Union of South Africa, Mozambique, Tanzania, Kenya, or many of these countries. If the ship eligible for the annual fee begins in the calendar year, more than ten trips to the countries listed above, or a trip to another country, the right under the first paragraph of this section becomes payable port of arrival, when returning to port in the customs territory.

If for some reason, the vessel shall be detained in port for six consecutive months of the year, the taxpayer may obtain a refund of half the fees paid. The tonnage tax is the net tonnage, indicated by the official documents of the vessel, ten rounded to the nearest barrel. Within twenty four hours of the arrival of the vessel, the captain (or his representative on the ground) must submit to Customs a declaration conforming to the model set by the Director General of Customs, providing all the information necessary for the liquidation of the tax. The ship and its cargo meet the payment of the navigation, which must be secured or paid at first port in Madagascar. However the ships came in ballast or with a full load of charcoal can, if they boarded a cargo is released to the output port.

Art.263 .- are exempt from the law here:

° 1 ° warships (including hospital ships) of all nationalities;

• 2 ° vessels operating exclusively within ports and harbors;

° 3 ° inbound and outbound ships in ballast;

° 4 ° ships coming in hard and not using any commercial operation other than unloading or refueling or charges necessitated by the condition of the ship;

° 5 ° vessels entered with a full load of coal and outbound in ballast;

° 6 ° recreational boats and ships engaged on cruises.

Chapter 5 - Other duties and taxes

Art.264 .- The Customs Department is also responsible, on liquidation issued by the competent authorities, to collect or to guarantee collection of all duties and taxes on imports or exports, including:

· Taxes verification, sealing and shifts control service packaging, access and security of ships;

· Rights marine sanitation.

It provides possibly the collection of stamp duties, including bills of lading.

Chapter 6 - Computer fees

A fee-Art.265. computer fixed, fixed by regulation, is levied on all transactions subject to a regulatory reporting for duty with a computerized customs office.

TITLE 10 - LITIGATION

Chapter 1 - Definition of customs offenses

Art.266.-For customs offenses are defined as violations of the requirements of this Code and those of the customs laws and regulations defined in Article I hereof.

Chapter 2 - Establishment of customs offenses

Section 1 - Recognition by input MINUTES

Section 1 - Persons required to carry out seizures - Rights and duties of striking

Art.267.-1 ° The customs offenses can be established by a customs officer;

2 ° Those who find a breach of customs have the right to seize any property subject to confiscation, withholding shipments and all other documents relating to seized items and to detain articles assigned to preventive safety penalties;

3 ° They can proceed with the capture of accused in cases of flagrante delicto, with placement in custody pursuant to the provisions of the Code of Criminal Procedure Madagascar.

Paragraph 2 - General Procedures and mandatory on pain of nullity for the drafting of the minutes of seizure.

Art.268 .- 1 ° a) To the extent that circumstances permit, the goods and vehicles seized are carried and deposited in the office or customs station nearest the place of seizure. When there, in the same locality, several offices and customs posts, the thing may be transported either in any one of them.

b) When you can not lead immediately to the office or position, or when there is no post office or in the locality, the thing may be in the custody of the accused or third , the scene of the seizure or to another location;

In this case, the defendant or the third party has custody and preservation of seized and will be held responsible for any loss of such items. It is forbidden to sell, move, replace them, use them for personal use.

Violation of these provisions constitute an offense and punishable by the provisions of Articles 406 and following of the Penal Code Malagasy (immediate his surrender of the accused to the prosecutor) without prejudice to the application of this Code.

2 ° The officers found a violation write the minutes without entertaining other acts, and, later, immediately after the transport and deposition of seized items;

3 ° a) The minutes can be written instead of filing of the articles seized, or instead of, as offenses.

It can also be prepared at the headquarters of the gendarmerie, an official in the office of Finance or the district office of the administrative position of the place or the mayor of the municipality;

b) When entering a house, the Minutes may be validly drawn.

Art.269 .- The minutes state the date and cause of the seizure, the statement was made to the accused, the name and address of the striking qualities and the person in charge of the proceedings, the nature of things seized and quantity, the presence of the accused to their description or summation that has been made to attend, the name and status of the custodian, the place of writing the minutes and the time of its closure.

Art.270.-1 When the seized goods are not prohibited, it is offered release of means of transport on bail or under solvent log value;

2 This offer and the response are mentioned in the minutes.

3 ° The release of the conveyance shall be granted without bond or deposit to the owner in good faith in concluding the contract of carriage, rent or lease the binder to the offender in accordance with laws and regulations in force and practices of the profession.

However, such release is subject to reimbursement of any costs incurred by the Customs to ensure the custody and preservation of seized conveyance.

Art.271.-1 If the accused is present, the Minutes states that it has been read, he was arrested to sign it, and he immediately received a copy;

2 When the defendant is absent, the copy is posted within twenty four hours at the door of the customs office or city hall or the office of the district or administrative position in the place of writing of the minutes if n ' not exist in this place of the customs office;

In this regard, the minutes drawn up in absence of the accused, has the same effect and the same validity as that written in his presence.

3 ° In both cases, these minutes has subpoena under the conditions specified in Article 310 below.

Paragraph 3 - Procedures for some specific input

A. Entered on the fake and altered shipments

Art.272. 1-If the reason for the seizure of false or alteration of shipments, the Minutes provides the kind of forgery, alteration, or overload.

2 ° Such expeditions, signed and initialed "ne varietur" by striking, are appended to the minutes containing the summons made to the accused to sign them and answer.

B. Seizures Home

Art.273.-1 In case of seizure at home, non-prohibited goods are not moved, provided the defendant gives security solvent value. If the accused does not guarantee, or is prohibited items, goods are transported to the nearest office or entrusted to third guard is formed at the site of the seizure, or in another locality.

2 ° In case of refusal by the accused, just for the regularity of operations, the record contains a reference to the refusal.

C. Seized on ships and deck boats

Art.274.-A against seizures of ships and deck boats when unloading can take place immediately, the striking affix seals on the panels and hatches of the buildings. The minutes, which is drawn in as and when unloading, mention the number, marks and numbers of bales, crates and barrels. The detailed description is made in the office, in the presence of the accused or after summons to attend, it is given a copy to each shift.

D. Captured outside the radius

Art.275.-1 Outside of the radius, the foregoing provisions shall apply to violations detected in offices, warehouses and other places subject to supervision by the Customs Administration.

2 Seizures can also be practiced anywhere in the event of continued custody, caught in the act, a violation of section 254 above, or unexpected discovery of fraudulent goods whose origin is evident from the statements of the holder or documentary evidence found in his possession.

3 ° In case of foreclosure proceedings in order, the Minutes should see:

• a) if the goods subject to the formality of the catwalk, that the goods have been implemented continuously since their crossing the inner boundary radius until they entered and were devoid of Shipping necessary for their transport into the customs radius;

• b) in the case of other goods, such goods have been implemented continuously since their crossing of the border until they are entered.

Paragraph 4 - Rules to be observed after the preparation of the minutes of seizure

Art.276 .- 1 ° complaint with a civil as well as the minutes noting the customs offenses are given to prosecutor or magistrate who shall act, and defendants are brought before him captured.

2 To this end, the civil and military authorities are required to lend a hand to customs officers at the first request.

Section 2 - Finding by the observation MINUTES

Art.277.-1 The results of checks carried out in accordance with Article 54 above and, in general, those investigations and interrogations by customs officers are recorded in the minutes of observation.

2 ° The minutes state the date and place of checks and investigations performed, the nature of the findings and information gathered, the seizure of documents and computer data collected as appropriate and the name, position residence and administrative enforcement officers. They indicate, moreover, that those in whom the investigation or monitoring has been carried out have been informed of the date and place of writing this report and their summation was made to attend this writing, if these people are present in the writing, they state that their reading was made and they were arrested to sign it.

Section 3 - Provisions common to the minutes of seizure and of finding MINUTES

Paragraph 1 - Stamp and registration

Art.278.-The minutes of Customs and the submissions and transactions are provided in lieu of the formalities of stamp and registration.

Paragraph 2 - MINUTES Evidentiary effect of regular and avenues for legal warned against the faith

Art.279.-1 Minutes customs written by two sworn officers of Customs are prima facie of forgery physical findings stated therein.

2 ° They are authentic proof to the contrary that the accuracy and truthfulness of confessions and statements they relate.

Art.280.-1 Minutes customs written by one sworn officer are prima facie evidence to the contrary.

2 ° In terms of violations by the finding in the report drawn up following an examination of writings, the evidence to the contrary can not be presented only through certain documents prior to the date of the survey carried out by agents verbalization.

Art.281.-The courts can not accept the minutes against customs other than those resulting nullity of the omission of the formalities prescribed by sections 268 and following of this Code.

Art.282.-1 Anyone who wants to argue against a report is required to make statement in writing, in person or by proxy special signed before a notary, on or before the hearing indicated by the summons to appear before the court needs to know the offense.

2 It must, within three days make the registry of that court filing means of false and names of the witnesses he wants to hear, on pain of forfeiture of the registration of false.

3 ° The declaration is received and signed by the President and the Registrar, if the declarant can write or sign.

Art.283.-1 ° In the case of an entry against a false report stating fraud, if registration is made within the time and in the form prescribed by the preceding article and assuming that the means false, if proven, would destroy the existence of fraud in relation to the registering, the prosecutor or the magistrate who shall act as did the due diligence in order to make a decision without delay.

2 ° It may be suspended, in accordance with Article 529 of the Code of Criminal Procedure, the trial of the offense until after the trial of false registration, in which case, the court of the offense interim order the sale of goods subject to decay and animals that have been transported.

Art.284.-When one of forgery was not made in time and in the manner determined by Article 282 above, it is, without any regard, proceeded to trial and trial of the case.

Art.285.-When an offender admits guilt and seeks the benefit of a transaction, the Customs may not draw up a report and then establishes a quote-trade, an act which contains the account of events, recognition of the offense by the accused and his statement to rely on the decision of the Authority.

The signature of the accused must be preceded by the words "read and approved", and that of the bond, the words "Approved for."

The act applies transactional basis, justifying the perception, the claim and the recovery of customs debts.

Chapter 3 - Prosecution and Recovery

Section 1 - General

Art.286.-All crimes and offenses under the customs laws and regulations, as defined by Articles I and 266 above, can be prosecuted and proved by all legal means even though no seizure could been made in the customs radius or outside this radius, or the goods have been the subject of a declaration would give rise to any observation.

As part of the Mutual Administrative Assistance International, as intended in Article 54-5 ° of this Code, the Customs Administration is authorized, subject to reciprocity, to collect customs authorities of the country Foreign further information, certificates, minutes and other documents in order to prosecute and punish violations of laws and regulations applicable to the entry and exit.

The objects of fraud seized or confiscated may be returned to the home country at the express request of the customs authority and with the consent of the other party. The costs for the return are the responsibility of the requesting State.

Art.287.-In terms of customs offenses, the competent court is seized not only the facts specified in the summons, but also those identified by the minutes, the basis of the prosecution, stating whether the articles it related.

Art.288 .- 1 ° The action for the application of penalties is exercised by the Crown.

2 The action for the application of tax penalties is exercised by the Customs;

3 ° In the Court of Appeal, the Court of First Instance or the Court Section in whose office is located Customs, the Customs Administration is represented by the Collector of Customs or his designated representative for this purpose.

Supreme Court, it is represented by the Head of Central Service in charge of litigation or his authorized representative.

If necessary, one or the other can validly exercise the function of representation in the courts of first degree or second degree and provides the hearing to defend the interests of the Treasury as a civil party, the prosecution.

4 In case of customs offenses or other offenses for which prosecution and diligence are recognized in the Customs, he may bring a civil action or during the survey, at the hearing, before all instances court.

Art.289.-When an offender dies customs intervention before a final decision or transaction, the Customs is entitled to exercise against the estate an action to decide the court confiscation of articles subject to the sanction or, if they could not be seized, the order to pay an amount equal to the value of those items is calculated using the market price within the time where fraud was committed.

Section 2 - Continued by compulsion

Section 1 - Application of the constraint

Art.290 .- The Director General of Customs and recipients may issue constraint for the recovery of duties and taxes of any kind that the Customs Department is responsible for collecting, for the payment of fees, fines and other amounts due in the event breach of the commitments contained in the receipts to deposit and often missions, and generally in all cases where they are able to establish that any sum is due to the Customs Administration .

Art.291 .- They can also award constraint in the case provided for in Article 42 above.

Paragraph 2 - Titles

Art.292 .- The constraint must include copy of the title which establishes the claim.

Art.293.-1 constraints are set free by the presiding judge or section;

2 Judges can not, under any pretext whatsoever, refuse the visa of all constraints presented to them, on pain of being in their name and private pre-pro, responsible for objects for which they are awarded.

Art.294 .- Constraints are served in accordance with Article 307 below.

Section 3 - Termination of rights and prosecuting

Paragraph 1 - The right transaction

Art.295.-1 The Customs Administration is authorized to negotiate with people prosecuted for customs violations;

Manner of exercise are set by decree of the Minister of Customs.

2 ° The transaction may occur before or after final decision;

3 ° In the second case, the transaction leaves corporal punishment.

4 ° The transaction can benefit only those for which it was granted. As a result, prosecutions remain possible against other offenders, they are co-authors, accomplices or interested. It is different for those

guarantees and civil liability with the understanding that responsibility flows directly from that of the author, in case it benefits from this regulation, and that their fate is inextricably linked to that of the last.

5 ° The transaction between the parties, the authority of res judicata. It can not be challenged for error of law or due to injury.

6 The same facts concerning the same person can not, as a result of a customs transaction which had the effect to extinguish the public action be pursued under another legal qualification.

Art.296.-To account for resources and expenditure accounts receivable or other special circumstances, to reconsider the sanctions may be granted by the Authority which issued the penalty.

2 - Provision of the action

Art.297.-The action of the Customs Administration is prescribed by law enforcement within five years under the same conditions as the prosecution for ordinary crimes.

Section 3 - Limitation of the rights of individuals and the Administration accountable

A. Prescription against the debtors

Art.298.-No person is entitled to bring against the Customs Administration, claims for restitution of rights and goods and payment of rent, two years after the time that the claims give the rights to payments, stocks of goods, rents and deadlines.

Art.299.-The Customs Administration is discharged to the parties responsible, three years after a year expired, custody records and other revenues of that year, without being required to represent them if there were instances still remaining for instructions and judgments which the said books and records were necessary.

B. Prescription against the administration

Art.300.-The Customs Administration is not entitled to bring any claim for payment of duties, four years after such rights should have been paid.

C. If the requirements of short duration did not take place

Art.301.-1 The requirements in sections 298, 299 and 300 above did not take place and when there becomes thirty, before the terms provided, awarded constraints, actions or claims made in court (Complaint Parquet, complaint with a civil action), sentences, pro-masses, conventions (submission litigation, acts or transaction submitted in lieu) or special obligations and special for the object that is repeated;

2 ° It is the same with respect to the requirement under section 300 where a fraudulent act by the debtor that the administration has ignored the existence of the event giving rise to the right and could not perform the action it proficient for its enforcement.

Chapter 4 - Procedure in court

Section 1 - Jurisdiction in respect of customs

Section 1 - Jurisdiction Award

Art.302 1 .- The Criminal Court has jurisdiction to prosecute violations customs, customs offenses, violations of exchange control violations joint customs and exchange customs and all matters raised by way of exception.

2 ° The civil court has jurisdiction in respect of disputes concerning the refusal to pay duties and taxes, the recovery of fees and charges, objections to the stress-stress, non-discharge of the receipts to deposit and Other customs affairs not under the jurisdiction of criminal courts.

3 ° The Administrative Court is competent to judge the actions and decisions of administrative

Paragraph 2 - Jurisdiction

Art.303. 1-territorial jurisdiction, the Tribunal will be the one in whose jurisdiction is located the customs office nearest the place of commission of the offense.

2 ° In cases of multiple offenses arising from a criminal act committed in several places on the one hand, and in case of finding by the office staff, on the other hand, the jurisdiction is in the whose jurisdiction is located the customs office nearest the place of writing the minutes of seizure.

3 In civil matters, the jurisdiction is within whose jurisdiction is located the office of the Service or the recipe, plaintiff or defendant in the action.

Section 2 - Proceedings before courts

Paragraph 1 - In the institution of proceedings

Art.304.-In civil cases, the proceeding is commenced either by request or by subpoena.

Paragraph 2 - Judgement

Art.305.-1 On the day appointed for the appearance, the judge hears the game, if present, and is required to issue a ruling.

2 ° If circumstances require a delay, except as provided in section 206 above, it can not exceed eight days and the trial court must authorize the sale for the goods subject to decay.

Paragraph 3 - Call of judgments by the courts

Art.306 .- All the judgments of the courts in customs matters may be appealed regardless of the amount in dispute in accordance with the rules of the Code of Civil Procedure.

Paragraph 4 - Service of judgments and other proceedings

Art.307 .- 1 ° meanings to the Customs are made to the agent to represent him;

2 ° to the other meanings are made pursuant to rules of the Code of Civil Procedure.

Section 3 - Procedures before the criminal courts

Art.308. 1-Continued Customs offenses is subject to the complaint with a civil service or the head of the customs collector on pain of nullity of the proceedings. In this regard, all acts of recognition established by agents other than customs administration must be submitted to the Customs for competence with regard to the prosecution.

2 ° The summons to appear before the Tribunal is given either by the record evidencing the same offense, either by summons or warnings.

Art.309.-The provisional release of accused persons residing abroad and arrested for the crime of smuggling is subject to the obligation to provide a bond guaranteeing payment of financial penalties incurred.

Art.310 .- The rules of procedure in force in the territory of the Republic shall apply to citations, judgments, objections and appeals.

Section 4 - Appeals to the Supreme Court

Art.311.-The rules in force in the territory of the Republic concerning appeals on points of law in civil and criminal cases are applicable to customs.

Section 5 - Miscellaneous

Subsection 1 - Rules of Procedure common to all instances

A. Instruction and fees

Art.312.-long appeal in the first instance, the statement is a simple verbal memory and no legal fees to repeat on either side.

B. Exploits

Art.313 .- Customs officers may, in respect of customs, all deeds and other acts of justice that the bailiffs are wont to do, but may have recourse to a bailiff, including sales of items seized , confiscated or abandoned.

Paragraph 2 - Fenders made to judge - Mitigating circumstances - Recurrence

Art.314.-1 Judge may, just to respond in a personal and private, moderated the rights or forfeitures and fines, in order not to prejudice the use of the Administration Customs;

However, notwithstanding this principle, they hold the mitigating circumstances, judges may:

· Free offenders confiscation of means of transport, however, these provisions are not applicable in cases where acts of smuggling or the like have been committed by concealment in hiding or in specially designed cavities or voids that are not normally for housing of the goods;

· Free offenders confiscation of objects used to hide the fraud.

2 ° In the case of smuggling prohibited goods on or subsequent offense, mitigating circumstances can not be granted.

Art.315.-It can not be released the seized goods in the final judging at all, on pain of nullity of judgments and damages in favor of the Customs Administration.

Art.316 .- It is forbidden to all judges, under the penalties under Article 293 above, provide no defense against the constraints or sessions, which will be null and void, unless the damages of Administration of Customs.

Art.317.-court judges and their clerks can not send receipt of payment or deposit, holidays, catwalks, receptions or discharge of bids, or make any judgments in lieu of shipments.

Paragraph 3 - Special provisions for offenses resulting from customs authorities

A. Evidence of non-infringement.

Art.318.-In any action on a seizure, evidence of non-infringement are the responsibility of

B. Action in warranty

Art.319 .- 1 Whatever the nature of the rules of the customs offense has been the subject of a report, at least one of the following administrative measures can be taken as security for payment of duties and taxes evaded or compromised and fines imposed or imposed:

· A) blocking of import transactions

· B) temporary or permanent withdrawal of approval of any kind on the decision of the Minister of Customs,

· C) closure for a term not exceeding three months, institutions, factories, workshops, warehouses, depots of the offender. To this end, the Customs may affix his lead or use any other means of closure.

• This measure is, after informing the administrative authority of the place of exercise of the activity or the regional representative of the state, imposed by decision of the Minister of Customs who delegates his power:

· In charge of the Head of Litigation and the Fight against fraud when the duration of the closure does not exceed one month,

· The Director General of Customs for more than a month.

After the period of three months, the Customs Administration reserves the right to decide the fate of the infringing goods in accordance with the Customs Code.

In no event shall such goods, rights and guarantees of taxes and fines, can not be exported.

During the duration of the penalty, the taxpayer is required to serve its employees wages, salaries, allowances and benefits of any kind to which he was right until then.

2 ° confiscation of the seized goods can be pursued against the driver or without reporting the Customs Administration is obliged to question the owners, even if they would be given him;

3 ° However, if the owners were involved or were known as security by those in which the seizures were made, the courts would rule and of law, or the intervention of third parties.

C. Forfeiture of seized goods and the minutiae of unknown

Art.320 .- 1 The Customs Administration may ask the court, upon request, the nature of the forfeiture of items seized or of unknown individuals who were not prosecuted due to limited major fraud;

2 A decision on that application by a single order, even if the request relates to several seizures separately.

D. Claiming items seized

Art.321.-1 The items seized or confiscated may be claimed by the owners or the price, whether recorded or not, claimed by creditors even privileged, saving their recourse against the perpetrators of fraud;

2 ° The times call for third party opposition and selling expired, all rehearsals and actions are inadmissible.

E. False statements

Art.322.-The truth or falsity of written or oral statements should be judged on what was first said.

Paragraph 4 - Legal nature of fines and confiscations

Art.323.-Fines and confiscations customs are the double character of penalties and civil damages and that the character of civil compensation predominates.

Art.324.-In addition to tax penalties, the courts order payment of the amounts defrauded

Chapter 5 - Enforcement of judgments of the constraints and obligations in customs matters

Section 1 - security for the performance

Section 1 - Lien

Art.325. In all cases, finding an infringement gross customs, means of transport and goods in question not liable to forfeiture may, as security for penalties, be retained until it is provided surety or paid deposit the amount of such penalties.

Paragraph 2 - Liens and Mortgages: subrogation

Art.326.-1 The Customs Administration has the rights, confiscation, fines and restitution, privilege and preference to all creditors on furniture and household effects of the royalties, with the exception of legal fees and other charges preferred what is due for six months rent only, and unless the claim as properly formed by the owners of goods in kind that are still packed

2 ° This Administration has similarly mortgage on the property of taxpayers and offenders as well as some furniture could Mortgage (ships, river boats, aircraft, belonging to the latter).

The Constitution Mortgage is a simple decision of the Director General of Customs, without writing a notarized. This decision can be made from the finding of infringement customs and / or financial and committed to follow the normal procedures for registration of the mortgage.

Art.327.-1 ° The approved customs agents who have paid for one third of duties, taxes or customs fines are subrogated to the lien of the Customs whatever the methods of collection observed by them in respect of the third party;

2 ° However, such subrogation shall in no case be opposed to government departments in charge for customs agents authorized to take action against the third party or their constituents.

Section 2 - enforcement procedures

Paragraph 1 - General Rules

Art.328.-1 The execution of judgments and rulings on customs matters may take place by all legal means.

2 ° The judgments sentencing for breach of customs laws and regulations are also performed by the body.

3 ° The constraints are enforceable by any legal means except by the body. The performance constraints may be suspended by any objection or other instrument.

4 Constraints customs prevail mortgage in the same way and under the same conditions as the sentences from the judiciary

5 ° When an offender customs dies before completing the settlement of fines, forfeitures and other financial penalties imposed against him by final decision or set forth in the transaction or litigation missions often accepted by him, recovery may be continued against the estate by any legal means, except by the body.

6 ° The customs fines and forfeitures, regardless of the court which pronounced them, shall be prescribed in the same time that correctional penalties under common law and under the same conditions as damages.

Paragraph 2 - Special rights reserved to the customs

Art.329 .- The Customs Administration is authorized to make any payment of judgments under attack by way of objection, appeal or cassation, unless at first those for whose benefit such judgments been made have been good and sufficient security as security for amounts awarded to them.

When Art.330.-release of seized for violations of laws and regulations whose implementation is entrusted to the Customs Administration is granted by decisions against which a remedy is made, delivery is not made those for whose benefit such judgments were made only in good and sufficient security of their value. Release can never be granted for goods whose entry is prohibited.

All-Art.331. seizures of duties, made the hands of receivers or those beholden to the Customs Administration are null and void, notwithstanding such seizures, the parties responsible are forced to pay the debt on their due.

Art.332.-In the case of sealing of the effects and papers of the accounting records and other revenues for the current year should not be enclosed in the sealed records are only those arrested and initialed by the the judge shall give the officer the recipe Acting, which notice guarantor as the trustee of justice, and it is mentioned in the minutes of sealing.

Art.333 .- 1 ° When customs offenses were regularly observed, and in case of emergency, the President of the Tribunal may, upon request of the Customs Administration, order the seizure of property as a precaution the defendant and that the cash held by third parties

2 ° The order of the President will be enforceable notwithstanding opposition or appeal. May be given release from arrest if the debtor provides a bond deemed sufficient.

3 Applications in validity or release from seizure are the responsibility of the presiding judge or section.

The sentence is immediate validation of attachments and seizures stop.

Art.334 .- All debtors and trustees of funds from the Head of taxpayers affected and the privilege provided for in Article 326-1 ° above are required, the request is made to them, to pay the acquired of taxpayers and the amount of money they have or are their hands up all or part of amounts due by them.

Paragraph 3-Year Advance imprisonment for debt

Art.335.-Anyone convicted of smuggling is, notwithstanding any appeal or further appeal, detained until he has paid the amount of the pecuniary sentence against him, however the length of detention may not exceed that fixed by the legislation on the attachment.

Paragraph 4 - Disposal of goods seized for violation of customs laws and regulations

Art.336.-1 In case of seizure of goods of fraud, the means used to conceal fraud and transportation, for the minutes of customs in good and due form, will be conducted at the behest of the Customs Administration before trial, the sale of items seized as security for fees and charges and financial penalties incurred after conversion of the seizure confiscation order of the judge of the place of commission of the offense or transactional decision, both in the absence and presence of the offender whose procedure will be established by decision of the Director General of Customs.

2 ° However, the sale may be suspended if the offender pays a bond deemed sufficient up to the value of seized cash to the customs collector one month later than the date of seizure;

3 ° the proceeds of the sale will be subject to claim, a claim by the offender or the owner.

Section 3 - Distribution of fines and confiscations

Art.337.-1 Total proceeds of fines and forfeitures resulting from ongoing business at the request of the Customs Administration supports above all share the following samples:

· A) the duties and taxes, if not paid by the purchasers of goods or offenders;

· B) the unrecovered costs of the defendants.

The surplus form the product available. The share of the State Budget for this product available is 25 percent.

2 ° The conditions under which the remainder is distributed are determined by decision of the Minister of Customs.

Chapter 6 - Accountability and Solidarity

Section 1 - Criminal Responsibility

Paragraph 1 - Holders

Art.338.-1 The owner of the fraudulent merchandise is deemed responsible for the fraud;

2 ° However, the carriers are not considered, they and their servants or agents, as offenders, when, for a regular and exact designation of their constituents, they put the Customs can exercise meaningful action against the real perpetrators of the fraud.

Paragraph 2 - Captains of ships, aircraft commander

Art.339.-1 Masters of vessels, ships, boats and aircraft commanders are deemed responsible for omissions and inaccuracies in the manifests and, in general, offenses committed on board their vessel;

2 ° However, prison sentences prescribed by this Code shall apply to the commanders of merchant ships or war or military aircraft or commercial in case of misconduct.

Art.340 .- The captain is relieved of all responsibility:

· A) for infringement under section 3672 ° below, if administered proof that it has fulfilled all its duties of supervision or if the offender is discovered;

· B) in the case of infringement under section 3673 ° below, if he is serious damage that required the diversion of the ship and provided that these events have been recorded in the logbook before the visit Administration of Customs.

Section 3 - Declaration

Art.341 .- 1 ° affidavit signers are responsible for omissions, inaccuracies and other irregularities in the statements, but their appeals against their constituents.

2 ° Where the declaration was drafted in accordance with written instructions given by his principal, it is liable to the same penalties as the person signing the declaration.

Paragraph 4 - Licensed Customs Brokers

Art.342.-1 ° The approved customs agents are responsible for customs operations performed by them;

2 ° the penalties of imprisonment prescribed by this Code does not apply to them in case of misconduct.

Paragraph 5 - Bidders

Art.343.-1 Bidders are responsible for the breach of commitments, but their actions against the carriers and other agents;

2 To this end, the service that the goods are presented does discharge for quantities for which commitments have been completed within the time and penalties to the offense continued to the issuing office against bidders and their guarantors.

Paragraph 6 - Complices

Art.344.-The provisions of Articles 59 and 60 of the Penal Code are applicable to accomplices in customs offenses.

Paragraph 7 - Interested in fraud

Art.345.-1 Those who participated in some way to a crime of smuggling or an offense to import or export without declaration are liable to the same penalties as the perpetrators of the offense, and Moreover, deprivation of rights enacted by section 374. below;

2 are deemed interested in:

· A) contractors, members of business, insurers, policyholders, lenders, owners of the goods and, in general, those who have a vested interest in fraud;

· B) those who have cooperated in some way to a set of acts performed by a number of individuals acting in concert, according to a plan of fraud stopped to achieve the result pursued in common;

· C) those who knowingly, or cover the acts of fraud or attempted to provide them with impunity, either purchased or held, even outside the radius of goods from a crime of smuggling or import without declaration;

3 ° The value of fraud can not be attributed to the person who acted out of necessity or as a result of error invincible.

Art.346 .- Those who bought or held, even outside the radius of goods smuggled or without a declaration, in quantities greater than the needs of their family consumption, are subject to the penalties for contraventions of the fourth class.

Section 2 - Liability

Paragraph 1-Liability of the Customs Administration

Art.347.-The Customs Administration is responsible for the acts of his employees in the exercise and only reason of their duties, saving its recourse against them or their sureties.

Art.348.-When a seizure made under article 267-2 ° above is not justified, the owner of the goods is entitled to compensation in an amount equal to 1 percent per month the value of items seized from the time of the reservoir until the date of delivery or the offer he was made.

Art.349. "If he is not found there is reason typing, it must be paid the sum of 100 Ar than in the home which the investigations were made under section 52 below above, except larger damages that the circumstances of the visit can potentially result

Section 2 - Liability of owners of goods

Art.350.-The cargo owners are legally responsible because of their employees with respect to the rights, confiscation, fines and costs.

Paragraph 3 - Liability of guarantors

Art.351 .- The sureties are required, as well as principals, to pay the fees and charges, monetary penalties and other amounts due by the debtors that they have bonded.

Section 3 - Solidarity

Art.352.-1 ° convictions against several individuals for the same act of fraud are interdependent, both for monetary penalties in lieu of confiscation for the fine and costs;

2 ° This does not apply only in respect of infringements of Articles 35-1 ° and 47-1 ° above, which are punishable by fines individual.

Art.353 .- The owners of the fraudulent merchandise, those who are responsible for import or export, the interest in fraud, accomplices and members are all united in body and compellable to pay the fine, amounts in lieu of forfeiture and costs.

Chapter 7 - Criminal Provisions

Section 1 - Classification of Customs Offences and penalties main

Section 1 - General

Art.354.-There are four classes of tickets customs and three classes of customs offenses.

Art. 355.-Any attempt to customs offense is considered the same offense.

Subsection 2 - Customs Violations

A. 1st class ticket

Art.356.-1 is liable to a fine of 100,000 to 1,000,000 Ar any breach of customs laws and regulations when the defect is not more severely punished by this Code;

2 ° fall, in particular, within the scope of the provisions of the preceding paragraph:

· A) Any omission or inaccuracy on one of the indications that the statements must contain the irregularity does not affect the application of duties or prohibitions;

· B) Failure to register for directories,

° C) while violations of Articles 47, 58-b), 60, 61, 64, 71-2 ° and 129-2 ° above or the provisions of the decrees for the application of Article 12-2 ° of this Code.

· Contravention of the second class.

Art.357 .- 1 is liable to a fine of between one and two-time duties and taxes evaded or impaired, the payment of duties and taxes, any breach of customs laws and regulations when the defect is to or effect of evading or to endanger the recovery of a right or any tax and is not specifically punishable under this Code;

2 ° fall, in particular, within the scope of the preceding paragraph, the offenses hereinafter as they relate to goods of the category of those subject to duties or taxes:

· A) deficits in the number of packages declared manifested consignee or transport catwalk with borrowing under the sea or acquired to bail;

· B) deficits on the quantity of goods placed under an economic system;

° C) the non-representation of goods placed in bonded warehouse or special warehouse in EPZs and Free Enterprises;

• d) the presentation for under seal broken or altered goods shipped under customs seals and stamps;

° E) the total or partial breach of the commitments acquired in the deposit and to bid;

· F) the excess weight, number or measure stated.

3 are also sanctioned by penalties for contraventions of the second class all offenses jeopardizing the recovery of navigational rights and duties on goods;

4 is also punishable by the penalties for contraventions of the second class the breach of Article 229-3 °, above where it is not more severely punished by this Code.

C. Contravention of the third class

Art.358.-are punishable by the confiscation of the infringing goods and a fine of between one and half times the value of the goods.

° 1 ° any act of smuggling as well as any act of import or export without a declaration when the offense involves goods from the category of those that are neither prohibited nor heavily taxed on entry or exit;

• 2 ° any false statement in this case, the value or origin of goods imported, exported or placed under an economic system where a customs duty or any tax is evaded or undermined by the false statement;

• 3 ° any false statement in the name of the actual recipient or sender real

• 4 ° any false declaration to obtain undue benefit of the exemption under section 240-1 °, 258 and 263 of this Code and any violation of the provisions of the decrees, if any, for the purposes of those sections;

° 5 ° any diversion of goods not prohibited their destination;

• 6 ° the nomination as a unit in the manifestos and statements by several bullets and other closed packages, meeting in any manner whatsoever;

° 7 ° the absence of manifest or non - performance of the original manifest; omission of goods in the clear or in the summary statements, and any difference in the nature of the cargo manifest or declared summarily.

Contravention · 4th Class

Art.359 .- 1 is liable to the confiscation of the infringing goods and a fine of between one and two times the value of such goods, any breach of customs laws and regulations when the defect is in respect of goods the category of those that are prohibited at the entrance or exit and is not specifically punishable under this Code;

2 ° fall, in particular, within the scope of provisions of the preceding offenses referred to in Article 357-2 ° above when they are to report goods to the category of those prohibited to the entry or exit.

Paragraph 3 - Customs Offences

A. Offense of first class

Art.360 .- are punishable by the confiscation of the object of fraud, confiscation of means of transport, the confiscation of objects used to conceal the fraud, and a fine of twice the value of subject to fraud and to imprisonment for one year to three years, all because of

smuggling as well as any act of import or export without a declaration when the offenses relate to merchandise the category of those that are prohibited or heavily taxed on entry or prohibited or heavily taxed at the exit.

B. Offense of second-class

Art.361 .- are liable for tax penalties provided in the preceding article and imprisonment for two years to three years of smuggling offenses committed by a meeting of three individuals and up to six inclusive, all wear or No, the fraudulent merchandise and are authors or co-authors interested in fraud.

All violations of Articles 351 °, 54 and 95 above, are subject to the same prison sentence and a fine of

100000-2500000 Ar

Also, are subject to the same prison sentence and a fine of 500,000 to

5,000,000 Ar, all violations of the provisions of Article 90-1 ° of this code, and any offense committed by a person who has been a withdrawal of approval, continues to do for others, directly or indirectly, customs formalities for the declaration for the goods.

C. Crime of the third class

Art.362 .- are punishable by the confiscation of the object of fraud, confiscation of means of transport, the confiscation of objects used to conceal the fraud, a fine of double and triple the value objects confiscated by imprisonment of at least two years and five years:

° 1 ° smuggling offenses committed by more than six people or three or more individuals on horseback or bicycle, all are not goods or fraud;

° 2 ° the crimes of smuggling by air, for self-propelled or towed vehicle, vessel or floating craft of less than one hundred tons net or by riverboat.

• 3 ° the means of transport used to carry out and deliberately commit the crimes in this category become the property of the state, represented by the Customs, after processing their input in confiscation of administrative and judicial decisions.

They can not be claimed by the owners or the price, whether recorded or not, claimed by creditors even privileged.

Paragraph 4 - Smuggling

Art.363. 1-Smuggling means of imports or exports outside the office and any violation of laws or regulations relating to detention and transport of goods within the territory 2 are, in particular facts of smuggling:

· A) violation of Articles 691 °, 72-1 °, 76, 251 and 252 above;

· B) payments fraud or fraudulent shipments made either in the confines of a port or on the coast with the exception of landings fraud referred to in Article 370-1 ° below;

° C) substitutions or subtractions during transport of goods shipped in economic systems, and all customs fraud in such transport;

• d) the violation of either legislative or regulatory prohibition on the export or re-export, or making the export or re-export to the payment of duties or taxes or the completion of special formalities when the fraud was made or attempted outside the office and is not specifically repressed by another provision of this Code.

· Art.364.-Goods of the category of those prohibited to entry or heavily taxed, are deemed to have been smuggled, and the goods of the category of those whose output is prohibited or subject to strong duties and taxes are deemed to be an attempt to export contraband in all cases of offense listed below:

° 1 ° when found in the terrestrial area of the radius without being provided with a receipt of payment, shipping or other free pass valid for the route they follow and the time in which the transport takes place, unless that 'they come from within the customs territory of the road that leads directly to the customs office nearest and be accompanied by the documents listed above and the orders made for the purposes of section 251 above ;

• 2 ° when even being accompanied by an expedition with the express obligation to do aim at an office of transit, they have exceeded this office without that obligation has been met.

• 3 ° when being brought to the office, they are deprived of the documents listed in Articles 251 and 252 above.

° 4 ° when found in the terrestrial area of the radius in violation of section 253 above.

Customs; Art.365.-1 goods referred to in Article 254 above shall be deemed to have been smuggled in the absence of proof of origin or if the documents presented are false, incomplete or not applicable;

2 ° They are captured wherever they are and the persons referred to in paragraphs 1 and 2 of Article 254 shall be prosecuted and punished in accordance with Articles 360 to 362 above;

3 When they informed that they issued the original justifications could not do it properly or that they sold, transferred, exchanged or given the goods was not able to justify their detention regular, holders and carriers will be condemned to the same penalties and the goods will be seized and forfeited under the same conditions as above regardless of the justifications that have been produced.

Paragraph 5 - Import and export without statements:

Art.366.-constitute imports or exports without a declaration:

° 1 ° imports or exports by customs offices, without accounting or under cover of a detailed declaration applicable to goods not provided;

° 2 ° subtractions or substitutions of bonded goods. 3 ° Any violation of the provisions of Article 247 above.

Art.367 .- · are deemed to be without an import declaration:

° 1 ° the goods declared for transport through the territory of the sea for the temporary export or to obtain a transit traffic within range, if nonreprésentation or differences in the nature or kind between such goods and those made at the outset;

• 2 ° prohibited or heavily taxed items found on board ships in the limits of ports and harbors to trade independently of the objects or components regularly manifested cargo and aircraft stores properly represented before visiting;

° 3 ° goods specially designated by order of the Minister of Customs discovered on ships or lying at anchor in the maritime zone of customs.

Art.368.-are deemed imported or exported without a declaration packages exceeding the number declared. It is the same deficits on the weight, number or measure stated.

Art.369 .- shall be deemed to import or export without a declaration of prohibited goods:

1 ° Any violation of the provisions of Article 283 ° above and the fact that for the issuance of one referred to in Article 28-3 ° above or by counterfeiting of public seals, or by false statements or by other fraudulent means and all violations of the provisions of Article 29 of this Code;

2 ° Any misrepresentation for the purpose or effect of evading the application of measures of prohibition.

However, prohibited goods at the entrance or exit that have been declared under a name by highlighting the prohibition that strikes are not captured, and those for import are sent abroad, and those whose output is are required in Madagascar;

3 ° misrepresentation in this case, the value or origin of goods or the recipient's real name or the actual sender, when the offenses were committed with bills, certificates or other documents false, inaccurate, incomplete or not applicable;

4 ° The declaration or act having the purpose or effect of obtaining, in whole or in part, a refund, an exemption, a reduced fee, or any benefit attached to the import or export;

5 ° Establishing, to establish or use an invoice, certificate or other document null and false, to obtain or to improperly obtain, in Madagascar or in a foreign country, the benefit of a preferential treatment provided, either by treaty or international agreement or by a provision of domestic law, for goods leaving the customs territory or entering Madagascar.

Art.370 .- are deemed tax-free import prohibited goods:

° 1 ° landing smuggled objects referred to in Article 367-2 °, above;

° 2 ° fraudulent naturalization of ships;

° 3 ° the registration of automobiles, motorcycles and aircraft without prior completion of customs formalities;

• 4 ° misuse of prohibited goods to their destination.

Art.371.-1 is deemed export prohibited goods without declaring any breach or legislative or regulatory prohibition on the export or re-export, or making the export or re-export to the payment of duties, taxes or the completion of special formalities, where fraud has been made or attempted by the office and it is not specifically repressed by another provision of this Code.

2 ° If the goods have been exported as an exception to a prohibition of output destined for a particular country, are, after arrival in this country, shipped to a third country, the exporter is liable to the penalties of export without a declaration if it is determined that the forwarding was done on his instructions, at the instigation or with its complicity, or if it is shown that he has benefited or had knowledge of the return projected at the time of export.

Section 2 - ADDITIONAL PENALTIES

Paragraph 1 - Confiscation

Art.372.-Notwithstanding any other penalties provided by this Code, shall be confiscated:

° 1 ° the goods that have been or were to be substituted as provided in sections 357-2 ° a), 363-2 ° C) and 366-2 °;

° 2 ° the goods originally presented as provided by article 367-1 ° above and 3 ° The means of transport in the cases provided for in Article 47-1 ° above.

Section 2 - Financial penalty

Art.373 .- Regardless of the fine for refusal to disclose in accordance with Articles 54 and 95 above, offenders should be sentenced to represent the books, papers and documents withheld under a penalty of 3000 Ar at least each day of delay. This penalty begins the day of the finding by the minutes of the refusal of communication, it continues until the day it is found, through an entry made by an agent of control over one of the key books of the company or institution, that the Authority has been able to get through orderly

Paragraph 3 - deprivation of rights

Art.374.-1 In addition to the penalties provided by this Code, those found to have participated as interested in any way with the crime of smuggling or an offense to import or export without statement are declared incapable of voters or elected chambers of commerce and commercial courts, as long as they have not been relieved of this disability.

2 To this end, the public prosecutor to the criminal court sent the Attorney General and the Director General of Customs, extracts from the judgments of the court for these individuals to be posted and made public audiences and in all places of commerce and to be inserted in newspapers, in accordance with Article 442 of the Commercial Code.

Art.375 .- 1 ° Anyone will be legally convicted of having abused an economic system, may, by decision of the Director General of Customs, with the possibility of delegation, be excluded from the regime of temporary and be deprived Faculty of transit and storage and removal of any credit.

2 ° one who lends his name to escape the effects of these provisions those who suffer, incur the same penalties.

Section 3 - Special cases of enforcement of sentences

Paragraph 1 - Confiscation

Art.376.-In cases of infringement under Articles 367-2 ° and 370-1 °, the forfeiture may be imposed only in respect of objects of fraud. However, fraud and concealing goods transport used in the landing and the removal of fraudulent items will be confiscated if it is established that the possessor of such transport is complicit in the fraud.

Art.377.-When the objects subject to forfeiture could not be seized or when, having been seized, the Customs Department so requests, the court shall, in lieu of forfeiture, ordered to pay are equal to the value represented by said objects and calculated from the value of the goods or cleared according to the statistics at the time the fraud was discovered.

Paragraph 2 - Special arrangements for calculating monetary penalties

Art.378.-1 Notwithstanding the provisions of Articles 23 and 26 of this Code, when the value of the infringing goods is denominated in foreign currency, the conversion rate to consider is that applicable on the date of the minutes finding, or seizure or any act in its stead highlighting the merits of the offense.

2 ° For the application of penalties, the value to be considered is the value in the domestic market as well as import and export.

3 The calculation of duties and taxes evaded or compromise is as follows:

· A) the Rights Agreement, the quotas of taxes and duties to be considered are those applicable at the date of the declaration of release for consumption;

· B) for unpaid taxes, the percentages of taxes and duties to be considered are those applicable at the date of the minutes of con-tat or seizure or act in lieu of emphasizing the merits of the offense.

Art.379.-1 Under no circumstances, fines of multiple rights or many of the value delivered for the purposes of this Code shall not be less than 50,000 per package or Ar Ar 50,000 per ton or fraction of a ton if These goods are not packed;

2 ° When a false statement in the name of the actual recipient was observed after removal of the goods, the sentences can not be less than 50,000 per package or Ar

Ar 50,000 per tonne or part tonne in the case of unpackaged goods.

Art.380 .- If the court is satisfied that the tenders, proposals for the purchase or sales agreements of any kind relating to the objects of fraud were made or contracted at a higher price in the domestic market, the time the fraud was committed, it can be based on that price to calculate the penalties set out in this Code based on the value of those objects.

Art.381 .- In the case of an offense under article 369-4 ° above, the penalties are determined from the value given for the calculation of the rebate, exemption from or reduced duty the advantage sought or obtained, whichever is higher than the actual value.

Paragraph 3 - Competition offenses

Art.382 .- 1 ° Any act falling within the scope of penal provisions enacted by this separate code should be considered in the highest sense it is likely that criminal;

2 ° In cases of multiple violations of customs offenses or the financial penalties are imposed for each offense duly established.

Art.383.-Without prejudice to the application of penalties laid down in this Code, the crime of abuse, assault, rebellion, corruption or maladministration and of smuggling gathering and carrying of arms are prosecuted, tried and punished according to law

SUPPLEMENTS

GOVERNEMNT CONTACTS

PRESIDENCE

Adresse
Lapam-Panjakana Ambohitsorohitra
BP 955 - 101 ANTANANARIVO

TEL : (261 20) 22 273 38
FAX : (261 20) 22 670 33

PRIMATURE

Adresse
Lapan'ny Mahazoarivo

TEL : (261 20) 22 331 13 / 22 650 10

VICE-PRIMATURE CHARGÉ DES PROGRAMMES ECONOMIQUES, MINISTRE DES TRANSPORTS, DES TRAVAUX PUBLICS ET DE L'AMENAGEMENT DU TERRRITOIRE

Adresse
BP 3378 Anosy
101 ANTANANARIVO

TEL : (261 20) 22 356 12

JUSTICE

Adresse
Rue Joel Rakotomalala
Faravohitra - 101 ANTANANARIVO

TEL : (261 20) 22 376 84
FAX : (261 20) 22 644 58

INTERIEUR ET REFORME ADMINISTRATIVE

Adresse
BP 833 - 101 ANTANANARIVO

TEL : (261 20) 22 230 84
FAX : (261 20) 22 277 77 (SG)
(261 20) 22 311 15 (DAF)

ENSEIGNEMENT SUPERIEUR ET RECHERCHE SCIENTIFIQUE

Adresse
BP 4163 Fiadanana
101 ANTANANARIVO

TEL : (261 20) 22 294 23
FAX : (261 20) 22 345 08

SECURITÉ PUBLIQUE

Adresse
BP 23 Bis - Anosy
101 ANTANANARIVO

TEL : (261 20) 22 210 29
(261 20) 22 376 14/18
FAX : (261 20) 22 318 61

AFFAIRES ETRANGERES

Adresse
BP 836 - Anosy
101 ANTANANARIVO

TEL : (261 20) 22 207 81
(261 20) 22 211 98
FAX : (261 20) 22 344 84

ENVIRONNEMENT, EAUX ET FORETS

Adresse
Rue Farafaty - Ampandrianomby
BP 571 - 101 ANTANANARIVO

TEL : (261 20) 22 409 08
FAX : (261 20) 22 419 19

DEFENSE NATIONALE

Adresse
BP 8 - Ampahibe
101 ANTANANARIVO

TEL : (261 20) 22 273 95
(261 20) 22 222 11 **FAX :** (261 20) 22 354 20
(261 20) 22 604 73

FONCTION PUBLIQUE

Adresse
67 Ha 101 ANTANANARIVO

TEL : (261 20) 22 230 82
(261 20)22 230 47
FAX : (261 20) 22 338 56

SANTE

Adresse
BP 88- Ambohidahy
101 ANTANANARIVO

TEL : (261 20) 22 631 21
FAX : (261 20) 22 642 28

POPULATION

Adresse
BP 723 - Ambohijatovo
101 ANTANANARIVO

TEL : (261 20) 22 276 91
FAX : (261 20) 22 648 23

DECENTRALISATION, DEVELOPPEMENT DES PROVINCES AUTONOMES ET DES COMMUNES (AUPRÈS DE LA PRÉSIDENCE DE LA RÉPUBLIQUE CHARGÉ)

Adresse
BP 24 Bis
101 ANTANANARIVO

TEL : (261 20) 22 358 81
(261 20) 22 375 16
FAX : (261 20) 22 375 16

CULTURE
^

Adresse
BP 305 - Antaninarenina
101 ANTANANARIVO

TEL : (261 20) 22 274 77
FAX : (261 20) 22 298 48

JEUNESSE, SPORTS ET LOISIRS

Adresse
Place Goulette - Ambohijatovo
BP 681 - 101 ANTANANARIVO

TEL : (261 20) 22 277 80
FAX : (261 20) 22 342 75

ENSEIGNEMENT SECONDAIRE ET EDUCATION DE BASE

Adresse
BP 267 - Anosy
101 ANTANANARIVO

TEL : (261 20) 22 629 11
(261 20)22 213 02
FAX : (261 20) 22 247 65

TELECOMMUNICATION, POSTES ET COMMUNICATION

Adresse
Antaninarenina
101 ANTANANARIVO

TEL : (261 20) 22 232 67
FAX : (261 20) 22 358 94

ECONOMIE FINANCES ET BUDGET

Adresse
BP 674 - Anosy
101 ANTANANARIVO

TEL : (261 20) 22 665 24
FAX : (261 20) 22 285 08

AGRICULTURE, ELEVAGE ET PECHE

Adresse
BP 301 - Ampandrianomby
101 ANTANANARIVO

TEL : (261 20) 22 272 27
FAX : (261 20) 22 265 61

INDUSTRIALISATION, COMMERCE ET DEVELOPPEMENT DU SECTEUR PRIVE

Adresse
Immeuble ARO Ampefiloha
BP 527- 101 ANTANANARIVO

TEL : (261 20) 22 322 51
FAX : (261 20) 22 280 24

ENERGIE ET MINES

Adresse
Ampandrianomby
- 101- ANTANANARIVO

TEL : (261 20) 22 289 28
FAX : (261 20) 22 325 54

TOURISME

Adresse
BP 610 - Tsimbazaza
101 ANTANANARIVO

TEL : (261 20) 22 262 98
(261 20)22 668 05
FAX : (261 20) 22 789 53

TRAVAIL ET LOIS SOCIALES

Adresse
Immeuble FOP - 67 Ha
101 ANTANANARIVO

TEL : (261 20) 22 338 59
(261 20) 22 213 09 (S.P.)

IMPORTANT GOVERNMENT AND BUSINESS CONTACTS

COUNTRY GOVERNMENT AGENCIES

Ministère des Finances et de l'Economie
P.O. Box 61
Antananarivo - Madagascar
Tel: (261 20) 22 216 32
Fax: (261 20) 22 345 30

Ministère de la Décentralisation et du Budget
P.O. Box 61
Antananarivo - Madagascar
Tel: (261 20) 22 301 73
Fax: (261 20) 22 345 30

Ministère du Commerce et de la Consommation
P.O. BOX 245
Antananarivo 101 - Madagascar
Tel: (261 20) 22 272 92
Fax: (261 20) 22 312 80

Ministère de la Promotion de l'Industrie et de l'Artisanat
P.O. BOX: 527
Antananarivo 101 - Madagascar
Tel: (261 20) 22 255 15
Fax: (261 20) 22 277 90

Ministère de l'Energie et des Mines
P.O. BOX 257
Antananarivo 101 - Madagascar
Tel: (261 20) 22 255 15
Fax: (261 20) 22 325 54

Ministère d'Etat à l'Agriculture et au Développement Rural
P.O. BOX 842
Antananarivo 101 - Madagascar
Tel: (261 20) 22 247 10
Fax: (261 20) 22 265 61

Ministère des Postes et Télécommunications
Antaninarenina
Antananarivo 101 - Madagascar
Tel: (261 20) 22 261 21
Fax: (261 20) 22 240 08

Ministère des Transports et de la Météorologie
Anosy
Antananarivo 101 - Madagascar
Tel: (261 20) 22 227 19
Fax: (261 20) 22 240 01

Banque Centrale de Madagascar
Antaninarenina
Antananarivo 101 - Madagascar
Tel: (261 20) 22 217 51
Fax: (261 20) 22 345 32

COUNTRY BUSINESS ASSOCIATIONS

Chambre de Commerce, d'Industrie et d'Agriculture d'Antananarivo
P.O. BOX 166
Antananarivo 101 - Madagascar
Tel: (261 20) 22 202 11
Fax: (261 20) 22 202 13

- FIVMPAMA (Association of Malagasy Businessmen)
12, rue Rainizanabololona - Antanimena
Antananarivo 101 - Madagascar
Tel: (261 20) 22 690 78
Fax: (261 20) 22 320 56

- GEM (Groupement des Entreprises de Madagascar)
P.O. Box 1695
Antananarivo 101 - Madagascar
Tel: (261 20) 22 238 41
Fax: (261 20) 22 219 65

- SIM (Syndicat des Industries de Madagascar)
c/o PAPMAD
P.O. Box 1756
Antananarivo - Madagascar
Tel: (261 20) 22 206 35
Fax: (261 20) 22 243 94

- GEFP (Groupement des Entreprises Franches et Partenaires)
Lot II B 1C
Amboditsiry – Andranobevava
Antananarivo 101 – Madagascar
Tel: (26120) 22 418 07
Fax: (26120) 22 403 73
E-Mail: gefpmg@dts.mg

COUNTRY MARKET RESEARCH FIRMS

Automated Data Analysis, Processing & Trading (ADAPT)
P.O. BOX 4212
Antananarivo 101 - Madagascar
Tel: (261 20) 22 291 92
Fax: (261 20) 22 291 92

Cabinet MICA
P.O. BOX 5258
Antananarivo 101 - Madagascar
Tel: (261 20) 22 243 62
Fax: (261 20) 22 259 31
E-Mail: narondro@dts.mg

Cabinet Fivoarana
P.O. BOX 3854 - Madagascar
Antananarivo 101
Tel: (261 20) 22 219 25
Fax: (261 20) 22 271 41

Cabinet d'Etudes, de Conseil et d'Assistance à la Réalisation
Lot IVD 17 Bis, Tsiazotafo
Antananarivo 101 - Madagascar
Tel: (261 20) 22 347 26
Fax: (261 20) 22 206 44

Cabinet Ravonison, Gast et Associés
Lot 1B 26-9, Rue de la Réunion
Isoraka
Antananarivo 101 - Madagascar
Tel: (261 20) 22 261 71
Fax: (261 20) 22 446 33

OSIRIS
P.O. BOX 3476
Antananarivo 101 - Madagascar
Tel: (261 20) 22 420 44
Fax: (261 20) 22 420 44

Ocean Consultants
P.O. Box 3528
Antananarivo 101 - Madagascar
Tel: (261 20) 22 428 06
Fax: (261 20) 22 271 26

USEFUL WEBSITES

Tourism: www.tourisme-madagascar.com
Intestment/Tourism: madagascar-guide.com
Industry: www.sinergic.mg/madagascar-industrie
General Information: www.embassy.org/madagascar
General/Economy: www.madagascar-contacts.com
National Assembly: www.an.online.mg
Economy: www.simicro.mg/sta
Malagasy Products: www.zoma.com
Privatization: www.madaprivat.org
Indian Ocean/Madagascar: www.lk-oi.com
Investment: www.bni.mg

EMBASSIS TO OTHER NATIONS

Embassy of Madagascar in Beijing, China - 3 Sanlitun Dong Jie, 100600 Tel: 6532-1353,6532-1643
Consulate of Madagascar in Hong Kong, Hong Kong - 14/F, East Ocean Centre, Penthhouse, 98 Granville Road, Tsim Sha Tsui East, Kowloon. Tel: 23160888
Embassy of Madagascar in Tokyo, Japan - 2-3-23, Moto-Azabu, Minato-ku. Post Code:106 Tel: 34467252/ 4 Fax: 34467078

Consulate General of Madagascar in Karachi, Pakistan - B-307,Block 6,Gulshan-e-Iqbal Karachi, Pakistan Tel: 467118, 464674

EMBASSIES OF OTHER NATIONS TO MADAGASCAR

Honorary Consulate of Belgium in Antananarivo, Madagascar - 19, Rue révérend Père Callet, Behoririka 101 Tananarive (Mailing : P.O. Box 3046, Antananarivo, Madagascar) Tel: 2220984 Fax: 2220368
Consulate of Canada in Antananarivo, Madagascar - c/o QIT-Madagascar Minerals Ltd.,Villa Paula Androhibe, Lot II-M62C, Villa 3H Ivandry, Antananarivo 101 (P. O. Box 4003, Antananarivo 101) Tel: 42559 Fax: 42506
Special Delegation of China in Antananarivo, Madagascar - Villa Bakoly VIII, Lot Pres VR 61 B Ambohidraserika, Ambohimiandra-Antananarivo, Madagascar (B.P. 3117, Antananarivo 101, Madagascar) Tel: 2234838 Fax: 2228971
Vice Consulate of Denmark in Toamasina, Madagascar - c/o La Ligne Scandinave, 2, Rue Lieutenant Berard, B.P. 18, Toamasina (Source from Udenrigsministeriet, check following URL for update information) Tel: 53 32548 Fax: 53 339-37 E-mail: sealtmm@bow.dts.mg
French Embassy in Tanandava, Madagascar - 3 rue Jean-Jaur? - Ambatomena - BP 204 Tel: 22 398 98 Fax: 22 399 27
Embassy of Indonesia in Antananarivo, Madagascar - 26-28 Rue Patrice Lumumba, Tsaralalana, B.P. 3969/3242 Tel: (261-20) 222-4915, 222-4825 Fax: (261-20) 223-2857
British Embassy in Antananarivo, Madagascar - First Floor, Immeuble "Ny Havana" Cite de 67 Ha, BP 167, Antananarivo Tel: 22 27749, 22 27370, 22 33765 Fax: 22 26690 E-mail: ukembant@simicro.mg
British Consulate in Toamasina, Madagascar - SEAL TAMATAVE Tel: 53 32548/32569 Fax: 53 33937 E-mail: sealtmm@bow.dts.mg

FOREIGN ORGANIZATIONS IN MADAGASCAR

Organization Name	Phone	FAX	Address (all in Antananarivo)
American Lutheran Mission	22-331-74 22-292-86	22-330-81	9 Rue de Belgique, Isoraka
Care International	22-320-75 22-332-65	22-349-11	11 Rue Radama 1er, Tsaralanana
Catholic Relief Services	22-265-34 22-206-66	22-316-96	II W 27 D, Ankorahotra
Conservation International	22-352-89	22-204-22	II L 1 A, Ankadivato
Rotary Club	22-414-65		Rue VVS, Andrainarivo
UNESCO	22-217-61		11 Rue Naka Rabemanantsoa, Behoririka
UNICEF	22-280-83 22-303-51	22-304-01	Rue Robert Ducrocq, Behoririka
UNPD	22-219-07 22-234-90 22-241-15	22-347-96	22 Rue Rainitovo, Antsahavola
USAID - US Agency for International Development	22-254-89	22-348-83	Immeuble Vonisoa, Ambohijanahary-Andrefana
US Cultural Center	22-202-38 22-202-39	22-213-97	4 Rue Razafindratandra, Ambohidahy
US Embassy	22-200-89 22-212-57	22-345-39	14 Rue Rainitovo, Antsahavola
US Peace Corps	22-313-30 22-313-54		II Y 14 bis, Ambaranjana
WWF - World Wildlife Fund	22-346-38 22-348-85	22-348-88	II M 85 ter, Antsakarivo

BANKS IN MADAGASCAR

Standard Bank of South Africa holds a minority shareholding in the Union Commercial Bank SA, Madagascar.
Tel.: 092612022 27262
Fax.: 092612022 28740

Bankin'Ny Tantsaha Mpamokatra (BTM)
(Banque Nationale pour le Développement Rural)
Place de l'Indépendance
BP 183
Antananarivo
tel: 20251
fax: 29408

Bank Pan Oceanic (BPO)
BP 21 bis
Antananarivo 101

Banky Fampandrosoana Ny Varotra (BFV)
(Banque Nationale pour le Commerce)
14 Lalana Jeneraly Rabehevitra
BP 196
Antananarivo
tel: 20691
fax: 34554

Banque Malgache de l'Océan Indien (BMOI)
BP 25 bis
Antananarivo 101
fax: 34610

BNI - Crédit Lyonnais Madagascar
74 Rue du 26 Juin 1960
BP 174
Antananarivo 101
tel: 22800
fax: 33749

Union Commercial Bank SA
77 rue Solombavambahoaka Frantsay
BP 197
Antananarivo
tel: 27262
fax: 28740

Chamber of Commerce, Industry and Agriculture of Antananarivo
Antananarivo 101
tel: 20211
fax: 20213

Fédération des Chambres de Commerce, d'Industrie et d'Agriculture
20, Rue Paul-Dussac
Antananarivo

Central Bank of Madagascar
Avenue de la Révolution Socialiste
BP 550
Antananarivo 101
tel: 21751
fax: 34532

Principal Commercial Centres

Antananarivo is the commercial and financial centre and also a major industrial centre.
Toamasina is the country's major port and an important industrial centre.
Other centres include Tulear, Antsiranana, Fianarantsoa, Antsirabe and Mahajanga.

SENATE MEMBERS

ANTANANARIVO

1 - ANDRIMIARISATRANA Noël Christian
2 - ANDRIANIRINA Lucien
3 - RABE François
4 - RABETSAROANA Sylvain Willy
5 - RAJEMISON RAKOTOMAHARO Guy
6 - RAHARIMINA Olga Emilienne
7 - RAKIVOLAHARIVONY Jeanine Hortense
8 - RAKOTOAMBOA Louis
9 - RAKOTOARIVENTINY Charlie
10 - RAKOTOMANANA Honoré
11 - RAKOTOZANANAY Augustin
12 - RAMAMONJISOA Benjamin
13 - RAMANANAKASINA Maurice
14 - RAMILISON Max Marie
15 - RANDRIAMIANDRISOA Philippe
16 - RANIRIHARINOSY Daniel
17 - RANOHISOA Seth.
18 - RASAMOELY Frederic

ANTSIRANANA

1 - ADINANY Jery
2 - BADADY Roland
3 - BENJAMIN Clovis
4 - BETIANA Bruno
5 - FAGNANO Andriana
6 - JAOTOMBO Ferdinand
7 - JOSEPH Yoland
8 - RAKOTO Julien
9 - RAKOTOMAMONJY Jean Max
10 - RAZANAMAHOLY Robia
11 - TOTOBESOLA Jean Pierre

12 - VAOVAO Benjamin

FIANARANTSOA

1 - ANDRIAMORA Paul Bernard
2 - JOSEPH Sylvain
3 - MAC TONG KI Jean Yves
4 - MANANJARA
5 - NDONGO Gabriel
6 - RAFAMANTANANTSOA Faniry
7 - RAKOTOMIHANTAHARIZAKA R.S Organès
8 - RAKOTOZANDRINDRAINY Raphaël
9 - RANDIMBISOA Jean Chrysostome
10 - RANDIMBISON André dit Jehovah
11 - RANDRIANANDRASANA Jean Louis
12 - RAVELOARISOA Olga
13 - RAZAFIMILY Constance
14 - VELONAODY Fabien

MAHAJANGA

1 - BEFENO
2 - HASSANY Bin Mohamady
3 - HOUSSAIN
4 - JAFASY Bruno
5 - JEAN Clément
6 - LININA Zoé
7 - MARINASY
8 - MOHAMED Abdou
9 - RALAIJAONA Alfred
10 - RAMBOASOLO Lucien
11 - RATIANARIVO Jeanson
12 - SAJY Pierre
13 - SOUDJAY Bachir Adehame
14 - SYRITIS Alexandre

TOAMASINA

1 - ANDRIAMASY née RAKOTOARIVO Marie Suzette
2 - BEKY née RAZAFITSALOVA Monique
3 - BOTOROA Romule
4 - JEAN Félicien
5 - KOTO Dauphin
6 - MORA Richard
7 - PAUL Samuel
8 - RAKOTOMANANA Henri
9 - RAKOTOSIHANAKA Andriamiandra
10 - RAMASY Adolphe
11 - RANDRIANARIMANANA Jérôme
12 - RAOELINA Médard
13 - RATOVOSON Seth Arsène
14 - VELO Arsène
15 - RANDRIAMARO Arme

TOLIARA

1 - ARMAND Jean
2 - BOTOTSAKO Augustin

3 - DIMBY Marie Naphtaline
4 - KOLO Roland Eugène Christophe
5 - MARA David
6 - MOSA David
7 - NAIKA Eliane veuve Abdoulanziz
8 - NANG-TCHEE Jean de Dieu
9 - RABERSON Emilien Jeannot
10 - RAHERIVELO Tantely Guinéus
11 - RAJAOFERA Charlesv
12 - RASANDRATRINIAVO Hozllaz
13 - RAZAFITOMBO née Alibena Elisa
14 - REBOZA Mahaforona Cyrille
15 - ROBERT Razaka
16 - SOJA Jean André

GLOSSARY -- MADAGASCAR (INDIAN OCEAN)

CFA
: Communauté Financière d'Afrique (African Financial Community). The CFA covers those African countries whose currencies are linked with the French Franc at a fixed rate of exchange.

Comoran franc (CF)
: One Comoran franc = 100 centimes; in June 1995 US$1.00 = CF363.98.

crown colony
: A colony of the British Commonwealth over which the crown maintains some control, as through appointment of the governor.

European Community (EC)
: See European Union.

European Currency Unit (ECU)
: Standard currency unit of the European Union; in April 1995 ECU1 = US$0.75.

European Union (EU)
: Formerly the European Community, it was established by the Maastricht Treaty of December 1991 to expand European cooperation from economic and commercial into monetary, security and judicial matters. It officially came into being at the end of 1993.

exclusive economic zone (EEZ)
: A wide belt of sea and seabed adjacent to the national boundaries where the state claims preferential fishing rights and control over the exploitation of mineral and other natural resources. Madagascar claims a 150-nautical-mile exclusive economic zone. Mauritius, Comoros, Seychelles, and Maldives all claim 200 nautical miles. Boundary situations with neighboring states sometimes prevent the extension of the exclusive economic zones to the full limits claimed.

fiscal year (FY)
: Same as the calendar year for all except Mauritius, in which it runs from July 1 to June 30.

Franc Zone
: A monetary union among countries whose currencies are linked to the French franc. Members are France and its overseas appendages and fourteen African countries, including Comoros.

gross domestic product (GDP)
: A value measure of the flow of domestic goods and services produced by an economy over a period of time, such as a year. Only output values of goods for final consumption and intermediate production are assumed to be included in the final prices. GDP is sometimes aggregated and shown at market prices, meaning that indirect taxes and subsidies have been eliminated, the result is GDP at factor cost. The word "gross"

indicates that deductions for depreciation of physical assets have not been made. *See also* gross national product.

gross national product (GNP)

Gross domestic product (*q.v.*) plus the net income or loss stemming from transactions with foreign countries. GNP is the broadest measurement of the output of goods and services by an economy. It can be calculated at market prices, which include indirect taxes and subsidies. Because indirect taxes and subsidies are only transfer payments, GNP is often calculated at factor cost, removing indirect taxes and subsidies.

import substitution

The replacement of imports by domestically produced goods, often supported by tariffs or import quotas, and motivated by foreign exchange considerations.

International Development Association (IDA)

See World Bank.

International Finance Corporation (IFC)

See World Bank.

International Monetary Fund (IMF)

Established along with the World Bank (*q.v.*) in 1945, the IMF is a specialized agency affiliated with the United Nations and is responsible for stabilizing international exchange rates and payments. The main business of the IMF is the provision of loans to its members (including industrialized and developing countries) when they experience balance of payments difficulties. These loans frequently carry conditions that require substantial internal economic adjustments by the recipients, most of which are developing countries.

Lomé Convention

The first Lomé Convention (Lomé I) came into force in 1976, Lomé II came into effect in 1981, and Lomé III came into force in 1985; Lomé IV came into effect in 1990. The convention covers economic relations between the members of the European Economic Community (EEC) and their former colonies in Africa, the Caribbean, and the Pacific (ACP). The convention allows most ACP exports to enter the EEC duty-free or at special rates and, among other things, provides funds through the Stabex system (*q.v.*) to offset adverse fluctuations in the prices of ACP exports.

London Club

An informal group of commercial banks that come together to negotiate a debt rescheduling agreement with a country. The group has two committees, an economics committee that develops economic data projections and a negotiating committee. Committee members usually come from the five principal banks that hold the largest amounts of a country's debt.

Malagasy franc (FMG)

1 Malagasy franc (franc malgache-FMG) = 100 centimes; in May 1995 US$1.00 = FMG4,236.9.

Mauritian rupee (MauR)

1 Mauritian rupee = 100 cents; in August 1995 US$1.00 = MauR14.43.

parastatal

A semi-autonomous, quasi-qovernmental, state-owned enterprise.

Paris Club

The informal name for a consortium of Western creditor countries (Belgium, Britain, Canada, France, Germany, Italy, Japan, the Netherlands, Sweden, Switzerland, and the United States) that have made loans or guaranteed export credits to developing nations and that meet in Paris to discuss borrowers' ability to repay debts. Paris Club deliberations often result in the tendering of emergency loans to countries in economic difficulty or in the rescheduling of debts. Formed in October 1962, the organization has no formal or institutional existence. Its secretariat is run by the French treasury. It has a close relationship with the International Monetary Fund (*q.v.*), to which all of its members except Switzerland belong, as well as with the World Bank (*q.v.*) and the United Nations

Conference on Trade and Development (UNCTAD). The Paris Club is also known as the Group of Ten (G-10).

rufiyaa (Rf)

Maldives currency; 1 rufiyaa = 100 laari; in June 1995 US$1.00 = Rf11.77.

Seychelles rupee (SRe)

1 Seychelles rupee = 100 cents; in August 1995 US$1.00 = SRe4.25.

Shia (from Shiat Ali, the Party or Ali)

A member of the smaller of the two great divisions of Islam. The Shia supported the claims of Ali and his line to presumptive right to the caliphate and leadership of the Muslim community, and on this issue they divided from the Sunni (*q.v.*) in the major schism within Islam. Later schisms have produced further divisions among the Shia over the identity and number of imams. Most Shia revere Twelve Imams, the last of whom is believed to be hidden from view.

South Asia Association for Regional Cooperation (SAARC)

Comprises the seven nations of South Asia: Bangladesh, Bhutan, India, Maldives, Nepal, Pakistan, and Sri Lanka; founded as South Asia Regional Cooperation (SARC) organization at a meeting of foreign ministers in New Delhi on August 1-2, 1983; a second organizational meeting of foreign ministers was held in Thimphu in May 1985; inaugural meeting of heads of state and government in Dhaka on December 7-8, 1985. The goal is to effect economic, technical, and cultural cooperation and to provide a forum for discussions of South Asia political problems.

special drawing rights (SDRs)

Monetary units of the International Monetary Fund (*q.v.*) based on a basket of international currencies including the United States dollar, the German deutsche mark, the Japanese yen, the British pound sterling, and the French franc.

Stabex system

A system of export earnings stabilization set up by the European Community (EC) in accordance with the African, Caribbean, and Pacific (ACP) states. Under the system, the EC helps developing countries withstand fluctuations in the price of their agricultural products by paying compensation for lost export earnings.

Sunni

The larger of the two great divisions of Islam. The Sunni, who rejected the claims of Ali's line, believe that they are the true followers of the sunna, the guide to proper behavior set forth by Muhammad's personal deeds and utterances. *See also* Shia.

World Bank

Informal name used to designate a group of four affiliated international institutions: the International Bank for Reconstruction and Development (IBRD), the International Development Association (IDA), the International Finance Corporation (IFC), and the Multilateral Investment Guarantee Agency (MIGA). The IBRD, established in 1945, has the primary purpose of providing loans to developing countries for productive projects. The IDA, a legally separate loan fund but administered by the staff of the IBRD, was set up in 1960 to furnish credits to the poorest developing countries on much easier terms than those of conventional IBRD loans. The IFC, founded in 1956, supplements the activities of the IBRD through loans and assistance specifically designed to encourage the growth of productive private enterprises in the less developed countries. The MIGA, founded in 1988, insures private foreign investment in developing countries against various noncommercial risks. The president and certain senior officers of the IBRD hold the same positions in the IFC. The four institutions are owned by the governments of the countries that subscribe their capital. To participate in the World Bank group, member states must first belong to the International Monetary Fund (IMF-- *q.v.*).

BASIC TITLES ON MADAGASCAR

Title	ISBN
Madagascar A "Spy" Guide - Strategic Information and Developments	1433031086
Madagascar A Spy" Guide"	1438730357
Madagascar Business and Investment Opportunities Yearbook	1433031094
Madagascar Business and Investment Opportunities Yearbook	1438730365
Madagascar Business and Investment Opportunities Yearbook Volume 1 Strategic Information and Opportunities	1438777248
Madagascar Business and Investment Opportunities Yearbook Volume 2 Leading Export-Import, Business, Investment Opportunities and Projects	1577519760
Madagascar Business Intelligence Report - Practical Information, Opportunities, Contacts	1433031108
Madagascar Business Intelligence Report - Practical Information, Opportunities, Contacts	1438730373
Madagascar Business Law Handbook - Strategic Information and Basic Laws	1438770375
Madagascar Business Law Handbook - Strategic Information and Basic Laws	1438770375
Madagascar Business Law Handbook - Strategic Information and Basic Laws	1433031116
Madagascar Business Law Handbook - Strategic Information and Basic Laws	1438730381
Madagascar Company Laws and Regulations Handbook	1433070243
Madagascar Constitution and Citizenship Laws Handbook - Strategic Information and Basic Laws	1438779372
Madagascar Country Study Guide - Strategic Information and Developments	1433031124
Madagascar Country Study Guide - Strategic Information and Developments	143873039X
Madagascar Country Study Guide - Strategic Information and Developments Volume 1 Strategic Information and Developments	1438774915
Madagascar Customs, Trade Regulations and Procedures Handbook	1433031132
Madagascar Customs, Trade Regulations and Procedures Handbook	1438730403
Madagascar Diplomatic Handbook - Strategic Information and Developments	1433031140
Madagascar Diplomatic Handbook - Strategic Information and Developments	1438730411
Madagascar Ecology & Nature Protection Handbook	1433031159
Madagascar Ecology & Nature Protection Handbook	143873042X
Madagascar Ecology & Nature Protection Laws and Regulation Handbook	1433074281
Madagascar Economic & Development Strategy Handbook	1433031167
Madagascar Economic & Development Strategy Handbook	1438730438
Madagascar Energy Policy, Laws and Regulation Handbook	1433072041
Madagascar Export-Import Trade and Business Directory	1433031175
Madagascar Export-Import Trade and Business Directory	1438730446
Madagascar Foreign Policy and Government Guide	1433031183
Madagascar Foreign Policy and Government Guide	1438730454
Madagascar Immigration Laws and Regulations Handbook - Strategic Information and Basic Laws	1438782985
Madagascar Industrial and Business Directory	1433031191
Madagascar Industrial and Business Directory	1438730462
Madagascar Insolvency (Bankruptcy) Laws and Regulations Handbook - Strategic Information and Basic Laws	9781433085468
Madagascar Internet and E-Commerce Investment and Business Guide -	1433031205

Title	ISBN
Strategic and Practical Information: Regulations and Opportunities	
Madagascar Internet and E-Commerce Investment and Business Guide - Strategic and Practical Information: Regulations and Opportunities	1438730470
Madagascar Investment and Business Guide - Strategic and Practical Information	1438768095
Madagascar Investment and Business Guide - Strategic and Practical Information	1438768095
Madagascar Investment and Business Guide - Strategic and Practical Information	1433031213
Madagascar Investment and Business Guide - Strategic and Practical Information	1438730489
Madagascar Investment and Business Guide Volume 2 Business, Investment Opportunities and Incentives	1577518721
Madagascar Investment and Trade Laws and Regulations Handbook	143307625X
Madagascar Labor Laws and Regulations Handbook - Strategic Information and Basic Laws	1438781180
Madagascar Land Ownership and Agriculture Laws Handbook	1438759487
Madagascar Mineral & Mining Sector Investment and Business Guide - Strategic and Practical Information	1433031221
Madagascar Mineral & Mining Sector Investment and Business Guide - Strategic and Practical Information	1438730497
Madagascar Mining Laws and Regulations Handbook	1433077795
Madagascar Recent Economic and Political Developments Yearbook	1433063441
Madagascar Recent Economic and Political Developments Yearbook	1433063441
Madagascar Recent Economic and Political Developments Yearbook	1433063441
Madagascar Starting Business (Incorporating) in....Guide	1433066998
Madagascar Taxation Laws and Regulations Handbook	143308032X
Madagascar Telecom Laws and Regulations Handbook	1433082136
Madagascar Telecommunication Industry Business Opportunities Handbook	143303123X
Madagascar Telecommunication Industry Business Opportunities Handbook	1438730500
Madagascar Transportation Policy and Regulations Handbook	1433067005
Madagascar: How to Invest, Start and Run Profitable Business in Madagascar Guide - Practical Information, Opportunities, Contacts	9781433083891

www.ingramcontent.com/pod-product-compliance
Ingram Content Group UK Ltd.
Pitfield, Milton Keynes, MK11 3LW, UK
UKHW051509290926
15471UKWH00008B/1526